PORSCHE CARRERA

THE WATER-COOLED ERA 1998–2018

PORSCHE
CARRERA

THE WATER-COOLED ERA 1998–2018

Johnny Tipler
Foreword by Richard Attwood

THE CROWOOD PRESS

First published in 2019 by
The Crowood Press Ltd
Ramsbury, Marlborough
Wiltshire SN8 2HR

www.crowood.com

British Library Cataloguing-in-Publication Data
A catalogue record for this book is available from the British Library.

ISBN 978 1 78500 529 9

Frontispiece: Caroline Llong is an artist based in Aix-en-Provence, specializing in
Porsche and Ferrari in particular, and loves working at the 24-Hours of Le Mans.
'My artworks are resolutely modern, colourful and imbued with movement,' she
says. 'You can perceive them in two ways: contemplate the artwork in its own right,
and study the details subjectively to uncover deeper and more intriguing meanings.
As an automobile aficionado you'll have fun decoding the detail.' It's fair to say that
all her paintings have a common bond: brilliance of colour, depth of light, dazzling
reflections, and an amazing energy. www.e-motion-art.fr CAROLINE LLONG

Title Page: artwork of the millionth Porsche 911 drawn specially for the book
by French watercolourist Laurence B. Henry. http://laurencehenry.hautetfort.com
LAURENCE B. HENRY

Typeset by Jean Cussons Typesetting, Diss, Norfolk

Printed and bound in India by Parksons Graphics

CONTENTS

ACKNOWLEDGEMENTS

I meet a great many enthusiasts in the course of my work as a car journalist, especially Porsche buffs, as I have backed myself down that particular cul-de-sac where I write about very little else these days, unless I'm covering an international rally or race meeting. Many have donated, directly and indirectly, to the compilation of this book. First up, many thanks to star driver and Porsche legend Richard Attwood for kindly penning the Foreword.

Probably the person who's contributed most is my regular colleague, Antony Fraser, who has unstintingly ransacked his personal archive in the interests of a fine spread of photos. He's one of the most accomplished of his ilk and his images raise the tone of the book. I've also worked with several other snappers over the past decade or so, and I'm delighted to include some examples of Amy Shore's highly characterful work. Peter Robain, with whom I worked in the early Noughties, also came up trumps with some very atmospheric photographs. It was a pleasure, too, working with Peter Meißner of Moment-fotodesign on the 9ff shoot. The illustrative material is graced by artworks from four extremely talented artists, Caroline Llong, Laurence B. Henry, Tanja Stagnic and Sonja Verducci, who very kindly provided paintings specially executed for the book.

As for the stock shots, I'm greatly indebted to archivist Jens Torner at the Porsche Photographic Library for providing a large quantity of original material on a cross-section of water-cooled 911s. As usual, I've tried to use shots that haven't been seen before – or at least are new to me. I've also received archive press photos from Tobias Mauler, and massive thanks to him too. On visits to the Porsche Museum I've been warmly welcomed by Jessica Fritzsch, who moved mountains to ensure photoshoots happened. Other helpful individuals at Zuffenhausen include Katja Leinweber, Conny von Buehler, Tobias Hütter, Tony Hatter and Dieter Landenberger. Without the generosity of the press officers at Porsche GB we wouldn't have had half the cars to drive and shoot that grace the pages of this book; so, many thanks indeed to Nick Perry, Rob Punchon and Rob Durrant for lending a fabulous variety of 996s, 997s and 991s for my delectation over the past ten years. And the bottom line is that none of this would have been possible without Steve Bennett, editor of *911&Porsche World*, commissioning features on these cars for the magazine.

Specialists who've enthusiastically made available cars from their showrooms, forecourts and collections for us to play with include, in no particular order, Paul and Rebecca Stephens, John and Tanya Hawkins at Specialist Cars of Malton, Ian Heward at Porscheshop, Adrian Crawford, Richard Williams and Louise Tope at Williams Crawford, Andy Moss at SCS Porsche, Andrew Mearns at Gmund Cars, Ollie Preston at RPM Technic, Simon Cockram at Cameron Cars, Mark Sumpter at Paragon Porsche, Martin Pearse at MCP Motorsport, Jonny Royle at Cambridge Motor Company, Jonathan Sturgess at Autostore, Joff Ward at Finlay Gorham, Phil Hindley at Tech9 Motorsport, Russ Rosenthal at JZM; Josh Sadler, Steve Woods and Mikey Wastie at Autofarm, Karl Chopra at Design911, Mike at Ashgood Porsche, Jon at Yorkshire Classic Porsche. Then we get on to our continental friends, beginning with tuner and builder extraordinaire Alois Ruf and his team, including Estonia (Mrs Ruf), Claudia Müller, Marcel Groos, Marc Pfeiffer, Michaela Stapfer, who always made our trips to Bavaria a pleasure. Next up, the genial Willy Brombacher and his FVD operation; Thomas Schnarr at Cargraphic, whose silencers adorned my 996. We've also been entertained by Tobias Sokoll at TechArt, Björn Striening at speedART, Oliver Eigner at Gemballa, Thomas Schmitz at TJS German Sportscars, Michael Roock at Roock Racing, Jan Fatthauer at 9ff, Dirk Sadlowski at PS Automobile, Eberhard Baunach and Markus Feist at Kremer Racing, and Manfred Hering at Early911S. I'd like to pay a special tribute to Johan Dirickx and Mike Van Dingenen of 911Motorsport for inviting me to the twice-yearly fun and games at Abbeville Circuit; and, by implication, Kobus Cantraine for providing 911s to have fun in. Likewise, Mark Wegh at Porsche Center Gelderland.

Constructive observations and encouragement from my PA, Emma Stuart, are much appreciated, and I want to mention a swathe of aficionados, colleagues and commissionaires with whom I spoke or drove, including Brent Jones, Mauritz Lange, Peter Bergqvist, Jürgen Barth, Hans-Joachim

Stuck, Jacky Ickx, Vic Elford, Mike Wilds, Mario Andretti, Ron Simons, Mark Mullen, Lee Maxted-Page, James Lipman, Simon Jackson (editor of *GT Porsche* magazine), Alastair Iles, Lee Sibley (editor of *Total 911*), Timo Bernhard, Peter Dumbreck, Wolf Henzler, Olaf Manthey, Brendon Hartley, Angelica Grey, Walter Röhrl, Andrea Kerr, Tim Havermans, Wayne Collins, Peter Offord, Alex Denham, Kenny Schachter, Ash Soan, Nick Bailey and Els van der Meer at Elan PR, Angie Voluti at AV PR, Sarah Bennett-Baggs, Mike Lane, Sarah Hall, Angelica Fuentes and Keith Mainland, Keith Seume (editor of *Classic Porsche* magazine), Max, Franziska and Theo Brombacher, Phil Churchill, Andy Prill and Bert Vanderbruggen – to name but a few.

Other benefactors who in no small way enabled the composition of the book include Chris Jones at Brittany Ferries, Frances Amissah at Stena Line, Michelle Ulyatt at DFDS Ferries, Natalie Benville at Eurotunnel, Natalie Hall at P&O Ferries, Simon and Jon Young at Phoenix Exhausts, Vredestein Tyres, Falken Tyres and Continental Tyres. Many thanks to all concerned, and hopefully I haven't left out too many people.

FOREWORD

Richard Attwood

I began racing Formula Junior Lolas in 1961, which included winning at Monaco in 1963, graduating to Formula 2 in 1964, and entering F1 with BRM the same year. At the same time I was also enjoying Sports and GT cars, driving John Wyer's Ford GT40s and Ferrari P330-P3/4s for David Piper and Maranello Concessionaires from the mid-1960s onwards. I was a member of the works Porsche team from 1969 to 1971, helming Martini-Salzburg and Gulf-JW-Automotive 917s and 908s, culminating in the 1970 Le Mans win alongside Hans Herrmann in the red 917/023.

I retired (temporarily) in 1972, since when I have worked with and raced various Porsche products to keep me fresh. Most recently, in 2017, I raced a 928S in the HSCC's Road Sports event at Croft circuit. Back in the day the Works drivers received 911s as their road cars. While the others tended to swap theirs every year for the latest evolution, I kept my 2.0S as I was rather fond of it.

I'm pleased to write the Foreword to Johnny Tipler's book on the most recent generation of 911s, the water-cooled Carreras, because I have been closely involved with them since their inception in 1997. I can still be found at the Porsche Experience Centre on odd days of the week. When the 996 came out and landed at Millbrook Proving Ground it was very apparent that it was the start of the 911 becoming a more sophisticated car: it was quieter, faster, more economical and more refined. Of course, with any new Porsche, it was also more expensive!

The same theme has continued with every successive model and Gen 2 evolution of each one, to the point that the current cars are totally user friendly for anyone to drive.

According to Richard Attwood, 'with all the traction aids and four-wheel drive, on the road the current 911 is almost ridiculously relaxed to drive.' ANTONY FRASER

1970 Le Mans winners Hans Herrmann and Richard Attwood are reacquainted at Classic Le Mans 2010. AUTHOR

Driving the red Porsche 917 #23, Richard Attwood and Hans Herrmann won the 1970 Le Mans 24-Hours. PORSCHE MUSEUM ARCHIVES

For instance, the big difference between the 997 and the 991 is that the later model is now very difficult to break away at the rear. Exactly how Porsche achieved this with two-wheel drive was very significant, and how they did that with the same wheel and tyre combination is amazing. Now, with all the traction aids and four-wheel drive, on the road the current 911 is almost ridiculously relaxed to drive. And yet they are still evolving, and as I jokingly say to my favourite customers, Porsche are still trying to get the 911 right.

Richard Attwood is a consultant on the Porsche Driving Experience at Millbrook and Silverstone. ANTONY FRASER

PREFACE

Porsche motoring became a reality for me in 2000 when I traded my Dad's Audi A4 against a left-hand-drive Prussian Blue 1984 3.2 Carrera. In those days Mrs T and I were involved in a cross-country school run, 40 miles (65km) each way, twice a day, and the kids – and the dog – were small enough to fit comfortably in the back of the 911. Only a Porsche could have made that episode pleasurable. It was a true family car: a couple of summers later I fitted a Thule top box and we drove through France and Spain to Portugal without significant discomfort. I also played in a band and my 911 accommodated the whole drum kit, even with my daughter Zoë buried in the back under the tom-toms.

That was a classic car even then, of course. But what of the modern 911? Launched in 1997, the water-cooled 996 was three or four years old by this time, and even though I'd started scribbling for the *Porsche* magazine in 2000, I was still not particularly enamoured of the new breed of '911'.

That was partly because it might as well have been in a different universe price-wise and, with its fried egg headlights (shared with the Boxster), curious liquid cooling (what was that all about?!) and overblown globule contours, it didn't look enough like a trad 911 to qualify for the honour of using the legendary moniker. That was down to CAD (computer-aided design), here employed at Zuffenhausen for the first time on the 996, generating a digital rendering before the three-dimensional clay buck was pared. Plenty of air-cooled buffs remained downright sceptical of 'the Kettle'.

The water-cooled 996 was firmly entrenched in the Porsche model line-up as we rolled into the twenty-first century, and the ensuing decade has seen two major evolutions of the 911 – the 997 and 991 – spawning a host of GT derivatives and special editions.

First of these was the 3.6-litre, 360bhp 996 GT3, beloved of my photographer colleague Antony Fraser. This is a light-

996 C2 'Pig Energy' at my house in the Douro, northern Portugal.
AUTHOR

996 C2 'Pig Energy' touring the Brittany coast. AUTHOR

Murky business: driving the Pass of the Cattle in north-west Scotland in a 996 Turbo. PETER ROBAIN

weight, lowered and stiffly sprung roustabout derived from the factory-built GT3 race cars, and based on the 4WD model's broader bodyshell. It was brought out in 1999 as a club racer and trackday hooligan with more than a passing nod to the GT3 motor sport category. The normally aspirated 3.6-litre water-cooled flat-six used the casings of the old 964, which were also utilized by the GT1 Le Mans car as well as the 996 Turbo unveiled in 2002. Both these models – the 996 GT3 Mk 1 and the 996 Turbo – subsequently provided two of my all-time motoring highlights. A few years ago Antony and I went to Zandvoort circuit in Holland to interview racer Jan Lammers, and he gave me an eye-opening run around the dunes in the GT3. Fraser is no slouch, but Lammers was a slammer, and I could see, as he hurled it from lock to lock in the context of an undulating race track, what this factory-tuned 996 comps car was really all about.

Going back a bit, in the early 2000s I drove a 996 C4S press car, courtesy of Porsche GB, up to Hadrian's Wall for a feature based on General Wade's military roads that flank

Gen 1 996 GT3 during a photoshoot in the underground car park at the Porsche Museum, Zuffenhausen. AUTHOR

those Roman bulwarks. This was an entirely competent car, or so I thought until on the way south, while the computerized fuel gauge told me there was at least 30 miles-worth left in the tank, I found myself stationary beside the A1 Doncaster by-pass as white vans honked in derision!

My next voyage in a 996 was rather more illuminating, driving a 996 Turbo up to the north of Scotland and negotiating the mesmerizing corkscrew of a road that crosses over to the Applecross peninsula on the west coast. This all-wheel drive, 420bhp twin-turbo missile revealed its Jekyll and Hyde personality in its blistering pace heading from Inverness to Wester Ross, and its restrained ability on the winding ascent (1:5) over the 2,000ft (626m) Pass of the Cattle and the descent to the sea. On the major arteries north and south, the Turbo was the most benign of companions, easing past other traffic without blinking. The 996 Turbo offered even more poke in S guise, for an extra £10 grand, punching out 430bhp.

This is essentially a 911 dissertation, but by way of taking us through Porsche actions in the 2000, I'll mention in passing that the Cayenne 4 × 4 SUV was launched in 2002, and I've enjoyed outings in this hugely capable trans-continental express to the Netherlands, the Nürburgring Old Timer and Spa-Francorchamps. Mrs T and I followed the progress of Vic Elford and David Stone's 911 on the 2008 Monte Carlo Historic Rally in a Cayenne Turbo, chauffeuring Mrs Elford (Anita) and Mrs Stone (Bibi) along the way. Luckily, they spoke French and could intercede with the implacable traffic cops. And then in 2009 Fraser and I took one to Zuffenhausen to attend the opening of Porsche's fabulous new museum. That same year Porsche's other four-door limo came out, the Panamera, with V6 and V8 power units and a hybrid in the pipeline.

Specialist tuning and parts purveyor FVD built a 4.0-litre 997 GT3 RS, seen here storming the Schauinsland hill climb in the Black Forest. ANTONY FRASER

A lot of the 911 story in the Noughties is about evolution; nothing stands still for long. It's also inevitable that there's more to say about the 996 models than the subsequent 997 and 991, because issues such as the intermediate shaft bearing (IMS), oil leaks and bore-scoring were ironed out during the earlier years. By the time of the 991 the model was, to all intents and purposes, faultless. And that is to the detriment of the 911's traditionally flawed concept: you loved it because of and in spite of its foibles. Talking of foibles, the GT3 lineage will always have a wilful streak – all competition-based cars do, though that again became increasingly subdued with successive incarnations.

The second-generation 997 GT3 RS appeared in 2009, with lightweight bodywork elements and powered by a 450bhp 3.8-litre engine, plus modified suspension and engine mounts and a titanium exhaust. Two years later the third-generation 997 GT3 RS appeared, with a long-stroke 4.0-litre flat-six in 2012, the largest flat-six to occupy the 911's engine bay, and developing 500bhp. Lightweight components included carbon fibre bonnet and front wings, bucket seats and plastic rear windows, while aerodynamic tweaks included lateral front air deflection vanes (used for the first time on a production Porsche) to increase downforce. I sampled one prepared by Willy Brombacher's FVD concern in 2012, rushing up the legendary Schauinsland hill climb. Staggeringly fast, with wheelspin in every gear that I dared explore up the damp Black Forest incline, it was a salutary lesson in top-end performance characteristics.

Porsche has come up with two supercars so far in the twenty-first century. With its origins in the 1996 GT1 WSC racing car, the mid-engined Carrera GT with its 5.7-litre V10 and carbon fibre chassis was in production between 2004 and 2007. Just 1,270 cars were made at Leipzig in a run that ended abruptly. This was followed in September 2013 by the Michael Mauer-styled mid-engined 918 Spyder and RSR coupé, each powered by a 563bhp 4.6-litre V8 supported by a pair of electric motors. A racing variant was shown at the North American International Auto Show in 2011. On-track success is a manufacturer's best advert in the showroom, and during this time Porsche's Carrera Cup has gone from strength to strength, with national series flourishing as well as the international brigade that's showcased at the F1 Grand Prix curtain-raiser. I will dip into that scene in Chapter 9.

For now, though, I hope you'll enjoy this journey through the evolution of the water-cooled 911s, from the prosaic to the exotic, bookmarked with driver and personality interviews, and illustrated with a glorious range of images from professional photographers and artists and the Porsche photo archive.

Distinctively liveried 997 GT3 at Lime Rock Circuit, Connecticut, during a round of the IMSA US Porsche Carrera Cup series, 2014. AUTHOR

INTRODUCTION

It was an incredibly brave move of Porsche to introduce a completely new model line of water-cooled 911s, at the same time as abandoning its stock-in-trade air-cooled models that dated back to the firm's inception – and indeed, dropping the front-engined (water-cooled) sports models entirely. True enough, in financial terms it was probably the way forward, and in environmental as well as performance terms there was no alternative. But still, it needed guts to make the call: the organizational shift from one production methodology to another, the admin, the marketing logistics and implementation were colossal.

The water-cooled Porsche Carreras were introduced in 1998 with the 996 model, following on from the Boxster 986, which shared much of the 996 componentry. While the Boxster is a mid-engined sports car, the 996 follows a similar pattern to the traditional 911, being a coupé with rear-mounted engine – liquid-cooled as opposed to air-cooled – with just as many spin-off variants. Indeed, Porsche still likes to call the Carrera models 911s; their internal designations are 996, 997 and 991.

Over the past 15 years or so I've driven a wide cross-section of water-cooled 911s, whether press cars or the products of Porsche specialists, offerings from motor traders and private owners, as well as running my own 996, and I've been able to drive them to some stunning locations in pursuit of feature articles. There's absolutely no substitute for getting behind the wheel and making a journey to fully gauge and comprehend what a car is capable of, and what defines its character, and that's what a large part of this book is comprised of: my on-the-road experiences in water-cooled 911s, illustrated by a wealth of superb photos provided by pros like Antony Fraser, Amy Shore, James Lipman and Peter Robain, together with my own contributions

My 996 C2 and Boxster 986 S, contemporary models that shared many components during production. AUTHOR

In mid-2018 Porsche produced its Millionth 911, creating a special one-off 991 to commemorate the achievement, pictured here on the concours at the Museum in Zuffenhausen. AUTHOR

The 600bhp 991 Turbo S Exclusive is finished in exclusive Golden Yellow Metallic paint, celebrated on canvas by artist Tanja Stagnic in her painting of the car, which was displayed at the International Frankfurt Show. Tanja uses acrylics, gold leaf and jewels to achieve the image, and the process of creating the painting can be viewed on YouTube. TANJA STAGNIC

Legendary Porsche racing driver Hans-Joachim Stuck samples a 997 Turbo Cabriolet. ANTONY FRASER

Hans-Joachim Stuck is a brand ambassador for Porsche and has scored countless wins for the marque during his 50-year professional racing career. ANTONY FRASER

and some stunning shots from the Porsche Photographic Archives, augmented by a few super artworks by talented automotive painters Caroline Llong, Laurence Henry, Tanja Stagnic and Sonja Verducci.

I no longer mind the fried egg headlights, but when the 997, the 996's replacement, came out in 2005 I welcomed the new model's tendency towards the classic 911 look. It's badged a Carrera, but I still can't accept that the name, once applied exclusively to paragons of Porsche performance like the 2.7 Carrera RS, is not diminished by being applied across the board to all but the GT2/3 and Turbo models, the very machines that actually merit the appellation. Anyhow, the 997 coupé contrived a lower drag coefficient (0.28) than the 996, its interior was agreeably redesigned, and it was said to have retained only a third of its predecessor's componentry.

The basic 997C2's 3.6-litre flat-six produced 325bhp and the 3.8-litre motor powering the 997C2S developed 355bhp. The latter was equipped with uprated suspension and PASM (Porsche Active Suspension Management) with electronically adjustable settings. It also came fitted with so-called Lobster Fork 19in alloys, bigger brakes with red calipers, and dazzling Xenon headlights. The all-wheel-drive C4 and C4S versions were announced for the 2006 model year, featuring the wider shells and fatter tyres.

The 997 Cabriolet was actually designed before the closed versions on the basis that the necessary chassis strengthening for the open-top car could be pared down for the coupé. Antony and I have had two or three forays in the 'hairdresser car', including a snowy run into Scotland to photograph a Turbo Cab beside the Falkirk Wheel, and motoring to

Porsche's chief test driver Walter Röhrl signs off every new model. Here he drives me up a hill road near Regensburg in his 997 GT3 RS. ANTONY FRASER

Frankfurt in a white one to persuade Hans-Joachim Stuck to take it for a drive. He didn't bat an eyelid.

More up Stucky's street, though, the 997 GT3 RS, launched in 2006, was a road-legal version of the FIA-homologated GT3 RSR race car using a GT3 driveline with a lightweight flywheel and closer gear ratios. There was a carbon rear wing and a front splitter, plus lightweight plexiglass rear windows and a factory roll cage. Another career highlight was being driven up a damp Bavarian hill road in a GT3 RS by none other than Walter Röhrl in 2010: caged and trussed like a cock pheasant bound for the Aga, I was hurtled skywards, the maestro unconcernedly getting two wheels on the verge when confronted by a giant combine harvester. After that Walter could do no wrong and I no longer feared for Antony Fraser's safety as he crouched on the apex of a turn to snap us sliding towards him. Walter's car was painted black with orange detailing, and he'd had his 964 RS similarly hued to match.

The 997 Targa model – in C4 and C4S spec – was relaunched in November 2006, bridging the gap between cabriolet and coupé with its clever sliding glass top pioneered in the 993 Targa. I had a couple of lengthy road trips in Targas, one to Münster with Brett Fraser to do a couple of magazine features on the 917 and 935 exotica in Jan Luehn's showroom, and another with Antony Fraser to cover the Monte Carlo Historic Rallye in 2010, when Bjorn Waldegård was the shooting star in the classic 911. Both times the 997 Targa's ingenious lid made stowing their extensive camera gear a piece of cake. Who said 911s weren't practical?

In July 2007 the 997 GT2 replaced the 996 version of

Porsche's hottest road car. Power came from the twin turboed 523bhp 3.6-litre flat-six, allied to a 6-speed manual gearbox and rear-drive transmission. Quoted top speed was 328km/h (204mph), making it the first road-legal 911 to break the double ton, although Ruf's Yellowbird 911 had managed 340km/h (211mph) twenty years earlier in the famous Ehra Lessien showdown with the Ferrari F40, Lamborghini Countach and the 959. The bonkers 620bhp GT2 RS appeared in 2010.

Subtle upgrades for the 997 in 2009 included Bluetooth mobile phone technology, a larger air intake in the front valance, new headlamps and rear lights and, far more cru-

The 997 Carrera Targa's rear hatch provided excellent storage for photographer Antony Fraser's camera equipment, pictured here on the Col de Turini during the Monte Carlo Rallye Historique in 2010. ANTONY FRASER

The 991 Turbo S 'Limited Edition 918 Spyder' commemorated the eponymous 981 Boxster model, with just 918 units produced. AUTHOR

The 991 Carrera S posed beside the former Funkturm Race Control building on the previously banked North Turn of the AVUS racetrack in Berlin. What remains of the original circuit is basically a 9km stretch of autobahn dual carriageway. ANTONY FRASER

cially, new common-rail direct engines married to the dual clutch PDK gearbox were installed. Changing gear in a 911 would never be the same again. The 997 Turbo unveiled in August 2009 was still configured as a four-wheel-drive chassis, incorporating a system related to the AWD Cayenne's, which was meant to improve all-weather handling rather than simply benefit traction, though the PTM facility was rearward biased. The Turbo used the same twin-turbo 3.6-litre flat-six as its predecessor, now rated up to 480bhp and 620Nm of torque, thanks to VTG (variable turbine geometry), which manages to combine the low-revs boost and swift response characteristics of a small turbo with the high-revs grunt of a big turbo. Not only was fuel consumption better, the 997 Turbo went from standstill to 100km/h (62mph) in 3.7s in manual mode, topping out at 310km/h (193mph). A year later the Turbo S was available, basically an all-options Turbo, cranking out 520bhp, and it's likely that the quoted 0–60mph time of 2.8s was facilitated by the PDK transmission because it provides a faster shift than it's possible to achieve with a manual box.

For the 997 GT3, the time-served Turbo motor descended from the 964/993 and GT1 Mezger race engine was replaced in 2009 by a new 493bhp, twin-turbo, 3.8-litre unit based on the 997 C2S's 3.8-litre unit, including uprated intercooler and fuel system. Paddle shift controls for the PDK double-clutch gearbox also appeared for the first time on the Turbo, with Sport, Sport Plus and launch control options displayed on the steering wheel when selected via the optional Sport Chrono package. There were stylistic tweaks too: like the 996 Turbo, the GT3's LED driving lights, parking and indicator lights were mounted horizontally across the front air intakes, while the rear wing was a retake on the 996's biplane spoiler.

Porsche was fond of claiming that virtually every constituent part of a new model was fresh, such as the 993 following on from the 964, and in 2012 the 991 was touted as only the third entirely new platform since the original 911 was released in 1963. Its chassis was indeed quite different to all its predecessors. The 991 was the first 911 to employ aluminium in its construction, being used for the floorpan, roof, door skins, bonnet, engine lid, luggage compartment, front crash structure and rear wings. That amounts to 45 per cent of the chassis, so even though the 991 was larger than the 997, it was 50kg lighter, enhancing performance figures in the process.

The 991 C2 was powered by a 350bhp 3.4-litre engine, while the sibling C2S's 3.8-litre produced 400bhp. A 3.9in (99mm) longer wheelbase accounted for an overall increase in length of 2.2in (56mm), while the rear axle shifted back-

The 385bhp 997 C2S provided superlative transport to the 2010 Le Mans Classic. ANTONY FRASER

wards towards the engine by an extraordinary 3in (76mm), and the front track of the C2S was 2.0in (51mm) wider. The PDK transmission was revised, and a ground-breaking 7-speed manual gearbox was available, double-declutching during downshifts when set in Sport Plus mode. Electro-mechanical power steering replaced the hydraulic set-up, while a stop-start system switched the engine off when stationary at red traffic lights, and a freewheeling system placed the engine at idle while coasting downhill, bringing environmental as well as economical benefits. A torque vectoring system braked the inner driven wheel during turn-in, while on-board stability aids PASM and PDCC improved ride quality and stiffened the suspension during fast cornering.

With the retirement of Harm Lagaaij in 2004, the in-house design team was now headed by Michael Mauer, whose first baby was the 991. But on the corporate front, Porsche was involved in major changes. CEO Wendelin Wiedeking, who'd lifted the firm onto its mass-production platform from his arrival in 1993, sought during the early 2000s to bring Porsche into a position where it could acquire Volkswagen, and by degrees the fiscal feelers fell into place. That would have been quite an irony, given that Professor Ferdinand Porsche designed the VW Beetle in 1936, and the 356 came into being in 1948 using Beetle components. Volkswagen, however, turned the tables, and the result of the financial chess game was that Porsche became a Volkswagen-owned company on 1 August 2012. Wiedeking was replaced as CEO by Michael Macht in 2009 and then Matthias Müller in 2010.

The 4WD versions of the 991 were introduced in January 2013, with the customary wider rear bodywork, fatter tyres and a red reflector strip between the tail lights. A significant bonus was that the intelligent 4 × 4 system now deployed drive to the front axle only when necessary, so there was more of the sensation of driving a more finely honed rear-wheel-drive car when conditions allowed, while dispensing power and torque up front when road and weather situations required it. As well as hiking the power output of the 991 Turbo and Turbo S to a whip-cracking 520 and 560bhp, among the innovations flagged up for the 2014 model year were a rear-wheel steering system for the Turbo models that basically works by rotating the rear wheels backwards at low speeds to sharpen handling.

As the Carrera models have evolved, you would expect that the most recent would be the best. Of course that's true in many ways, although the more complicated they get and the more attuned they have to be to the demands of safety and emissions legislation, the less delicate and tactile they become. The middle ground was probably reached in the 997 era, though one tries to keep an open mind. For instance, the 991 Cabriolet that Antony and I took to Bavaria in 2014 was a fabulous machine, civilized at high speeds on the unrestricted German autobahn – we saw 170mph (274km/h) more than once and could still hold a normal conversation – and it was just as entertaining on the winding sub-Alpine hairpins. It was also amusing to lower and raise the canvas-clad magnesium roof at 25mph (40km/h) to catch the farmyard aromas as we glided through the Bavarian countryside. We agreed it was quite possibly the most capable Porsche all-rounder we'd ever been let loose in. Whether that assertion stands up by the time you get to the end of the book is another matter.

The 991 C4S was launched in 2012 at the Paris Motor Show, powered by the 400bhp 3.8-litre flat-six engine, with a facelift coming in 2014. The Gen 2 version debuted in October 2015, running with smaller 3.0-litre twin-turbo engines, developing 420bhp. This was the first time that 911 Carreras were fitted with turbochargers, apart from the specifically designated Turbo models. ANTONY FRASER

CHAPTER ONE

DESIGN AND CONCEPT OF THE 996

BOILING THE KETTLE

Not many Porsches polarized enthusiast opinion as markedly as the 996-model Carrera. Its Boxster stablemate trod new ground, while the 996 sought to recreate the 911; and propositions do not come much more audacious than that. Unveiled at the Frankfurt Show in September 1997 and on sale from late autumn that year, the 996 was, from the outset, a love-it or loathe-it car. Not surprisingly, given fifty years of air-cooled antecedents, many Porsche buffs were prepared to loathe it with an almost sectarian fanaticism. Air-cooled diehards considered it to be little short of an abomination. Never mind that it looked a bit like an overbaked 993, or that, from the front at least, it looked very much like its junior sibling, the entry-level Boxster, with which it shared most of its frontal body panels and hardware. Never mind that it maintained the marque's tradition of a rear-mounted flat-six power plant: what really upset the nay-sayers was the fact that its engine was nothing less than water-cooled. Whatever next? An all-wheel-drive off-roader? And that is

Anatomical cutaway reveals the inner workings and componentry layout of the Gen I 996 C2. PORSCHE MUSEUM ARCHIVES

why the water-cooled (liquid-cooled) 911s are known disparagingly as 'kettles'. Never mind the fact that models such as the 924, 944 and 928 had been thus chilled since the late 1970s.

The cognoscenti knew that, for several reasons, Porsche simply couldn't carry on building air-cooled engines, or indeed the adorable 993, and so they welcomed the 996 with open arms. It was as modern, as contemporary, as aesthetically stylish and, above all, as fresh as Porsche devotees could have realistically hoped for, and had just the right blend of restrained aggression and timeless elegance to make it appear as much at home in Knightsbridge as the Nürburgring. No wonder that, by the time production ended in early 2005, the 996 had sold well over 150,000 units of all derivatives. More significantly on a corporate level, in consort with the 986-model Boxster, it transformed Porsche from its mid-1990s status as one of the world's most endangered independent car companies to the most profitable of all.

The 996 was no slouch, even in base 3.4-litre format. The first water-cooled 911 went, and still goes, remarkably well, too. From standstill to 62mph in 5.2s, and on up to a maximum of 174mph (280km/h); allied with flawless brakes, and

Featuring three eras of 911, the 2015 Jerry Judah sculpture that soars over the roundabout at the heart of Porsche's Zuffenhausen factory and museum complex. AUTHOR

Launched in 1998, and retrospectively identified as Gen 1, the 996 was an entirely new take on the 911 concept, with fresh styling cues including the 'fried egg' headlights, frowned upon by purists at the time. PORSCHE MUSEUM ARCHIVES

Getting the aero just right: a 996 GT2 is in for assessment in the factory wind tunnel. PORSCHE MUSEUM ARCHIVES

a poise that belied a quarter of a tonne of engine slung out behind the rear wheels. It sounded good, too. Here was a 911 you could drive every day and in all weathers, and which, with 10,000-mile (16,000km) service intervals, wouldn't cost an arm and a leg to maintain. To this day it remains every inch a proper Porsche. The 997 is better – marginally, perhaps significantly – in just about every respect, and you'd expect nothing less, but only because of what the company learned and acted on while it was building the 996. There are plenty out there just waiting to be bought and enjoyed. The 996 performs and handles just as well as it ever did and,

The 996 Turbo came out at the Frankfurt Show in September 1999, while the facelifted Gen 2 996 C2 appeared in 2002, complete with an engine capacity hike from 3.4 to 3.6 litres. PORSCHE MUSEUM ARCHIVES

like any 911, makes you feel better about yourself than you would imagine any car ever could. A good 996 represents amazing value for money, too. They've stopped depreciating and by 2016 values were climbing. Like all resuscitated classics, if you choose the right car, previous owners will have picked up the tab for your driving pleasure. Twenty years ago you'd have paid rather more than £50,000 for a basic UK-spec Carrera 2, but now that same car, with less than 100,000 miles on the clock, with all-important full service history, could be bought for between £15,000 and £20,000. Now, as in its heyday, there's a 996 for everyone, including the mainstream models and specials such as the Turbo, GT2 and GT3.

The 996 Carrera 2 was launched in rear-drive format, and with either a six-speed manual gearbox or a five-speed Tiptronic S automatic. This makes a superb system, if a little tardy, especially compared with its PDK successor. The all-wheel-drive and Porsche Stability Management-equipped C4 followed in 1999, closely followed by the rear-drive and manual-only GT3. That particular masterpiece was followed a year later by both the 420bhp 4WD 996 Turbo model and, to celebrate the new millennium, the limited-edition normally aspirated Millennium model.

In early 2001 the 462bhp twin-turbo GT2 was released, featuring PCCB ceramic brakes, and the following year Porsche broadened the range's appeal with the glass-roofed

The 484bhp twin-turbo 996 GT2 was unveiled in 2003, configured with rear-wheel drive only in order to be eligible for the GT2 racing category. PORSCHE MUSEUM ARCHIVES

The Gen I 996 coupé shares its front end with the 986 Boxster, including the so-called 'fried egg' headlights. PORSCHE MUSEUM ARCHIVES

Targa, an intriguing configuration developed from that of the air-cooled 993 model, where the glass roof panel retracted into the rear screen, which also doubled as a hatch. The same year also ushered in the wide-bodied Carrera 4S. A few months later, in the spring of 2003, along with a significant facelift and revised engine capacity, came a new GT3; these paragons have become designated unofficially as Gen I and Gen 2. During 2004 one launch followed another, including brand-new Cabriolet versions of the C4S and Turbo, a 381bhp GT3 RS, another special-edition anniversary C2 to celebrate forty years of the 911, the 450bhp Turbo S, and an uprated GT2.

The 996's replacement, the 997 Carrera, was first seen in mid-2004, but that wasn't the end of the line for the first water-cooled 911. Production of the more mainstream models would be phased out by the end of the year, but both the Carrera 4S and the Turbo – in the absence of 997 versions of the same – continued to be built well into 2005. No less prolific were improvements to the cars' specification and appearance. The 1999 model year brought POSIP, the Porsche Side Impact Protection System, plus an exhaust system tuned for a better sound, and clear lenses front and rear, instead of the previous orange, for the indicators. This saw the end of the original so-called 'fried egg' headlights – though you could just as easily describe the facelift headlights as fried eggs, depending on your cooking technique. This simple step usefully distanced the 996 from the 986 Boxster, though the 987 Boxster gained headlights similar to those of the 997. For a while the Gen 2 headlamp upgrade was a popular, if expensive, aftermarket upgrade for an earlier 3.4 car. Now nobody minds much either way; as traditional 911 headlights fade

into history, the fried egg versions have a character all their own.

For 2000 Porsche upgraded the Carrera 2 with the C4's drive-by-wire electronic throttle mechanism (E-Gas), an improved engine management system, and not least the option of Porsche Stability Management (PSM); early cars have only a basic traction-control system. In 2001 the cars gained sill-mounted electric switches to open the front and rear lids in place of the earlier mechanical levers. This useful refinement also allowed the front lid to be opened remotely with the electronic key fob.

The Gen 2 996 coupé received a facelift, which included installation of Turbo headlights and consequently revised front panel. Capacity rose from 3.4 to 3.6 litres. AUTHOR

The 996 Cabriolet was available with a flush-fitting detachable aluminium hardtop, weighing 33kg (76lb). A stand while it's not in use is also desirable, rather than leant against a wall. PORSCHE MUSEUM ARCHIVES

Extracted from the car and bereft of ancillaries, a 3.6-litre flat-six is a remarkably compact unit. PORSCHE MUSEUM ARCHIVES

By far the biggest changes, however, came about in the 2002 model year. Externally the cars received revised front and rear aprons with improved aerodynamics and, most obviously, the teardrop-style headlamps that served to distance the 996 from the 986 Boxster. Inside there was a new three-spoke steering wheel and, for the first time, an opening glovebox – with cup-holders, too.

The 996 Cabriolet, although never criticized for its plastic rear window as much as the early pre-2003 Boxster, gained a glass screen. Way more significant than all that, though, were the changes to the engine.

The previous 3.4-litre VarioCam unit was abandoned in favour of a much-improved 3.6-litre motor with Porsche's ingenious VarioCam Plus technology, previously reserved for the Turbo. This not only gave the basic models more low-speed punch, but also seemed ultimately more reliable. It certainly made these subsequent cars more desirable on the second-hand market. Other factors influencing desirability include bore-scoring and IMS bearing failure, which I deal with later, and crankshaft-seal oil leaks, but these prob-

The sleek lines of the Gen 2 996 coupé, in this instance sporting aerodynamic sill covers and optional five-spoke Carrera wheels. AUTHOR

Cabin interior of the 996 Gen 2 is a harmonious blend of practicality, comfort, efficiency and sports car spartan. AUTHOR

Rear quarters of the 996 Gen 2 encompass the sloping rear tail, engine-lid grille that doubles as spoiler, plus twin exhaust tips and back window wiper. AUTHOR

---

996 CARRERA C2 (1998–2002)

Layout and chassis
Two-plus-two coupé and cabriolet, with unit-construction steel body/chassis

Engine

Type	M96/22 6-cylinder, horizontally opposed, rear-mounted
Block material	aluminium
Head material	aluminium
Cylinders	flat-six
Cooling	water
Bore and stroke	96 × 78mm
Capacity	3387cc
Valves	4 valves per cylinder
Compression ratio	11.3:1
Fuel supply	multi-point injection
Max. power (DIN)	300bhp @ 6,800rpm
Max. torque	265lb ft @ 4,600rpm
Fuel capacity	64 litres (14.07 gallons)

Transmission

Gearbox	Getrag G96/00 rear drive 6-speed; ZF 5HP19 automatic; M-B 5G Tiptronic
Clutch	hydraulic single dry plate
Ratios	1st 3.82
	2nd 2.20
	3rd 1.52
	4th 1.22
	5th 1.02
	6th 0.84
	Reverse 3.44
	Final drive 3.89

Suspension and steering

Front	independent by MacPherson struts, aluminium links, longitudinal and transverse links, coil springs, gas dampers, anti-roll bar
Rear	independent by MacPherson struts, aluminium links, lateral and transverse links, coil springs, gas dampers, anti-roll bar
Steering	rack-and-pinion
Tyres	225/40 × 18 front, 265/35 × 18 rear
Wheels	aluminium alloy
Rim width	7.5in J front, 10.0in J rear

Brakes

Type	front and rear vented discs with four-piston calipers
Size	298 × 24mm front; 292 × 20mm rear

Dimensions

Track	
Front	1,455mm (57.28in)
Rear	1,500mm (59.05in)
Wheelbase	2,350mm (92.51in)
Overall length	4,430mm (174.4in)
Overall width	1,765mm (69.48in)
Overall height	1,305mm (51.3in)
Unladen weight	1,320kg (2,910lb)

Performance

Top speed	280km/h (173.9mph)
0–60mph	5.6s

lems by no means affect all cars and there are now well-known solutions and cures for most of the major maladies. Typical prices for the earlier models are still relatively low, so they're worth taking a chance on. Paradoxically for such an accomplished modern car, the 996 is now hailed as a classic, even though production volumes alone mean it far outstrips its hallowed air-cooled predecessors in terms of availability. Perhaps one shouldn't be surprised, since it has everything else going for it: looks, handling, performance, build quality, comfort and sheer practicality for a sports car, making it fantastic value in the market that the Germans call 'young-timer' classics.

Shared platform

Proposed by Wendelin Wiedeking, the 996 and 986 Boxster were manufactured in far greater numbers than previous models, and their success literally saved the company, which was in serious financial difficulties in the early 1990s.

The two strands of Porsche sports car soon went their own separate ways, metamorphosing into the 997 and 987 series. Stylists involved with the water-cooled Carreras include Harm Lagaaij, Pinky Lai and Michael Mauer. The evolution of the Boxster and its Cayman sibling may be found in *Porsche Boxster and Cayman: The Complete Story* (The Crowood Press, 2016).

No previous 911 was built in as many different guises as the 996 – and that's also true of its successors, the 997 and 991. Top of the tree in the performance and price stakes has to be the GT2, essentially a tweaked, race-proven Turbo with ceramic brakes as standard, which then cost nearly £130,000. Even though it was originally priced at roughly

A 996 Cabriolet outside Werk I building at Zuffenhausen: note the building's northern light architecture, which provides a more consistent light to work by. PORSCHE MUSEUM ARCHIVES

£75,000, the GT3 was – and probably remains – the one to have, especially now that you can buy a high-mileage one for as little as £40,000. There are few better trackday machines, even in its slightly sanitized 'Gen 2' form – with the possible exception of a genuine Supercup car – and it's no surprise that many ordinary 996s are now sprouting copycat GT3-style wings, skirts and wheels. The glass-roofed Targa is a very pleasant machine indeed, offering a real sense of cabin space, but with all the security and weather protection of a proper coupé, and the wide-bodied Carrera 4S has a certain appeal too – although understandably a Turbo is more desirable.

The 996 quickly diverged into a cluster of different models, ranging from rear-drive C2 to four-wheel-drive C4,

Rivals in the top-down motoring department: the 996 Cabriolet and the 986 Boxster. The 996 model offers a pair of child-friendly rear seats and is more of a touring car, while the Boxster provides proper sports car motoring and dynamic handling.
ANTONY FRASER

begetting the S version, Cabriolet, Targa, Turbo, GT2 and GT3. The 996 range was in production until 2005, superseded by the 997, encompassing a similar range of models – S, GTS, Cabriolet, Targa, Turbo and GT3 – and coinciding with the replacement of the 986 Boxster with the 987 Boxster and new Cayman model. A major revision in 2009 included the implementation of the highly efficient PDK transmission, which replaced the long-standing Tiptronic automatic shift.

Next revision was the 991, introduced in 2011, with similar diversions into S, GTS, Cabriolet, Targa 4, 4S, Turbo, Turbo S, GT3, GT3 RS and R models (though not GT2).

Each evolution, 996, 997, and 991, has received a facelift and mechanical upgrades, and so they are divided into Gen 1 and Gen 2 cars. These models have all participated in the Porsche Carrera Cup and are known as Cup Cars. This is

an important means of developing technical advancements to pass on to road cars. I have interviewed people involved with racing these cars, such as top tuner Olaf Manthey and drivers Mike Wilds and Peter Dumbreck, and we'll hear from some of these aces in due course. There is a healthy aftermarket for tuning and modifying road cars, and I make a point of visiting specialists and tuners such as Alois Ruf at least once a year to review their innovations. In most cases, especially Ruf, their evolutions are seriously worthwhile advances on the Porsche formula.

Meanwhile, the 991 continues in production (as are the 718-model Boxster and Cayman). I recently saw the one-millionth 911 at the Porsche Museum, Zuffenhausen. It's actually a 991, though Porsche likes to carry on calling the Carrera the 911 for continuity's sake.

996 GT2 (2000–2005)

Layout and chassis
Two-plus-two coupé, unit-construction steel body/chassis

Engine

Type	M96/72 'Mezger' dry sump, horizontally opposed, rear-mounted 6-cylinder
Block material	aluminium
Head material	aluminium
Cylinders	flat-six
Cooling	water
Bore and stroke	100mm × 76.4mm
Capacity	3600cc
Valves	4 valves-per-cylinder
Compression ratio	11.7:1
Fuel system	multi-point injection, 2 KKK K24 turbochargers
Max. power (DIN)	462bhp @ 5,700rpm
Max. torque	457lb ft @ 3,500rpm
Fuel capacity	64 litres (14 gallons)

Transmission

Gearbox	Getrag G96/00 rear drive, 6-speed
Clutch	Hydraulic single dry plate
Ratios	1st 3.82
	2nd 2.20
	3rd 1.52
	4th 1.22
	5th 1.02
	6th 0.84
	Reverse 3.44
	Final drive 3.89

Suspension and steering

Front	independent by MacPherson struts, aluminium links, longitudinal and transverse links, coil springs, gas dampers, anti-roll bar
Rear	independent by MacPherson struts, aluminium links, lateral and transverse links, coil springs, gas dampers, anti-roll bar
Steering	rack-and-pinion
Tyres	225/40 × R18 front, 295/30 × R18 rear
Wheels	aluminium alloy
Rim width	7.5in J front, 10.0in J rear

Brakes

Type	front and rear vented discs with six-piston calipers; optional M450 ceramic discs
Size	380 × 24mm front; 350 × 20mm rear

Dimensions

Track	
Front	1,455mm (57.28in)
Rear	1,500mm (59.05in)
Wheelbase	2,350mm (92.51in)
Overall length	4,430mm (174.4in)
Overall width	1,765mm (69.48in)
Overall height	1,305mm (51.3in)
Unladen weight	1,540kg (3,395lb)

Performance

Top speed	305km/h (189.5mph)
0–60mph	4.2s

HARM LAGAAIJ INTERVIEW

The process of designing the 996 is an intriguing topic, imbued as it is with the reputation of having saved the company as well as taking the sanctified 911 model line into previously uncharted territory. Porsche's Head of Design at the time, the Dutch designer Harm Lagaaij, talked me through the mechanics of styling the car. He had two stints in the Porsche design studios, first as an assistant stylist from 1971 to 1977 and again from 1989 to 2004. His standout car during his first stint was the 924, for which he was entirely responsible, with input into detailing on the 928. In the interim he was design manager for Ford Cologne (Sierra, Scorpio) and chief designer at BMW (Z1). Then, in his second round at Porsche, he was head of design, in charge of the final revamp of the air-cooled 911 in the shape of the 993, and the company's launch into liquid-cooled cars with the Boxster 986 and 996 series, as well as subsequent models up to his retirement in 2004. His favourite design for Porsche? If pressed, he cites the 997. I caught up with him at the Spa Six Hours race weekend where he was racing his Shadow Mk 1 Can-Am car, and we chatted about the Porsche design process.

JT: Who is your favourite stylist? Historically, whom do you admire or who got you into car design in the first place?

HL: I've always been into cars although my background in terms of automobile styling is purely self-taught. At the end of the 1960s and early '70s, whoever you were, you couldn't get a job without a state permit in Italy because there wasn't a European Union yet. Pininfarina and Bertone looked at my portfolios but they couldn't give me a job because of the state permit problem. The Italian design studios, which have now more or less disappeared, were extremely influential for me, and standing out is, of course, Giorgetto Giugiaro, who for me is the most influential designer from the 1960s, '70s and '80s. However, after that, I would say the most influential things in car design spring from the internal studios. If you ask me, 'who is your inspiration from the 1990s to now?' I have to say it's the fantastic studios which each company has now, and how they are led and what their cars look like. And that's also the reason why studios like Bertone and Vignale, one by one, went out of business; not because they were not good enough but because the design studios at the car companies became so sophisticated, so professional and large.

JT: When you joined Porsche in 1971, what was your view of the company at the time?

HL: I was a junior designer and it was really the beginning of my career and so I didn't fully understand exactly what was going on. But my observation was that the 911 was in a difficult period for many reasons. Even then the 911 was not considered modern enough, and you have to have something to replace it with, and therefore the 928 project started off and, because of the circumstances, the 924 was a project like the 914 which we did for VW. Porsche had a very healthy

Renderings for the 996 demonstrate the desire to maintain the 911 lines in general, showing logical similarities with the 993. PORSCHE MUSEUM ARCHIVES

Many and varied ideas for the detailing of the 996, including the Targa and Cabriolet, even hinting at the VW-derived Porsche 64 Berlin–Rome record breaker from 1938. PORSCHE MUSEUM ARCHIVES

(continued overleaf)

HARM LAGAAIJ INTERVIEW (continued)

income from research and development for VW, which was a very nice situation when it comes to covering motor sport expenses. That was more or less the financial purpose of the projects which were given to Porsche by VW at the time, to fund motor racing.

JT: When you were given the job of styling the 924, did you think front engines were the way forward, or did you somewhat regret it?

HL: No, not at all. Three designers were asked to do a proposal for this VW sports car. I was one of the three and I won the competition. And that was the 924, and although I was supported by a senior designer in how to develop it and address the technical feasibility and the package feasibility, the design was mine from the beginning, even though I was very young and inexperienced.

JT: When you came back to Porsche in 1989 the 964 was already launched.

HL: Yes, the 964 was launched, but in a very difficult period and it wasn't selling very well.

JT: So was your first task then to revamp the 964 into the 993?

HL: Yes. It was done in a very short period. So my life as far as the 911 is concerned was very much influenced by 'please, Mr Lagaaij, could you change it?' I love 911s but I'm not nostalgic about them. I look at each of them and say, okay, well the next step could be this or that, and the current 991, which my successor was responsible for, I look at it and say, 'Okay, I understand. What's the next step?' And all around me I see the old 911s becoming more popular by the day, and even my designer colleagues are buying them even though they don't work for Porsche. They all have a 911 tucked away somewhere but I'm one of those who hasn't done it yet, though it will happen one day. But I'm not sure whether I want to spend so much money on one. I'm not nostalgic, you see. I love historic racing; I love going to the concours parades and I love judging them because I know a bit about the history of each car, and I always try to understand exactly what context they were designed in, engineered and produced in.

Harm Lagaaij and Pinky Lai of Porsche Design discuss the buck for the 996 as the clay is shaved to perfect the contours. PORSCHE MUSEUM ARCHIVES

JT: There's a paradox there, because historic racing is about nostalgia to a great extent. Seeing and hearing a 2.0-litre short wheelbase, narrow-bodied 911 being put through its paces at Spa Six Hours is like going back in time to a truly halcyon era even though it's happening today.

HL: Sure, but even though I've been involved in historic racing for five years I'm still not nostalgic about it. I do it because the budget is lower – or at least in the beginning the budget was much lower to go racing than with modern racing cars, and because you can improve them so much within the spirit of the rules. You can make them faster than they ever were in period. It's a combination of many things being improved, and that's what I love about it. I love improving the cars but once they are finished I want to move on to the next project.

JT: At what point could you see the transition from air-cooled to water-cooled coming up? When were you given a brief to draw the 996 and Boxster?

HL: The car development process is extremely structured and today, even more so than ten, fifteen, twenty years ago, its become extremely well organized, so it's not just that somebody throws in an idea, it's a huge amount of work before any drawing pen is moved. In the case of Porsche in the beginning of the 1990s it was completely clear that it could not continue as it was with the car line-up we had

A contraption of inexplicable complexity is mounted on the front of the 996 chassis in readiness for crash test evaluation during the process of obtaining TüV type approval. PORSCHE MUSEUM ARCHIVES

The crash test dummy sits, oblivious to the blow that's been targeted at the back of the 996. The circular marker points indicate the extent to which the bodywork has been affected by the impact. PORSCHE MUSEUM ARCHIVES

and therefore a very interesting two-year period began, deciding what to do next. In that period there was a group of people comprising engineers, concept engineers, design engineers, and the sales and marketing people who decided what it could be. We shouldn't forget that Porsche was a very small company, even then, compared to today, and therefore it was a relatively small group of people trying to come up with a solution. They came up with a lot of concept sports cars and four-seater sports cars. Then the head of R&D came up with the brilliant idea of making the Boxster and the 996 based on commonality up to the windscreen. That was an incredible breakthrough because it not only meant that we had two completely different cars in terms of their concept but also a completely different financial

basis, plus the fact that Mr Wiedekin was obsessed about lowering the production costs as much as possible. So the commonality of platform between Boxster and 996 was a stroke of a genius because it meant that Porsche was back. It had the potential to become a healthy company again and the Boxster and the 996 were an incredible breakthrough in the history of Porsche. Putting those two models into production, we were making money again, so that was the turning point in the company's history.

JT: What was in your mind when you were drawing those cars? Were you thinking, yes, we must go back to Porsche's racing heritage, to the 550 Spyder or the 718 RSK, to get some of these styling cues into the Boxster?

Sheer artistry: the full-size 996 model is mounted on a turntable, the better for Porsche designers, including Pinky Lai and Harm Lagaaij (left), to contemplate the contours. PORSCHE MUSEUM ARCHIVES

996s pass through the spray booth; this one will be finished in Zanzibar Red. PORSCHE MUSEUM ARCHIVES

(continued overleaf)

HARM LAGAAIJ INTERVIEW *(continued)*

HL: Not directly. By coming up with the concept of two cars with commonality, one of which would be the mid-engined two-seater car, then you can start looking back in time. But until that moment in the beginning of the 1990s we didn't actually know that we would be going for a mid-engined car again. But when that decision was taken then of course you start looking back at the form of the Spyders and the RSK, so there is some form language from those cars, but the Boxster is a very individual shape. It's lovely to look at that motor sport period, but the Boxster is very much a reflection of how much fun a two-seater mid-engined sports car could be for Porsche again.

JT: Talk us through the mechanics of styling a car. Do you go from pen-and-paper renderings to clay buck and so on?

HL: It's a very structural process. First of all, you need to know whether it is going to be a completely new car or an evolution. For instance, a completely new car is the Panamera. An evolution is the 991. So they start off very differently. The big difference between the design process in the 1970s, '80s and '90s was that in a '90s project, you'd have a 911 group of people and a Cayenne group of people, then you have the Panamera group, and each faculty is represented in this group; so you have a project leader, you have a group of engineers who, for instance, if it's the Boxster, they only specialize in the Boxster. There's a group of designers, and I decide which designers are going to be in that group, and then they start work. If it's an evolution, say, of the next Boxster, then it's a continuous development, where you have a certain amount of time available to develop it from how it is now and what it's going to consist of as a face-lift, or as a major face-lift.

But if it's a completely new car then it's a totally different story. Then the design process starts with an advanced design period, which can take from one to three years if you don't know what the car is going to be like. The Cayenne went through an extremely long period of advanced design and engineering to find out which particular car would suit Porsche best. So those two projects are very different in terms of the time they take and the people involved, and the budget you have available. Each project group has a lot of authority to move on as necessary, therefore these groups stay together for quite a long time. The Boxster group, for instance, goes from the very beginning right up to the current Boxster, because they specialize in that car. The project leader of the Boxster has been the same for fifteen years now, I think, and they protect and they develop their baby as best and as competently as possible within budget. Everything is very well structured on how to develop it, the time frame and for how much money.

So it's very much a conceptual period when you are not certain of what particular form the car should be. In the case of the Cayenne, as you can imagine, Porsche, having always been a sports car company, deciding to go for an SUV was almost unthinkable but in hindsight it was the best decision it made. Fortunately after asking quite a lot of other car companies whether they would like to do a car together with us, we found VW willing and able to do so. We would develop two SUVs, one with a VW badge and one with a Porsche badge, and the best part was that VW actually paid Porsche to develop it, so that was a win-win situation.

Tony Hatter, pictured at Classics at the Castle, is a prominent member of the Porsche Design team and is now Director of the Design Quality Style department. His wife was responsible for designing Porsche cabin upholstery. AUTHOR

Pre-launch testing involved high-speed running at Mugello in Tuscany, Italy, where the climate is favourable all year round. Both 996 and Boxster 986 were trialled simultaneously. PORSCHE MUSEUM ARCHIVES

Prototypes of the 996 were subjected to hot weather trials in arid conditions in the USA. PORSCHE MUSEUM ARCHIVES

JT: At what point was it proposed to turn the Boxster into a coupé? When did you start thinking about the Cayman?

HL: It was very simple, because you always try to find synergies within one particular car. The best example is the 911 having so many derivatives. The 911 was developed from the very beginning as a Coupé and the next step is a Targa version, then all the motor sport versions, then the Cabriolet, then the four-wheel drive; you have so many derivatives just in the 911 range. The same vision should be applicable to a Boxster. However, on the Boxster it's more difficult, because you cannot do four-wheel drive because of the mid-engine. And then we found out that a lot of people, especially in hot countries, don't ever open up their roof, so then you say, 'why don't we do a coupé?' So it's a very logical step, and you always try to find an original, attractive synergy to enhance the production volumes of a Boxster. And that is the Cayman, which will never sell as well as a 911 Coupé but it's a fantastic car that's underrated at the moment. It's a phenomenal car. It

has a tauter chassis and more space than a normal Boxster and it does everything even better. So that's how derivatives are started.

JT: Of all the Porsches you've designed what's your favourite?

HL: All of them have merit in some way. But if pressed, I would say the 997.

Apart from racing histories (like his ground-hugging Shadow Mk1 Can-Am car), Harm Lagaaij loves nothing better today than riding his KTM Supermoto around remote and challenging European mountain passes, using his Cayenne to transport the bike there.

The 996 pauses at an outpost of civilization while undergoing extreme cold weather testing at Tatchun Centre in the Klondike, Yukon territory, Canada.

PORSCHE MUSEUM ARCHIVES

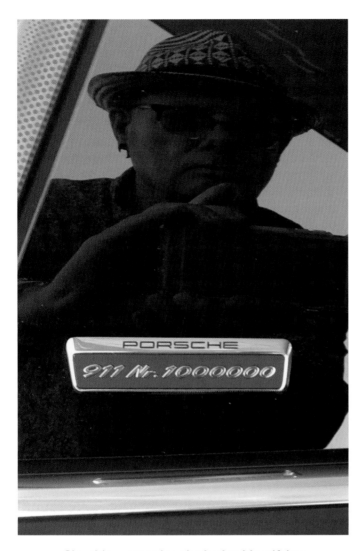

Sleuthing: snapping the badge identifying this 991 as the 1,000,000th 911. AUTHOR

version of the 3.6-litre water-cooled flat-six. It's normally aspirated, so there's no 'artificial' boost and no extraneous ducting about the bodywork: just pure aerodynamic functionality to the splitter, side-skirts and biplane rear wing.

The Gen 1 GT3 appeared in May 1999 and lasted a couple of years until Gen 2 came out. The general spec differs from the basic 996 in having 30mm lower and firmer suspension, 330mm cross-drilled ventilated discs, four-pot calipers and specially adapted ABS brakes. Anti-roll bars are adjustable, and ten-spoke 18in wheels – 8in and 10in – shod with 225/40ZR 18 and 285/30 ZR 18 rubber are complemented by 5mm spacers for extra track width. The dry-sump GT3

The 996 GT3 was introduced in 1999 and powered by the naturally aspirated 3.6-litre flat-six version of the Le Mans-winning Mezger engine, developing 3,600bhp. Here the author is let loose in Antony Fraser's car at Zandvoort Circuit. ANTONY FRASER

THE 996 GT3

Every era of Porsche production has included a rarefied top-line model, usually with competition aspirations or descended from a race car, and badged as an RS. For the first couple of years of its life, the 996 lacked a standard-bearer, but that was addressed by the introduction of the GT3, named after the FIA race category it was eligible for, blending a higher performance, normally aspirated engine with a lighter body, and sports-tuned suspension with a track-focused demeanour: an RS in disguise. Soon enough, the GT3 was massaged into an RS in its own right.

The GT3 is the most sublime evolution of the basic 996 model, created using the narrow-body C4 chassis – in rear-drive only format – and powered by the unburstable Mezger

The photographer's Mk 1 996 GT3 quayside at the Hook of Holland; the swan-neck rear wing is a prominent aerodynamic aid on this model, aimed at exerting downforce on the back of the car at high speed. ANTONY FRASER

The 360bhp 996 GT3 engine looks purposeful even out of the car.
PORSCHE MUSEUM ARCHIVES

engine features nitrided crank, titanium con rods, dual-mass flywheel allied to a 6-speed geabox, and develops 360bhp. In the cabin, the standard GT3 offers bucket seats for driver and passenger but none in the rear, with sound deadening and hi-fi speakers deleted as well in order to save weight, while the Clubsport option provides race seats, a half roll cage, six-speed transmission with single-mass flywheel, fire extinguisher and air bags deleted.

In production from 2002 to 2005, the 381bhp Gen 2 GT3 bore revised headlamps and front and rear detailing, including a new fixed wing. It delivered more power and was even tauter in the suspension department, with better brakes to match. The jury's still out on which is the better car, though either does the business in fine style. On a fast, rural A-road the GT3 really feels planted, rock solid in its ability to go the distance whatever the journey. It's a tour de force and thoroughly merits its place in the Porsche pantheon. As for which version to choose, that's another matter.

Playing a motorized version of the generation game, I had the opportunity to try a pair of 996 GT3s back to back. There were several choices to make: Comfort or Clubsport, tuned or standard, a case of age over beauty, Mk 1 or Mk 2? As much as any other model, the 996 GT3 epitomizes Porsche's design and manufacturing philosophy. A perfect blend of road-going sports car and track-oriented elaborations, it's a direct manifestation of a philosophy that goes back way beyond the much vaunted 1973 2.7 RS to evolutions of the 356, such as the 356 Carrera of 1955. The company has always sought to implant lessons learned on the track in its road-going models. The 996 GT3 was announced at the Geneva salon in April 1999. It unites a higher performance, normally aspirated engine with a track-tuned chassis, and augments the lineage of Porsche thoroughbreds in the RS

idiom. It certainly looks the part with its deep front spoiler and airdam, aerodynamically configured sills, and fixed double-decker 'swan neck' wing on the engine lid (in Mk 1 guise) instead of the retractable wing of the standard 996.

With a nod to the FIA's GT3 endurance racing class, it was immediately seized on as the vehicle of choice for the Carrera Cup and Porsche Supercup series and, from 2000, the N-GT class of the FIA GT Championship, as well as international races like the Nürburgring 24-Hours. It was an immediate sensation. Manthey Racing's GT3 won the GT class at the 1999 Le Mans 24-Hours with drivers Uwe Alzen/Patrick Huisman/Luca Riccitelli at the wheel. Shortly afterwards, Porsche's test driver Walter Röhrl took a GT3 around the 14-mile (22.5km) Nürburgring Nordschleife in 7mins 56s, notably under the crucial 8.00-minute mark, the first time ever for a production car, much to the glee of the Porsche PR department.

Porsche's chief test driver Walter Röhrl making it look effortless at the wheel of his 997 GT3 RS. ANTONY FRASER

The 996 GT3 is the offspring of Andreas Preuninger, head of Porsche's GT series production department and manager of Porsche High Performance Cars. A renowned purist, he designed a specification that would encourage maximum driver involvement, and for that reason Tiptronic and PDK transmissions were off the menu. The 996 GT3 uses the then-new Carrera 4's narrow (as opposed to wider C4S) bodyshell, adapted to house the GT3's dry-sump oil tank, different engine mounts and larger fuel tank. At the time, normal 996 Carreras used the 3.4-litre flat-six, but in order to stand the strains and stresses of on-track use, the GT3 was fitted with a new 6-cylinder unit, the 3.6-litre 'Mezger' engine. This unit was based on the crankcase of the 964, allied to a pair of water-cooled cylinder banks and camshafts in a configuration similar to that of the 959 Supercar, Group

The ten-spoke split rim wheel characterizes the 996 Gen I GT3. AMY SHORE

Andreas Preuninger is known as the Godfather of the GT3. After joining the company in 2000, he oversaw every subsequent incarnation of the model, as well as the GT3 RS variants, GT2 and Cayman GT4. PORSCHE MUSEUM ARCHIVES

C 956 and 962 racing cars, and the GT1 Le Mans winner – heady stuff indeed.

The Mezger engine, named for the legendary Porsche race design engineer Hans Mezger, was installed in normally aspirated format so it would have wider race homologation potential. It came with a higher 11.7:1 compression ratio, VarioCam timing adjustment and four valves per cylinder, and its plasma-nitrided crankshaft and titanium con rods allowed it to rev significantly higher than the standard engine. The six-speed GT2-based G96/50 transmission and dual-mass flywheel with 40 per cent limited slip differential were sourced from the 993 GT2. Capable of 360bhp at 7,200rpm (273lb ft torque at 5,000rpm) when it came out, the GT3 was the most powerful non-turbo 911 ever made. The 0–60mph rush took 4.7s, with a top speed of 300km/h (187mph). Counting on engine upgrades rather than turbocharging to accomplish a higher performance, the GT3 body lacked 996 Turbo- or GT2-style vents in its rear wheel arches, enabling a coherent overall neatness of design – no doubt overseen by Harm Lagaaij.

The handling matches the power and looks. The GT3 sits 30mm lower than standard and its suspension consists of adjustable dampers, shorter, stiffer springs and adjustable anti-roll bars, with cross-drilled and ventilated 330mm disc brakes with red-painted four-piston calipers and ABS 5.3. They inserted 5mm spacers for slightly wider track, and fitted lightweight ten-spoke Speed Design split-rim 18in wheels (8in rims front, 10in rear), shod with 225/40 × 18 and 285/30 ZR × 18 tyres.

On the assumption that owners would want to take their GT3 on track at some point, two trim levels were offered: Comfort, with lighter sports seats and no rear seats, but

The Gen 2 996 GT3 has more linear front air-intake scoops, and the headlights contrast with those of the Gen I car to the right. AMY SHORE

The swan-neck analogy of the Gen I GT3's double-decker rear wing is clear when viewed in profile. AMY SHORE

otherwise virtually identical to the 996 C2; and the Club-sport, which is equipped with a single-mass flywheel, allowing the revs to rise and fall more rapidly, while the cabin features racing seats and bolted-in rear roll cage tied in to the rear shock towers for added chassis stiffness. Both the rear seats and side airbags are absent. In both versions the space-saver spare is replaced by a puncture repair kit and inflator. The Mk I is the last road-going Porsche to be built on the motor sport production line, and is the last Porsche to have a throttle cable; apart from ABS it has no other driver aids. Although it's a heavier car than the standard 996 Carrera, the Mk 2 GT3 is heavier still. There was the odd downside: the Mk I gained a reputation for worn synchro rings, but then a second batch of cars incorporated steel synchro rings, an upgrade extended to the Mk 2.

The Mk 2 GT3 appeared on the scene in 2004 at the same time as the GT3 RS. Model buffs reckon the Mk 2 was toned down to provide more of a contrast with the hardcore GT3 RS (the Mk 2's cup holders were a sign). For the first time the GT3 was available in the USA, a market historically wary of hotter evolutions. The Mk 2 presents several stylistic changes too. The 'teardrop' headlights are sourced from the Turbo – and applied to the rest of the 996 range – to replace the Mk I's 'fried eggs' and further differentiate it from the Boxster, and the front and rear PU skirts have revised slope angles to the inlets and air ducts, with subtly different curves and splitter. It is the same with the back panel, which also displays revised contours. The 18in ten-spoke wheels are simplified, side skirts moulded to enhance the aero, and the rear wing configured as a platform on a pair of struts – an ironing board instead of the Mk I's swan-neck biplane. It's also 30kg heavier than its predecessor.

The ten spokes of the 996 Gen 2 GT3's colour-coded wheels are grouped in five pairs. The supports for the rear wing are also angular, rather than curved. AMY SHORE

In the performance stakes, power rises to 381bhp with torque up to 284lb ft, available from 2,000rpm, and it's also shorter geared in 5th and 6th. The suspension is lowered and firmed, brakes beefed up with six-pot calipers up front; Porsche's ceramic composite brake system was a £5,356 optional extra. Bespoke semi-slick Michelin Pilot Sport N1 tyres were developed specifically for the Mk 2 GT3.

The pair of 996 GT3s seen here near Duxford, Cambridgeshire, are a Mk I Comfort and a Mk 2 in Clubsport trim. A back-to-back road test was an interesting proposition in itself, but the cars had been modified by the tune-up experts Manthey and Parr, respectively, which made this an even juicier prospect. First up is the left-hand-drive 1999 GT3 Mk I finished in Basalt Black Metallic with a black

A pair of 996 GT3s, with the Gen 1 car in front of the Gen 2 version, tracking along a Cambridgeshire country road. AMY SHORE

Engine bay of the Gen 1 996 GT3 reveals the aftermarket BMC GT3 Cup air filter and the Manthey-tuned 3.6-litre flat-six, consisting of exhaust, carbon air intake and ECU remap, yielding 400bhp. AMY SHORE

leather cabin, in which the only mod is an aluminium foot-rest beside the clutch pedal. It's fitted with 18in GT3 Sport Design alloy wheels, wearing 225/40 × 18 and 285/30 ZR × 18 Pirelli P-Zeros. It's got Litronic headlights, aluminium gearshift and handbrake levers, matching black-painted centre console, climate control and GT3 sports seats with blue belts. The clincher is a full Manthey K400 package consisting of exhaust, carbon air intake and ECU remap, installed by Steve McHale's JZM workshop and yielding 400bhp. Like a lot of Mk 1s, it's also received Mk 2 six-piston front brake calipers with Alcon floating discs. The front brakes have cooling ducting too. The gearbox has been fully rebuilt with steel Motorsport Synchros also fitted by JZM, and an RS-spec differential with single mass flywheel and clutch.

There's also an interesting aerodynamic tweak: like the 996 RS, the radiator has been set at an angle for efficiency and to create downforce by means of the RS-style air vents cut into the top of the front PU panel. The engine lid with its swan-neck wing is noticeably lighter than the Mk 2 car's and incorporates a carbon fibre duct that, when closed, channels air directly to the single K&N mushroom filter. It's done 101,000 miles (162,550km) and appears to have been a money-no-object passion for the previous owner. The K400 conversion and gearbox rebuild was carried out just 3,000 miles (4,830km) ago and the annual service stamps show the car has been meticulously maintained all its life.

Next up is the 2003 GT3 MK 2 with Clubsport spec and Parr Motorsport engine performance upgrade. This too is painted Basalt Black Metallic and features all the aesthetic changes wrought on the Gen 2 cars. The cockpit is fitted with black leather bucket seats with the Porsche crest embossed in the headrests, plus Schroth five-point racing harness in red, along with red seat belts, and protected by a stainless-steel Porsche Tequipment half-cage in the rear cabin.

The 18in GT3 alloy wheels are the ten-spoke design, painted grey and lacking the split-rim bolts of the earlier Sport Design wheels. They're shod with 225/40 × 18 and 295/30 ZR × 18 Michelins. Front brakes consist of GT3 RS six-pot calipers, operating on Alcon floating discs via Pagid RS pads. A full set of KW coil-over suspension is fitted, along with one of Thomas Schnarr's magnificent CarGraphic sports exhausts. This one's covered 41,000 miles (66,000km) with a full Porsche main dealer service history, and the last service was carried out by Parr at Crawley, where it underwent the Parr engine tune and ECU remap, logging 400bhp on the rolling road dyno.

Cockpit of the Gen 2 996 GT3, revealing the regular no-frills steering wheel and the rear cabin's roll cage. AMY SHORE

The author motoring in the Gen 1 996 GT3, a great driving experience. AMY SHORE

The differences between the rear wings of Gen 1 (right) and Gen 2 996 GT3s are clear when viewed from behind. AMY SHORE

The black beauties are eased out onto the back roads to see what's what. I'm in the Mk 1 to start with. It's such a wonderfully lithe car: there's so much torque that it needs minimal accelerator pedal pressure to get going. At 4–5,000rpm it's really starting to zing, pelting along the flat-land straights and soaking up the undulations with ease. On fast corners, it's effortless with completely smooth turn-in and faultless handling. It's a very elegantly balanced chassis. And that makes it a much better compromise as a road car, although the Mk 2 seems marginally faster around the lanes.

Next I try the right-hand-drive Mk 2 with its more sports-oriented Clubsport cabin, which immediately makes a psychological difference to one's perception and expectations of the car. It's louder, stiffer and more focused in a business-like way, tauter, more planted and less balletic. It turns in sharply, but it is bobbing about on the bumps, with a bit more of a tendency to tramline. All this is in response to driving

on B-roads, where there's less traffic, but if you're bent on doing trackdays, the Mk 2 is definitely better because of its firmer set-up.

They both look great with their lowered suspension – that's a great stance for a 996. The Gen 2, with its roll cage cabin bracing, is a tauter car and delivers a harder, more uncompromising ride. It's the older version, however, that meets the criteria of real-world driving. Without question, the less modified Mk 1 is the car that I'd prefer to take home: it's a sweetie on a winding B-road, quick enough in acceleration and cruising, a tad less torquey than its younger sibling but you'd catch up in short order. It's difficult to see how you'd better this as a road car. Does it need the additional 40bhp? Not particularly, though I don't have any issues with a little light tuning. The quirkier aesthetics of the Mk 1 over the Mk 2 are also more intriguing, and that confirms my view.

996 GT3 'GEN 1' (2000–2001)

Layout and chassis
Two-plus-two coupé, unit-construction steel body/chassis

Engine

Type	M96/72 'Mezger' dry sump, horizontally opposed, rear-mounted 6-cylinder
Block material	aluminium
Head material	aluminium
Cylinders	flat-six
Cooling	water
Bore and stroke	100 × 76.4mm
Capacity	3600cc
Valves	4 valves per cylinder
Compression ratio	11.7:1
Fuel supply	Multi-point injection
Max. power (DIN)	381bhp @ 6,800rpm
Max. torque	273lb ft @ 4,250rpm
Fuel capacity	89 litres (19.5 gallons)

Transmission

Gearbox	Getrag G96/00 rear drive 6-speed; ZF 5HP19 automatic; M-B 5G Tiptronic
Clutch	Hydraulic single dry plate
Ratios	1st 3.82
	2nd 2.20
	3rd 1.52
	4th 1.22
	5th 1.02
	6th 0.84
	Reverse 3.44
	Final drive 3.89

Suspension and steering

Front	independent by MacPherson struts, aluminium links, longitudinal and transverse links, coil springs, gas dampers, anti-roll bar
Rear	independent by MacPherson struts, aluminium links, lateral and transverse links, coil springs, gas dampers, anti-roll bar
Steering	rack-and-pinion
Tyres	225/40 × 18 front, 285/30 × 18 rear
Wheels	Aluminium alloy
Rim width	7.5in J front, 10.0in J rear

Brakes

Type	front and rear vented discs with four-piston calipers
Size	298 × 24mm front; 292 × 20mm rear

Dimensions

Track	
Front	1,455mm (57.28in)
Rear	1,500mm (59.05in)
Wheelbase	2,350mm (92.51in)
Overall length	4,430mm (174.4in)
Overall width	1,765mm (69.48in)
Overall height	1,305mm (51.3in)
Unladen weight	1,350kg (2,976lb)

Performance

Top speed	302km/h (187.6mph)
0–60mph	4.8s

996 CARRERA 2 CABRIOLET

At the other end of the macho image scale, from the Turbo at least, is the 996 Carrera 2 Cabriolet. In 2017 I sampled a 2003 model that had done just 51,570 miles and was on sale for £16,995, less than half the price of the equivalent 996 Turbo. Convertibles don't come much more groovy than this with the top down on a balmy summer's day. It's a post-facelift Gen2 and its four previous owners have covered on average only about 3,600 miles (5,800km) per year. Its overall condition suggests that it's been an exclusively summertime car, although it does have a matching factory hardtop to turn it into a curvaceous coupé for the winter. That particular look emphasizes the front end of the car, and from some angles it appears more lithe, whereas the

The 996 Carrera Cabriolet was available from 1998. The dedicated hardtop fitted was almost a match for the 996 coupé model, aesthetically, while offering the benefit of cruising in convertible mode. AUTHOR

996 TURBO (2000–2005)

Layout and chassis
Two-plus-two coupé, unit-construction steel body/chassis

Engine

Type	M96/72 'Mezger' dry sump, horizontally opposed, rear-mounted 6-cylinder
Block material	aluminium
Head material	aluminium
Cylinders	flat-six
Cooling	water
Bore and stroke	100 × 76.4mm
Capacity	3600cc
Valves	4 valves per cylinder
Compression ratio	11.7:1
Fuel system	Multi-point injection, 2 KKK K16 turbochargers
Max. power (DIN)	420bhp @ 6,800rpm
Max. torque	413lb ft @ 4,250rpm
Fuel capacity	64 litres (14 gallons)

Transmission

Gearbox	Getrag G96/00 rear drive 6-speed; ZF 5HP19 automatic; M-B 5G Tiptronic; all-wheel drive
Clutch	Hydraulic single dry plate
Ratios	1st 3.82
	2nd 2.20
	3rd 1.52
	4th 1.22
	5th 1.02
	6th 0.84
	Reverse 3.44
	Final drive 3.89

Suspension and steering

Front	independent by MacPherson struts, aluminium links, longitudinal and transverse links, coil springs, gas dampers, anti-roll bar
Rear	independent by MacPherson struts, aluminium links, lateral and transverse links, coil springs, gas dampers, anti-roll bar
Steering	rack-and-pinion
Tyres	225/40 × R18 front, 295/30 × R18 rear
Wheels	aluminium alloy
Rim width	7.5in J front, 10.0in J rear

Brakes

Type	front and rear vented discs with four-piston calipers
Size	350 × 24mm front; 330 × 20mm rear

Dimensions

Track	
Front	1,455mm (57.28in)
Rear	1,500mm (59.05in)
Wheelbase	2,350mm (92.51in)
Overall length	4,430mm (174.4in)
Overall width	1,765mm (69.48in)
Overall height	1,305mm (51.3in)
Unladen weight	1,540kg (3,395lb)

Performance

Top speed	305km/h (189.5mph)
0–60mph	4.2s

traditional 911 coupé is sufficiently hump-backed to draw the volume of the shape rearwards. The hardtop is far from essential, though, as the normal rag-roof is perfectly capable of withstanding the rigours of the northern European winter, while not giving as much insulation.

Detaching the hardtop involves undoing the Allen bolts located in the speakers in the rear parcel shelf with the spanner provided, and then it becomes a two-person lift-off, as it encompasses a two-plus-two cockpit, and is accordingly too weighty for one. You then need somewhere to store it. Anyway, it's there if you want it. The point of the Cab is to get involved with the fresh air, whether in the countryside or cruising the esplanade of some coastal paradise.

The 996 two-plus-two rag-roof grand tourer was launched as a 3.4-litre model in April 1998, receiving the 3.6-litre engine in 2002, and was superseded by the 997 Cab in the 2005 model year. Its hull is finished in a rich, deep Lapis Blue, a gorgeous colour, with a grey leather cockpit interior, which I find a little sombre and not my personal choice. A thick pile grey carpet clads the floors. I suppose there are enough variations in texture and shape to negate what could be a sea of grey, and it may be advantageous on an extremely hot day when black would be murder. Our subject car is on a set of 18in Porsche Sport Design split-rim alloy wheels. There's no doubt that it's in pretty good shape for its mileage, with scarcely a stone chip to be seen. There's a full OPC and Porsche specialist service history, 12 months' MoT and has recently had a major service.

Detachable hardtop for the 996 Cabriolet really needs two people to lift off. AUTHOR

Rear seats in the 996 Cabriolet cockpit are identical to those of the coupé, providing comfortable accommodation for young children, while an adult has to make the best of things. Alternatively, the backrests fold down to provide a useful luggage platform. PORSCHE MUSEUM ARCHIVES

The canopy is the Cabriolet's *raison d'être* and it's simplicity itself to retract, being operated entirely electronically. To lower it in preparation for an excursion, I press the switch on the centre console and hold it down. This releases the catch that secures the rigid front hoop of the hood on the windscreen header-rail. The canopy arches back overhead to the accompaniment of a mechanical whirr, while the door windows lower themselves and the rear three-quarter side windows also retract into the slots either side of the cockpit. The folding roof then buries itself snugly into the hold to the rear of the cockpit and is neatly hidden away from view by the closing lid. Raising the roof is the

The canopy roof of the 996 Carrera Cabriolet retracts electrically into a well behind the rear of the cockpit, where it is neatly accommodated. AUTHOR

same in reverse: you keep your finger on the button throughout the whole procedure, which lasts around 15 seconds. There's a delay of a second or so after pressing the button before the erection process starts. The lid rises behind the cockpit and the canopy emerges skywards, arcing overhead, while the rear-three-quarter triangular panes pop up and the side windows retract slightly in anticipation as the canopy lowers itself down to the windscreen, where it settles neatly on the header rail and locks itself into position.

The Cabriolet's controls and six-speed shift are totally familiar from my 996 C2 – just a tad grey. It's an easy rider in the grand touring manner, capable of accommodating four people as long as two of them are children, which is good for the school holidays, as I know from hustling my own kids to Portugal a couple of times in 911s.

The 996 Gen 2 3.6-litre delivers everything you'd expect from a 996, turning in nicely in the bends and well equipped for a cross-country dash should you require it, though it isn't in the slightest bit demanding like a GT3 could be. It's literally a breath of fresh air when top down, and it inspires the laid-back approach to a leisurely jaunt. If I'm right and this has been a high-days-and-holidays car all its life, that's a good indication as to where its appropriate future lies too. It would be perfect for insouciant sauntering at the weekend or crossing the Continent to soak up some sun.

The 996 Carrera Targa represents the best of both worlds, being a coupé with a retractable glass ceiling, opening up a large expanse of the car's roof to the elements. PORSCHE MUSEUM ARCHIVES

996 TARGA C4S

Cabriolets are all very well – most have electric canopies these days – but they do lack the solidity of a hardtop roof, one that you can tap without it giving against your finger. That'll be the Targa, then. We've had hard-lidded 911 Targas since 1968, when the debutant soft-window version gave way to the heated greenhouse-glassed Targa, a design that held sway till the advent of the 993 Targa in 1995. The original Targa concept endured for almost three decades, but even that was relatively cumbersome. You may not have had to struggle with the taut canvas, recalcitrant hood frames and press studs that bedevilled traditional roadsters, but lifting off a Targa top was almost a two-person job – and once removed you then had to stash it in the luggage compartment. The glazed roof panel of the 996 Targa may not have been quite the macho fresh-air aperture of the classic models, but who needs macho when ease of operation means accessing the elements is just the touch of a button away?

Available from 2001 to 2005, the 996 Targa inherited the sophisticated sliding glass roof panel premiered in the 993, and it was a technological tour de force as well: the 996's pane is an expansive canopy occupying the car's entire roof space – twice the area of the normal sunroof. This means there's a constant awareness of celestial surroundings and a feeling of increased luminosity, visibility and perception, and a casual upward glance is a more convivial, un-buffeted event. There's a sunshade tint to the glass, so occupants aren't quite so exposed to ultraviolet rays and the public gaze, and a full-length roller blind extends the length of the roof at the press of a button. A button on the centre console erects the wind deflector, and a second touch activates the retraction mechanism that operates the glass panel. It can

also be triggered via the key fob. The glazed roof eases its way rearwards and is stowed discreetly inside the rear window, forming two layers of glass in the process, while leaving the aperture over the cabin wide open. The 996 Targa roof also offers a hatchback rear window for ease of stowage.

Targas have always been something of a law unto themselves, attracting a particular fan base, and the 996 version doesn't break that particular mould. There are visual clues in the body lines as to the 996 Targa's origins. Take a look at the sharp point where the long, elegant sweep of the roof edge meets the delicate upsweep of the rear wing, turning the rear three-quarter window into a pointed shield shape rather than having a rounded trailing end like the coupé does. It's what a 996 Cabriolet looks like when it's fitted with a hardtop, and that's where the Targa hails from. But while the Cab could be specified as a C2 and all-wheel drive

This 996 Carrera Targa features black powder-coated spokes to its Porsche Classic split-rim wheels. AUTHOR

dark grey spokes. The dark grey theme was carried through to the door mirrors and sculpted aero sill skirts. The engine lid grille and, by implication, the rear wing were also painted dark grey to match. Body colour was Arctic silver, which is slightly darker than the rarer Polar.

When put to the test, I found the familiar 996 cabin was pure and simple, though I had to fiddle with the seat and steering wheel adjusters to come up with a suitable driving position, which is half the battle in evaluating any car. It was diverting to play with the button shifts on the steering wheel, and it accelerated smartly enough, though it didn't seem as swift as a manual. It ducked and dived into the bends nicely, though I felt it lacked a spring in its step. However, on a sunny day it was nice to have the Targa top open to enjoy direct contact with the countryside. The growl from the exhaust was more audible with the top open too. I'd label it as a cruiser, a touring car rather than a sports car.

Timo Bernhard

Not only does the 996 Targa roof open wider than a normal sunroof, the model also features a hatchback rear window. AUTHOR

C4, the Targas were all fashioned on the narrow-bodied C2 driveline. Historically Targas have always been roughly 50kg (110lb) heavier than their coupé counterparts due to the structural enhancements, and the same is true of the 996 coupé and 996 Targa: at 1,470kg the latter weighs 50kg more, but more surprisingly the 996 Cabriolet is 10kg heavier than the Targa.

I recently tried out a 2004 996 Targa C4 that had done just under 140,000 miles (225,300km) and was on sale for £18,000. Was it worth the money? All 996 values are on the rise, and what makes a Targa more special is both its ingenious fresh air format and the fact they only built 2,693 of them. It can be argued that a Porsche purist will always want a coupé because that's the 911 heritage, but Targas are in vogue again and there has been a big impact on their prices. The upholstery on this 996 Targa was in very good condition and the doors shut properly. It had integral dash-mounted satnav and telephone. Transmission was via Tiptronic shift and, despite its relatively high miles, it was in very good shape. Tyres were Continental Sport Contacts, 285/30 × 18 on the back and 225/40 × 18 on the front, cladding attractive Porsche Design split-rim wheels enhanced with contrasting

Timo Bernhard: a Porsche pilot through and through. PORSCHE MUSEUM ARCHIVES

Headhunted by the Porsche Racing Department, Timo Bernhard, here seen driving a 996 GT3, was champion in the 2001 German Carrera Cup. PORSCHE MUSEUM ARCHIVES

Three times winner of the Nürburgring 24-Hours in a 997 GT3 RSR, Timo Bernhard also won the 2007 ALMS (American Le Mans Series) in the Porsche RS Spyder. He was born in Homburg, Saarland, and has been a mainstay on the works Porsche driver roster since he signed for them in 1999 at the age of just eighteen. Timo progressed from 996 GT3 to full-on Spyder in six years, and has remained wedded to the Stuttgart marque, happy to race for Porsche in different disciplines on both sides of the Atlantic.

In 2008 I interviewed him in the Drivers' Club garden at the Festival of Speed, just after he'd run up the Goodwood Hill in the ALMS LMP2 Spyder;

It's great to do this for fun. The track is narrow, but the surface is very good, so it isn't a problem to run here with these cars. At first, I didn't know the track, and at every corner I slowed down a long way ahead. I spun the tyres on purpose, because the fans love the smoke and the wheelspin. They love a bit of showboating!

Maybe so, but Timo is extremely serious about his racing.

It's my first time here, but once I started to learn the track I could go quicker. I feel like I'm in the 1960s – the tracks with no Armco and the straw bales! It's good for all modern young drivers to see circumstances like this to get a bit of perspective on the past. I enjoy driving here because of the atmosphere – on the one hand it gives you the feeling like you're at a professional race because all these famous cars and legendary drivers are here, but on the other it's a bit like a real hill climb. The fans appreciate the proximity, too. They can get right up close and almost touch the cars in the paddock. When you go up the hill you don't see the crowd, but on the way back down you see all the people are waving – and that's a real buzz.

If Timo Bernhard isn't a household name in the UK, it's because his triumphs have been in continental Europe and

Perceived by pundits as the Achilles heel of the 996 and 997 engines, the intermediate shaft (IMS) bearing can occasionally fail, resulting in a costly strip down to replace it or even an internal catastrophe within the engine. The IMS bearing evolved over the life of the 996 and 997, with some bearings being stronger than others, but a replacement always brings peace of mind. ANTONY FRASER

The original 996 Gen 2 IMS bearing race before replacement. ANTONY FRASER

the entire engine suffers from the disbursed swarf, while the cam timing can also be affected, causing valve-to-piston contact – and a consequent need to replace or rebuild the engine. So why does this sometimes happen? There's no definitive agreement, but it's likely that heat generated by the engine makes the seals of the bearing race harden over time, and the grease contained within seeps out, leaving the balls destitute of lubricant, while, conversely, the seals prevent engine oil accessing the race to lubricate the balls. It's been suggested by some specialists that the seal on the outer edge of the bearing should be removed, allowing the engine oil access, but just removing the seal alone doesn't ensure a reliable supply of lubricant.

There are four ways to counter this scenario. First, replace the vulnerable bearing every 50,000 miles (80,000km) and hope for the best. Second, go for a Direct Oil Feed kit, as I did with my 996, which takes an oil line off the crankcase directly to the bearing race. This includes a new bearing (and, at 40,000 miles (64,000km), I have to report that there was nothing wrong with the existing bearing) and thus ensuring a constant flow of lubricant. A more complex route is to fit the LN Engineering ceramic replacement dual-row or single-row bearing sets. What appears to be a more comprehensive solution, however, is available from Autofarm at Weston-on-the-Green, Oxfordshire, where Matt Wiltshire explained the options:

Three types of IMS bearings have been used in M96 and M97 engines A dual-row bearing race was fitted from 1997 model-year to 1999, and that can be changed without having to strip the engine. Then, from the 2002 model-year to 2005, a single-row bearing race was used, and although that can be swapped for a new one without stripping down the engine, it is now seen as a retrograde feature. So, between model-year 1999 to 2002, either of these bearings could be used. Then, from model-year 2006 to 2008, the bearing is bigger and it can't be removed without removing and stripping the engine.

Autofarm co-owner Steve Wood took up the story:

We now use a cylindrical bearing with thrust control that can take both radial and axial loadings. From an engineering point of view, we believe this is the most robust and well-designed bearing we've seen to date. We've actually had one installed in a 996 that does a lot of miles backwards and forwards to Scotland. After a year we removed it to inspect it, and couldn't witness any wear or markings. But the innovation with this method is in the IMS shaft, and where the other solutions just allow oil into the bearing, this method allows pressurized oil drawn from the oil pump (after the modification) to go through the IMS shaft and into the bearing. That wouldn't be the case with the standard bearing, of course, which shouldn't allow any oil into the IMS cavity, but it sometimes did, and that was very likely to be dissolving the grease from the original bearing.

Steve thinks there are various possible causes: 'Once the grease is washed out of the bearing race you'll get a bit of slop in the bearings, and they'll get a bit hot from the friction of picking up slightly on the race. So the danger time is early in the morning when people start their cars up, that's often when they let go.'

Autofarm's solution is more involved and requires more labour, but Steve believes the benefit of allowing oil into the bearing internally is worthwhile:

The cylindrical roller bearing is made specially for this application, and its manufacturer claims it is five times stronger because it has more surface area to take up the load. With ball bearings, at low rpm only three of the ball bearings are actually making contact with the outer race, so at low rpm it's actually not quite as stable as it is at 5,000rpm because of the inertia taking all the balls out of play. As the shaft spins up, inertia takes effect and pushes the ball bearings out onto the outer surface of the race. In 2006 the 997 received an IMS bearing that's nearly twice as big, and the LN ceramic bearing is very similar to that, size-wise, but it relies just on engine oil to lubricate the bearings, which is the same principle as the Direct Oil Feed kit – but that employs steel rather than ceramic bearings.

We looked at the bearings and thought, what would we want in our own engines … that's a steel

Regular maintenance is vital to the ongoing survival of the water-cooled flat-six engine: here the 996 receives an oil change. AUTHOR

bearing and I think I'd rather have that than the ceramic one. Some people say you shouldn't put a needle-roller in that location because they don't like side loadings and a needle-roller will wear on the edge slightly, while a ball bearing takes the loading in that point where a needle-roller can wear slightly on one side if they are subjected to side loadings. But the manufacturers of this solution have been quite clever in the way they've made the bearing, because it's got thrust control built in; it is allowed a small amount of end float.

Autofarm's method also involves tapping a tiny hole in the end of the IMS shaft to allow oil to pass along its length 'so you get a bit of oil flow. We're not talking about much. There'll be oil crank pressure, which will allow oil to go into the IMS shaft, so you've actually got oil at the back and front of it, whereas these other grease bearings only have oil at the front.'

Matt described the procedure:

You can normally do them in situ, but if the engine has to come out, normally a C4 is slightly easier to drop out. We'll always do an inspection to highlight anything else that is worth doing while we've got an opportunity to take the engine out, one of them being the brake pipe that goes over the top of the gearbox; there's a clip that holds the pipe on, and it corrodes right at that point, so it's obviously worth renewing if it looks suspect. I've just seen a car that's got over 300,000 miles on the clock with the original bearing, and I think the high mileage cars would probably be alright because they've survived, while on the other hand I've seen low mileage cars go, so there's no rhyme or reason to it. Probably lower mileage cars are more prone to go because they are the ones that are sitting around, the bearings not being used, but no one has actually pinpointed why it happens.

They're great cars, and it's a real shame the bearing issue happened. They still had the issue with the IMS bearing in 997s up to 2006; that's when the big IMS bearing came in. We've not seen any issues with the bigger one. If I bought a 996 tomorrow I would change it, because there's that possibility it could happen, so why take a chance for that sort of money, especially if it's a manual gearbox and it's come in for a clutch. It's actually not that expensive to do the rest of the stuff, so why wouldn't you do it? It's about having complete confidence in your car to go and enjoy it.

Steve then explained how much Autofarm charges to install the IMS solution:

> You're looking at around £1,850 to do just the bearing: that's labour to take everything out, then you check to see if it needs a flywheel, which we test to see if it's springing back OK – they're about £400 – and then obviously the clutch kit. Including the IMS bearing, clutch and flywheel, when that's all done you could be driving out of here for £2,500 plus VAT.

It's an expensive business if it goes wrong, so would you rather spend that kind of money on the replacement bearing or £12,000 for a new engine? I think it's a sensible move, especially if you're planning on keeping the car. Nonetheless, Steve advised a rain-check before committing:

> We say to customers, before you go steaming in there and change it, take the oil filter off, with the housing off, and have a look inside. If there is a problem, you'll see something that looks like gold dust in the bottom of the pot, and if the bearing is really starting to break up you'll see metal filings in the filter too. So we pull the filter apart and check that first. Keep changing the oil regularly, and if you see any signs of gold dust or metal filings, then you've got to bite the bullet.

There's no such thing as a wild goose chase with an IMS bearing swap because, even if it's OK when checked, there's every possibility it could shatter a year hence. It turned out that the one in our subject car had no play in it whatsoever, despite what was seen when looking into the oil filter. A special tool is used to press the bearing out. Being the original

bearing from a 3.4, it's the dual-row race and this was the first time it had been removed. A snap-ring at the front has to be removed before it's pressed out. As he removed the old bearing Matt found traces of oil, and when he pulled out the intermediate shaft there was about an eggcup's worth of oil in the tunnel, confirming the suspicion that this is how the grease gets leached out of the bearing race, with the oil getting through the bearing itself and then into the shaft. This could have happened a week before or a couple of years ago, but it couldn't have drained out during an oil change, so it's important to soak up all the oil while the shaft and bearings are out, even though the intention is to get fresh oil running through the system. As Matt explained:

> The oil pump is actuated by an intermediate shaft that's driven by the crankshaft and we fit a modified drive that sends the oil through a little gully, and then when it's rotating the oil passes through the shaft. As part of our modification, we make an insertion in the end of the oil pump end of the intermediate shaft and then the oil comes through as it's spinning and will actually feed the bearing itself.

The oil then drains from there into the sump.

There's nothing terribly sophisticated about inserting the bearing race, though Autofarm uses a special insertion tool, a kind of collar that is placed over the top of the race and, when absolutely sure it's squarely in the entrance to the tunnel, is tapped fully home with a mallet.

There's one more surprising task to perform. Matt took off the oil pump cover and removed the pump and the gears. He also took the drive out of the end of the intermediate shaft, then tapped a tiny hole in the end of the actual shaft,

Special tools are employed to access and withdraw the IMS bearing race in the 996 engine. ANTONY FRASER

Autofarm's solution to the IMS bearing replacement scenario is to fit a race containing roller bearings instead of ball bearings. ANTONY FRASER

which enables the oil to travel along inside the shaft and feed the vulnerable bearing. Who knew the metal was so thin at this point? As it is, the other bearing at the back of the pump is never short of lubricant: 'There'd be oil gathered up there and it'll come through the little gully in the end of the oil pump, so it also lubricates the bearing and the shaft, and now oil will go down through the intermediate shaft and down to the other end.' It's such a straightforward solution that one can't help wondering why the manufacturer didn't implement it. All that now remained was to reassemble the engine and ancillaries and reinstate it in the car.

It's a very short step from watching to wanting. As I would be away for a month, I left my 996 'Pig Energy' in the care of Autofarm with a wish list that included a fresh IMS bearing. It's hard to evaluate 'peace of mind', but I am confident that the potential IMS bearing issue is now a thing of the past for this car, and if I came to part company with it that would surely be a strong selling point. According to Autofarm, people looking to buy a 996 or an early 997 will usually go for one that's had the bearing upgrade. Now that 996 prices are hardening, it's not a bad idea to go for the IMS upgrade to consolidate their value.

996 CARRERA C2 'GEN 2' (2002–2004)

Layout and chassis
Two-plus-two coupé, Targa and cabriolet, with unit-construction steel body/chassis

Engine

Type	M96/22 6-cylinder, horizontally opposed, rear-mounted
Block material	aluminium
Head material	aluminium
Cylinders	flat-six
Cooling	water
Bore and stroke	96 × 82.8mm
Capacity	3596cc
Valves	4 valves per cylinder
Compression ratio	11.3:1
Fuel supply	multi-point injection
Max. power (DIN)	320bhp @ 6,800rpm
Max. torque	273lb ft @ 4,250rpm
Fuel capacity	64 litres (14.07 gallons)

Transmission

Gearbox	Getrag G96/00 rear drive 6-speed; ZF 5HP19 automatic; M-B 5G Tiptronic
Clutch	Hydraulic single dry plate
Ratios	1st 3.82
	2nd 2.20
	3rd 1.52
	4th 1.22
	5th 1.02
	6th 0.84
	Reverse 3.44
	Final drive 3.89

Suspension and steering

Front	independent by MacPherson struts, aluminium links, longitudinal and transverse links, coil springs, gas dampers, anti-roll bar
Rear	independent by MacPherson struts, aluminium links, lateral and transverse links, coil springs, gas dampers, anti-roll bar
Steering	rack-and-pinion
Tyres	225/40 × 18 front, 285/30 × 18 rear
Wheels	aluminium alloy
Rim width	7.5in J front, 10.0in J rear

Brakes

Type	front and rear vented discs with four-piston calipers
Size	298 × 24mm front; 292 × 20mm rear

Dimensions

Track	
Front	1,455mm (57.28in)
Rear	1,500mm (59.05in)
Wheelbase	2,350mm (92.51in)
Overall length	4,430mm (174.4in)
Overall width	1,765mm (69.48in)
Overall height	1,305mm (51.3in)
Unladen weight	1,320kg (2,910lb)

Performance

Top speed	285km/h (177.09mph)
0–60mph	5.0s

CHAPTER TWO

EVOLUTION OF THE 996

In order to illustrate how the 996 range unfolded, I shall recount a catalogue of driving experiences, in no particular order, and based on various cars I've handled on assignment. It's only when you're behind the wheel and operating the controls that you truly comprehend a car's handling and on-road behaviour, and this is where its true character emerges. First off, let me take you back to the 'New Millennium'.

Porsche celebrated the new millennium with a special edition of the Mk 1 996 C4 to mark the passage of time, but it was some years later before I parted with number 556 out of the 911 cars that were made. Dubbed the Millennium, all are finished in Violet Chromaflair, an enigmatic dark auber-gine hue that perplexingly contrives to look green, blue or purple, depending on the light.

It's a sort of 'coming-of-age' 996. It isn't just the shape-shifting external colour scheme that made the Millennium special; the leather upholstery and deep-pile carpet inside the cabin were toned a warm tan shade, and the standout feature was the burr-maple veneer that bound sections of the steering wheel rim and the door pocket lids that double

The 996 Millennium limited edition model came out in 2000 to mark the dawning of the 21st Century; 911 units of the Gen 1 car were made. ANTONY FRASER

as arm-rests. It was an expensive car, costing DM185,000 at the turn of the century (that's €94,500 or £73,400), while the standard 996 C4 cost DM147,000 (€72,000 or £56,000). A further DM5,000 would buy the optional five-speed Tiptronic transmission, as was found on our subject car, instead of the six-speed manual. This was quite a mark-up for an aesthetic upgrade with no special mechanical tweaks. To put this in proportion, in 1999 the Mk 1 996 GT3 cost DM179,500, an astonishing DM5,000 less than the Millennium C4. You might think it would now be difficult to flog a Millennium C4 for proportionally more than a 996 Mk 1 GT3, but the market for limited editions can be unpredicatable: a 996 Millennium C4 was recently offered for £60,000, which is indeed more than the very cheapest GT3. It's equally amazing that this Millennium C4 may be worth twice as much as a good C4S (£30,000).

But it looked the part, and the sandy brown cabin with its clubby woodcraft detailing was a breath of fresh air in the

The plaque below the '911' in front of the gear lever indicates that this is number 556 out of the 911 cars. Satnav and in-car phone were state-of-the-art communication at the time. ANTONY FRASER

torpid sea of sombre black leather that pervaded most 996 interiors, although I find the chosen exterior colour was rather gloomy for something that was meant to be heralding the hope and optimism of a new era. They could have gone with something more radical or jazzy, but perhaps, with the high-profile 996 Turbo waiting in the wings, it wouldn't have done to proclaim the merits of the standard car too loudly.

Millenniums don't come on the market very often, but there was an opportunity to try one in Belgium when Bert Vanderbruggen bought number 556 (though you need a magnifying glass to read the tiny silver plaque on the centre console behind the gear-lever). They all bear the 911 badge on the engine lid, as well as lettering on the door sills. The four-wheel-drive running gear, mated to the 3.4-litre water-cooled flat-six, means the narrow-bodied Millennium C4 is quick enough, conveying secure, stable handling in corners and on wet roads, its performance sparkling though not devastating. Top speed was rated at 174mph (280km/h) – 171mph (275km/h) with Tiptronic – and a 0–60mph time of 5.2s, or 6.0s in Tiptronic mode. In that respect it's no different to the Gen 1 996 C4. The suspension is the same up front too, consisting of wishbones, MacPherson struts, anti-roll bar, coil springs and twin-tube gas dampers, with the LSA (Lightweight, Stability, Agility) concoction of five wishbones per side at the rear, plus anti-roll bar, coil springs and single-tube gas dampers. The sleek narrow body has no aerodynamic excrescences, apart from the electric spoiler that emerges from the rear engine lid at 50mph and retracts at 5mph. Overall, it's quite unassuming and is certainly an appealing package.

This Tiptronic S-equipped Millennium C4 was delivered to the Porsche main dealer in Padua, Italy, in November 1999 and was taken to Belgium in 2004. It's now done 100,000km. The Millennium's dome sports a sunroof with comfy Alcantara headlining, and it also boasts a satnav, a top-line radio and CD changer, Bose speakers, leather-clad telephone, rear wiper and chrome tailpipes.

All the controls operate smoothly; the wood-rim wheel is nice to twirl, the shift knob agreeable to handle and the driving seat is comfortable and supportive. It looks and feels really classy: everything works just as it should and the cabin provides a pleasant, unpretentious environment, whatever your take on the veneered sections. It has all the electric seat adjustments and first-edition 996 equipment, including the natty little telephone handset, presumably a bit special in 2000 before hands-free became a legal necessity. There's no glove locker, leaving just the door pockets for the receipts and oddments that inevitably accrue while the car's in use. It's a simplification to call the upholstery 'tan', because it is quite an orangey colour. The gear knob and handbrake lever

The cabin of the 996 Millennium was opulently upholstered in tan leather. ANTONY FRASER

Overhead rear view demonstrates the Gen I 996's clean, uncluttered lines. AUTHOR

surround are also in wood trim, inset with the gearshift pattern and Porsche logo in silver. The main dials, on-board computer and vents are in black, providing an overall effect of restrained opulence.

So how does it fare on the road in comparison to my 996 C2? Comparative weights are 1,320kg for the 996 C2 against 1,375kg for the C4 Millennium, and this is manifest in a slightly more athletic performance by the rear-drive C2, though the all-wheel-drive car's poise and control ensures confidence-inspiring security when the surface is damp. It's less enthralling than the C2, though rewarding in its own competent way. Instantly the steering feels much heavier than the C2, thanks to the front-wheel driveline as I pull away, and the additional weight makes it seem slightly bulkier. While it lacks the sprightly character of the C2, it does feel more planted and placid on smooth straights. The four-wheel drive becomes even more obvious in manoeuvres such as a simple turn-around (a constant, repetitive aspect of all photoshoots), asserting itself as I power the car

back into a straight line. This is a feeling that's completely absent in the more delicate steering response of the C2. On fast A-road bends the four-wheel traction is amazing: it just sticks and goes. It is extremely efficient, but I have to say that the C4 driveline means it rather lacks the soul of the C2. Pondering the club class cabin, the Millennium could almost win me over to an all-wheel-drive 996 – but not quite.

996 GT3 GEN 2

A visit to the West Country in 2017 provided the opportunity to compare two examples of the 996 GT3 Gen 2, starting with one offered by Simon Cockram at Cameron Cars, near Bath. The car, which had last been on the market in 2013, has the basic Gen 2 Comfort specification, but with fibreglass hard-back Clubsport-style bucket seats with crested headrests. This offers leather upholstery, including a leather-clad dash, door cards and seats, and it's

**Gen 2 996 GT3 Clubsport fitted with
additional front splitter.** AUTHOR

fitted with climate control. The finish is Polar Silver, which is a bluey sort of silver, as opposed to Arctic, which is lighter and brighter.

In Simon's opinion the market for both 996 and 997 GT3s has improved in recent years. Historically the GT3s were always a slower market and examples might hang around longer in stock, but when the market took off the prices of 996 GT3s pretty much doubled. This has now calmed down a bit, but it seems prices are unlikely to drop back to their former level. A one-owner, 3.8-litre 997 Gen 2 GT3 at Cameron Cars that has done just 4,000 miles (6,440km) was priced at £120,000, which suggests that the market is still strong for the right models.

The other 996 GT3 Gen 2 on offer was with Williams Crawford at Saltash in Cornwall. Its almost unbelievably

low mileage – 20,660 miles (33,250km) since it was first registered in June 2004 – and pristine condition explain its expensive asking price of £97,000. It has right-hand drive, a metallic Arctic Silver finish and full leather interior, including factory-fitted Recaro seats. It's fronted by Xenon headlights with headlamp wash, and runs on 18in GT3 alloys.

In both the Gen 1 and slightly more refined Gen 2 guise, the 996 GT3 is a perfect blend of road-going sports car and track-oriented incarnations, epitomizing Porsche's design and manufacturing philosophy. The GT3 Gen 2 appeared on the scene in 2004, and some say it was toned down to provide a contrast with the more hard-core GT3 RS. The Gen 2 presents several stylistic changes too. The 'teardrop' headlights were sourced from the Turbo and replaced the Gen 1's 'fried eggs', and the front and rear bumper panels have revised slope angles to the inlets and air ducts, with subtly different curves and splitter. The back panel also displays revised contours that are a matter of taste, though there must be some practical substance to the alterations. The 18in ten-spoke wheels are simplified, side skirts moulded to enhance the aero, and the rear wing configured as a platform on a pair of struts instead of the Gen 1's elegant swan-neck biplane. It's also 30kg heavier than its predecessor. In the performance stakes, power rises to 381bhp with torque up to 284lb ft, available from 2,000rpm, and it's also shorter geared in 5th and 6th. The suspension is lowered and firmed up, brakes beefier with six-pot calipers in front, while bespoke semi-slick Michelin Pilot Sport N1 tyres were developed specifically for the Gen 2 GT3.

The low mileage over the course of thirteen years places the previous owner in the category of a collector who wants as few miles as possible. This is crucial for buyers wanting a

**With its lowered
suspension, front splitter
and ten-spoke alloy
wheels, the Gen 2 996
GT3 adopts a purposeful
stance.** LOUISE TOPE

The Gen 2 version of the 996 GT3 sports the fixed two-tier horizontal rear wing on its engine lid. LOUISE TOPE

This Gen 2 996 GT3 is equipped with highly contoured and supportive Sports seats, which have apertures above the shoulders for fitting full race harnesses. LOUISE TOPE

car they can salt away for another decade as prices escalate. Other punters don't care about this and require a trackable car. This can lead to a wild disparity in GT3 values.

This example is in its original first paint, exactly as it left the factory, making it a really good target for investment or a collector's item, but I think GT3s are built to be driven hard and enjoyed, not preserved in a bubble. If you have a racing car you should be out there racing it. According to Adrian Crawford, 'a lot of people are parking money, and they pick a low production, top spec car, whether that's top technical spec or low production, and then they want every box ticked: history, provenance, condition, mileage'. The gap between collector quality and the enthusiasts' car has been getting bigger, but both categories can be a winner, because you are doing what you want to do with your car.

I know how these cars go, and how fantastic they are in any context. It's a real powerhouse, dispensing the throaty Mezger roar, depth of performance and tautness of handling

that's unique to the GT3. It doesn't take a day on the track to realize that. In deference to its showroom status I limited myself to a short run, fervently hoping that it gets bought by someone who recognizes its fabulous quality and will put it to use without worrying too much about knocking up the miles.

FORCED INDUCTION

I've had a lot of work done on my 996 by the Oxfordshire-based company Autofarm, which was founded in the late 1960s (*see* Chapter 10). On one of my visits I tried out a 996 Turbo they were offering.

The 996 Turbo was launched in 2000, replacing the air-cooled 993 version, and was related to its 996 GT3 sibling

The 996 Turbo is a comfortable, civilized way of travelling very fast. It is capable of reaching 60mph in 4.2s, and has a top speed of 190mph (305km/h). AUTHOR

The street version of the Le Mans-winning 911 GT1 provided inspiration for the GT3 and Turbo's Mezger engine – the 'unburstable' flat-six unit named after Hans Mezger, head of Porsche's race design office from 1965. AUTHOR

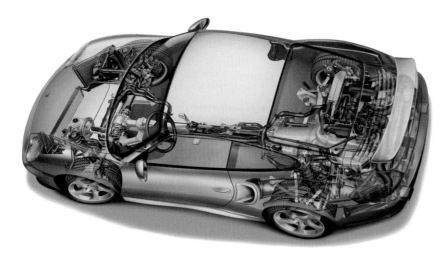

Cutaway illustration of the 996 Turbo, revealing the all-wheel-drive layout. PORSCHE MUSEUM ARCHIVES

The 996 Turbo engine develops 420bhp at 4,800rpm. The twin turbochargers are located either side of the crankcase. PORSCHE MUSEUM ARCHIVES

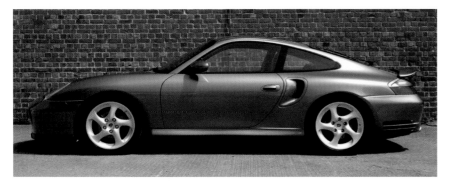

Viewed in profile, the 996 Turbo's front splitter is just visible. The vents in the lower rear bumper panel are another distinctive Turbo feature. AUTHOR

by virtue of its 'Mezger' dry-sump engine. This revered power plant, which is, by common consent, a stronger unit than the normally aspirated 996 flat-six, originated in the aluminium-cased flat-sixes powering the 930 Turbo, 3.0 SC and the partly water-cooled 962 4-valve engine, with cylinder heads derived from the 959 supercar. It was then engineered to debut as a 3.2-litre chain-cam twin-turbo in the Le Mans-winning 1998 GT1.

It was a bold, if pragmatic, move to shoehorn this engine into the rear quarters of the 996. The 996 Turbo can deliver 420bhp at 6,000rpm, enabling genuine 190mph performance and 4.2s acceleration to 62mph. Only the rear-drive 462bhp 996 GT2 and run-out Turbo S with the 450bhp X-51 performance upgrade kit are more powerful examples of the 996, and so worth investigating if you seek a greater surge factor, and of course the Turbo Cabriolet if you're a sun worshipper.

This particular example was finished in Seal Grey, which makes a change from Polar or Arctic Silver, and its metal finish is quite fetching. The cabin is also upholstered in dark grey leather. Although I prefer black – certainly a black wheel – this complements the general hue of the car rather well. It is endowed with the full original factory specification, including Recaro sports seats, electric sunroof, PSM (Porsche Stability Management), front and side airbags, bi-Xenon headlights, the on-board computer that computes fuel range, oil level, outside temperature and so on, plus inertia belts in the rear and standard extras such as air conditioning.

Some three-quarters of its mileage had been in the hands of a single long-standing Autofarm customer. Its fully documented service history recorded a suspension overhaul, including fitment of Bilstein B6 shock absorbers in 2012 (at 55,000 miles/88,500km); a brake overhaul that included new discs in 2013 (at 64,000 miles/103,000km); and in 2014 the air-con system was overhauled with new radiators fitted; while its idiosyncratic Turbo-twist 'throwing star' wheels had been refurbished and a set of Michelin Pilot Sport tyres fitted, with mileage logged at 77,000 miles (124,000km).

Ideally you need an unrestricted Autobahn to light up a 996 Turbo and head like a rocketship for the vanishing point, but I had to make do with the local back roads. Sliding into the cabin, the electrically adjustable seats quickly locate a favourable driving position. It has done just shy of 80,000 miles (128,750km), so all the mechanisms – steering, six-speed shift, switchgear, levers – are precise and in excellent shape. The steering feels nicely weighted, the six-speed stick moves slickly through the gate, and it delivers awesome acceleration. The chassis is hugely competent, reassuring and confidence inspiring.

It handles very nicely, and I'm not conscious that the Turbo's front powertrain is as prominent as it can be in a C4 driveline. On these back roads its towering pace is less evident than its multifaceted ability. The compliant ride, fluent steering, easy shift, confidence-inspiring brakes and sure-footed 4 × 4 traction and grip around the corners combine to provide an easy, almost languid ride. It may be a 420bhp twin-turbo salvo-server, but its schizophrenic personality is well concealed on these sinuous lanes. But it also delivers a slug of grunt with aplomb, prompting a glorious sensation of indomitability. On a short stretch of dual carriageway I can floor the throttle with impunity and the Turbo kicks in instantaneously, as the 996 hurls itself forward with the velocity of a howitzer shell before the ultra-efficient brakes pull it back once more.

It's the all-round competence of the car that's the making of it – surfeits of power, finely honed handling and all-wheel-drive competence, governed from the supremely comfortable and efficient 996 cockpit. It's the unsung supercar hero, awesomely capable, robust and reliable, a trans-continental express par excellence.

The 996 Turbo rear wing is a two-tier device with an upper aerofoil that rose on hydraulic struts. PORSCHE MUSEUM ARCHIVES

A 996 Turbo posed at Harewood House, Yorkshire – scene of the famous hill climb event. The standout characteristics are the wide-arched body, so-called Turbo wheels, and front panel with large ovoid cooling apertures. AUTHOR

996 TURBO

A well-maintained 2001 996 Turbo available from West Yorkshire Classic Porsche, near Wetherby, caught my attention partly because of its slightly more affordable asking price. It had a six-speed manual gearbox and was finished in Arctic Silver, with grey extended leather interior, and a highly detailed service record. Standard equipment included 18in Turbo pattern alloy wheels, Xenon headlights, electric memory seats, extended leather, Alcantara headlining, the upgraded Porsche sound package including PCM navigation module with a hands-free phone system. There was a sunroof, automatic anti-dazzle rear view mirror, anti-dazzle driver's mirror, upper-part tinted screen and a six-disc remote CD changer. It was also fitted with the 997 short-shift kit. The sales pitch emphasized that a 996 Turbo was a 'rock solid investment. More civilized than a GT3. It's the safest car to buy at the moment. Anything that's up at £350 grand could come tumbling down, but these won't.'

This 996 Turbo has been around a bit, but it has been serviced every year regardless of mileage, from 2001 right up to 62,000 miles (99,800km), when everything imaginable was done, including spark plugs and pollen filter, and the wheels were refurbished. Even though this was a right-hand-drive car, it was manufactured as part of the Exclusive programme and used as the demonstrator at Porsche OPC Gothenburg, Sweden, before being exported to Britain in 2003 at 36,000 miles (57,950km). It is almost certain it was ultimately destined for the UK and the original owner bought it however he could to circumvent the massive waiting list. In later years its service records document its travels from Wilmslow to Newcastle and Harrogate, before four years in Essex and on to Yorkshire.

Few cars look more purposeful on the road than the 996 Turbo with its broad rear quarters. The hill climb at Harewood seemed an appropriate excursion. The electrically adjustable seats quickly provide a position similar to that which I'm accustomed in my 996 C2 – only faster! The predominantly grey leather cabin interior works well enough with the Arctic Silver shell. As it's done only 63,000 miles (101,000km) everything is crisp and in very good condition; the steering is spot on, the six-speed shift precise and the towering performance is evident. The chassis is hugely competent, reassuring and confidence inspiring. It handles very nicely, and the front powertrain is less dominant than it can be in a C4 driveline. It engenders a feeling of invincibility, such is its colossal velocity and all-round ability, given its muscle-toning brakes and the surefootedness of the all-wheel-drive traction and grip through the bends, abetted by its Bridgestone Potenzas. Steering is fluent into and out of corners, and the ride is relaxed. Short-shift gearchange kits can be slick and pleasant to use, as on this Turbo, or they can be unduly notchy (like the one in my 996 C2). This all-wheel drive, 420bhp twin-turbo missile demonstrates both blistering on-boost pace and a restrained ability on winding back roads. On major arteries the Turbo is the most benign of companions, easing past other traffic without blinking.

Historically, the 996 Turbo offered even more poke in its later S guise, punching out 430bhp for an extra £10,000. The X51 power kit can lift the standard Turbo's power even further from 420bhp to 450bhp at 5,700rpm, a significant hike that brings it close to the 996 GT2's 462bhp at the same revs. Having said that, there is absolutely nothing lacking in the regular 996 Turbo, and this one certainly lives up to expectations.

ZANZI BAR

I'm driving Zanzi, a Zanzibar Red 996 GT3 trackday special, and it's possibly the fastest Porsche I've ever handled on the road. Mindful of my licence, I don't extract anything like its maximum potential, but it certainly feels mind-blowing. Hugging the verge, the GT3's rotund red left-hand wing tucks in with a mix of resolute authority and graceful serenity, powering relentlessly out of the curve and onto the upcoming straight.

An offer from Jonathan Sturgess of the Cambridge Motor Company to have a taster of a madcap Zanzibar Red GT3 could not be refused. This is a dish indeed, and one that hap-

Zanzibar Red is one of Porsche's more eye-catching hues. When applied to a 440bhp 996 GT3 it is positively eye-watering. AMY SHORE

pens to run a 4.1-litre flat-six, pushing out almost 500bhp – over 100bhp more than the standard Mk I GT3. The latter's spec was advocated by Andreas Preuninger, head of Porsche's GT series production department, and designed to provide maximum driver involvement and serve as a flagship model for the new millennium; what we have here exceeds that definition by some way!

Before venturing out, I run through the inventory. There's a suede-rimmed Momo steering wheel, dished back towards the driver, and I'm surrounded by a hefty web of bars comprising a full roll cage, padded along the sections where you are likely to knock your head. The roll cage originated in a Porsche 996 Cup Car, testified by a sticker at the bottom of a downpipe. There's an intercom system in the cabin, so driver and co-driver can communicate on special stages when wearing appropriate lids.

Its JRZ suspension cells are attached to the rear downtubes of the cage; there's one for each damper, so there are another two under the front lid. The JRZ dampers provide adjustable bounce and rebound, and because the cells are in remote reservoirs they don't overheat when racing around a track. It's also been equipped with £8,000-worth of Elephant Racing suspension components, which explains its distinctively shaped arms. Each of the ten arms cost about £600, so the bits that can't be seen were almost as expensive as what's on show. The power steering reservoir has been relocated to the nose just ahead of the fuel tank, together with the remote reservoirs and the adjusters for the front shocks – damp and squat on both, and hardness directly on the top. Altogether the parts came to roughly £12,000 before fitting, which was a lot more than the equivalents from KW or H&R.

The Zanzibar Red 996 GT3 with contrasting black multi-spoke wheels is one of the finest examples of the marque's earlier water-cooled models. AMY SHORE

The cage is united with the shell of the car by fillets of metal reminiscent of knuckledusters. These reinforcements then run down the 'A' post and 'B' post where they're welded onto the body. There's a fire extinguisher in the passenger footwell. Five-point Schroth harnesses straddle the Porsche Recaro race seats, though the regular 996 shoulder belts are also usable. Incongruously for such a firecracker of a car, there's also a CD changer.

Most of us would be extremely content with an untouched 3.6-litre Mezger engine, but not this owner who wanted the ultimate and was prepared to lavish about £50,000 on it. The oil filter has been relocated for simple servicing and there many details that are very different to a normal GT3, such as custom-built throttle bodies, to which the air filters inside the engine bay are attached, and a custom air-scoop, all in

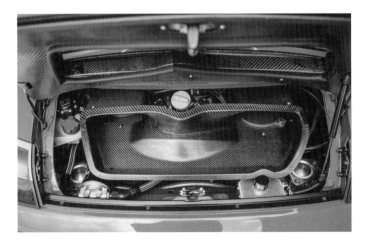

The Kevlar scoop feeds air into the GT3's big-bore 3.9-litre Manthey-tuned and equipped flat-six engine. AMY SHORE

carbon fibre. There are solid engine mounts, a relocated dry sump oil reservoir, and a custom-made exhaust – part titanium, part stainless steel – which apparently cost a little under £12,000 and was chosen after trying four different systems on the rolling road.

Time to hit the road. It's not the easiest of starters: hold the key over and keep the motor churning till it fires. After that there's no problem, though it is ticking over quite fast at 1,200rpm. The sintered clutch, however, makes it a difficult car to get off the line when I come to release it. They are manufactured using iron as a friction material because it can tolerate more abuse, hence their use in racing applications. The steering is light enough once I'm up and running, but it is hard work hauling it around to get out of a parking situation.

The 440bhp Zanzibar GT3 is one of the fastest cars that the author has ever driven. AMY SHORE

Soon enough I come to terms with the sintered clutch; it is just a matter of balancing the revs on the accelerator and releasing as delicately as possible with tensioned left leg muscles. When opening up it is quite brutish in character, and the enormous power that it can deliver is immediately obvious. On a straight it's violently fast and feels as quick as a GT2, though of course you have to work at it as there's no turbo. That also means there's a heck of a roar from the exhaust: from 4,000rpm to 5,000rpm in 3rd and 4th it's positively roaring. The rev limiter is set at 9,300rpm, so there's no chance of challenging that round here. All the time though, no matter what the revs, there's a hint of backfiring on the over-run, which is quite seductive and adds to the charm. It's compliant too. It's going where I'm steering it, with immaculate turn-in, inviolable, poised cornering and handling.

Hugging the verge at speed, the Zanzibar GT3 turn-in and handling is utterly peerless. AMY SHORE

The ride is what you'd expect of a GT3. The suspension is particularly hard, along the lines of the Clubsport but rather more so, which means I'm feeling all the bumps. There's slight tramlining but nothing you wouldn't get with a regular GT3. Anchoring hard for each bend, the brakes respond dramatically well, albeit squealing in agony. I'm keeping the power on as I'm storming the corners. Most Porsches impart the feeling that you could actually take on the world, I know, but this one does it in spades.

Jonathan's account of the car's provenance was laced with jaw-dropping numbers as the sums spent on it mounted up. Zanzi has an interesting and comprehensive history file. It's metamorphosed through three major engine rebuilds in the quest for more power, all of which added way more than the price of the car. The current engine build tots up to £90,000. Before that the best part of £25,000 was spent on the Manthey rebuild to bring it up to 3.9 litres and 440bhp. That was preceded by the 400bhp conversion by JZM, which was another £10,000 to £12,000. Altogether about £140,000 has probably been spent on a car that's on sale for £75,000, but if the market continues its trend, the time may not be so far off when 996 GT3s are worth that kind of money anyway.

So, what has all that been spent on? As a standard car, the GT3 was first taken to JZM at King's Langley in 2005, where a Manthey K400 package was installed, consisting of exhaust, carbon air intake, ECU remap, and yielding 400bhp. In 2007 it had tuning work done by Fearnsport at Silverstone. The following year it was packed off to Manthey in Germany and, at 65,000-miles (104,600km), had a €26,700 full engine rebuild to M440 spec (440bhp), which entailed rods, valves, chains and tensioners, and taken out to 3.9 litres. That still didn't give enough power, so it went to CTR Developments at Huntingdon, which have a reputation for making race engines in small numbers. Here it was fitted with a Motec M600 engine management system, custom throttle bodies, Schrick cams, a 4.0-litre crank from the 997, Capricorn rods and Cup RSR heads, liners and pistons:

> The crank, rods, liners and pistons were around £15,000, the heads were £5,000, induction kit £6,000, loom and ECU £6,000, extra head work £3,000 and machining for all of the components £3,000. The bill for the custom exhaust is £10,000 including titanium silencer £6,500. Then another £7,000 just for the dyno work, which seems a lot of money for running a car up on a dyno.

The suspension set-up installed consists of the Elephant arms plus three-way adjustable motor sport JRZ 1231 dampers, costing €7,500 for the kit. It also runs 18in forged magnesium BBS Manthey wheels, the full cage described above, Momo sports steering wheel with air bags, Mk 2 GT3 RS floating discs and six-pot calipers. The total spend on this occasion was £46,988, which resulted in 489bhp at 8,800rpm. By comparison a standard Gen I GT3 is 360bhp, so that's a pretty impressive hike.

Being a Gen 1 996 GT3, the Zanzibar express retains the two-tier swan-neck rear wing. The black Gurney spoiler at the trailing edge of the lower wing is a small but significant sophistication. AMY SHORE

Despite its stratospheric spec, Jonathan concedes that there's a paradox about Zanzi Candy's position in the marketplace, because most buyers don't want modified cars unless what's already been done matches their own aspirations. Money spent on restoration and performance tuning is never recovered in the sale price. An original Zanzibar would have sold much sooner. If a potential buyer is told that the engine cost £50,000, they might think, 'if it breaks, do I have to spend that much to fix it?' In reality, however, a car with this spec such as this is built for racing all day, every day, so it's unlikely to have any engine problems.

Some of my acquaintances have upgraded their GT3s just as Zanzi has evolved, but they have espoused newer incarnations in the shape of the 997 and 991 GT3, and that might be the rub. Persuading such a person to travel back in time requires them to countenance older tech and an older image. It wasn't that long ago that I was modifying a 964, so there shouldn't be a problem in that respect. The look of the original 996 GT3, with its deep front spoiler and airdam, aerodynamically sculpted sills, and fixed double-decker swan-neck wing on the engine lid, shows the model at its purest and most elegant – less aggressive too – before the introduction of the ironing-board rear wing of the Mk 2 and the more muddled ducts, gaping vents and prominent splitter of the 997 GT3. The Mk1's styling is captivating in itself, but what of the colour? Zanzibar Red – paint code 1A8/1A9/N1 – is a rich, dense, ambiguous hue that looks orange by day and red by night. It's subtly adrift of red, having an exotic quality straight out of a spice market, redolent of paprika, water melon or achiote (*Bixa orellana*) seeds, famed for their red pigment when crushed. Having featured as the colour

of the first 996 GT3 sales brochure in 1999, it was available on the Porsche colour chart until 2004, so you'll find a few Zanzibar 996s, Boxsters and even the odd Carrera GT, but they're rare, and mainly confined to GT3s and Turbos.

You would certainly want to experience this car on the racetrack, which is where the sintered clutch would make sense, given those aggressive power-down wheel-spinning starts, but it's a very different matter on the road. I once drove FVD's 4.0-litre 997 GT3 RS up the tortuous Schauinsland hill climb, but it was raining so I had to hold myself in check. While that is surely the fastest incarnation of that generation of GT3s, and therefore in theory the fastest Porsche I've driven on the road, in fact it's the Zanzibar car that now occupies top spot in my speed sensory memory bank. For a bit of trackday fun the Zanzi would give even a 997 GT3 RS a run for its money, but otherwise it may be too much of a good thing, although there's always that gorgeous curry-paste colour.

The Zanzibar 996 GT3 craves the open road on which to deploy its stratospheric spec. AMY SHORE

RUF 2017 CTR YELLOWBIRD

In recent years Alois Ruf has directed his company towards promoting what he calls 'neo-classics', designs that may go back more than fifty years but never look outdated, and will stay that way forever. They are aimed at those who have a hunger for the older cars that their father or grandfather drove and now wish to share that experience.

The Ultimate may have been based on the 964 and the SCR 4.2 on the 993, but radical changes were made to pro-

The master of the performance boost, Alois Ruf, with his latest creation, the 2017 Yellowbird. The monocoque has front and rear wings, doors and lids all in carbon fibre, with integral roll cage, horizontal pushrod inboard springs and dampers, powered by a water-cooled 997 twin-turbo 3.6-litre flat-six.
ANTONY FRASER

vide the former with a carbon fibre chassis frame, while the chassis of the latter was extended by 20mm at the front and 50mm at the rear (see Chapter 8). The overall dimensions of the glasshouse remained the same, with only the position of the wheels changed. Both cars were steps in the direction of applying modern technology, materials and components to secure the future of the design by installing a water-cooled engine that meets Euro 5 and 6 type regulations. It's never going to be mass-produced, but will always be something for the connoisseur.

Ruf's latest development has been based on the wheelbase of the 996 and 997, which he believes was a great improvement over the early 911s and provides excellent performance. This was chosen in preference to the extended wheelbase of the 991, which was only needed for rear-wheel steering. It was also decided to keep the car as simple as possible, without too many electronic gimmicks: 'The more electronics you put in the less soul the car has. And a car needs to have a soul.'

Ruf's early reputation was consolidated by the Yellowbird CTR-1, which trounced the world's supercars in a track test at VW's Ehra-Lessien proving ground in 1987. Thirty years later the latest Yellowbird, the 2017 CTR, was introduced at the Geneva Show. It is just as innovative as the Ultimate and the SCR 4.2. The thinking was to recreate the whole Yellowbird philosophy in a modern way, based on a central monocoque with built-in roll cage and front and rear subframes carrying powertrain and suspension running gear, clad with carbon fibre body panels. According to Alois:

The 2017 CTR Yellowbird has a very strong central monocoque. You see the crash structure in the front, a subframe made in lightweight steel; this is also where the supports are for the front axle and the wishbones. This is bolted onto the monocoque just like the rear subframe structure. This is all new, so it borrows nothing from the existing 911s, apart from the silhouette; it's an entirely new car. The yellow car in the showroom is the same structure as we have here.

Like the Ultimate and the SCR 4.2, you have the impression that you're looking at a classic 964-era 911, but beneath the skin lives the integral roll cage within the monocoque, which serves to stiffen the body structure. The chassis is a carbon monocoque with carbon skin, and the front and rear wings, doors and lids are in carbon fibre. The rear subframe cradles the engine. At the front there are three water radiators and the oil is cooled via a heat exchanger. Horizontal inboard springs and damper units are operated by pushrods, similar to the mid-engined CTR-3, and there are drop link pick-up points for the anti-roll bar. The engine is a water-cooled twin-turbo 3.6-litre flat-six. The horizontal spring and damper units have separate reservoirs to stop them getting too hot, operated by a pushrod arrangement from the front suspension, which keeps the unsprung weight inboard and also allows more room between the structure of the car and the wheel, so the unequal length double wishbones are unimpeded. This ensures a direct response to the longitudinally mounted shock absorbers, which also give more space in the boot.

Fortunately Ruf, as a small volume manufacturer, doesn't have to crash a car to comply with TüV approval, so a virtual crash on a computer, together with all the detailed and expensive engineering work and calculations, is sufficient.

The 2017 CTR encapsulates the latest concepts in race car design, rendered roadable, yet ostensibly it recalls an early 1990s 911. The original Yellowbird from 1987 was the first car that didn't have rain gutters, so of course this feature has been retained by the 2017 car. A pair of NACA ducts either side of the rear wings below the three-quarter windows are new features for the combustion, allowing the engine to breathe, with one providing air intake just for the intercoolers. Slats in the rear bumper panel recall the Yellowbird too.

The Yellowbird door is about 30mm thicker than a regular 911. The wings are wider than the 930's; in fact, they are the same width as a 959, but it's not that obvious because the extra body and curves still leave it looking subtle and they improve the aerodynamics. The headlamps have been moved 20mm further outwards to slim the appearance of the front wings.

Moving the rear axle back by 50mm provided the additional 70mm wheelbase difference between the 993 and the longer 997. This allowed 50mm more bodywork ahead of the rear wheel arch, 50mm less behind the rear wheel arch, and 70mm behind the front wheel arch, disguised by making the door longer.

Features carried over from the first CTR include the flush door handles and oil filler in the right-hand rear wing, which simplifies putting the oil in and checking the oil level. The newly designed headlamps, turn signals and tail lights use LED technology. Another subtle difference is that the tail lights are 40mm larger and the whole fender was moved outwards so it doesn't project such a huge arch. The wheels are 19in Ruf wheels shod with Michelin Pilot Sport Cup 2s: 245/35 ZR 19 on the front and 305/30 19s on the back.

Ruf plans to produce just thirty of the 2017 CTR Yellowbirds over two years. Alois is enthusiastic about his vision:

It's classic, but it's ultra-modern. The suspension, the chassis, the structure, these are all things that have never been available in a 911 previously; this is all entirely new, it only has the familiar shape. It has been my dream to come up with this combination of a car that carries the spirit of something that we originated thirty years ago, and combine it with more modern technology. I call it an analogue car because it will be minimalistic as far as electronic devices are

concerned. It will have ABS and a stability system and the rest is in the driver's brain and butt! This car was built from my heart for the people who feel it with their heart.

FULL FRONTAL MASQUERADE

Not every 996 that you might see with the awe-inspiring Turbo front is actually turbocharged. Here are two normally aspirated pretenders – and one's even a C2.

A fortieth birthday is traditionally a sign that one has reached a certain maturity to be marked by partying down hard; Porsche celebrated the fortieth birthday of the 911 in 2003 by launching an Anniversary edition of the 996 C2, going for broke with a tuned-up engine and suspension package, topped off with the front panel from the 996 Turbo to hint at latent virility and vitality.

The concept of adding a Turbo front wasn't novel; the 996 Turbo had been out since 2000, and the 996 C4S, which inherited the Turbo's wide body in 2001 to better incorporate the four-wheel-drive transmission system, was also given the Turbo's more aggressive front panel, with its gaping nostrils as well as the slatted lower rear panel. These wide-mouthed coupés are by no means sheep in wolves' clothing; they're both class acts with attributes that far transcend such a demeaning position. You might expect a narrow-body 996 with a prominent Turbo facade to look a bit pudgy-nosed, but helped by the aero sills and body-coloured slats within the side intakes (replacing the usual black holes), it gets away with it aesthetically.

Special dark grey finish on the Anniversary model's five-spoke Carrera wheel contrasts nicely with the Carrera Silver body colour.
ANTONY FRASER

A pair of 996 Turbo-fronted cars that aren't turbocharged: the 40th Anniversary model and C4S. ANTONY FRASER

This is number 1,068 of the 1,963 Anniversary cars made in 2003, reflecting the date of the 911's introduction. ANTONY FRASER

The 996 40th Anniversary models were all painted Carrera GT Silver – like the 986 Boxster S '550 Spyder 50th Anniversary' model, which was also available in 2004 – and the five-spoke wheels presented either with a chrome effect, achieved by shot-blasting and polishing, or painted grey in a similar way to the Boxster S 550, although only the latter's spokes were painted. Just as Boxster 550 Anniversary production numbered 1,953 units as a nod to the year in which the 550 Spyder was introduced, so the 996's '911 40th Anniversary' special edition numbered 1,963 units, the year the 911 was launched.

On the central console there is a tiny silver plaque bearing the number of the Anniversary run, which in the case of our subject car is 1,068, plus an emblem on the rear deck stating '40-Jahre Limited Edition'. Like the aubergine 996 Millennium special edition of 1999/2000, the 40th Anniversary 996 declares its lineage with a simple 911 badge on the engine lid. The cabin is upholstered in the familiar black leather, although most 40th Anniversary cars were furnished in dark

In 2003 Porsche brought out another special edition 996 C2, known as the Anniversary model, to celebrate 40 years of the 911. It was finished in Carrera Silver with special wheel finish and the front panel from the 996 Turbo. ANTONY FRASER

grey leather. Silver bezel trims surround the Bose speakers and silver centre console detail. Costing £68,000 new, the 40th Anniversary car has a Porsche telephone, now a curious relic of the days before it was illegal to be other than hands-free. The built-in satnav system was well ahead of the game when it came out, though it would struggle a bit today unless refreshed.

Both the 996 40th Anniversary and the C4S were supplied by Specialist Cars at Malton, North Yorkshire, and taken through their paces in the vicinity of Castle Howard.

Setting off first in the 996 'Annie', I can instantly feel the more notchy short-throw action of the gear selector, as well as the harder, more focused ride of the M030 suspension. The short-shift I could live without, but the M030 coil-over set and 10mm lower ride is a welcome addition to the 996 spec in my opinion. It has a sports exhaust as well, so it's sounding good. The 3.6-litre flat-six produces 345bhp thanks to the X51 power kit, which consists of reworked inlet and exhaust ports and manifolds, machined cylinder-heads, revised camshafts, valves and timing, plus the limited slip differential normally found on the GT3 and Turbo. That means it runs a close second to the 360bhp 996 GT3 in the normally aspirated power stakes; by comparison the 996 Turbo delivers 420bhp. It may not feel any quicker than the standard 3.6-litre 996, but it is slicker and keener to get off the mark, and the acceleration feels brisker. Tyres are Michelin Pilot Sports, 225/40 ZR 18 and 285/30 ZR 18, and it grips well and tracks true through successions of rural curves as I head towards Castle Howard.

Having grown accustomed to the Anniversary's eager performance and lithe dynamics, I switch over to the black bomber, the C4S. The methodology is relatively straightforward: drive one car from the showroom to the environs of Castle Howard, do the photoshoot, switch over and drive the other one back. The road out of Malton offers a few miles of rippling asphalt through open country, barely wide enough for two vehicles, but relatively underused. Both C2 and C4S are very quick along here, one a wee bit flighty, the other stern and taciturn. It's punctuated by sets of sharp bends where I guide the livelier C2 in and out of the nicely cambered curves. Its darting quality evokes a certain satisfaction at its fluency, while in the C4S it's as if someone else is taking charge of the proceedings, even though I'm still at the controls. It's less thrilling than the C2, though rewarding in its own competent way.

Sure-footed and confidence inspiring, the C4S boasts 4 × 4 traction. ANTONY FRASER

Taking a tight line in the 996 40th Anniversary model: lowered by 10mm, handling is more focused, and with the X51 performance pack it is also quicker. ANTONY FRASER

The approach to Castle Howard is a spectacular switch-back of smooth-ish tarmac, a majestic avenue of mature beech trees rising and falling through rolling farmland. The dips and troughs are so steep that crests are totally blind, so it's essential to keep to the correct side of the road, while the descents are heart-in-mouth fairground stomach churners. The surface is eroded in places where cars have bottomed out, though our two suffered no such indignities even when going hard. Happily it's off-season, so there's no tourist traffic and I can savour each car's power a little bit and assess their relative virtues.

There are no great differences between the two cars inside their cabins, and the controls are just as familiar, but as I pull away in the C4S it immediately feels twice as heavy as the C2 in terms of steering and the whole weight of it makes it seem a bulkier beast. While it lacks the sprightlier character of the C2 it does feel more planted: an agile mid-dleweight boxer compared with a gazelle-like ballet dancer. The Annie C2 tips the scales at 1,370kg, whereas the C4S is 1,470kg, or 1,525kg with the Tiptronic transmission. That's one reason why there's a slight hiatus in its get-up-and-go compared with the Annie C2. Performance stats state

Cabin of the 996 C4S manual. ANTONY FRASER

Blue leather upholstery blends well with the special edition Anniversary 996 C2. ANTONY FRASER

that the 345bhp Annie C2 takes 4.9s to go from 0–60mph, maxing at 180mph (290km/h), while the 320bhp C4S does 0–60mph in 5.0s and tops out at 178mph (286km/h). There's not much in it on paper, but the main benefit of the C4S is that it inspires confidence, no matter what the weather and road conditions. On a smooth straight the C4S feels more placid than the C2. In a few instances, such as a simple turn-around, the four-wheel drive becomes even more obvious, asserting itself as I power back into a straight line, and of course this is a feeling completely absent in the steering response of the C2. The four-wheel traction is amazing on really fast up-and-down A-road bends – it just sticks and goes. It's extremely efficient, but it lacks the soul of the C2.

When the wide-bodied 4 × 4 C4S was launched in 2001 it was at a premium of £2,610 over the normal 996 C4, which today makes it seem like a bargain. It certainly would have been money well spent if you'd kept it, such is the exalted value and status of the Turbo-bodied car over the narrow one. This C4S is running Bridgestone Potenzas 225/40 ZR 18 and 295/30 ZR 18s, the same size as the 996 Turbo. It also benefits from having had a new 3.6-litre engine, fitted under guarantee by Porsche Centre Newcastle (at a cost of £11,583), so there are no longer any concerns about IMS bearing failure. It received new air-con condensers, discs and pads at the same time, and it has the freshness of a new car, certainly in its mechanical responsiveness.

Finished in Basalt Black with black wheels (the original standard alloy-look wheels are stored with the car) and black leather cabin upholstery, the options list includes seat heating, rear wiper and integral windscreen aerial, plus top tint, coloured wheel crests, parking sensors and in-car telephony. The car was first registered in Nicosia, Cyprus, in August 2005, and then immediately shipped to England.

The C4S and 40th Anniversary model are highly desirable versions of the 996 that are unlikely to be found abandoned in barns. ANTONY FRASER

With four owners and a service history ranging from Sussex to Aberdeen via Newcastle, its mileage is 28,366, and the £33,000 price tag makes it look extremely good value indeed. That mileage might seem low, but this particular Anniversary model has done just 8,000 miles (12,875km), so it's not even run-in. It's already been grabbed by a buyer in the Far East, but with 1,963 units signed off other examples are about. The model generally fetches up to £30,000, which, given the very desirable factory mods it carries, makes it even more of a Porsche bargain.

The only 996 model to bear the 911 badge on its engine lid, just 1,963 units of the 40th Anniversary were released. ANTONY FRASER

While these are by no means the most radical versions of the 996, they do represent opposite ends of what's usable as well as being affordable, and each is extremely competent in its own way. For absolute poise and control, take the C4S, while basking in the knowledge that, in this particular case, your engine is unlikely to let you down. Visually, people love the C4S's front panel and broad-in-the-beam Turbo haunches. When it's down to degrees of on-road aptitude, the C2 Anniversary's exhilarating adrenaline rush stands out. It's the unsung hero of the 996 line-up; apart from a few aficionados, who have their own Facebook page, few of us are aware of it, swept along by more exalted GT3s and Turbo versions. This well-run Facebook site provides a link to a regularly updated DropBox containing a comprehensive chronology of most of the 1,963 cars, identifying each one's last known whereabouts and current owner. A separate listing of cars whose current location is unknown makes interesting reading. Conversely, the C4S has a strong cohort of devoted followers, though there isn't a dedicated online fraternity or a specific forum within Porsche Club GB's 996 section.

For a taste of the obscure, the 40th Anniversary car is the more fascinating and, as I've speculated, the limited-edition status car with its enhanced specification should appreciate in value. Either, though, would be an attractive purchase.

THE 996 GT3 RS

The 996 GT3 RS is as scintillating a performer as you could wish for, but what about one set up for the track? The showroom of Specialist Cars at Malton, crammed with tantalizing exotica, including a quartet of Carrera GTs and a 996 Carrera Cup race car that proprietor John Hawkins declares undriveable on the road, provided the opportunity to find out for myself.

They say that you can wait ages for a London bus, and then two come along together. The same seems to hold true of GT3 RSs, because here I'm let loose in two ostensibly identical 996 GT3 RSs, although this is limited to their traditional red-on-white livery. Exceptional cars by any standards, these bolides are as different as Dr Jekyll and Mr Hyde: one's a biddable 'standard' GT3 RS, with two previous owners, the other's a wilful GT3 RS track machine. In the way it delivers its performance the standard RS is as compliant as you could desire, while the worked-over wonder is a race car that, even on a tight rein, is apt to want its own way. By default, that makes it the star car of this duo because it's so outrageous. Based on the 996 GT3, the RS began life in 2003 as a homologation model, a competition car with its sights

Two ostensibly identical 996 GT3 RSs: one's a regular GT3 RS, the other's a GT3 RS track machine. ANTONY FRASER

set on the FIA GT3 category, pitching it against rivals like the Dodge Viper and Ferrari 360 Modena, as well as providing rolling stock for the Carrera Cup race series.

Its RS suffix also endowed it with the iconic trappings of the 1972 Carrera 2.7 RS – hence the obligatory white

There's not much in it, but the track version of the GT3 RS sits lower than the touring model. ANTONY FRASER

bodywork with red or blue graphics. Output of the 996 GT3 RS totalled 682 units, with just 140 configured in right-hand drive; 113 of the latter were officially imported into Great Britain. The RS simply wasn't available in North America. While the GT3 Clubsport version weighs in at 1,380kg, the RS tips the scales, fuelled up, at 1,360kg, a 4 per cent improvement on its power-to-weight ratio. The RS develops 381bhp at 7,300rpm, officially identical to the regular GT3, though 400bhp is rather more likely. As a measure of its greater performance potential, look no further than Walter Röhrl, Porsche's official test pilot, who lapped the Nürburgring Nordschleife with the 996 GT3 RS in 7mins 43s, an amazing 13 seconds quicker than he managed in an 'ordinary' 996 GT3.

Everything happens very fast in this car: the GT3 RS can accelerate from standstill to 60mph in 4.3s, topping out at 306km/h (190mph). Torque is rated at 284lb ft @5,000rpm. Like its Turbo, GT2 and stock GT3 siblings, the 3.6-litre flat-six engine (designated the M79/80) is based on the time-served Mezger 964 split-casings, incorporating dry-sump

Wry and spry, the 996 GT3 RS is as quick as you can get on the serpentine moorland roads. ANTONY FRASER

lubrication and liquid cooling, with a system similar to the 962 and GT1 racing cars that involves separate water jackets on each side of the crankcase, cooling each bank of three cylinders via a radiator. The cylinder heads' intake and exhaust ports are reconfigured for racing homologation, with titanium con rods attaching the pistons to the crank, while the compression ratio rises from 11.3:1 to 11.7:1. Between the engine and gearbox there is a single-mass flywheel that has a lower rotating mass than the double-mass version.

One is never sure quite how effective rear wings are, but officially that of the RS harnesses 35kg (77lb) of downforce on the car when it's doing 201km/h (125mph). The rear wing isn't just about optimizing downforce: at high speed the engine draws extra air from a pressurized collector situated under the rear wing, ducting 18Mb of pressure into the intake when it's running at 301km/h (187mph). This is surely hypothetical in a real-world scenario, but the Mulsanne Straight at Le Mans might be a different matter. It's said to produce an extra 15bhp (11kW) at such a velocity.

Another legacy of the air-cooled 911s is that the engine-to-transmission mounting flange means the GT3 RS is obliged to use a manual gearbox, while interchangeable ratios make it more suitable for racing applications than the standard 996 gearbox. In 2004 the RSR version featured a sequential gearbox, and the following year this evolution proved highly effective in the VLN endurance series in events such as the Spa 24-Hours.

A polycarbonate rear window, a carbon fibre reinforced front lid and that distinctive rear wing contribute to the quest for lightness. Devoid of most sound-deadening and upholstered with lightweight carpet, the cabin is dominated by its sporting accoutrements: a full roll cage that disallows

access to the rear of the cockpit, barring much more than stuffing a coat behind the sports seats. These are by Recaro, criss-crossed by Schroth harnesses that double up with regular diagonal and lap belts. The steering wheel is rimmed with tactile suede, with similar suede cladding around the gear stick,

Certain technical features are shared with the racing version, including complete wheel hub assemblies, divided front and rear lateral suspension control arms, and optimized rear-axle geometry. The RS sits 3mm (0.1in) lower than the normal GT3; both front and rear control arms are adjustable and the suspension top mounts can be rotated 120 degrees to a Cup Car setting. The RS is fitted with progressive rather than linear springs, while uprated dampers are between 10 and 15 per cent stiffer in bounce and rebound than the GT3. Carbon fibre-reinforced silicon-carbide ceramic composite brakes are an attractive option, being more heat- and fade-resistant than the standard cast-iron units. Tyres are 235/40 ZR18 at the front and 295/30 ZR18 at the rear. The 996 GT3 RS was superseded in 2006 by the far more plentiful 997 GT3 RS.

The trackable tearaway under consideration started life in 2004 with identical credentials to the standard model, but has had a further £80,000 lavished on it, which is not far removed from its original £85,000 sticker price. It was developed by Parr Motorsport in conjunction with BTCC and Porsche Supercup hero Kelvin Burt and Carrera Cup and Supercup champion Richard Westbrook, and competed in the Porsche Speed Championship, as a result of which it held the Croft lap record, and gained numerous Time Attack trophies. Between 2004 and 2006 it was modified to include Carnewal corner weights, BBS LM wheels, solid suspension bushes, 350mm Brembo floating disc brakes,

Ventilated rear three-quarter windows are a telling feature in the profile of the track version of the GT3 RS. ANTONY FRASER

ECU upgrade, a new splitter with brake air duct, plastic rear quarter-light windows and a new carbon driver's seat. And yet that doesn't make it substantially quicker on the road. I can easily keep up with Antony Fraser on our short blasts over to the moors, implying that the racer isn't appreciably faster. He does look to be trying hard, and the soundtrack is impressively raucous, but you probably wouldn't want to gun the racer so hard for very long: the on-board computer suggests that the standard RS has been gulping fuel at a rate of 14.8mpg (19.08ltr/100km).

We occupy ourselves blasting one RS and then the other over the wilderness. The standard one is still very spartan, and because there's no sound deadening the transmission whine and the engine's mechanicals are broadcast loud and clear from the rear of the car. You can't rush the six-speed gearchange, otherwise you get a slight baulking, but, satisfyingly, the power comes instantly in great surges. From the outset unless I'm judicious with the throttle the back wants

Panning shot of the road version of the 996 GT3 RS. ANTONY FRASER

to step out. Steering is absolutely positive and direct, though it's quite nervous and a little skittish in the corners.

The road surface has doubtless been compromised by annual frosts, and the car's tramlining all over the place, following the dips and humps every which way, while I feel every bump from the rock-hard suspension. There's masses of acceleration and power available, allied with sublime handling, and this is a hugely enjoyable car, but more so on a smooth surface.

It's now my turn to tackle the racer. The hotter car differs visually from its stablemate in its multi-spoke road wheels, but it's the plastic windows and less finely finished closure panels that give the game away – plus there's the more comprehensive cage inside the no-frills cabin.

Clambering over the side-impact bars is a knack that never leaves you. The RS's Carrera Cup clutch bites instantly, and it's so sharp it demands extreme left-leg muscle action to control the pedal. That makes it murder in traffic, even

Engine bay of the 996 GT3 RS track car. ANTONY FRASER

Purposeful head-on tracking shot of the pair of 996 GT3 RSs. The tow eye of the track car is the most obvious distinguishing feature. ANTONY FRASER

Keen concentration is required helming the track version of the 996 GT3 RS, with its three-spoke dished Momo competition wheel. ANTONY FRASER

The austere cabin of the track car has drilled pedals, fire extinguisher and timer. The carpet, centre console and tunnel capping have been removed. ANTONY FRASER

The track version of the GT3 RS makes short work of the winding lanes on the North York Moors. ANTONY FRASER

though we are merely passing through small Yorkshire market towns. The driver's bucket seat is fixed in position so there's no opportunity to adjust my proximity to the controls, though it actually corresponds reasonably well for me. Because I'm so close to the steering wheel, however, I adopt a crouched, pugilistic position with my elbows by my waist, forearms at 45 degrees to the wheel. It's fearsomely fast, dispensing absolutely raw and brutal power when I floor the throttle in 3rd gear.

It's nervous as a scalded cat and all over the place on this serpentine moorland road, constantly weaving on the bumps and wanting to go its own way. After a tooth-loosening cattle grid I hurtle ever upwards, taking a chance at blind crests

– will there be a left or a right over the top – and will there be sheep in the road? It's a scruff-of-the-neck car, but one that needs a healthy dose of caution in the process. Reassuringly, the brakes are just as sharp as its forward motion. Antony's reaction was 'exhilarating, yes, and somehow we managed not to crash!'

This is certainly one of the wildest Porsches I have ever driven on the road, and clearly not one for everyday use: as we can judge from the specification, this animal belongs on a racetrack. If justification were needed, here is a car that you could drive to the circuit for a competition and, all being well, drive home again. It points up the relative refinements of the standard RS, a car that seems quite a normal proposition after driving the racer for a while. I welcome its meagre creature comforts and I enjoy its precision steering and instant throttle response while having fun coming down the back lanes to Rosedale. It's apparent that the race car's gearing is different to the standard car's, but again in this tight environment it seems they are well matched for speed and handling.

The 996 GT3 RS is an amazing car by any standards and I am spoiled for choice. Which of these icons would I wish to own? If I were to come into some money I would go home with the standard version, though anyone bent on Track Attack participation would have a fabulous weapon at their disposal in the racer. Hold the red mist, though. Let either of them get the better of you on the public road and you are hailing those London buses while you ride out your driving ban.

CHAPTER THREE

ADVENTURES IN THE 996

HIGHLAND FLING

When evaluating the various models of any car, in this case the 996, it is not just the design and specification that should be examined, but most profoundly the driving experience. Let's start at the top with the 996 Turbo. It is powered by the 3616cc liquid-cooled flat-six, allied with twin turbochargers, VarioCam Plus, and driving through a six-speed manual gearbox with permanent four-wheel drive. Suspension is by MacPherson struts, with coil springs, gas-pressure twin-tube dampers and anti-roll bar at the front, and five-link arms, coil springs, single-tube dampers and anti-roll bar at the rear, modulated by Porsche Stability Management (PSM). It's shod with Pirelli P Zeros: 225/40ZR18 (front), 295/30ZR18 (rear). Brakes consist of 330mm vented discs all round, and the 3.6 Turbo develops 420bhp at 6,000rpm and 415lb ft torque between 2,700 and 4,600rpm. It goes from 0–100km/h (62mph) in 3.9 seconds, pressing on to 190mph (306km/h). Fuel consumption averaged 24.1mpg (11.72ltr/100km) for the trip described here. When new the 996 Turbo cost £90,360.

Where better to put this beauty through its paces than one of the most foreboding and remote places in the UK: the Pass of the Cattle – Bealach na Ba – on the Applecross peninsula in Wester Ross in the highlands of north-west Scotland. Impossibly tight hairpin bends and sheer drops mean that you cannot afford to divert your attention from road to view for even a second. The slightest error would have you over the edge in a trice. To put a car and my skills to the test, I brought a 996 Turbo, one of the fastest cars on the planet, which would have to be tightly reined in. Punching out 420bhp, the Turbo is a big-time A-road car and would surely be like a fish out of water in the constricted mountain passes. But at least its four-wheel-drive transmission would ease the pain in the direst of circumstances.

I started from the Muir of Ord in undulating countryside 10 miles north of Inverness. The east-to-west route here presented some impressive driving roads, where a Porsche might be given its head, and the freshness of the air lifted the spirits. As I prepared for the run I took stock of the car's interior. Everything about the controls is refined and still recognizably 911. The cabin is well designed, its switch-

The Road to the Isles: a 996 Turbo press car passing through some of Scotland's most spectacular scenery between Muir of Ord and Applecross. The 911 HUL number plate is reserved for Turbos on the Porsche GB press fleet. PETER ROBAIN

gear more coherently sited than in the early days. The silver-finished dashboard air vents are an amusing contrast to the dark-leather upholstery. The electrically operated seats were more comfortable than in the 996 Carrera 4S, although they didn't cuddle as fondly as the sports seats in my old Carrera 3.2. Every time I stopped for any length of time they returned to their original attitude – doubtless there was a memory function that I didn't find – but it was a simple matter to find my ideal position once more.

The car came into its own immediately. Power delivery was instant, even alarming. Clutch take-up was light, although it needed a few thousand revs to get it off the line. Between shifts, the right foot had to be completely removed from the accelerator before depressing the clutch pedal, otherwise the revs soared. That was a mark of the eagerness of the gear shift as much as anything. It was as well oiled and slick as any, and the six ratios were perfectly spaced. The twin-turbos came in around 3,000rpm, surging car and occupants forward with great gobbets of energy. On a clear stretch of motorway at night its alleged 190mph maximum seemed entirely plausible. Overtaking moves that would ordinarily give pause for thought were possible, especially valuable when making time on congested A-roads. The fast road was flanked by stonewalled woods and bright-yellow gorse and broom, with thrilling ups and downs bookmarked by action-packed corners.

The 996 Turbo tackled the empty roads with a sense of urgency, the power-assisted steering civilized and well weighted, even through the tightest corners. Flanked by a single-track railway line, the road colour changed from blue-black to faded grey asphalt, sometimes without markings or catseyes, presenting a succession of sweeping, 60mph, top-gear bends and long straights. Highland weather is notoriously fickle, and I hit rain showers. Already it was looking bleak and inhospitable, and I shivered at the prospect of the vertiginous climb ahead. I opted for the left fork along Glen Carron, signposted to Kyle of Lochalsh and thence the Isle of Skye. This is still a quick two-lane road, although you need to be aware of the presence of sheep on the roadside, especially since the Turbo's rev counter read 4,000rpm in sixth gear.

The 'wow' factor kicked in just short of Loch Carron when, browing a crest, the long waterway heading towards the sea came into view. The twisty, grey-granite surface of the road, which stretched away for a mile or two ahead, was lined by Scots pines, larch and silver birch. None of these bends was to be underestimated. My technique was typically slow in, fast out, in true 911 style, but that comparison was relative considering you could be going appreciably faster in the 996 Turbo. Power-assisted steering enabled total accu-

Cockpit of the 996 Turbo is familiar to all devotees of the 996, though a six-speed manual is not the normal choice of shift. PETER ROBAIN

racy of line through corners, and effortless turn-in to tighter bends, facilitated by unshakable grip from the low-profile rubber and its four-wheel-drive traction. Negotiating fast turns, the whole car bucked and heaved, just like a classic 911, and to a degree could be given its head without any wheel-wrestling. In slower corners – hairpins, even – I could wind it effortlessly round, although the armrest sometimes intruded. The door pocket was a convenient ergonomic device on the long run.

The downside of the 996 Turbo was the noise created by its wide tyres. To an extent that depended on the nature of the road surface: the smoother the asphalt, the quieter the ride. Particularly on the motorway or one of those high-adhesion surfaces it was difficult to hold a conversation or hear the radio, but why would you want to? As with all 911s, this car is all about the thrill of corners well taken, and the pleasure of driving. It may be a problem for the neglected passenger, but certainly not for the enthusiastic driver. I drove along the north shore of Loch Carron and turned west onto the brown-signed Wester Ross Coastal Trail. Abruptly the road turned into a single track with passing places, and the parlous surface quality was demonstrated by the Land Rover Discovery in front dropping one of its rear wheels up to the axle in a pothole. The single-track road climbed swiftly to bleak, heather-clad moorland, bare rock interspersed with sheep and giving our first taste of being in the clouds, before dropping down again into a craggy ravine.

A prominent road sign exhorted caravans, learners and inexperienced motorists to refrain from taking the turn, but here was my chance to emulate the great German mountain-climb aces from the late 1930s. The start of the climb

The 996 Turbo takes a breather before tackling the Pass of the Cattle, which winds its way over the Grampians between Loch Kishorn and Applecross on the Atlantic coast. PETER ROBAIN

was a gentle gradient, and to my passenger's dismay I rushed up it a little too zealously. The first of many hairpin bends came up all too soon. As we wound our way ever higher, I didn't see much of the islands down in the loch because my attention had to be 100 per cent focused on the road rather than taking in the view, since all that might restrain a wayward vehicle was a yard of tussocky rock at the edge of the road. Further on, though, a few short stretches had been fitted with a deeply reassuring Armco barrier. The passing places were roughly 100 metres apart on left and right, but if an approaching vehicle was unsighted behind a hairpin higher up, it meant backing down to the last lay-by. Pulling in to a passing place on the left, that's to say the side with the perpendicular plunge, demanded extreme caution to ensure the

nearside wheels didn't slide over the edge. As we became shrouded in cloud, and the higher we climbed, so it became apparent that the scree tumbling down the mountainsides was composed of huge boulders, any one of which would flatten a car roof.

Instead of the Armco barriers, there were now painted white lines along the side of the road and it was impossible to discern whether a sheer drop lay to either side. Faced by more unfeasibly constricted first-gear hairpins, our progress was conducted at less than 25mph (40km/h), with headlights and windscreen wipers on permanently. The electric windows and sunroof were one-touch operations, but the incentive to open the top was negated by an uncomfortable drumming in the ears. During the ascent, I had my window open, but the rain highlighted the lack of guttering on the modern Porsche, allowing water to drip in from roof and door mirror. With visibility reduced to 20m in the swirling mists, we reached the summit of the pass. The trig point told us that we were 15 miles (24km) from Portree on the Isle of Skye and 57 miles (92km) from Inverness, but in these conditions we couldn't even see Beinn Bhan, the highest peak on the peninsula.

Despite the fact that high-speed cornering was out of the question, I think this is the most daunting and demanding drive anywhere in the British Isles. Fortunately there wasn't the same sense that we were about to meet our maker on the way down the other side. The clouds cleared, revealing the splendour of the Applecross landscape. The terrain mellowed, the hillsides became less precipitous and the road ahead was now visible as it wound down through bracken and heather towards Applecross House, our destination.

Stopping and passing places provide a welcome opportunity to contemplate the amazing landscape from the highest points of the Pass of the Cattle, looking out over the sea to the Inner Hebrides. PETER ROBAIN

The 997 Turbo, beached at Applecross, having crossed the Pass of the Cattle. PETER ROBAIN

After lunch we elected to do a circuit of the peninsula, taking the winding, undulating, 14-mile (23km) single-track coast road from Applecross to Shieldaig. Around every turn some fresh spectacle delighted the eye. We continued on through Glen Torridon. There were plenty of lovely corners to indulge the compliant 996 Turbo on the Targa Torridon's ups and downs and blind brows, but I was always conscious that sheep and lambs might be on the other side. The road wiggled up the valley, yet it was clear that there was nothing coming towards us. The Porsche wasn't fazed by any of the irregularities and undulations or camber changes. If we did meet something coming the other way, it could stop in very short order.

Glen Docherty was less harsh, with gorse, bracken and heather usurping the bare rock. A new two-lane highway was being constructed, with contractors hard at work to complete it in the summer months. The section that had been completed was terrific: smooth, with fast curves, lined with new stone walls and barriers along the side of Loch a'Chroisg; it was a relief to be on a proper two-lane road again. Now that we better knew the road back to the Muir of Ord, our progress was swifter and more assured. In that respect the 996 Turbo was exemplary and inspired confidence, hardly surprising given its four-wheel drive and Porsche Stability Management systems, but it meant that I could perform more or less any manoeuvre I felt like. It handled superbly, provided all the acceleration, braking and high-speed cruising ability one could wish for, and it was comfortable to sit in throughout the 12-hour run between Norwich and Inverness.

Handsome and purposeful, the 996 Turbo looks like it means business. One of the views I like best is of its rear flanks when seen in the rear-view mirrors – much more muscular than classic models, almost equine, like the shoulders of a cob horse. At 72in (1,829km) wide, the Turbo body is 2.3in (58mm) broader than the regular 996 coupé – and, crucially, only a shade narrower than the new normally aspirated 997 Carreras. If it were mine I'd probably fit an aftermarket exhaust to give it a little more presence to override a slightly muted personality. The only malfunction was the windscreen washers, which appeared to run dry after a few hundred miles, producing only a strong smell that meant opening the windows to clear the aroma from the cabin. When I topped the reservoir it needed hardly any liquid, but since I couldn't imagine poking around the jets with a needle would do any good, I left it alone and just made use of a car-cleaning kit. The satnav was helpful in urban situations, at the expense of self-reliance; where I chose to deviate from the designated path, ignoring exhortations to turn around, it very soon adapted itself with a new plan of action.

At the end of the journey the car had done 4,209 miles (6,774km), of which this trip accounted for 1,550 miles (2,494km), averaging 51mph (82km/h) and 24.1mpg (11.72km/100ltr). Our expedition from Muir of Ord to Applecross covered 73 miles (117km), which is not far, but undoubtedly took us on some of the most arduous roads and through breathtaking scenery. This was a truly fabulous car. Ultimately I forgave the massive road noise because of the performance and handling pleasure it returned. But isn't that what this car is all about? High-speed touring. It was that very ability that allowed a three-day run to the far north of Scotland and back, even if the car couldn't demonstrate much of its awesome prowess at our destination.

Stranger in a strange land: the 996 Turbo may be superlative at covering ground, but on the narrow roads of the Scottish Highlands its role is that of Grand Tourer. PETER ROBAIN

How to turn a 996 C2 into a GT3 Carrera Cup replica: fit an aftermarket front – and put up with the inevitable contretemps with traffic-calming humps. AUTHOR

MORE FRONT THAN SAINSBURY'S

It was only a matter of time before I swapped the front panel of my 996 C2 for something rather more racy – switched the wheels too. Sure, the hot GT3 is subtly different from the standard 996 in the looks department and not difficult to imitate. But why stop there? You see, I wanted an even harder-edged image than the GT3 front end, without venturing into the realms of the body-art specialists orbiting Zuffenhausen, such as Gemballa, speedART, CarGraphic and TechArt, however exotic they may be. Closer to home, Design 911 offered just the look I wanted, though it's not absolutely specific to any particular hotted up 996, which makes it even better. I'm not seeking to emulate anything precisely, just give the car more of a sporting image to match its Porscheshop power upgrades. Having ordered up the new fibreglass nose, 'Pig Energy' was booked in with Wayne Parker at Norfolk Premier Coachworks in Norwich for its transformation.

There's much more to this than whipping the old nose off, sloshing a coat of silver over the new panel and bolting it on. The paint code says Arctic Silver, but it turns out there are at least half-a-dozen shades of Arctic Silver, so Wayne had to experiment to be sure of getting the right one. The meticulous methodology adopted by Wayne is to remove the original front bumper PU panel, then offer up the replacement piece. The fitter marks out where all the existing holes align with the new spoiler, which is then removed from the car

and the marked holes drilled out with a 5mm bit. The nose is then refitted and checked for alignment, with all points marked that need modifying. Once these have been attended to, it's refitted once again just to be sure, then taken off and prepped for first stage primer – that means all repaired areas as a consequence of the modifications. Next, a primer guide coat is applied before block sanding. This highlights any imperfections in the primer when sanding, and these blemishes can now be attended to. After sanding the panel is cleaned up with degreaser, and the complete front bumper is primed with a fine surface coat.

The nosecone is now prepped and block sanded so it's ready for the topcoat, with a final blow-down and thorough degrease. It is mounted on a panel stand in the painting booth, wiped down with a tag cloth, and the first coat of Arctic Silver is applied. This normally takes about three applications of basecoat to cover, and then a fourth and final drop-coat is sprayed on to even out the metallic hue. That gets a 15-minute flash-off in the oven, then the painter applies the first clear-coat, followed by one more full wet-coat to finish off. After flash-off it is baked in the oven for 40 minutes at 65°C. After it's cooled down the painter flattens out any tiny imperfections in the clear-coat with 1500-grade wet-and-dry paper. It's then polished back until all scratches have been removed.

Another facet to the front panel of any water-cooled Porsche is the air ducts and channels. I resolved to fix this with the new nose and ordered a sheet of black mesh from Design 911 along with the front panel. This was cut to fit and bonded in place to the rear of the ducts. It looks very smart as well as keeping out extraneous garbage.

The GT2/3 Carrera Cup-style nosecone being prepped for the 996 C2 at Norfolk Coachworks. Aftermarket panels such as these require a lot of work to ensure tight panel gaps when painted and applied to the car. AUTHOR

The Gen 2 996 Carrera C2 'Pig Energy' at Arègos beside the author's Douro riverside home, northern Portugal. AUTHOR

The author's Gen 2 996 C2 'Pig Energy' on the quay at Santander. ZOË TIPLER

Only now could the new panel be attached to the car again, along with all bumper fixtures and fittings including side indicators, tow-eye cap and number plate. A last polish and wax, and the job was complete. I am thrilled! It's just the appearance I was after.

The car was ready just in time for a mad dash down to Plymouth with daughter Zoë, the overnight sail to Santander and the drive to our Portuguese holiday home in the Douro. But first, Pig Energy's wheels were swapped for a set of genuine 18in Porsche Classic II spokes, along with a new set of ContiSport Contact boots.

These sexy, competition-style split-rim wheels are also set off with coloured centre caps bearing the Porsche crest. I'd pondered having the spoked centres painted a contrasting colour, but they look just fine in plain aluminium alloy, though they're difficult to clean.

Embarking on the ferry demanded great care traversing the ramps so as not to damage the new nose's front splitter. It's the same on speed bumps, where a new vigilance is required. Having arrived in Spain, we headed west and south across the Castilian plateau towards Benavente along the fabulous *autovia*. Smooth as glass, the *autovia* are a delight for the Porsche motorist: light on traffic and toll-free, they provide a sublime route over the Cantabrian mountains down to Portugal, driving footloose and fancy-free.

We stayed the night in the frontier town of Puebla de Sanabria and then set out on the most spectacular section of the journey, the trans-moorland run over the Parque Natural da Montesinho towards Braganza in Portugal, through mists and then breaking out into brilliant sunlight and autumnal shadows, on a succession of bleak hairpins, mostly Armco lined and flanked by gorse, heather and gum-cistus; amazing scenery. We encountered just one other car,

Destination achieved, the 996 C2 parked beside the River Douro at Arègos, northern Portugal. AUTHOR

though I only straightlined the corners I could see around, and it was an exhilarating workout for both me and 'Pig Energy'. The Portuguese *autovia* then tracks southwest over the barren, boulder-strewn peaks of the Tras-os-Montes. We were aiming for Vila Real where they held an international sports car street race in the 1960s, and Peso da Régua, the world's port wine capital. There are two kinds of highway on our journey. In northern Portugal, as in Spain, the EU-funded motorways are equally new and billiard-table blacktop; traffic is sparse, and foreign plates meaningless to electronic tolls. Breathtaking stilted sections soar majestically across valleys and chasms, with long, artfully cambered curves provoking the Porsche driver to go ever harder. Though the maximum speed limits are similar to the rest of Europe, Germany excepted, these motorways are without doubt the most congenial on the continent, enabling the kind of progress that took us from Santander to Puebla de Sanabria in such short order. Although they're perfectly decent, designated service areas are not so numerous, and instead, adjacent villages are often signposted as sources of services, which is true of Puebla de Sanabria.

It's staggeringly rugged country, and the first glimpse of the mighty river from on high is breathtaking. It's obsessively terraced in the port-wine district, an amazing landscape with a network of great driving roads incised into the hills, rising ever higher into the remote Serra da Estrela (max altitude 1,993m) to the south and Serra de Marão (1,415m) to the north, distant, intersecting horizons pinned by lines of wind turbines.

The broad River Douro is half-a-mile wide and a powerful little ferry whisked us over to Caldas d'Aregos on the south side. After closing the shutters for the winter, the return run was an easy five-hour stint, with stops at León and Ribadesella. At Santander we were first on board, putting 'Pig Energy' in pole position for Portsmouth.

NUMBER CRUNCHING

Production of Mk 1 GT3s totalled 1,868 cars, including Comfort and Clubsport variants, against 2,300 Mk 2 GT3s. The UK imported 103 Mk 1s and 246 Mk 2s, while more than 900 Mk 2 GT3s were exported to the USA. There were just 200 examples of the 996 GT3 RSs. According to the Porsche press office, the respective numbers of Clubsport and Comfort models were never recorded.

996 GT3 MK 1 AND MK 2

As I explained above, the GT3 was Porsche's first crack at a spicy, RS-style version of the 996. More than once I have sampled both Mk 1 and Mk 2 versions in the course of compiling magazine features. Sleek, purposeful: no other Porsche has quite the same pared-back, shark-like demeanour as the 996 GT3. The company's radical evolution from air-cooled, hand-crafted cars to robotized production line, water-cooled models from 1996 demanded a flagship, something to lead the charge, a competition-oriented car along the lines of the 1973 2.7 RS and its 964 and 993 RS successors. Launched in May 1999, the 996 GT3 did the business straightaway, combining a higher performance, normally aspirated engine with a sports-tuned, track-focused

The 996's door-pull and opening lever almost echo the GT3's swan-neck wing for elegance. AMY SHORE

Centre console and radio surround of the Gen 1 996 GT3 have a sports-oriented carbon fibre fascia. AMY SHORE

There's not that much to choose between the two incarnations of the 996 GT3, Gen 1 or Gen 2, in terms of performance, ride and handling, though the Gen 1 is quirkier and more characterful. AMY SHORE

suspension to produce a highly strung thoroughbred. Like RSs from previous generations, the GT3 demands to be put through its paces every time it's fired up and, as we'll find out, it never disappoints.

Road-going models come in two trim levels: Comfort or Clubsport, the latter featuring racing seats and rear roll cage at no extra charge. Clubsport versions also employ a single-mass flywheel, allowing the revs to rise and fall more rapidly. The Comfort features leather-upholstered bucket seats, but no rear seats or centre console.

In both cases the space-saver spare is replaced by a puncture repair kit and inflator, which is all very well if you detect your tyre deflating but useless if it's shredded by the time you come to a standstill. The Mk 1 was the last Porsche to have a throttle cable, and apart from ABS it had no other driver aids. It was also the last road-going Porsche to be built on the motor sport production line. Though it's a heavier car than the standard 996 Carrera, the Mk 2 is heavier still. The Mk 1 had a reputation for worn synchro rings, but a second batch of cars incorporated steel synchro rings, which the Mk 2 received as a matter of course.

In 2004 the Mk 2 appeared on the scene, along with the GT3 RS. There's a school of thought that the GT3 was softened to produce more of a contrast with the hard-edged GT3 RS version introduced at the same time and, if nothing else, the presence of cup holders perhaps hints at such a revised status. The Mk 2 (you'll now also see them referred to as Gen 1 and Gen 2) was the first GT3 to be available in the USA, traditionally legislatively averse to tuned versions. Externally the Mk 2 displays several stylistic changes too, some subtle, some not so subtle. They are less exaggerated, kind of like art deco's rigidity against art nouveau's floridity – or, more simply, visually it was toned down. The headlights were modified to differentiate it from the Boxster, and to expand the fried egg simile, the Mk 2's eggs occupied less of the frying pan. The front and rear aprons are different too, earning the Mk 2 some maturity in the process, with slightly different geometry and slope angles to the inlets and air ducts, which should ideally have mesh behind them to stop ingress of garbage. The 18in ten-spoke wheels were simplified, side skirts massaged to provide more aero, and the rear wing configured as a platform on a pair of struts instead of the Mk 1's elegant swan-neck biplane.

More significantly, power rose to 381bhp with torque up to 284lb ft, most of which was available from 2,000rpm, and it was shorter geared in fifth and sixth. Suspension was further lowered and firmed, brakes were beefed up with six-pot calipers up front, with Porsche's optional ceramic composite brake system for an extra £5,356. When track-testing a GT3 with ceramic brakes, *Autocar* magazine's test team discovered that, 'not even several committed laps of the Nürburgring could induce any fade'. Sticky tyres aided traction too: bespoke semi-slick Michelin Pilot Sport N1 tyres were developed specifically for the GT3.

The GT3 was well received by *Autocar* at its launch: 'A joy to use, but no quicker than the standard 911.' Testing the car at Millbrook proving ground, they reckoned this was due to the fact that the GT3 weighed 30kg more than the regular 996 Carrera and 'it wasn't as quick as we'd hoped'. Nevertheless, there were few other gripes: braking, they reported, 'is chest-crushing from any speed'. At low speeds and in town it was not an illuminating experience, though there were compensations: 'For an engine that offers 100bhp per litre, it has an unnatural dose of deportment at low speeds.' And handling too: 'the payback is stunning body control on any given road, just grip and composure.' Turn-in was found to be much sharper than the standard model, 'more on its toes with front-end bite'.

The rear wing of the Gen 2 996 GT3 is a much more straightforward affair than that of its Gen 1 predecessor. AMY SHORE

The swan-neck profile of the Gen 1 996 GT3 is a work of art in its own right. AMY SHORE

From a distance the Gen 1 (left) and Gen 2 996 GT3 look pretty much identical, and only when close up do the subtle differences become apparent. AMY SHORE

When the Mk 2 GT3 became available, *Autocar* was on the case again: 'the latest GT3 is in a different league from its ancestor when it comes to straight-line go … so it qualifies as a genuine supercar.' They ventured that it was more compliant than its predecessor: 'Rock hard and very noisy over anything other than billiard-table smooth surfaces. But when the GT3's handling moment arrives it is a truly devastating thing to experience.'

Despite the pundits' assertive views, there's still an underlying element of connoisseurship among 996 GT3 owners and aspirants, manifest in niggling light-hearted rivalry, traffic-light jousting, and conflicting views on the relative values of earlier and later models, as Mk I owners contend their cars are better than Mk 2s, and vice versa. It goes without saying that the more evolved Mk 2 version is an improved car, yet, on paper at least, the two cars seem so alike that we are in hair-splitting territory. There's much to commend about the first series of any car in terms of purity of concept and specification, and however rationally applied, improvements don't necessarily bring a more desirable result. So, what are the disputed points? Some claim Mk Is are slightly more involving to drive, others cite the Mk 2's ability to rev more freely, produce more torque, sound better, with a more positive feel to the gearshift. We'll discover the truth for ourselves in a minute.

I have been drawn to Cambridge Motor Company's showroom by the prospect of two 996 GT3s owned by well-known promoters of the Porsche marque: Martin Pearse of MCP Motorsport and Jonathan Sturgess of Autostore. The yellow Mk I GT3 gracing the showroom has recently been bought by Martin in Sicily and driven back to Cambridge, where it is now on sale. The GT3 has had two wealthy owners since 1999 and been stored for a long time, hence less than 30,000 miles (48,280km) on the clock (though the speedo is in km/h). It's been repainted, though you wouldn't guess; it just looks like an immaculate Mk I. Martin checked it out at Porsche Palermo and it ticked all the boxes so he did the deal. It has black leather sport seats with yellow belts, plus the usual features like climate control, carbon pack, CDR 22 Radio, stainless-steel kick-plates embossed with the GT3 logo, and 18in GT3 alloy wheels. Its Porsche service history includes the most recent service, along with a new MOT, when a brand new set of Pirelli PZERO Tyres was fitted. It's priced at £69,750 and appears to be the only Mk I GT3 for sale in Great Britain at the time of writing while owners wait to see what happens to the marketplace. It's also a matter of logical market progression; as air-cooled RSs disappear over the fiscal horizon, the GT3 is obviously the next best thing.

Today's Mk 2 version, also yellow, is Jonathan Sturgess's pride and joy. He bought the car from an owner in the Scottish Highlands and claims to have been the only punter prepared to make the journey to this remote location on the off-chance it would be worth buying. It turned out to be a cracker that he keeps strictly for high days and holidays.

The yellow twosome are eased out onto the web of country lanes, marked by long straights, shallow curves and acute field boundary corners. It's been sunny and dry for days so the surfaces are ideal, and where there's a clear view I straightline the bends for sustained velocity potential.

The left-hand-drive Mk I feels very comfortable in what for me is the 'correct' driving position. Its purposeful stance suggests that a GT3 might be a daunting prospect, but this one doesn't overawe, it's not a hostile, unfriendly car. At a standstill there's a much looser, rattley sound about the exhaust and transmission, quite different to a normal 996's flat-six. The growl it emits from 3,500rpm upwards becomes

The author reflects on the prowess of the 996 GT3. AMY SHORE

Carbon fibre weave clads the Gen 2 996 GT3 centre console. AMY SHORE

Yellow peril: a pair of 996 GT3s, Gen 1 and Gen 2, finished in Speed Yellow, let loose on the Cambridgeshire back roads. AMY SHORE

a roar at 5,000rpm. Steering is sharp and nicely weighted so there's some resistance to it, but it's effortless as well. I'm absolutely in touch with the road; the front end is feeling every nuance of the camber, nosing around like a hunting hound, though at speed on the straight ahead it does jink and weave a little. On the other hand, it also rides and absorbs bumps such as railway level crossings very well. This chassis is supremely alive, communicative and out for a game; if you're up for a thrill, it's right there with you.

I'm not expecting any major differences in the driving experience when we swap over, in spite of *Autocar*'s earlier verdicts, but it turns out there is a big surprise in store. The first thing I'm aware of in the Mk 2 is how much firmer this one feels; it's not that the Mk 1 is in any way loose, just that the Mk 2 is tauter. It's more planted, less inclined to dance around. In hard cornering the Mk 2 is much better controlled, less wilful. The smoothness and awesomely fast acceleration are impressive. I think it's a significantly more compliant car than the Mk 1, though Martin proposes getting his charge's suspension reviewed by Centre Gravity. In fact, a number of Mk 1s have Mk 2 calipers fitted retrospectively,

and though the 381bhp Mk 2 has another 21bhp, mild engine work would enable a Mk 1 to match that.

The gearshift of the Mk 1 feels notchy, a bit 'clink, clunk', though never recalcitrant, while the Mk 2 is a bit slicker. This Mk 2's actually a Comfort that's had most of the Clubsport kit fitted retrospectively, so I'm aware of the roll cage in the back and the classy racing bucket seats and Schroth harnesses. I wonder if it feels a tauter chassis because of the roll cage adding structural rigidity. Visually I prefer the quirkier aesthetics of the Mk 1, which make it a bit more purposeful, other-worldly even, while the Mk 2 looks standardized by comparison. Some might perceive that the Mk 2 looks cleaner cut. As for driving them, the Mk 2 will be the easier of the two to live with; it's like a top-notch Olympic sprinter compared with a gutsy amateur club-class athlete. And the verdict? As for *Autocar*'s scribes, they reckoned the Mk 2 GT3 'is one of, if not the most, exciting handlers this magazine has ever tested'. I couldn't agree more. It's the one I'd have, money no object, at least in water-cooled terms. And though it would be the Mk 2, I'd fuss about with the detailing so at least it had that elegant Mk 1 swan-neck wing.

Rear tracking along a straight road is all very well, but it's on the twists and turns that the GT3s really come into their own. AMY SHORE

NEED FOR SPEED

The Mk 2 wins the speed table stats, though not significantly. The biggest difference is at 100mph.

Mk 1 996 GT3
0–30mph: 1.8s
0–60mph: 4.8s
0–100mph: 10.9s
Standing kilometre: 23.4s, clocked at 226.9km/h (141mph)

Mk 2 996 GT3
0–30mph: 1.7s
0–60mph: 4.5s
0–100mph: 9.3s
Standing kilometre: 22.1s, clocked at 238.2km/h (148mph)

The journey back from Cambridgeshire gave me an opportunity to put these reactions into perspective. The Boxster S is so effective cross-country that I don't reckon either GT3 would have done it any quicker – and I had the top down all the way. But much as I like the Boxster's imagery and flexibility, it's the 996 GT3 that does it for me.

TOP TABLE

The 996 is now seen by many adherents as the up-and-coming, must-have Porsche; but which is the ultimate version? John Hawkins of Specialist Cars, Malton, supplied three fabulous range-topping 996 supercars to test in spring-like weather out on the moors. This is the ideal environment as each is subjected to our regular repertoire of on-road actions. Inevitably the contest throws up a host of paradoxes and tantalizing alternatives, much like a *MasterChef* semi-final.

A trio of Porsche's finest: the 996 GT2, the Gen 2 996 GT3 and 996 Turbo with X51 engine upgrade. ANTONY FRASER

MARKET WATCH: 996 GT3

We've seen the prices of air-cooled cars go stratospheric, and now the water-cooled ones are taking off too – especially the 996 GT3. Jonny Royle of Cambridge Motor Company explains some of the background to this:

The market for 996 GT3s has really firmed up over the past year, and they are now between £65,000 and £85,000. The economy's doing well; banks are lending money, people are beginning to recognize what they represent and snapping them up. Another thing that seems to be happening is that people are cashing in their pensions early and salting away a GT3 to offset their pension until they really do need it, and by then they'll have made a better return than they would on their pension. And that's one factor in the cars going up in price. It may flatten out, but it's not going to crash, because people realize they didn't make so many of these cars and they are pretty special. With GT3 RSs now fetching £160 grand, that affects the price of the GT3, and they are simply following the trend. And as GT3 values rise, so that drags the basic 996 C2s and C4s along on their coat-tails. There's no doubt the 996 GT3 should be a sure-fire investment.

Making a splash: the 996 Turbo's X51 performance package includes revised 74mm plenum, throttle body and Y-branch air intake, and raises power from 420bhp to 450bhp. ANTONY FRASER

Three of the most likely candidates for the title of most desirable iteration of the 996 are the GT2 and GT3 Clubsport, and a Turbo that's laden with ex-factory X51 accessories. The Gen 2 GT3 is owned by one of Specialist Cars' customers, while the equally desirable GT2 and X51 Turbo are both in stock.

The GT2 is metallic Basalt Black with silver wheels, white-faced dials and silver central tunnel cover, with Kevlar detailing on the handbrake lever and gear knob, and Alcantara roof lining. Recaro race seats are encased in Schroth six-point harnesses, behind which is a comprehensive bolted-in half-cage, occupying the rear of the cabin in true Clubsport fashion. Doubtless the cage adds significant structural rigidity to the bodyshell too, though it also brings weight to the package. In a trackday context the Clubsport is a no-brainer and, in similar vein, a huge Werner fire extinguisher is stored in the passenger leg-well.

The Arctic Silver 996 Turbo brings an entirely different set of features. In the cabin – sorry, saloon, surely – there's particularly soft leather upholstery of the seduction couch variety, and the steering wheel features a Kevlar-and-leather rim, while the carbon effect translates through to the handbrake and gearshift levers as well as the central tunnel and centre console trim, door pulls and cubby lids. Perhaps it's a bit over the top, but others might not agree. There's a sunroof, satnav and a telephone handset of somewhat dubious legality, though the passenger may be allowed to use it. Otherwise the Turbo's interior is not fundamentally different to the 996 C2 that I drove up to Yorkshire, though perhaps a swankier version. The X51 power kit lifts the Turbo's power from 420bhp to 450bhp at 5,700rpm, a significant hike, since it brings it close to the GT2's 462bhp at the same revs.

What's not to like about a Guard's Red 996 GT3? This one belongs to William Miers, who wanted something for the track:

I've enjoyed every minute of it. I've done a lot of Porsche Club trackdays, from Goodwood to Silverstone, and our local circuit at Croft, a couple at Spa and about eight at the Nordschleife. So, I've done probably 100 laps of the Nordschleife! I've never kept any car more than six years and I'm more than happy with it, so this one's a keeper. It's a better car than I am a driver, so there's no reason to change it.

His Mk 2 GT3 has done 33,000 miles (53,100km), and the only relatively major replacement is a set of rear shock absorbers.

Both the Turbo and the GT3 have steel discs, while the GT2 has ceramic composite brake discs. The Turbo's tyres are Michelin Pilot Sport, 225/40 ZR18 front and 295/30 ZR18 back; the GT3's are similar-sized P-Zeros. The GT2 is also on Michelins, but 235/40 ZR18 front and 315/30 ZR18 back.

A river runs through it: the 996 GT3 Gen 2 fords a stream on the North York Moors. ANTONY FRASER

John Hawkins knows all three cars well. His firm has serviced the GT2 every year. He considers the GT3 a raw beast, though slightly less so than the Mk I version. The X51 Turbo is a rare example with that power kit, but it will do anything you want it to. The Turbo was always the most expensive model in the line-up, at £120,000, but then they brought out the GT2, which seems to bring out the worst in some drivers. According to John:

> there aren't that many about that are undamaged. We've sold three in the past that have subsequently been smashed up. But they're not the Widow Maker that people claim, they're just a car at the end of the day, and some people are in over their heads with them; they just have to be treated with respect.

The 996 GT2 is a ferociously powerful car, delivering 462bhp from its 3.6-litre twin-turbo engine. It has a deeper front panel than the regular 996 Turbo, with additional chin-spoiler and a differently configured, permanently fixed rear wing. It has bigger turbochargers and intercooler and, crucially, it is rear-wheel-drive only. ANTONY FRASER

If cars could be 'listed' like historic buildings, the GT2 would be Grade I. Released in 2001, the 996 GT2 turned out not to be the anticipated hard-core cage fighter, rather something rather less uncompromising, more user-friendly, which came as something of a surprise. Not that it takes any prisoners, just that, provided you don't abuse what it has to offer, it's eminently usable, even in this moorland setting. While the preceding 993 GT2 was a competition car, Porsche elected to concentrate on using the GT3 for motor sport. Although the GT2 uses a twin-turbo version of the GT3's 3.6-litre flat-six (rising from 462bhp to 483bhp against the GT3's 360bhp), it is more closely related to the 996 Turbo in terms of road-going set-up. Giveaways to the GT2's identity are the distinctive bisected air intakes in the front panel and the air ducts feeding its turbo intercoolers in the

Cockpit of the 996 GT2 is a more austere environment than ordinary 996s, with plain metal centre tunnel, six-point harnesses and competition seats. ANTONY FRASER

Rear three-quarter shot of the 996 GT2 demonstrates the cantilevered rear wing bridging the entire width of the car's rump. AUTHOR

leading edges of the rear wheel arches. The rear wing is different too, cantilevered from the engine lid with downswept fins on either end. But despite a 10mm lower ride height than the 996 Turbo, which explains why the tyres touch the inner wheel arches on full lock, the GT2's drag coefficient is slightly higher – 0.34Cd against the Turbo's 0.33 – due to the larger expanse of the fixed rear wing.

Clamber into the Recaro chair and at once the GT2 feels raw. The seats are not adjustable, but that's not an issue, such are the figure-hugging contours, and in any case they are part of the Clubsport experience. It's a way more sporty proposition than the X51 Turbo, combining the stark rawness of the GT3 with added poke. Talk about moorland magic: there's no shortage of great driving roads around Malton to put the trinity to the test, and we target the moors above Pickering and over to Whitby. We have a great cross-section of asphalt to power down, including cattle-gridded moorland single-track and two-lane A- and B-roads, interspersed with myriad bends, convoluted cambers, rollercoaster dips and troughs; all in all, an exhilarating prospect in these super cars.

First up is the GT2. It leaps athletically into action. It's heftier than a 996 C2 in terms of the bulk of car I'm throwing down the road, though it has way more than enough power to do that. There's a madness about the delivery – floor it, and it gets cracking without hanging around, and though at first I think I detect a slight lag, that notion is soon dispensed with. Lift off abruptly and the violent forward dash is punctuated by a sideways twitch. The gear lever action is light and feels reasonably slick, and because it's rear drive it's not constrained by the front axle drivetrain. I'm mean-

Eschewing the race harness in favour of the normal diagonal seat belt – in matching red – the author takes the 996 GT2 for a run on the North York Moors. ANTONY FRASER

dering along the A64 towards Whitby, 1,800rpm cruising at 50mph in 6th, and there's enough torque to encourage it to get a move on if an opportunity arises – but I have to drop two cogs to inspire it, and at 3,000rpm in 4th it starts to go. Flooring it across the B-road all hell breaks loose and it reveals itself as the crazy monster that I knew it would be. So much power on tap! I'm following the rapidly accelerating X51 Turbo, and I'm holding him, but it's abundantly clear that the four-wheel-drive chassis is the more secure and that I'm in the perilous projectile.

But oh, the thrill of it, switching from 3rd to 4th, maybe 5th on a long straight, with the power instantly there. It's a firm-ish ride, though softer than the GT3, and the ratios are closer than the GT3, and all but 2nd are the same as the Turbo's. I love the way the front wheels are following all the undulations on the moorland road, feeling its way along. The delicacy of control going round some very tight corners on the wooded hill roads is wonderful. It is interesting having the boost gauge in the bottom segment of the rev counter: I see 0.8 bar, accelerating in 2nd gear at 5,000rpm, though I'm mainly concentrating on watching the road ahead – it's that kind of car.

Hydroplane racing? The 996 Turbo was not designed as such, but it creates one hell of a bow wave as it navigates a ford. Luckily the water level is barely a couple of inches deep. It's all done for the benefit of the camera, obviously, because in the general rule of things we take the ultimate care when traversing adverse surroundings.

After a stop we change cars. The shift on the GT3 is slightly notchier than the GT2 and the steering is slightly more sensitive, which could be due to the camber settings. The performance is markedly less aggressive than the turbocharged car, but on the other hand it's a livelier chassis and maybe that's also to do with lower weight – 1,380kg against 1,420kg (the Turbo is 1,585kg). The all-black interior of the GT3 is conventional with contrasting red seatbelts. As they are both Clubsports, the GT3 and GT2 have identical Recaro racing seats, five-belt Schroth harnesses and half cages occupying the rear of the shell.

The full-on speed and agility of the GT3 makes me more amorous of it than the nuttiness of the power-crazed GT2, as seductive as the turbo power is. Its handling through the corners is sublime: steer it in and keep on the gas, and it just goes round, and of course the brakes are instantaneous to slow it down. If push came to shove, which of the Clubsports would the GT3 owner William take home?

I like that the GT3 is so alert, so responsive. On the other hand, the GT2 is really powerful and so relaxed. It covers the ground so easily. I'm also surprised how

Cornering in the 996 GT2 on the wilds of the North York Moors is an exhilarating experience, calling for deft application of the throttle. ANTONY FRASER

comfortable it is too. I expected it to be harsher like the GT3, but it's smoother. The suspension is firmer on the GT3; you've got more feel of the road, whereas the GT2 seems softer in the damping. The X51 Turbo with its short shift goes amazingly well, of course, though anybody could order the short-shift linkage, but in fact it's not as slick as the GT2, which is more refined. If you don't want to slip the clutch it stalls very easily, and I think that's because of the Clubsport's lighter flywheel that spins up and slows down faster. Once it's hot, the GT3 shift eases up, but otherwise it's a bit notchy.

996 Turbo at speed on the moorland road. ANTONY FRASER

All of which serves to confirm why the GT3 is the more purposeful of the two Clubsports, given its race-focused appellation.

Despite their respective mileages (33,000 versus 10,000 miles), the GT2, which has seen less use, feels the more run-in of the two. The GT3 is a tauter, more responsive vehicle in the first place. In view of its role in the 996 line-up, it's perhaps not surprising that the GT2 feels less hard-core than the GT3, and it's more like a light, leery Turbo than a GT3. As William remarks, 'When the day comes that you tire of the roar of 7,000rpm, maybe that's the time to get a GT2!'

The X51 Turbo is somewhat stolid by comparison with the other two, but evaluating it on its attributes, it's quite as quick, it has four-wheel-drive security, and the luxurious soft leather comfort factor – and a sunshine roof, which I have open today. The carbon detailing in the cabin seems bogus, given the company it's keeping here, an unnecessary ostentation, and in fact I don't care for the feel of the carbon fibre rim of the steering wheel at all. Although it matches the GT2 in power, the manner of delivery is far less dramatic. I don't sense the liveliness of the rear-drive GT2, and William agrees: 'You can call the Turbo a lazy car because it's got so much torque and grip, whereas the GT3 is nearly as fast, but you have to use the gears much more.' A different animal, in other words. The Turbo X51 may have a close-ratio box, but it is on the notchy side, unfeasibly laborious, and less pleasant to use than the GT2 and GT3. However, by working the 'box, it can be as much of a hooligan as the other two,

OLAF MANTHEY INTERVIEW

Olaf Manthey formed his team in 1996, winning the Porsche Supercup every year from 1997 to 2000. Manthey also ran one of the two development 996 GT3-Rs at the 1999 Le Mans 24-Hours, and has won the Nürburgring 24-Hours five times. JAMES LIPMAN

Few independent Porsche specialists have enjoyed quite as much success in international competition as Olaf Manthey, to the extent that Manthey Racing virtually owned the awesome Nürburgring 24-Hours race a few years ago.

The team was established in 1996 to contest the Porsche Supercup and Porsche Carrera Cup in Germany, winning the Supercup four consecutive years with Patrick Huisman (1997–2000). Manthey also ran one of the two development 996 GT3-Rs at the 1999 Le Mans 24-Hours, and has won the Nürburgring 24-Hours five times consecutively, also being on the podium numerous times.

   In December 2013 Porsche bought a 51 per cent shareholding in the Manthey team, since it represents the manufacturer in the GTE Pro and GTE Am classes of the World Endurance Championship. This came about after Olaf approached Porsche and asked if they would be interested in more commitment. Porsche Development at Weissach works closely with his team in building and setting up the 470bhp 991 RSR that competes in the GTE Am class. I interviewed Olaf Manthey in the Drivers' Lounge at the 2015 Goodwood Festival of Speed.

JT: Is this your first run up the Hill?

OM: Yes, my first time at Goodwood and first run up the Hill!

JT: So, what's your impression? It's not really a hill climb like Schauinsland, is it?

OM: No, it is too short for that, but it's tricky because the track is not so wide, and when you go fast in the car then the track will seem much smaller then, because you haven't enough space to manoeuvre if you come sliding into a corner. You have to take it very carefully so you don't damage the car – and their wall of straw bales!

JT: Do they let you practice first?

OM: I have had one practice run already, and in the afternoon I have a second practice run, then tomorrow (Friday) is the qualifying, and that's it.

JT: Are you quick compared with some of the other cars going up?

OM: Yeah, quick, but I'm not giving it 100 per cent; I think it is better to go at nearly 80 per cent, so that you always have enough space if you come in sliding. But first you have to learn where the braking points are, what corner is coming up next – is it a short corner, is it a long corner, fast corner, middle fast or slow corner – you have to learn all these things before you can go quickly.

JT: But this is a fun occasion, isn't it? It's not as serious as if you were in the N-24, say.

OM: Yes, of course, it's more of a fun event. Although it is a big corporate occasion, it's not a promotional event for us as such. We have been invited because this car is the winner of the Nürburgring 24-Hours in 2007 and 2008, so they asked us to come over here and participate in the hill climb.

JT: Yes, it's very exciting to see your 997 GT3 RSR here. I recall the winning drivers were Timo Bernhard, Marc Lieb, Romain Dumas and Marcel Tiemann, three of them very much in the Porsche driver hierarchy now.

OM: Right – you could say they developed their careers at Manthey!

JT: Can we go back to the beginning of your career? When did you get involved, and what did your interest in motor racing stem from?

OM: I started off as a young driver aged 18, beginning with hill climb races, and then going to normal race tracks, and I started entering the German Touring Car Championship (DTM). I have done the DTM in a Rover Vitesse, and I was DTM champion twice in the Bastos Rover V8.

JT: That's a strange car for a man whose name is synonymous with Porsche!

OM: Yes, but this was the beginning of the DTM in 1984–5, and I was Champion those years with the SD1. Don't forget that it was a very competitive car at that time, with people like Kurt Thiim, Tom Walkinshaw, Steve Soper and Jeff Allam winning lots of races with it in the DTM and the ETCC. Then I switched to a BMW M3 until 1992. And then I went over to Mercedes-Benz until 1996, when I started up my own company to go racing in the Porsche Supercup with the 993 RS Cup Car. The Manthey team won the championship four years running, from 1997 to 2000.

JT: So, the cars would be 993 and then 996?

OM: In 1996 it was the 993 RS Cup Car, and in 1998 it was the new water-cooled 996 GT3 RS Cup Car, yes.

JT: What did you make of the transition from 993 to 996?

OM: It's a bigger car of course, more complicated, and the spec is much more evolved from the days of the 993 and 964 Cup Cars. My first contact with Porsche was in 1990 in the 964; up to this time I had been driving an M3 in the DTM, and on the same weekend there was a Porsche Carrera Cup race. So I got into the Carrera Cup, and I was the first champion of the German series, yeah, and from the beginning of 1990, it was a love story for me with Porsche cars!

JT: And then you started your own race team in 1996. You must have originally come from an engineering background to be able to see what was needed?

OM: Yeah, most of the cars I've driven I have also built myself. And I was not only the driver, I was also the race engineer and the mechanic on the car, and that's better for me because it gives me a better understanding about the technical aspect of the car's set up, its chassis, its engine … because it makes my life a lot easier when I have an advantage over the other teams and drivers, and to achieve this you have to work on the mechanics and the set-up so that you make the car better and better.

JT: So, you know how it feels yourself from driving the car round, let's say Hockenheim, and you know that, if you tweak this and adjust that, you can make the car work better?

OM: Yeah, it made things much easier when I became Team chief and I was on the other side of the pit wall and not actually driving the car myself, that because I had all this experience myself, when I'm speaking with a driver about the car I have a better understanding of what he means that he wants from the car, because I was a race driver and also an engineer and mechanic too.

JT: I understand that your operation consists of four departments: Manthey Racing, Manthey Motors, Manthey TZN and Raeder Motorsport; where is your headquarters located?

OM: Originally it was at Rheinbreitbach, and then in 2000 we moved to the Meuspath industrial estate just below the Nürburgring Nordschleife.

One of the Manthey Porsche 991 GT3 RSRs in the pits garage ahead of the 2016 Le Mans 24-Hours. AUTHOR

(continued overleaf)

OLAF MANTHEY INTERVIEW *(continued)*

JT: Of course, so that's a very convenient place to be able to say, OK, we've done this to the car, let's take it over to the Nordschleife and see if it works.

OM: Absolutely! There you have the best test opportunity in the world. You can test the race cars on the Grand Prix circuit, and you can test them on the Nordschleife, and for street cars, making a set of shock absorbers or a better spring set-up, you can also use the back roads in the Eifel, which are like the Nordschleife in character but a bit bumpier. The rest I have always done at the Nürburgring Nordschleife.

JT: And that's to your advantage when it comes to a race like the N-24, because you know it so well.

OM: Yes, it's my home, the Nürburgring Nordschleife. I first rode there aged 16 with a moped, then with a small Fiat 500, and then step by step into bigger and faster cars. We have won the N-24 five times outright.

JT: This year the Porsche factory 991 R-GTE has been developed by Manthey.

OM: Well, it is actually developed by Porsche in Weissach, together with us as a joint effort, and we run the cars at all the races, we take care of the handling, the repairs of the car, and the race engineer at the races is from my team.

JT: How many people in the Manthey team now?

OM: We have sixty-four permanent employees now, and about eighteen freelancers.

JT: The working relationship that you have with Porsche, how does that work in practice? Do you go to Weissach or do they come to you?

OM: The cars are built up at Weissach and afterwards they come up to us, and ahead of the races and in between the races they will be with us in our workshop.

JT: That means you have a direct hands-on role in how the work's car performs, and it's really down to Manthey that the car is a success.

OM: Yeah, we do all the maintenance, and we share our knowledge with the Porsche engineers at Weissach, and they share theirs with us. Then we combine what we have, and that brings the best out of the cars.

JT: How many cars are the Manthey squad running and racing at the moment?

OM: We have two cars in the WEC, and then we have six cars that we look after in the VLN races and the Nürburgring 24-Hour race.

It seems Manthey can do no wrong; everything he touches with a Porsche badge comes good. Currently, Manthey's input into the Porsche 991 RSR GT race programme is paying off – the most recent success has been a double victory in the Watkins Glen Six Hours. Meanwhile, Olaf can rest on his laurels at events like the Goodwood Festival of Speed.

In 2013 Porsche acquired a 51 per cent stake in Manthey, since it represents the Zuffenhausen manufacturer in the WEC's GTE Pro and GTE Am classes. AUTHOR

with a bit more security thrown into the mix. It steers very nicely, and I'm not feeling the front powertrain as dominant as it can feel in a C4 driveline. Steering is fluent into and out of corners, and the ride is the most relaxed of the three, as you'd expect. Put another way, the chassis is less playful, though it is hugely competent, reassuring and confidence inspiring, while the other two – and the GT2 in particular – are most definitely a walk on the wild side, in which I can explore the outer limits of handling and performance, not to mention my personal driving skills. That's where the big thrills are.

Back in the black GT2 again, and excitement doesn't come any more raw than this – it literally takes my breath away on this undulating, twisting, moorland B-road. It seems that the higher the gear the quicker it goes: pop it into the next one up and it goes even faster, while the intensity of engine note crescendos into a shrill baritone. Fuel consumption might not be your first concern, but zeroing the computers before the start showed the GT2 and GT3 recording a frugal 21mpg, while the X51 Turbo is a thirstier 14mpg. It's also amusing to contemplate the different sounds they emit: you can make anything more fruity by fitting an aftermarket exhaust, but the GT2 is quite rorty despite the turbo mute,

though it's not as sharp as the GT3's bark. The X51 Turbo has more to say for itself than a 'regular' Turbo, which is relatively muffled, but it's still flatter in tone than the GTs.

The fundamental question is whether the Turbo can live with the GT2 and GT3. I think it can; in its way it is the most competent of the three, but it is the least exhilarating – and it's not often you can say that about a Porsche Turbo. Price comes into the equation too. The GT3 and X51 Turbo are worth pretty much the same, £75,000, but you'd have to add another £100,000 to own the GT2, and that makes the big question harder to answer. In pure performance and usability terms, as well as thrills-per-mile, assuming we're picking a winner, it has to be the GT2, just on account of its extravagant wayward madness. The GT3 runs it a very close second in the drivability department, lacking nothing in the normally aspirated Mezger-engined track-oriented handling department; in a different contest it would come top – and certainly does in the value-for-money stakes. And if it were pouring with rain, the X51 Turbo would be favourite for its ability to dispense usable performance and for its luxurious mile-munching ability. Though there are just three items on the menu, selecting the dish of the day is more complicated than expected, and I am spoilt for choice.

Follow my leader: 996 GT3 Gen 2 heads 996 GT2 and 996 Turbo X51. ANTONY FRASER

CHAPTER FOUR

INTRODUCTION AND EVOLUTION OF THE 997

First mooted in late 1998 as the next phase in the 911 saga, the 997 was in the design process by February 1999, with full-sized clay models being created in the styling studio in 2000 and 2001.

The closeness in date to the introduction of the 996 raises eyebrows, since one might imagine that more time would have elapsed before they got stuck into developing the next model, but those are the bare facts. Based on an in-house design by Grant Larson, the standard base model 997 was broader at the rear by 88mm (3.5in) than the 996, but, more dramatically, the headlights were much more reminiscent of the old air-cooled 911s – like those of the contemporary 987 Boxster – which many felt realigned the 997 with the characteristic 911 appearance. Things moved quickly: prototypes of the 997 were under test by late 2001, with the first public unveiling in September 2004.

A clay modeller sculpts what will become the front bumper panel of the Porsche 997. The final design was credited to Grant Larson in 2001. PORSCHE MUSEUM ARCHIVES

The 997 C2 Gen 1 went into production in 2004.
PORSCHE MUSEUM ARCHIVES

The airstream flows in an arc over the 997's roof in the wind tunnel, performing a straight line over the car's extended rear wing. PORSCHE MUSEUM ARCHIVES

Driving a 997 C2 on a Devon moorland road. ANTONY FRASER

The 997 C2 demonstrates impeccable handling and cornering ability. ANTONY FRASER

The 996-model Carrera may have gained a mixed reputation since it went out of production, but its successor, the 997, became the undisputed hero of the used water-cooled 911 market. In production from 2004 for the 2005 model year until superseded by the 991 in 2012, the 997 Carrera is in good supply on the secondhand market and, at the time of writing, probably represents the best water-cooled 911 that Porsche has produced.

Solid, as in the hewn from stone simile, yet dispensing enough feel and feedback to satisfy the most discerning driver, the 997 is superior to its predecessor in terms of build quality, yet of lighter touch and response than the 991 that succeeded it. Whatever its detractors say about the 997's most immediate ancestor, the 996, the fact remains that it too was an extremely good car, but with the benefit of hindsight it's as if that first water-cooled 911 was a dress rehearsal, an inevitable by-product of the company flexing its muscles before the main event. At first glance there are few major differences between the 996 and 997, and it was hard to grasp that the 997 was 80 per cent new, compared to the 996. The Gen 1 997 was fitted with the 3.6-litre flat-six inherited from the Gen 2 996.

Despite the Carrera 'S' version developing around 40bhp and 20Nm more from its 3.8-litre engine over the previous 3.6-litre 996, the official figures showed the 997 'S' to be only marginally quicker to 62mph than the 996 – at 4.8s compared with the 996's 5.0s, and with much the same difference in 0–100mph times, at 11s for the 996, and 10.7s for the 997. Gradually, though, and crucially, without having to justify its existence in quite the same way as the 996 did, the 997 became an established facet of the Porsche landscape, universally accepted and respected in a similar way to the previous air-cooled generation's 993 and 964, representing an awesome blend of performance, style, usability and quality.

Anatomy of the 997 Turbo engine revealed in this cutaway illustration. PORSCHE MUSEUM ARCHIVES

Gen I 997s were fitted with the 3.6-litre flat-six, fundamentally the same as the 996 they replaced, and viewed by some specialists as better in terms of reliability than the forthcoming 3.8-litre unit. ANTONY FRASER

Cabin interior and controls of the 997 have a rather better feel of quality and construction than the 996, though the layout is very similar apart from the steering wheel, with its integrated fingertip controls. ANTONY FRASER

The 997 moved on stylistically from the 996 with its more traditional 911 headlights – of the Bi-Xenon Litronic persuasion (with attendant washers), and so incomparably brighter than the air-cooled candle power – as well as revised rear lamp clusters. Despite a broad similarity with the 996 bodyshell, the 997 coupé contrived a lower drag coefficient (0.28) than its predecessor, and it was said to have retained only a third of its predecessor's componentry, while its interior was also agreeably redesigned.

Power outputs of the basic models – without getting into GT2, GT3 or Turbo – stayed much the same as the 996.

The basic 997 C2's 3.6 flat-six produced 325bhp and the 3.8-litre motor powering the 997 C2S developed 355bhp. The latter was equipped with uprated suspension and PASM with electronically adjustable settings. It also came fitted with so-called Lobster Fork 19in alloys, bigger brakes with red calipers, and dazzling Xenon headlights. The all-wheel-drive C4 and C4S versions were announced for the 2006 model year, featuring the wider shells and fatter tyres. The 997 Cabriolet was actually designed before the closed versions on the basis that the necessary chassis strengthening for the open-top car could be pared down for the coupé. Subtle upgrades for the 997 in 2009 included a larger air intake in the front valance, new headlamps and rear lights, Bluetooth mobile phone ability, and, far more crucially, new common-rail direct engines married to the dual clutch PDK gearbox.

Despite obvious similarities, the 997 manifests quite a different personality to the 996. It's solidly built and largely dependable when ranged against the earlier car's relative fragility. Despite one or two minor diversions such as SportChrono, it's equipped only with hard-core systems and equipment that a car of this calibre needs to have in its spec to be taken seriously: if it doesn't have it on board, you don't need it. The 997 does have a few known but generally minor issues, such as bore-scoring in the 3.8-litre motor, but for the most part it's a question of deciding which model to buy in the first place, which optional extras are worth having and, crucially, where to buy your car. There are nine mainstream models, ranging from C2, C2S, C4, C4S, in coupé, Targa and Cabriolet format, plus the GTS, GT2, GT3, GT3 RS and Turbo.

The all-wheel-drive version, the 997 C4, was in the showrooms in November 2005. AUTHOR

THE 997 TIMELINE

April 2004

The 997 Carrera S was unveiled to the press in the Puglia region of southern Italy, though the story was embargoed until July 2004.

September 2004

The 997 was officially launched to the public at the Paris Salon. The 2005 model year cars went on sale in the UK on 18 September 2004, priced from £58,380 for the Carrera 3.6 and £65,000 for the Carrera 'S' 3.8. Standard equipment for both included air-conditioning and full leather trim, Porsche Stability Management (PSM), Porsche Com-

munication Management (PCM), an on-board computer and the Porsche Sound Pack. The Carrera was fitted with 18in wheels as standard. The 'S' model also featured a number of optional extras from the base Carrera, including Xenon headlights, Porsche Active Suspension Management (PASM), Sports Chassis, and 19in wheels. Ceramic brakes (PCCB) were available for both cars as a cost-option – £5,349 – together with Tiptronic 'S' automatic transmission, sports seats, electric adjustment for the front seats, sunroof, navigation module for the PCM and metallic paintwork.

Rigorous winter testing of the 997 C4S, fitted with intercom for communication between engineers and technicians. PORSCHE MUSEUM ARCHIVES

The 997 C2 Carrera's rear bodywork was 88mm (3.5in) wider than its predecessor, the 996 C2 Carrera. ANTONY FRASER

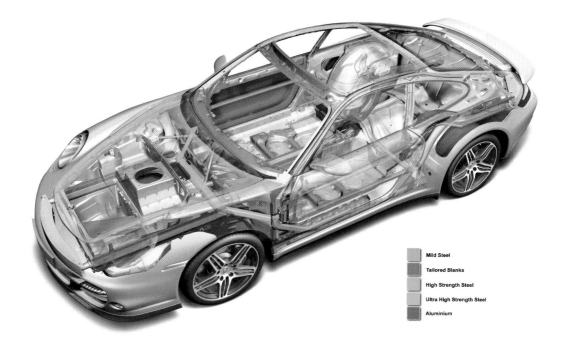

Cutaway drawing of the 997, indicating what elements of the skeleton are steel, and of what grade, and aluminium too. PORSCHE MUSEUM ARCHIVES

Mild Steel
Tailored Blanks
High Strength Steel
Ultra High Strength Steel
Aluminium

December 2004

Porsche announced that full Cabriolet versions of both the Carrera and Carrera 'S' would go on sale during April 2005, priced in the UK at £65,260 and £72,230, respectively, quickly bringing to four the number of 997 variants available. Equipment-wise, they would closely mirror the two coupés, as well as featuring the comprehensive Porsche Side Impact Protection system (POSIP) and pop-up roll-over bars carried over from the previous 996-model Cabriolets.

April 2005

In addition to launching the 997 Cabriolets, Porsche stole a march on the independent tuning companies with the introduction of an aerodynamic styling kit for 997 coupés. It was based on the 2005 season's SuperCup racing cars, but with a smaller rear wing for road use.

June 2005

Porsche announced that four-wheel-drive 'C4' versions of the Carrera and Carrera S coupés would go on sale for the 2006-model year in Germany and the UK on 22 October, while US sales would begin soon afterwards. UK prices would start from £69,000 and £76,800 for the 3.6-litre Carrera 4 and 3.8-litre Carrera 4S, respectively. Both cars would have wider-than-standard bodies, gaining an additional 44mm across the rear wheel arches, and a 10mm lower ride height than their rear-drive counterparts. This introduction brought to six the number of 997 variants available.

Harmonious lines of the Gen 2 997 C4 S coupé viewed in profile. Introduced in 2009, the new flat-six engine featured direct fuel injection and was mounted 10mm lower in the engine bay. AUTHOR

July 2005

Less than a month after unveiling the wide-bodied Carrera 4 and Carrera 4S coupés, Porsche released details of the broadly similar drop-top versions of the 2006-model C4 and C4S Cabriolets, on sale alongside the coupé versions on 22 October. Their UK price tags were almost identical, at £69,000 and £76,880, respectively, boasting broadly comparable levels of equipment and optional extras.

The cabriolet version of the 997 came out ahead of the coupé model in 2004 for model-year 2005. AUTHOR

August 2005

Celebrating fifty years of the Porsche Club of America, a special Azure Blue, limited edition Carrera 2 coupé sporting the X51 power kit was available in the USA.

1978 F1 World Champion Mario Andretti gave circuit rides at Sonoma in a GT3, posed here at Donington with a 997 GT3. ANTONY FRASER

February 2006

Porsche unveiled the long-anticipated 997 Turbo at the Geneva Salon, available in in the UK from 24 June 2006. Priced at £97,840, it was around £7,500 more than the 996 Turbo. The US launch was set for 8 July, with prices starting at $122,900. Also at Geneva, the new 997 GT3 was revealed, delivering 415bhp from its naturally aspirated 3.6-litre flat-six, still derived from the Le Mans-winning Mezger GT1 engine, rolling on to a maximum speed of around 194mph (312km/h). The GT3 went on sale in May 2006 in mainland Europe, and in August in the UK and USA. The UK price was £79,540 (nearly £5,000 cheaper than the 996-based GT3 RS) and in the USA at $106,000.

With large decals on its rear flanks proclaiming its pedigree, the 997 GT3 RS developed 450bhp and had shorter gear ratios than its GT3 sibling for swifter acceleration. PORSCHE MUSEUM ARCHIVES

Test driver Walter Röhrl assesses and fine-tunes every Porsche model, including the 997 Turbo featured here, until he is satisfied it is up to scratch before it goes into production. PORSCHE MUSEUM ARCHIVES

Pictured in 2008, a 997 GT3, powered by the 3.6-litre normally aspirated Mezger 964/GT1 engine, developing 409bhp. PORSCHE MUSEUM ARCHIVES

July 2006

The limited edition 997 GT3 RS went on sale in the UK in October 2006, a month after its public debut at the Paris Salon, priced at £94,280.

August 2006

The ninth mainstream 997 derivative, the glass-roofed Targa, was announced in August 2006. Based on the existing wide-bodied Carrera 4 and Carrera 4S models, and at the same time using essentially the same sliding glass roof as in the previous 996-model Targas, it was available in the UK from 18 November, priced at £70,320 and £77,370, respectively.

Enjoying the fresh air and sunshine aboard a 997 Targa. PORSCHE MUSEUM ARCHIVES

The Gen 2 997 Turbo was unveiled at the Frankfurt Show in 2009, powered by the 500bhp 3.8-litre twin-turbo flat-six. ANTONY FRASER

The 997-based 911 Speedster was available in 2011. Only 356 examples were produced, painted Pure Blue or Carrara White. They followed on historically from the 356, 930 and 964 Speedsters. PORSCHE MUSEUM ARCHIVES

May 2007

The soft-top version of the 997 Turbo was launched, the Cabriolet managing to be virtually as quick as the Turbo coupé.

November 2007

The rear-wheel-drive 997 GT2 became the fastest and most powerful 911 ever, taking 3.6s to accelerate from 0–60mph and passing 100mph in 7.4s, with a top speed of 204mph (328km/h). As well as being rear-drive only, as opposed to four-wheel drive, the GT2 differed from the 997 Turbo visually: its front bumper panel lacked foglights and it had twin air intakes either side of the central intake, plus larger rear wing and twin titanium tail pipes.

April 2009

Revisions announced for the 997 range included a facelift, direct injection engines and the PDK dual clutch transmission, plus torque vectoring system for the Turbo.

September 2010

Last hurrah for the 997 series was the GTS: the 408bhp power kit engine in the wide body, but rear-wheel drive only. It was an alternative to the special-edition Sport Classic or 997 Speedster, launched December 2010.

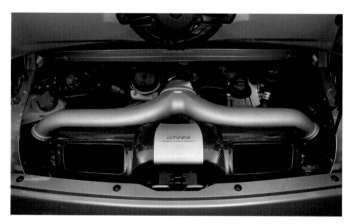

Engine bay of the 997 GT2 RS with prominent Y-pipe induction system and carbon cladding. PORSCHE MUSEUM ARCHIVES

The 3.8-litre 997 Carrera GTS of 2011 and 2012 was a halfway house between Carrera 2 and GT3, built on the wide body/chassis. It could be ordered in C2 and C4 format. PORSCHE MUSEUM ARCHIVES

Johan Dirickx powers his 493bhp 997 RS 4.0 into one of the tighter turns at Abbeville circuit, Picardy. AUTHOR

Cabin interior of this 997 Carrera C2 S is upholstered in blue leather with matching blue carpet, floormats and trim. AUTHOR

April 2011

The GT3 RS 4.0 was the final incarnation of the 997 GT3 RS, with only 600 units made, and the last Mezger flat-six, which, at 4.0 litres, was the largest displacement 911 engine ever.

997 CARRERA C2S

As far as prices for used models are concerned, water-cooled 911s are the snips of the Porsche coupé genre, and as 996 values continue to rise, a 997 C2S at £30,000 in pristine condition and with low miles looks like something of a steal.

I've come to components specialists PorscheShop at their premises between Kidderminster and Worcester. The building is a converted Second World War bomb-making

The 997 Carrera C2 S coupé body was reasonably aerodynamic, with a drag coefficient of Cd0.28. AUTHOR

factory, with appropriately substantial walls and a nod to pre-war art deco architecture. As well as offering parts of all descriptions, PorscheShop handles car sales and my eye is drawn to a svelte-looking 997 Carrera 2S, a 3.8-litre car delivered in 2005. It is finished in Arctic Silver with Ocean Blue leather cabin upholstery, which some might say is the ideal combination of hues; black's all very well, but dark blue raises the game. It's had just two owners, the last one for nine years, who have between them notched up a modest 29,700 miles (47,800km) in twelve years, and it has a full service history based on OPC Porsche Solihull.

It's endowed with the majority of 997 ancillaries, including switchable Sports exhaust system, reversing sensor, sunshine roof, heated seats with memory (not that I ever manage to get that to recall my own particular driving position).

While the 996 controls have a basic simplicity to them, in the same way as the 986 Boxster does, the 997 switchgear raised the game into a slightly more complicated mode. There's also a satnav, and again a modest TomTom appears to provide more up-to-date mapping and guidance than the inbuilt system, at least when regularly updated. An increasing number of drivers seem to be employing their smartphones for route instruction and I wonder about the legality of that, in a non-Bluetooth situation, though I suppose it will do so long as you're not chatting at the same time. This 997 also has a phone installed, as well as a six-CD player and eleven-speaker Bose surround sound system, plus the useful on-board computer gives the outside temperature, fuel range and other readings. It's recently had new front discs and pads, plus two new front tyres, and a full MoT.

This style of alloy wheel was a standard fitting on 997 Carrera C2 Ss. AUTHOR

The Gen 1 997 C2S is a sophisticated drive and it's a highly efficient ground coverer, totally untroubled by any twist and turn, no matter how quickly I'm going. It turns in and sticks to a given line like a suckered snail, though immeasurably faster. The ride on these undulating cross-country B-roads is controlled and composed, and it's equally as taut and positive as my hunkered down 996. The rear-drive C2S provides optimum steering feel and the ride is agreeable. It's as secure a driving platform as you could wish for.

997 CARRERA C4S 3.8

While I've been more than happy with the performance of my 996, I've always had a sneaking hankering after a 997, in the belief that they are extremely robust structurally

and bulletproof mechanically. Joff Ward of Finlay Gorham, based near Bury St Edmunds, rebuilds every 3.8-litre Gen 1 997 engine that he sells, as a matter of course, although not everyone fully appreciates the necessity: 'I need to get across to people the significance of what we're doing to Gen 1 997s, because otherwise people will not pay me the extra money for them because they haven't seen the point of why we do it.' He's referring to the 3.8-litre water-cooled flat-six, as fitted to 997s, Gen 1 S4s and C2 Ss, and Gen 2 C2s.

It's not a question of if the engine is going to go, it's when the engine's going to go. We're even finding some of the Gen 2s are scoring their bores. They haven't got an intermediate shaft so they can't damage that, which is something. And the timing chains on these Gen 1s are stretching over an inch, not even over big miles, and we take them out and find they're about an inch longer than a new one.

Just to get this straight, this is all about the 3.8-litre 997s; it doesn't apply to 996s, apparently, and all 3.6-litre 997s are fine.

A bore scope test will not necessarily indicate a problem; it could be fine and a month later it will score the bores There's no warning; I can't risk putting the bore scope down and telling customer it's all clear, because there's a good chance they'll be back six months later. And this is happening all the time.

For that reason Joff will only buy in 997 3.8s with damaged

Joff Ward of Finlay Gorham cautions that when buying a 3.8-litre 997 S, such as this C4S, it's wise to have the cylinder bores inspected for scoring. AUTHOR

engines – relatively cheaply, of course – and rebuild them, which makes the asking price start to look like a bargain. There speaks someone who's specialized in Porsches for forty years and reckons to have traded some 10,000 Porsches in that time: 'To me, the C4S is the best of the Gen 1s, and I love the way they drive.'

On the road I'm immediately aware of the additional power of the 3.8 engine over the 3.6. The C4S handles so well too, biddable and compliant despite the presence of the front drivetrain, and it feels more refined than the previous 996 version. There's the all-wheel-drive safety blanket too and its amazing grip, which Joff particularly welcomes in the snow: 'I almost prefer them to the C2s because I like the way they handle, especially in the wet when you've got that extra bit of grip.' It's also got PSM, but Joff turns that off most of the time:

as it spoils the fun. Suddenly the blurred edges of the standard 996 have gone; it's sharper and more reminiscent of a 993. I can do things in this that I would never dare do in a 996, in terms of handling. On the other hand, a GT3 is just bloody uncomfortable and to be honest I think I can get one of these quicker from A-to-B than in a GT3. I don't find the GT3 particularly user friendly; they're a trackday car rather than a road car.

Indeed, my outing in this fighter-jet of a car is edifying in that sense too: it is a fantastic ground-coverer, swift, secure and comfortable as well.

As for the upholstery, that's intriguing too: it's Cocoa brown, specified by the original owner, Irish interior designer Helen Turkington, and first registered in Porto.

997 CARRERA 4S (2005–2012)

Layout and chassis
Two-plus-two coupé, Targa and cabriolet, unit-construction steel body/chassis

Engine
Type	M97, horizontally opposed, rear-mounted 6-cylinder; 9A1 direct-injection from 2009
Block material	aluminium
Head material	aluminium
Cylinders	flat-six
Cooling	water
Bore and stroke	99 × 82.8mm
Capacity	3824cc
Valves	4 valves per cylinder
Compression ratio	10.0:1
Fuel system	Multi-point injection
Max. power (DIN)	355bhp @ 6,600rpm
Max. torque	295lb ft @ 4,600rpm
Fuel capacity	67 litres (14.7 gallons)

Transmission
Gearbox	Getrag G97/00 rear drive, 6-speed; PDK 7-speed from 2009; all-wheel drive
Clutch	hydraulic single dry plate
Ratios	1st 3.82
	2nd 2.20
	3rd 1.52
	4th 1.22
	5th 1.02
	6th 0.84
	Reverse 3.44
	Final drive 3.89

Suspension and steering
Front	independent by MacPherson struts, aluminium links, longitudinal and transverse links, coil springs, gas dampers, anti-roll bar
Rear	independent by MacPherson struts, aluminium links, lateral and transverse links, coil springs, gas dampers, anti-roll bar
Steering	rack-and-pinion
Tyres	235/35R × 19ZR front, 295/30ZR × 19ZR rear
Wheels	19in aluminium alloy
Rim width	7.5in J front, 10.0in J rear

Brakes
Type	front and rear vented discs with six-piston calipers; optional M450 ceramic discs
Size	330 × 24mm front; 330 × 20mm rear

Dimensions
Track	
Front	1,465mm (57.28in)
Rear	1,500mm (59.05in)
Wheelbase	2,350mm (92.51in)
Overall length	4,430mm (174.4in)
Overall width	1,808mm (69.48in)
Overall height	1,300mm (51.3in)
Unladen weight	1,515kg (3,340lb)

Performance
Top speed	298km/h (185mph)
0–60mph	4.5s

A 997 C4S at Finlay Gorham, with cabin upholstery in Cocoa brown, originally specified by interior designer Helen Turkington. AUTHOR

Pictured on the north Norfolk coast, the 997 C4S is a highly sophisticated touring car. AUTHOR

997 CARRERA 4S CABRIOLET

This is the car to enjoy the sunshine in. Supremely competent, the 997 C4S supplies the most efficient chassis dynamics, coupled with confidence-inspiring all-wheel-drive roadholding and, most of all in this particular incarnation, a fully automatic, electrically powered blue fabric canopy. The example on offer at Cameron Cars in rural north Somerset is finished in vivid Baltic Blue, one of those gorgeous hues that come alive in the sun. The cockpit – if a cabriolet can be said to have a cockpit rather than a cabin – is upholstered in deep Ocean

The rear of the 997 Cabriolet is slightly higher than the coupé version to compensate for differences in airflow over the canvas top against the smoother coupé shape. AUTHOR

Blue leather. Entry to the cockpit passes over stainless-steel shields and within are the electrically operated and heated sports seats that remember the driver's favoured position, and the instrument gauges have white dials.

The C4S is built on the broad-shouldered Turbo version of the 997 body, and the S derivative is powered by a 355bhp, 3.8-litre liquid-cooled flat-six, and this car is equipped with the six-speed manual gearbox. Some might say that Tiptronic transmission would better suit this car, given its raison d'être, but the manual box is also perfectly fine in the context of relaxed top-down touring because the flat-six is so torquey. Like all top-line modern Porsches it features Porsche Active Suspension Management (PASM) and Porsche Stability Management (PSM) to handle adverse driving conditions, and as you'd expect it has all the usual h-fi and connectivity equipment on board. It runs on 19in Carrera Classic five-spoke alloy wheels with coloured centre crests, shod with newish Bridgestone Potenzas. The 997 S also boasts bigger brakes and red painted calipers, plus Bi-Xenon headlights, and the comprehensive spec is finished off with four tailpipes. This is the third time that it's passed through Cameron Cars' premises, a reflection of the faith that customers place in them, rather than a brisk turnover of owners. It has a full OPC and Porsche specialist service history.

Cameron Cars generally have around twenty Porsches in stock, plus a handful of exotics. The firm was set up in 2003 by Simon Cockram and Ian Cameron. There are workshops on site for servicing and mechanical work, while paint and trim is outsourced locally. Much of their business is by word of mouth, so they don't advertise heavily.

For a road test I drive the 997 Cabriolet a couple of miles to the National Trust's Dyrham Park. These cars feel like they're particularly well built, whether open-top or coupé, and it drives as superbly and fluently as a new car. I operate the top and it retracts and erects itself with no fuss, though I keep it up for the photos so as not to attract attention in the grounds. It's such a distinctive car that my bid to remain inconspicuous fails totally and an attendant warns that I might have to pay a photographic fee. Fair enough; it certainly is a photogenic car, roof up or down.

997 TARGA C4S 3.8

These cars are so sophisticated with their sliding glass sunroofs. Porsche's latter-day Targas, such as the 997 C4S Targa, provide an unrestricted view of the heavens, rain or shine, open or closed. That's all very well, but on the move our perception of what's going on above our heads is mostly perfunctory, impressionistic, because our eyes are glued to the road ahead. The 997 Targa changes that. Available only with four-wheel drive, the 997 Targa came on line in autumn 2006 for the 2007 model year and was superseded in 2009 by the Gen 2 range, which lasted until 2012.

In 1996 the last evolution of the preceding 993, the Targa version, ushered in this very sophisticated sliding glass roof panel – positively 007 sci-fi in its ingenuity – a facility inherited and manifested in hatchback form by its water-cooled successors, such as this one. It was quite unlike the classic lift-off panel last seen on the 964. Unlike some overhead apertures where a glazed or perspex panel allows an aerial view, the 997's pane is an expansive canopy occupying the

The 997 Carrera 4S Targa's rear three-quarter windows are shaped differently to those of the normal 997 coupé, having sharply pointed rearmost ends instead of being more gently rounded. PORSCHE MUSEUM ARCHIVES

car's entire roof space. This means there's a constant awareness of celestial surroundings and a feeling of increased luminosity, visibility and perception, and a casual upward glance is a more convivial event. One's surroundings are viewed through a glass darkly (with apologies to Ingmar Bergman via the Bible), since there's a fashionable Mediterranean-style sunshades tint to the glass, meaning that occupants aren't quite so exposed to ultraviolet rays and the proletarian gaze. Indeed, a full-length roller blind extends the length of the roof at the press of a button, should more conventional privacy or insulation be required. The glass roof panel is made from high-strength laminated safety glass, and is operated by a button on the centre console ahead of the gear lever, one touch erecting the wind deflector, a second touch activating the retraction mechanism. The glazed roof eases its way rearwards and is stowed discreetly inside the rear window, forming two layers of glass in the process, while leaving the aperture over the cabin wide open and the occupants free as a bird.

The 997 and 996 Targas operate in a similar way to the 993, with the benefit of a hatchback rear window, which makes them very convenient for stowing luggage or camera gear, for example. The latest 991 Targa is a modern take on the original 911 Targa: while it loosely resembles the appearance of the 911 Targa, in practice the roof lifts off electrically and retracts like a docking space module, out of sight underneath the rear greenhouse. The 997 Targa roof consists of three glass elements: the wind deflector, the retractable roof section and the rear window, as well as the two body-coloured longitudinal steel members, which

Bird's-eye view of the Gen 2 997 Targa C4, demonstrating the extent and tinting of the car's glazed roof panels. PORSCHE MUSEUM ARCHIVES

provide rollover protection in the absence of the traditional Targa hoop. It's a best-of-both-worlds car, offering the swooping coupé profile allied to the convertible's tops-off, wind-in-the-hair exposure. The glass lid weighs more than the standard coupé steel roof – 60kg (132lb) – so the suspension is set up accordingly.

So, what's it like in practice? Around field-boundary lanes and on B-roads the C4 is swift enough, but frankly not particularly in its element. It's a grand touring car, a long-distance ground coverer that's more at home on the open road, or, indeed, soaking up the sun on the Grande Corniche. It's a decent enough day though for an open-roof blast up to Castle Howard and the 997 is as able and sure-footed as they come. I relish the glimpses of the tree branches overhead and the odd experience of being inside the building as the road shoots under the lodge at the periphery of the estate; you only get lingering views like these in a Cab or a Targa: a normal sunroof is too much of a postage stamp. And then I'm confronted by a series of interesting bends, so I drop into 2nd gear and apply some power, and that's when the 997 comes to life: I can feel the chassis working and, for a few delicious moments, I experience the thrills it's capable of providing.

The superannuated sunroof model lacks the purity and homogeneity of the sublime 997 Coupé, and you don't get the full wind-in-the-hair experience of the Cabriolet. It was always going to be a halfway house – that's always been the lot of the 911 Targa – but it's so well engineered and harmonious a design that it more than validates its position in the 997 line-up.

997 TURBO

For anyone addicted to straight-line speed, the 997 Turbo answers their dreams. The inexorable surge under boost to 198mph (318km/h) – on an unrestricted autobahn, of course – is sublime. It rushes from 0 to 62mph in 3.7s too. The finely honed 997 chassis is no slouch around the bends either, as was confirmed by a thrilling run over the Scottish Borders to visit Falkirk's Kelpies. It's four-wheel drive, as is the norm now, and when Gen 2 arrived in 2009, transmission was standardized with the seven-speed dual-clutch PDK paddle shift system. It's such an accomplished car that even the 997 Turbo could be construed as boring compared with air-cooled models. Horses for courses, and we'll give it the benefit of the doubt as it's such amazing value for such an accomplished car.

The 997 Turbo was unveiled at the 2006 Geneva Salon and was in production from 2006 for the 2007 model-year to 2014, when it was superseded by the 991. Stylistically it differs from the preceding 996 in having conventional ovoid headlights instead of the 'fried egg' look, and features LED indicator strips in the new front panel's air intakes, while fog lamps relocate to the outer ends of the panel. The trademark air vents in the leading and trailing edges of the rear

The 997 Turbo was unveiled at the Geneva Show in 2006, and here are two being put through their paces.
PORSCHE MUSEUM ARCHIVES

Cutaway illustration of the 997 Turbo Gen 2, revealing the all-wheel-drive transmission layout and turbo locations.
PORSCHE MUSEUM ARCHIVES

flanks are also different, while the retractable rear wing functions on similar lines to the 996 version.

The power plant is the much-vaunted 3.6-litre Mezger flat-six, which employs the casings of the GT1 racing car, developing 480bhp though its twin Borg-Warner VTG turbos that deploy Variable Vane Technology to reduce lag under boost. The Sport Chrono option can also override boost control to provide more torque over a short 10s period and a narrow rev range. Gen 2 also ushered in revised 'torque vectoring', meaning the differential dispenses varying amounts of power to the driven wheels according to road and weather conditions. Even the 997 Turbo Cabriolet

can perform at this level, in spite of its frivolous canopy, as I have found when being able to hold an almost normal conversation at 170mph (274km/h) on an autobahn.

In some ways the 997 Turbo isn't so very different from its siblings. There's always been a homogeneity about Porsche cockpits, and the 997 Turbo is no exception, being agreeably familiar with a dash that's recognizably akin to the Boxster's. Compared with classic models, however, it seems like the gauges and controls have been rationalized and simplified for the twenty-first century. The 997 Turbo has a more modern steering wheel with the shifter paddles on the two upper arms of the wheel. Electric seat adjustment

The rear-wheel-drive 996 GT2 was the fastest road-going Porsche ever to go on sale, though its spec was derived from WEC GT2 regulations. AUTHOR

The 997 Turbo press car used to cover the 2011 Roger Albert Clark RAC Rally. Its all-wheel-drive chassis certainly helped in the snowy back roads of the Scottish borders. ANTONY FRASER

997 TURBO GEN I (2006–2009)

Layout and chassis
Two-plus-two coupé and cabriolet, unit-construction steel body/chassis

Engine

Type	M96/72 'Mezger' dry sump, horizontally opposed, rear-mounted 6-cylinder
Block material	aluminium
Head material	aluminium
Cylinders	flat-six
Cooling	water
Bore and stroke	100 × 76.4mm
Capacity	3600cc
Valves	4 valves per cylinder
Compression ratio	9.4:1
Fuel system	multi-point injection; 2 Borg-Warner VTG turbochargers
Max. power (DIN)	480bhp @ 6,000rpm
Max. torque	295lb ft @ 4,600rpm
Fuel capacity	67 litres (14.7 gallons)

Transmission

Gearbox	Getrag G97/00 rear drive, 6-speed; all-wheel drive
Clutch	hydraulic single dry plate
Ratios	1st 3.91
	2nd 2.32
	3rd 1.61
	4th 1.28
	5th 1.08
	6th 0.88
	Reverse 3.44
	Final drive 3.89

Suspension and steering

Front	independent by MacPherson struts, aluminium links, longitudinal and transverse links, coil springs, gas dampers, anti-roll bar
Rear	independent by MacPherson struts, aluminium links, lateral and transverse links, coil springs, gas dampers, anti-roll bar
Steering	rack-and-pinion
Tyres	235/35R × 19ZR front, 295/30ZR × 19ZR rear
Wheels	19in aluminium alloy
Rim width	8.5in J front, 11.5in J rear

Brakes

Type	front and rear vented discs with six-piston calipers; optional M450 ceramic discs
Size	330 × 24mm front; 330 × 20mm rear

Dimensions

Track	
Front	1,465mm (57.67in)
Rear	1,500mm (59.05in)
Wheelbase	2,350mm (92.51in)
Overall length	4,450mm (175.1in)
Overall width	1,852mm (72.91in)
Overall height	1,300mm (51.2in)
Unladen weight	1,660kg (3,659lb)

Performance

Top speed	310km/h (192.6mph)
0–60mph	4.7s

makes it very easy to find a comfortable travelling position. In sports damper setting the ride is too harsh for country roads, though the sports exhaust is fun to play with in a context where you can hear it. Composed, serene, yet still fun.

ROADGOING RACERS

They don't get much hotter than the 997 GT2 CS and GT3 RS. With the help of F1 and Group C veteran Mike Wilds, who's a race driving instructor as well, I subjected these towering titans to a torrid track test around Silverstone's broad blacktop.

Preliminaries done, Mike takes me out for a lesson in cir-

cuit driving. Through Beckett's tricky left-right-left complex the slicks are well and truly squirming as they fight the chassis – they do not want to relinquish their grip, but staying on the circuit requires three rapid changes of direction. The faster we go the more the arm-wrestle takes hold. We're in the exalted performance domain of a 997 GT2, and a Clubsport to boot, and this is about as quick as a top-line Porsche road car gets on a racetrack. Having said that, there is nothing here apart from a Ferrari 458 race car and a couple of Radicals that can live with its towering performance.

The reality is that both cars are pretty docile at low revs, but when stirred into action they are savage performers indeed. On the premise that these two 997s represent the zenith of that model line, we reckon there's a viable motive

The Gen 2 997 GT3 RS was marketed from 2010 to 2012 and embraced a number of new features, including the more powerful 445bhp engine, shorter gear ratios, wider front and rear track and aero improvements, intended for homologation in the GT3 race cars. ANTONY FRASER

One of life's more engaging experiences, a trip behind the wheel of a 997 GT3 RS. ANTONY FRASER

Hard cornering on Salisbury Plain, the 997 GT3 RS turns in beautifully and exhibits no body roll. ANTONY FRASER

During his 50th anniversary year as a top-line racing driver, Mike Wilds ran this 997 GT2 CS, here in Silverstone's old pit lane, finished in the same colour as his crash helmet. AUTHOR

for comparing and contrasting them head to head. Although the GT2 isn't an RS, the brutal nature of its turbocharged performance places it in line with the normally aspirated 997 GT3 RS, making this encounter a bona fide track test. Although values have escalated sharply, like almost everything with a Porsche badge, they are still relatively affordable for someone with the wherewithal to go serious trackday motoring. We are at Silverstone on an RMA Trackday. It's a serious business: about a hundred 'drivers' have signed on, and Graham Clarke banishes the half-dozen who show up late for his briefing. Afterwards we return to the pits garage on the old National pits complex, where the cars have been delivered by JZM's Steve McHale.

This yellow GT2 is a rather special car. The standard GT2 was launched in 2007 and served as the chariot of fire for speed freaks and optimists running in national GT series; on the international racing front, Porsche had already flipped over to the GT3 as the weapon of choice. The GT2 is a twin-turbo rear-wheel-drive chassis pushing out 523bhp at 6,500rpm, and is capable of 0–60mph in 3.3s. Its top speed of 338km/h (210mph) was good enough for Walter Röhrl to lap the Nordschleife on a public day in 7m 32s. This example offers even more as it is a Manthey 600 conversion. (For the link between Manthey Racing and Porsche Weissach, see Chapter 3.) The M600 kit consists of an Akrapovič exhaust system including sports silencers, headers and cats; a different pressure sensor on the engine with programming by Manthey, and Manthey intercoolers serving the turbos. The GT2 clutch was replaced with a meatier 890 Newton clutch and 40/60 lock ratio locking differential from GT Gears, Cup Car diff, and Surface Transforms ceramic discs. According

to Steve, these ceramic discs are used for track as they are 6.5kg lighter than a standard disc and they don't burn out like Porsche discs. They are run with Pagid RSCI pads, race fluid and steel flexible hoses. The car still has the traction control connected, though there are plans to disconnect it. It produces 600bhp and 71Nm more torque than a GT2 RS in the mid-range, although to get that sort of power it is necessary to change the exhaust headers and cats, because the standard ones are too restrictive and it would simply melt the cats.

The car also features a sequential gearshift. This is an interesting proposition because you still need to clutch with each shift; it just allows you to go straight back and forward into each gear – with reverse at the far end ahead of neutral. With a normal manual box, if you're coming into a corner and you're in 6th and you know it's a 3rd gear corner, you'd go on the brakes and throw it straight into 3rd, but with the sequential lever you have to go through every interim notch to get there. At least there's a digital display that tells you which gear you're pulling – assuming you have time to glance at it. It's made by SQS, and works through a conventional gearbox; the lever itself is like a scale model of Blackpool Tower. It doesn't matter how quick your shift is, it will only shift at its own speed, though that is pretty nifty. It's also a pleasant enough feeling, working through the box.

The revised suspension consists of new tie rods, steering arms, RSS lower wishbones, KW Clubsport variant 3, which is only two-way adjustable because of the HLS hydraulic lift system, installed to elevate the front end over traffic humps and operational up to 50km/h. It also boasts a Manthey carbon splitter and Manthey carbon gurney flap, all of which was developed in the wind tunnel to obtain more downforce in racing and provide more vacuum at the front end of the wheel arches, and better brake cooling. It runs on BBS Cup Car rims and the tyres are Michelin Porsche Cup M1 slicks, 24/64 × 18 on the front and 27/68 × 18 on the back, although Steve notes that these only make you go faster: you can have just as much fun on road tyres. Other embellishments include a Cup Car steering wheel and carbon detailed interior. Otherwise, the body is standard, with ClubSport interior featuring Sports seats, Nomex and Kevlar detailing, and, by contrast, air con and carpets, and a half-cage in the rear of the cabin. Steve is enthusiastic about his charge:

It has got a massive spread of grunt. It doesn't matter if you've got 2,000rpm or 5,000rpm, it pulls just the same. Just change gear and use the torque. It will rev to 8,000rpm, and it will easily spin its wheels in every gear, and you can actually powerslide it despite its all-wheel drive because it's got so much torque.

Erstwhile F1, F5000 and WEC driver Mike Wilds prepares to give the author some circuit driving lessons in the 997 GT3 RS. ANTONY FRASER

I don my race suit, helmet and gloves, squeeze into the bucket seat and buckle up the five-point Schroth harness. It is such a beguiling environment: a combination of GT3 and race car. What a joy; the throttle is smooth, the wheel easy on the wrists. I motor smoothly, leisurely almost, out of the pit lane, keeping inside the white line, check mirrors, toe down and the revs soar. In an instant we're flowing through the five curves comprising Maggotts, Becketts, Chapel, taken in 3rd and on the throttle. It's here that the sheer power of the GT2 becomes evident, opening it up on the entry to Hangar straight. A few seconds in 6th before going down to 4th for Stowe, more technical than you think, then bustling into Vale in 3rd, performing a series of weird apexes at Club before hitting the modern Pit straight. There's hardly a lift in 5th as the track curves right at Abbey, hugging the

Mike Wilds instructs the author on Silverstone's braking points, turn-ins, apexes and exit points as he helms the 997 GT3 RS. ANTONY FRASER

left-hand side before massive braking and 3rd for the sharp right at Village, hooking right then arcing round The Loop. Another short shift then a blast in 6th to the Brooklands-Luffield complex, and soon enough I'm back on the old pits straight and going hard for Copse. I'm sometimes turning in too soon and understeering out, and that's a good lesson in track craft. It's also important not to allow other traffic to blow my concentration. The interesting sensations going through Becketts when the car is trying to get away is down to the slicks and the pace, and with gritted teeth I do my best to let it do what it wants, rather than fight it. It's also surprising how delicate it is to control; it's not down to brute force, even though its persona suggests its disposition could take no prisoners. Relax into it.

There's another dimension here too. Slicks are an acquired taste. When they're hot the pressures go up and you can tell because you start to lose front end grip, the car starts to understeer and therefore you lose grip, and subsequently as you start getting the power on early in the corners it loses rear end grip. I'm running with traction control off all the time at Steve's behest, simply because it's better for the rear discs and pads as they're not being asked to grip all the time, and it allows me to be more progressive with the throttle. When I come in Steve resets the tyre pressures and the car goes back to its sharp self again, with a hint of understeer, but it doesn't take long before they've gone up again, and the understeer is starting to come back. I'm also pumping the brake pedal once or twice because it may have a tiny air bubble in the line, and Steve takes a little squirt out of each caliper. After I've pitted I feel the slick treads: they're the consistency of hot chewing gum, and it smells of very hot brakes. In summary, the GT2's performance is effortless and, curiously, that makes it somehow less involving.

Our second contender is the blue GT3 RS, which has a similar KW three-way adjustable Clubsport suspension set-up to the GT2, which top drivers prefer as it is more sophisticated than two-way. Steve agains talks me though the spec:

> It comes with a cage as standard, unless you order it without, Service Transforms ceramic discs, competition pads, steel flex brake hoses, competition brake fluid. It has the same lock ratio on the diff – that's 40/60 Cup Car diff pack, plus Cup Car steering wheel, sequential shift, but standard GT3 RS engine and standard exhaust, giving 450bhp. We could make the engine bigger, and we can fit an Akrapovič exhaust, which gives you about 8 more horsepower for about £9,000; trouble is, you can't get them onto track days as they're too loud. Manthey do a 4.4-litre conversion which is 530bhp, but it's 55,000 euros!

The 997 GT3 RS prepared by JZM, ready for an outing at Silverstone in the hands of racer and instructor Mike Wilds. AUTHOR

I bend double to avoid hitting my helmet and duck into the left-hand-drive GT3 RS. Similar in layout, the cabin's a familiar environment. There's the same procedure to access the circuit, but the immediate sensation is of a lithe, snarling beast, with a much more aggressive disposition. It's lighter too, and apparently more chuckable. I change gear at 5,000rpm and when I want to go really fast it's 5,500rpm, but actually I don't think it makes much difference. I can use all the power because it hasn't got the onslaught of the turbo car, but in any case, it handles better because it's lighter, it doesn't need as much weight management. I can get it through the turns by revving it harder, working the gears more, though aiming for apexes is the same challenge in both cars, no harder in one than the other. Powering out of a corner, the GT2 is so quick, violent even, but actually at the apex, because of its weight, it's slower than the GT3 RS. The

normally aspirated car is nicely balanced and I can accelerate through the turns more easily, carrying more cornering speed, so in that sense it's less effort. It has a more familiar performance delivery, which makes it the more pleasurable experience of the two. It is incredible to see what it's capable of on track and know that it can do that on the road, because essentially it is a road car.

I'm breathless. At the end of the day, these two 997s are astonishing cars by any standards. They are formidable performers on track, yet they are actually road cars. What a pair! But if it's finder's keepers, I'll have the GT3 RS, thanks.

Mike Wilds, my instructor for the day, is of a similar mind. He describes the GT2 as sensational, but cannot resist the GT3 RS:

> Porsches are a commitment car, so you give a little to allow the car to work; you don't go into a corner too quickly, you drive it, let it do its job. They talk to you, and if you get it wrong they don't like you and they'll bite you, but if you drive them as they need to be driven, they love you and they'll give you more grip level than you could ever imagine a GT car could give you. And, as a racing driver, it's nice to drive something that talks to you and you can utilize the skills you've learnt over fifty years.
>
> As for the GT3 RS, this is the best one I've ever driven! It's absolutely fantastic, though you miss the pull on the straight. I love power and although I miss the turbo pulling me down the straight, as a racing driver I love the GT3 because it's a challenge to go quickly. I love the GT2 but if I was going to buy one or the other I'd probably buy the GT3 RS; it's just a much nicer balanced motor car, but they are two of the best GT cars in the world.

The 997 GT3 RS hurtles past Silverstone's spectacular Wing building during a trackday session with Mike Wilds. ANTONY FRASER

Hurrying across the MoD's Salisbury Plain battle training area in the 997 GT3 RS. The cantilevered rear wing is an unmissable feature. ANTONY FRASER

997 GT2 CLUBSPORT (2008)

Engine

Capacity	3.6 litres, M96/70
Compression ratio	9.0:1
Max. power (DIN)	600bhp @ 5,700rpm
Max. torque	680Nm @ 2,200rpm
Modifications	Manthey M600 kit, Akrapovič exhaust & Manthey intercoolers

Transmission

Gearbox	6-speed, G96/88 (SQS sequential)

Suspension and steering

Front	KW racing dampers and 3-way Clubsport coil-overs, adjustable anti-roll bar
Rear	KW racing dampers and 3-way Clubsport coil-overs, adjustable anti-roll bar
Tyres	235/35 ZR 19 front, 325/30 ZR 19 + 5mm spacers rear
Wheels	19 × 9in alloys front, 19 × 12in alloys rear

Dimensions

Overall length	4,469mm (179.5in)
Overall width	1,852mm (72.9in)
Weight	1,438kg (3,172lb)

Performance

Top speed	328km/h (204mph)
0–62mph	3.7s

997 GT3 RS (2008)

Engine

Capacity	3.6 litres, M96/70
Compression ratio	9.0:1
Max. power (DIN)	450bhp @ 7,600rpm
Max. torque	405Nm @ 5,500rpm
Modifications	None

Transmission

Gearbox	6-speed, G96/88 (SQS sequential)

Suspension and steering

Front	KW racing dampers and 3-way Clubsport coil-overs, adjustable anti-roll bar
Rear	KW racing dampers and 3-way Clubsport coil-overs, adjustable anti-roll bar
Wheels	19 × 8.5in front, 19 × 12in rear

Dimensions

Overall length	4,427mm (174.3in)
Overall width	1,852mm (72.9in)
Weight	1,375kg (3,031lb)

Performance

Top speed	309km/h (192.2mph)
0–62mph	4.0s

The Richard Westbrook Interview

Winning the Porsche Mobil 1 Supercup Championship in 2006 and 2007 as a member of Porsche's crack 997 GT3 RSR squad, Richard Westbrook joined the all-time greats on the roster of Porsche works drivers. In 2009 I caught up with the 2004 Carrera Cup GB champion over lunch. 'No, I don't come from Chelmsford,' he laughs. 'I just happen to have been born there.' His origins are nothing to be ashamed of, though. There's a perfectly respectable precedent for an Essex Boy with a Porsche factory drive in the shape of Jackie Oliver: and those are the sort of footsteps that Richard is following – Siffert, Rodriguez, Ickx, Bell, Redman – all inextricably wedded to Weissach.

Richard grew up in Ipswich, Suffolk, but moved to London aged sixteen. His father raced a silhouette-bodied, Cosworth-engined Mini in special saloon events in the 1970s and one year was British Champion, but then he didn't have time to do it any more. Racing was in the blood:

I remember Autosport *being delivered every Thursday, and Formula 1 took centre stage on a Sunday afternoon. Every birthday and Christmas I was bought toy racing cars. It wasn't pushed on me; I just loved it from an early age. One of my earliest recollections is being at Brands Hatch and asking, 'When can we go home?' and my mum would say, 'When Daddy comes past once more'. I can remember it so vividly, and little things like playing in the pits and getting told off for getting covered in oil. That would have been when I was about three or four.*

Richard Westbrook describes his career as a successful driver in Porsche Carrera Cup and Supercup. ANTONY FRASER

A Porsche driver to the core, Richard Westbrook at the wheel of his 981 Boxster S. ANTONY FRASER

Richard was ten when he started karting.

It was always dad's plan to put me in a go-kart when I was big enough to fit in one. There used to be a great kart track at Snetterton. I got my first glimpse of the karts going round there and I had no idea how quick they were. He bought one for my brother and me, with a view to us sharing it: I would do one race and he would do another. My brother is eighteen months older than me, but after a couple of days testing he realized it wasn't for him and, in any case, I was a bit quicker. The first couple of years were very tough, it was so competitive. But something clicked and I started winning races on a national level – and then at international level. I loved the karting days; it was so much fun, and a nice way of growing up with other kids of the same age. It was exciting, travelling the whole of Europe, and I really miss it.

Having won the British title aged fifteen in 1990, Richard took a two-year sabbatical from the sport. In 1993 he made the big step up from karting by scraping together enough money to do the Vauxhall Lotus Series with Martin Donnelly, skipping Formula Ford:

I was up against some really good drivers, like Ralph Firman and Darren Manning, but knew if I failed, then that would be it, and I would have to look for other work. But we ended up winning it. It was amazingly competitive – pretty much everyone who was in that series has gone on to be a professional driver.

The publicity brought Richard a ride with David Lloyd Motorsport in the European Opel Lotus Series. 'I had two fantastic years, but with not a lot of success. We were up against the cream of Europe and we were on a really tight budget. We came fourth and third in the championship, which is no disgrace.'

In 1996 Richard was signed up as a Benetton Junior driver:

They did a big test in Europe with me and Jarno Trulli. I thought all my dreams had come true – there was a two-year deal on the table, and there was a chance of putting some kilometres on the F1 car. But, just before the first race, the team said they wouldn't be doing it because the sponsors didn't want an English driver and they'd got to take a paying driver for the second car, so it all got cancelled.

It was no consolation that the German paying driver amounted to nothing, or that Richard beat Trulli (and Nick Heidfeld) in a non-championship F3 race at Hockenheim later in 1996. Over the next couple of years he drove a few Formula 3 races in Austria and Germany and did some F3000 testing. 'That was it. I'd hit a brick wall and it seemed my career was over, so I set up the taxi advertising business in London with my brother, which is still going strong.' He also started training to be a chef, but the course was interrupted by a chance to do the Porsche Supercup.

The offer to drive a 996 in the 2002 Mobil 1 Supercup series came from Kadach Racing, but the promised sponsors failed to step up and Richard was obliged to sell his London house to fund the drive.

> There was no way we were going to get a free deal after being out of racing for five years, as no one knew who the hell I was – and until then I had never raced anything with a roof over my head. I completely underestimated how different it would be and how long it takes to get your head around this car. A lot of guys who go into Supercup have either done a couple of years of Carrera Cup or they have done GT or Touring Car racing.

At that point the only Porsche he had ever been in was a 928, so he was straight in at the deep end. However, natural ability shone through, and he came to grips with racing a 911 very quickly, although he struggled initially because his car had no data logging to pinpoint where he could make up time on the circuits, unlike teammate Stephane Ortelli. This was a learning year, although there were two wins:

> The Carrera Cup was starting in the UK in 2003, and since I hadn't raced in England since 1993, it was a great opportunity as I had some experience in the Porsche to start with, making it more of an even playing field. A dear friend of mine, Alison Fydler, a Porsche enthusiast with a 993, bought me the car and obviously it had to be sold at the end of the year to pay her back. We then had to scrape together the money to run the car, and if we hadn't missed the first two rounds I would probably have won the Championship.

The following year was the turning point. Having chalked up nine wins in 2003, Richard was hot property and signed for Red Line Racing. The scene was set for a great season in 2004, spurred on by the prospect of a road-going 997 for the series winner. With seven victories under his belt,

Richard Westbrook takes the chequered flag in a Supercup round in his 997 GT3 Cup. PORSCHE MUSEUM ARCHIVES

Richard emerged Carrera Cup champion. 'I had such a good fight with Tim Harvey all year, then getting that car as a prize helped me to get out of debt, because by this point I was a long way below sea level!'

The Red Line deal carried on for 2005, with Richard logging thirteen wins to place second in the season's-end Carrera Cup classifications. His time was split between the UK series and the Porsche Supercup, however, having picked up a drive with Walter Lechner Racing, which he'd known since the Opel Lotus days.

> I was working for Philip Taysom's Track Share operation, teaching very wealthy Middle Eastern people how to drive a Porsche round Bahrain circuit, and Walter Lechner happened to be there at the same time, because Round 1 of the 2005 Supercup was scheduled for Bahrain as a curtain-raiser for the Grand Prix. Walter said, 'I'd love to get you in the car for Bahrain, do you think you can find a bit of sponsorship?' I knew that the Bahrain race was important if I wanted to make the step from Carrera Cup to Supercup, and I had to do something special. So I had a word with the guys I'd been instructing and they said, 'Yeah, no problem, we'll pay for that.' And then I saw the artwork for the car, which was a beautiful design – green with the Saudi Arabian flag and the words 'Qu'ran, peace from the land of Islam' on the bonnet. They wanted to promote a more positive message about Islam, and I was really proud to drive that car once I understood what they were trying to get across, though I wasn't looking forward to racing it in Indianapolis; fortunately, the Supercup didn't extend to that race.

Richard won in Bahrain, leaving Lechner no option but to run him at Imola, where the Brit triumphed again.

Imola is my favourite circuit because for a start it's anti-clockwise, and I have always gone well on anti-clockwise circuits. I was there in the support race the weekend Ayrton Senna died in 1994, which was awful, and we came back in 1995 when I had my best-ever win, romping away from everyone in the wet. Anyway, in 2005 I put Walter in the position where he had to keep me in for the rest of the season.

Though Supercup results tailed off in 2005, as much down to the car as anything, Richard signed as number one driver with the Dutch Jet Stream Morellato squad on an expenses-paid, winner-takes-all deal for 2006.

This was the first time in my life I didn't have to worry about money, and it was the most incredible season. We finished every race on the podium, which I don't think has ever been done before or since, and we set all sorts of records. We won the title by a country mile, with four races to go. Until then, Jet Stream had never had any success in the Supercup and we completely gelled. They are such lovely guys, a lot of smiles and a hell of a lot of success.

After such a convincing win, Richard wanted to move out of the Supercup and looked at the possibility of a Porsche works drive.

They tested me at Weissach and it went really well, but for whatever reason I wasn't offered a contract,

so it meant doing another season in Supercup. People in the right places at Porsche said: .Just do another year and see what happens; don't jump ship yet.' So I did it with a new team, HISAQ Competition, which was a bit of a gamble. But we ended up winning it, only just — it went down to the last corner on the last lap of the last race, which was horrible. It wasn't as convincing as 2006 — but who cares, we won it.

How about the competition? What's the needle like in a one-make series?

You're never that friendly with the drivers you're racing against, especially the ones you're fighting for the championship with. I've had some good races with Damian [Faulkner] over the years, and then we had that altercation last year on the last lap at the chicane at Spa. Even if he'd overtaken me, I was still

Richard Westbrook ran his 997 GT3 Cup Car in the GT2 category in the Le Mans Series in 2005. The class was designated GT2 to distinguish it from the quicker GT1 cars. PORSCHE MUSEUM ARCHIVES

Richard Westbrook takes his 997 GT3 Cup into the Port Chicane in a Supercup round at Monaco, curtain raiser for the F1 Grand Prix. PORSCHE MUSEUM ARCHIVES

Richard Westbrook exits Nürburgring's dramatic Karussell corner in the Manthey-prepped Haribo 997 GT3 Cup during the N-24 Hours. ANTONY FRASER

going to win the championship [Richard was lying third in the race, while his rival needed to win to take the title without Richard scoring any further points]. I wanted to finish that race on the podium and celebrate winning the championship with my team, but he took that away and I wasn't happy about it, but we get on well enough now. As I said at the time, when you wake up the next morning, all you think is, 'I am the champion'. Nothing else matters.

Another driver Richard regards as a serious rival is Uwe Altzen.

He's one of the toughest competitors I've ever been up against: he's a very hard no-nonsense driver and he's upset a lot of people in the past. But I have to say that all the close battles I've had with Uwe have been 100 per cent clean, so there's a lot of mutual respect between us, and there are not many people that you can race that closely with without touching. I can second-guess his moves and he can do the same with me. We did a 24-hour race in Dubai, and you're told to take it easy, but it was just like a Supercup race to begin with. I think the lead changed between me and him eighteen times in the first hour. Engineers on the pit wall were pulling their hair out, saying: 'It's a 24-hour race, what are you doing?' We were putting on a show because I knew he would give me room when I needed it, and vice versa if it came to it. We were having a lot of fun. That doesn't happen very often with anybody, and I'm not saying I'm friends with Uwe; I speak to him very rarely, but on track I have a lot of respect for him. He is regarded in Germany as a bit of a maverick: he was famous for telling his boss at Mercedes to f**k off, and he got the sack for that. But that's what he's like, and he's a really good driver.

When you've got a gridful of twenty cars that are to all intents and purposes identical, are some less equal than others?

When all the cars are the same, the only way you're going to get an advantage is if you set the car up correctly. You have to make your own advantage, and it's very important how the driver works with his engineer. The factors that make your Porsche go quickly are the driver, the tyres, the engineers and the team environment – and if one is wrong you won't win in the Supercup. It's as simple as that, everything has

to be right. It's a really tough championship and I'm going to miss it.

Richard signed to drive the works GT3 RSRs in 2008 in the FIA GT championship and the Le Mans series.

I like to think I put them in a situation where they had to take me. I had lots of other offers but this one felt right, the natural progression. At the penultimate Supercup round in Monza, Hartmut Kristen [Head of Porsche Motor Sport] came to see me and we had a short discussion about my plans for 2008. We agreed to speak again in November, and I was delighted to sign. It vindicates everything. I never thought, after so many years out, that I could come back at this level and achieve so much.

Richard came second in the first race of 2008, the Grand Am Daytona 24-Hours:

That was a little bit hard to take. When you come second in the Supercup, it's great: you've got 18 points, you can look at the points table and count how many people didn't score. In an endurance race, you've slogged your guts out for 24 hours and you're completely drained, but people only remember who won. No one remembers who came second, and that was totally apparent when I was on the podium. The winners got their Rolex watches and all we got was a baseball cap. We had been in a strong position to win it, but sand coming onto the track caused an overheating issue, which pegged us back a bit.

The programme for this year [2009] is to drive the RSR with Manu [Emmanuel] Collard as my teammate. We get on really well. He's won the Le Mans series twice and knows the championship inside out – and obviously, because I'm new to the championship, I need someone like him to learn from. He's one of the best Porsche drivers in the world, and that's why he's been a factory driver for so long, so it's great to be paired with someone like him. The RSR had a very tough season in 2007; it got beaten comprehensively by the Ferrari, and it's very important that the RSR is successful. It's a very important part of Porsche's racing programme and we gave it our all to get it back to where it deserves to be. There was a feeling that Ferrari had done enough to beat Porsche, but we wanted to prove the pundits wrong. Two great brands with a lot of racing tradition fighting it out head to head, with Aston Martin coming into it, as well.

A tight fit and much to comprehend: Richard Westbrook in the cockpit of his 991R. PORSCHE MUSEUM ARCHIVES

Tempted across the Atlantic in 2011, Richard raced with considerable success for the Corvette and Chip Ganassi teams, most recently winning the Rolex 24-Hours at Daytona in 2018 in a Ford GT. He's had enough success with Porsche, however, to call himself a dyed-in-the-wool Porsche driver and he enjoys driving his road car. He has also always been aware of Porsche's history, particularly its racing history, including Steve McQueen's 1971 film *Le Mans*. His experiences racing Porsches, however, has increased his exposure to their history and heritage, and he has enjoyed becoming part of that. It's no coincidence that one of his heroes is the iconic Pedro Rodriguez, who too was supreme in the wet.

997 GT3 GEN 2 (2009–2012)

Layout and chassis
Two-plus-two coupé, unit-construction steel body/chassis

Engine
Type	M96/72 'Mezger' dry sump, horizontally opposed, rear-mounted 6-cylinder
Block material	aluminium
Head material	aluminium
Cylinders	flat-six
Cooling	water
Bore and stroke	102.7 × 76.4mm
Capacity	3800cc
Valves	4 valves per cylinder
Compression ratio	12:1
Fuel system	multi-point injection
Max. power (DIN)	435bhp @ 7,600rpm
Max. torque	317lb ft @ 6,250rpm
Fuel capacity	67 litres (14.7 gallons)

Transmission
Gearbox	Aisin G97/92, rear drive, 6-speed
Clutch	hydraulic single dry plate
Ratios	1st 3.82
	2nd 2.26
	3rd 1.64
	4th 1.29
	5th 0.94
	6th 0.88
	Reverse 3.44
	Final drive 4.00

Suspension and steering
Front	independent by MacPherson struts, aluminium links, longitudinal and transverse links, coil springs, gas dampers, anti-roll bar
Rear	independent by MacPherson struts, aluminium links, lateral and transverse links, coil springs, gas dampers, anti-roll bar
Steering	rack-and-pinion
Tyres	235/35R × 19ZR front, 305/30ZR × 19ZR rear
Wheels	19in aluminium alloy
Rim width	8.5in J front, 11.5in J rear

Brakes
Type	front and rear vented discs with six-piston calipers; optional M450 ceramic discs
Size	330 × 24mm front; 330 × 20mm rear

Dimensions
Track	
Front	1,465mm (57.67in)
Rear	1,500mm (59.05in)
Wheelbase	2,350mm (92.51in)
Overall length	4,465mm (175.7in)
Overall width	1,808mm (71.18in)
Overall height	1,280mm (50.3in)
Unladen weight	1,470kg (3,240lb)

Performance
Top speed	312km/h (194mph)
0–60mph	4.1s

CHAPTER FIVE

LAUNCH AND EVOLUTION OF THE 991

Remarkably, the 991 generation of 911 is only the third all-new design that Porsche has implemented for the 911 in its 54-year history, and only the second since the arrival of the first liquid-cooled 911, the 996, in 1997. The 991 became public knowledge in late August 2011 and was unveiled at the Frankfurt Show on 15 September 2011. Being Porsche, the 991 was all about evolution, but even so the 991 was bordering on revolutionary when compared to its forebears, even its immediate predecessors. Styled in-house by chief designer Michael Mauer, the basic 911 shape and layout were familiar, as were the rear-mounted flat-six engines, but the 991 was loaded with even more technology and, most significantly, was dimensionally bigger than the 996 and 997.

This was in keeping with buyers' expectations for a contemporary car: every evolution expands, one way or another. The roofline was less arched than the 997, sloping into the more pert engine-lid, while the front wings (fenders) were proud of the luggage boot lid. The car now measured 4,490mm (176.8in), an increase of 70mm over the 997. Significantly, the wheelbase of the 991 was also extended by 100mm (3.9in) to 2,450mm (96.5in – a tad over 8ft) to create the most stable 911 yet. This was partly achieved by installing

A 991 C4S Gen 2 on the concourse in front of the Porsche Museum at Zuffenhausen. AUTHOR

Cutaway illustration of the Gen 2 991 Carrera C4S, revealing the powertrain, running gear, cockpit and controls. PORSCHE MUSEUM ARCHIVES

Naked: the 4 × 4 driveline of the 991 C4S revealing the flat-six, transmission, propshaft and suspension locations. PORSCHE MUSEUM ARCHIVES

The 991 Gen 1 Cabriolet was unveiled in Carrera and Carrera S versions at the Los Angeles Motor Show in November 2011. PORSCHE MUSEUM ARCHIVES

a new transaxle that enabled the rear wheels to be located 76mm (3in) rearward, relative to the position of the engine.

Allied to a wider track front and rear, any of the 911's less desirable residual handling traits were removed, while retaining massive grip levels, thanks to the rearward weight bias, because a longer track equals better stability. The weight factor came into play too. The 991 is also lighter than the 997, at 1,455kg, against 1,415kg for a similarly PDK-equipped C2S. A base-model 991 C2 weighs even less, at 1,380kg. This was achieved by extensive use of aluminium – another first in street 911 manufacture – manifest in the doors, bonnet, front wings and roof, plus the incorporation of high-strength steel and judicious weight saving on components throughout. At the other end of the scale, the all-wheel-drive Turbo with PDK transmission tipped the scales at 1,605kg (3,538lb). More controversial was the addition of electronic power steering, which exasperated some 911 purists, but could be justified by the need for marginal gains in fuel economy that such a system delivers, not to mention ease of packaging, with no need to worry about hydraulic lines.

At launch the 991 range consisted of just the base Carrera and the Carrera 2S in both coupé and cabriolet styles; a year later the all-wheel drive C4 and C4S were revealed at the Paris Salon. Prices started at £71,000 in the UK for the base C2 model, but lifting the standard 991 to a specification acceptable to potential wealthy and discerning owners meant adding another £20,000-worth of options. Typically the C2 and C2S came with two different engines. Unusually, perhaps, the C2 arrived with an engine capacity smaller than that of the outgoing 997 C2 – 3.4 litres as opposed to 3.6 litres – but Porsche pointed out that it produced more power, at 350bhp over the 997 C2's 345bhp. Torque was down, though, at 287lb ft at 5,600rpm, compared to 288lb ft at 4,400rpm for the 997 C2. The difference was only slight, but it's where the power was delivered that counted, or, in the case of the 991, more than 1,000rpm up the rev range, which was noticeable on the road. The 991 was quite peaky compared with the 997 C2, in that you had to work it just too hard on public roads, and it became relatively tiresome.

Cockpit of the 991 Carrera Cabriolet, featuring carbon trim detailing and characteristic chrome voids in the steering wheel spokes. PORSCHE MUSEUM ARCHIVES

drive 991 Turbo and Turbo S were released in May 2013, the 'basic' Turbo powered by a twin-turbocharged 3.8-litre motor developing 513bhp and 620Nm (457lb ft) torque. The Turbo S topped that with 552bhp and 516lb ft torque; of course the torque figure could be increased by turning up the boost. The S was able to go from 0–100km/h (62mph) in 3.1s, topping out at 318.6km/h (198mph). Both versions were equipped with seven-speed PDK transmission. Potentially the chassis of the 991 has it all, depending on the option boxes that have been ticked. The most likely of the suspension options to be chosen is PASM (Porsche Active Suspension Management), while PDCC (active anti-roll bars) and PTV (Porsche Torque Vectoring) are a bit esoteric.

Like the 996 and 997, the 991 also spawned a GT3 derivative, which came out at the Geneva Show in March 2013.

The Gen 1 991 Carrera GTS was introduced in November 2014 at the Los Angeles Motor Show, featuring 424bhp PowerKit engine, Sport Chrono Package, sports exhaust, 10mm lowered suspension, Sport Design front spoiler and side mirrors, and 20in centre-lock wheels. PORSCHE MUSEUM ARCHIVES

The 991 Targa and Targa S were launched at the 2014 Detroit Show, featuring a roof-lowering method way more complex than previous generations of Targa, though commensurate with technological advances in power hood technology. PORSCHE MUSEUM ARCHIVES

In a simultaneous and sophisticated action, the 991 Targa roof lifts off while the rear glasshouse rises up, and the roof panel is deposited in the niche behind the car's cockpit. PORSCHE MUSEUM ARCHIVES

This was not the case with the 3.8-litre 991 C2S engine, however, which featured a much more effusive 400bhp and 325lb ft of torque at 5,600rpm. Porsche didn't give up on the manual gearbox for the 991 and developed a manual version of the seven-speed PDK, with seventh like an overdrive for better economy, although some pundits averred that it was not one of Porsche's finest manual gearboxes.

Almost predictably, the 991 settled into Porsche's established launch pattern, with the Carrera 4 and Carrera 4S arriving in 2013. Both featured identical power outputs, while the C4S had the wider bodyshell that would also clad the forthcoming Turbo. Various performance options were available, taking power up to 425bhp. The four-wheel-

Its sparky performance was enhanced by active rear steering effected depending on entry speeds into corners, which determined whether and to what extent the rear wheels steered in the same or the opposite direction to the front wheels. This was claimed to offer higher lateral dynamics than previous versions. The 3.8-litre GT3 developed an astounding 500bhp at 8,250rpm and 460Nm torque at 6,000rpm. A year later, however, two fires in quick succession at the plant halted GT3 production and the engines of all 785 cars built up to that point were recalled and replaced.

The GT3 RS was unveiled at Geneva in 2015, featuring magnesium roof and louvres in the front wings above the wheels, plus Turbo-esque air intakes in the leading edge of the rear wing panels. Its carbon bucket seats were based on those of the 918 Spyder, and the Clubsport package included a bolted-in rear cage and six-point harnesses and ignition cut-out master switch. The RS capacity was raised to 4.0 litres, producing 500bhp and 339lb ft torque, delivered via PDK transmission allied to Porsche Torque Vectoring Plus, rear axle steering and fully variable rear axle diff-lock.

Perhaps the biggest surprise, however, was the arrival at the Detroit Show in January 2014 of the 991 Targa 4 and 4S, with its retrospective Targa hoop styling and complex retractable roof system, which offered a quantum leap from the Boxster's. For years the Targa had been a slightly left-field niche model in the 911 line-up, and suddenly it was feted as the best-looking model in the range. Completing the model line-up were the 991 Turbo and GT3, plus the GTS, launched at the Los Angeles Motor Show in November 2014. This more driver-focused 991 was available in two- and four-wheel drive as well as Cabriolet incarnations, with wide-body styling and 425bhp.

The final model to appear in the 991 Gen 1 range was the 911R, a reference to the pared-down, competition-focused 911R of 1967. In reality, the two models were as different as chalk and cheese, but it was good to see the company acknowledging its more exalted and esoteric models of the past. R stands for RennSport or Race. As you'll read in Chapter 6, I have driven two examples of the 991-based 911R (as well as five out of twenty of the 1967 competition version), and my opinion is that it is a rather more finely tuned iteration of the GT3. It is enough to say for now that it shares most of its underpinnings with the GT3 RS, minus roll cage and rear wing, making it lighter by 50kg. Its lower drag coefficient enables a top speed in excess of 200mph (322km), deployed via a six-speed manual gearbox. All the 991 units produced were snapped up by connoisseurs, collectors and investors, and prices quickly attracted a premium, which seems a shame when it is such a good car for enthusiasts.

Just as the 997's cabin interior was a step up from the 996, so the 991 moved the goalposts again, with superb build quality and materials, all dominated by the signature Porsche-style centre console. Most buyers would have upped the spec to include leather dash and door cards, plus the essential PCM nav/radio/iPod system. The overall effect was to make the 911 cabin, controls and switchgear seem way more complicated than the 997, let alone the austere 996.

Returning to the powertrain specs, Gen 1 991 engines came in 3.4-litre and 3.8-litre variants. As is usually the way, the larger-capacity S model was the more popular. It's not so much the extra 50bhp (400bhp, rather than 350bhp) that makes it more attractive, and indeed it's all relative in the context of crowded speed-camera ridden roads, but the extra torque is noticeable. Both versions provide serious performance, but the smaller engine needs to be worked a lot harder, and being in the upper reaches of the rev range all the time is wearying. The S will crack 190mph (305km/h) on an autobahn, while the C2 will almost get there. Both will hit 0–60mph comfortably in less than 5s, though the 3.4 engine will need whipping like a racehorse to get there. Both engines are fed by direct fuel injection, on-demand oil pumps and other efficiency-benefiting technologies, including stop-start. This generation of Porsche engines appears to have conquered the shortcomings of the M96 and M97 engines in terms of reliability.

The seven-speed PDK or seven-speed manual both provide the same ratios, but the PDK option is superior because it is swifter in operation; the manual just isn't an intuitive gearbox to use, which spoils the whole interaction. Around a tight circuit, like the specially built one at Porsche's Centre adjacent to Silverstone Circuit, a 991, Boxster or Cayman is significantly faster in PDK mode than manual, and this is a hard lesson to take for anyone brought up with manual boxes and who was encouraged as a child to regard auto-

The 911R is the sportiest road-focused – as opposed to track-biased – incarnation of the 991. ANTONY FRASER

Rear tracking shot of the 2017 Gen 2 991 Carrera GTS with rear spoiler extended, which is capable of 194mph (312km/h), thanks to its 3.0-litre twin turbo flat-six. PORSCHE MUSEUM ARCHIVES

matic transmission as somehow lazy or even effete. The PDK, meanwhile, maximizes performance and economy worked across two to three different modes, depending on whether Sport Chrono has been specified, and features a coasting function, whereby the gearbox decouples from the engine when you lift off the throttle at motorway speeds.

In 2015 the Gen 2 versions of the 991, referred to internally as the 991.2 models, appeared at the Frankfurt Show and ushered in new styling revisions and options. The most significant innovation across the whole Carrera range was the new 3.0-litre flat-six, employing twin turbos. This was the first time Carreras were fitted with turbochargers instead of normally aspirated engines. Both base Carrera and Carrera S were available as coupé and cabriolet ver-

sions, in C2, C4, C2S, C4S Targa 4 and Targa 4S, and from December that year (slightly perplexingly, given the fitment of turbochargers across the board) in Turbo and Turbo S format.

In January 2017 Porsche released five new GTS versions. The new facelifted GT3 was centre stage at the Geneva Show in March, powered by a 4.0-litre flat-six and optional six-speed manual gearbox. In June that year the Turbo S Exclusive series was unveiled, sporting a power kit and revised peripheral bodywork, plus optional braided carbon fibre wheels. Then at the Goodwood Festival of Speed, a GT2 RS was announced, featuring the so-called 'Weissach performance package', weighing in at 1,470kg to give a bhp/kg power-to-weight ratio of 2.1kg. Next revelation was the GT3 Touring, a touring spec GT3 with manual transmission and no fixed rear wing. That was supplemented in October 2017 by the Carrera T, harking back to the more basic 911T and RS models of the 1960s and early 1970s, with pared-down cabin furniture, shorter rear axle ratio and mechanical diff-lock, PASM, Sport Chrono, lowered suspension and sports exhaust. Aimed at the enthusiast market, creature comforts such as the in-car communication system could be installed as no-cost options.

Overall, the 991 is a more composed 911, more 'grand tourer' than outright sports car, which is what customers demand nowadays. It doesn't excite in all situations in the same way as its predecessors may have done, and to get the full 911 effect it needs to be worked hard, but then that's no bad thing. At a recent back-to-back at Chobham test track in Surrey involving a 996 Turbo, a 997 C4S and a 991 C2S I concluded that the car I would most like to drive home was the 991, and that is some kind of progress.

From 2017 all Porsche 991 Carreras were turbocharged, including the 911T model. PORSCHE MUSEUM ARCHIVES

991 CARRERA C2 GEN 1 (2011–2016)

Layout and chassis
Two-plus-two coupé and cabriolet, unit-construction steel body/chassis

Engine

Type	horizontally opposed, rear-mounted 3.4-litre 6-cylinder
Block material	aluminium
Head material	aluminium
Cylinders	flat-six
Cooling	water
Bore and stroke	97 × 77.5mm
Capacity	3436cc
Valves	4 valves per cylinder
Compression ratio	12.5:1
Fuel system	multi-point injection
Max. power (DIN)	345bhp @ 7,400rpm
Max. torque	288lb ft @ 5,600rpm
Fuel capacity	64 litres (14.0 gallons)

Transmission

Gearbox	rear drive, 6-speed manual; 7-speed ZF PDK (Doppelkupplung) semi-automatic
Clutch	hydraulic two plate
Ratios	1st 3.91
	2nd 2.29
	3rd 1.58
	4th 1.18
	5th 0.94
	6th 0.79
	7th 0.62 (PDK)
	Reverse 3.44
	Final drive 4.00

Suspension and steering

Front	independent by MacPherson struts, aluminium links, longitudinal and transverse links, coil springs, gas dampers, anti-roll bar
Rear	independent by MacPherson struts, aluminium links, lateral and transverse links, coil springs, gas dampers, anti-roll bar
Steering	rack-and-pinion
Tyres	235/40R × 19ZR front, 295/35ZR × 19ZR rear
Wheels	19in aluminium alloy
Rim width	8.5in J front, 11.5in J rear

Brakes

Type	front and rear vented discs with six-piston calipers
Size	330 × 34mm front; 330 × 28mm rear

Dimensions

Track	
Front	1,541mm (60.6in)
Rear	1,540mm (60.6in)
Wheelbase	2,450mm (96.4in)
Overall length	4,491mm (176.6in)
Overall width	1,808mm (71.2in)
Overall height	1,303mm (51.3in)
Unladen weight	1,435kg (3,164lb)

Performance

Top speed	289km/h (180mph)
0–60mph	4.8s

POMP AND CIRCUMSTANCE

You can't beat a long trip with a 911 to get to know the upsides and downsides of the car – not that there are any real howlers, other than straying into winter without the right tyres, but that's hardly the car's fault. All our destinations are fascinating in their own way, but one that had particularly eye-popping connotations was the Norisring circuit at Nuremberg, south-east Germany.

I've visited several old or redundant tracks where Porsche enjoyed a measure of success, including Dundrod, Rouen, Reims, Solitude and the Avus, and now it's the turn of Nuremberg's Norisring. There's little to match the aura of an international race meeting: the noise, the smells, the cars,

the celebs, the crowds; yet it's also rewarding to wander a racetrack on an off-day without all that razzmatazz, savouring the nature of the circuit, its setting and facilities. Founded in the arena where Hitler once saluted his marching Youth brigade, the Norisring is a fast street circuit with a substantial history of Porsche successes, and I lapped a brilliant blue 991 Cabriolet around its hallowed hairpins. Although it was only 7.00am when we did our shoot, there was still a bit of normal traffic, so I was being cautious but still provided a succession of demon laps, cocking both inside wheels over the red and white kerbs.

The route to Bavaria in the 991 Cabriolet includes stretches of unrestricted autobahns that bring out its qualities, with silky smooth acceleration and the gearchange nicely notchy.

991 TURBO (2013–2018)

Layout and chassis
Two-plus-two coupé and cabriolet, lightweight unit-construction steel/aluminium body/chassis

Engine

Type	dry sump, horizontally opposed, mid-mounted 6-cylinder
Block material	aluminium
Head material	aluminium
Cylinders	flat-six
Cooling	water
Bore and stroke	102 × 77.5mm
Capacity	3800cc
Valves	4 valves per cylinder
Compression ratio	9.8:1
Fuel system	multi-point injection, twin turbochargers
Max. power (DIN)	540bhp @ 6,400rpm
Max. torque	523lb ft @ 4,000rpm
Fuel capacity	68 litres (14.9 gallons)

Transmission

Gearbox	all-wheel drive, 7-speed ZF PDK (Doppelkupplung)
Clutch	hydraulic multi-plate
Ratios	1st 3.91
	2nd 2.29
	3rd 1.58
	4th 1.18
	5th 0.94
	6th 0.79
	7th 0.62
	Reverse 3.55
	Final drive 3.44 front, 3.33 rear

Suspension and steering

Front	independent by MacPherson struts, aluminium links, longitudinal and transverse links, coil springs, gas dampers, anti-roll bar; PASM
Rear	independent by MacPherson struts, aluminium links, lateral and transverse links, coil springs, gas dampers, anti-roll bar; PASM
Steering	rack-and-pinion
Tyres	235/35R × 20ZR front, 305/30ZR × 20ZR rear
Wheels	20in aluminium alloy
Rim width	9in J front, 11.5in J rear

Brakes

Type	front and rear vented discs with six-piston calipers; optional M450 ceramic discs
Size	380 × 34mm front; 380 × 30mm rear

Dimensions

Track	
Front	1,541mm (60.66in)
Rear	1,590mm (62.59in)
Wheelbase	2,450mm (96.45in)
Overall length	4,507mm (177.4in)
Overall width	1,880mm (74.01in)
Overall height	1,297mm (51.06in)
Unladen weight	1,595kg (3,516lb)

Performance

Top speed	320km/h (199mph)
0–60mph	2.9s

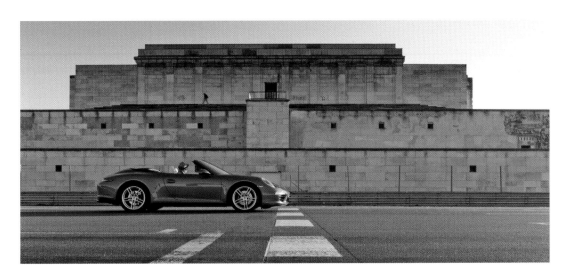

A monumental performer and monumental architecture: the 991 C2 Cabriolet at the Norisring, Nuremberg's city circuit, fronting the Zeppelinhaupttribüne designed by Albert Speer in 1935 in homage to the Temple of Pergamon of classical antiquity. ANTONY FRASER

991 C2 GEN 2 (2016–2018)

Layout and chassis
Two-plus-two coupé and cabriolet, unit-construction steel body/chassis

Engine

Type	horizontally opposed, rear-mounted 6-cylinder
Block material	aluminium
Head material	aluminium
Cylinders	flat-six
Cooling	water
Bore and stroke	91 × 76.4mm
Capacity	2981cc
Valves	4 valves per cylinder
Compression ratio	10:1
Fuel system	multi-point injection; two turbochargers
Max. power (DIN)	370bhp @ 6,500rpm
Max. torque	332lb ft @ 5,600rpm
Fuel capacity	64 litres (14.0 gallons)

Transmission

Gearbox	7-speed, rear drive manual; 7-speed ZF PDK (Doppelkupplung) semi-automatic
Clutch	hydraulic two plate
Ratios	1st 3.91
	2nd 2.29
	3rd 1.58
	4th 1.18
	5th 0.94
	6th 0.79
	7th 0.62
	Reverse 3.44
	Final drive 4.00

Suspension and steering

Front	independent by MacPherson struts, aluminium links, longitudinal and transverse links, coil springs, gas dampers, anti-roll bar
Rear	independent by MacPherson struts, aluminium links, lateral and transverse links, coil springs, gas dampers, anti-roll bar
Steering	rack-and-pinion
Tyres	235/40R × 19ZR front, 295/35ZR × 19ZR rear
Wheels	19in aluminium alloy
Rim width	8.5in J front, 11.5in J rear

Brakes

Type	front and rear vented discs with six-piston calipers; optional M450 ceramic discs
Size	330 × 34mm front; 330 × 28mm rear

Dimensions

Track	
Front	1,541mm (60.6in)
Rear	1,518mm (59.7in)
Wheelbase	2,450mm (96.4in)
Overall length	4,499mm (177.1in)
Overall width	1,808mm (71.18in)
Overall height	1,303mm (56.2in)
Unladen weight	1,430kg (3,152lb)

Performance

Top speed	295km/h (183mph)
0–60mph	4.2s

It grips in corners and holds the road perfectly, with precisely weighted steering and predictable turn-in, and while it may not have all the whistles and bells of fully specified Porsches, it is a lovely car to drive. Winding lock on going into the hairpins I can sight the car very nicely, even though we're in a right-hooker in a left-hand-drive country. Some say the cabriolet ought to have the PDK transmission, but in fact it's perfect as far as I'm concerned, having a stick shift for our Norisring re-enactment.

On the autobahn in our fantastic Blue Streak missile there is a fairly constant switching between 6th and 7th gears to springboard past the few recalcitrant outside laners, and though the speed limit is governed by overtaking trucks and the dodderers passing them, we're capitalizing on the three-lane sections, such as the long stretch around Augsburg, until all too soon we're plunged back into two-lane dual-carriageway, reduced to a 100km/h crawl instead of 160km/h cruise. Still, top down, we have magnificent scenery and sunshine to bask in, and we're scudding along a mature autobahn, judging by the vegetation in the central reservation. It's quite an aerodynamic car once we're up in the higher echelons of the rev band, but it is a base model and, given the hood mechanism, it's probably as heavy as a 911 coupé. All things considered, though, we are probably going much faster than most people would ever drive it.

We've been told by the Motorsport Club that the all-important start-finish straight of the Norisring racetrack is closed off, so we need to find a way in somehow. Arriving

The 991 Carrera C2 Cabriolet's 3.4-litre 345bhp flat-six engine propelled it from 0–60mph in 4.8s and on to an autobahn top speed of 180mph (290km/h). ANTONY FRASER

in Nuremberg at dusk, we look about and find there's a gap just wide enough for the Porsche between the barriers, and we're in. Next morning, I'm sitting in the 991 Cabriolet on Beuthenerstrasse, which is the start-finish straight, contemplating the soaring tribunes or viewing platforms that dominate the environment. Yellow painted rectangles define the starting grid, and the main straight is delineated by concrete barriers and catch fencing. Behind these barriers is a further expanse of tarmac, with a sports field beyond, all enclosed by tiers of overgrown pre-war seating. To my left is the centrepiece of the former Fascist stadium, a vast monolith apparently constructed from huge blocks of stone. The main building has two main levels where the Nazi hierarchy disported themselves, with a projecting balcony and railings where the Führer and his aides would have stood, and this podium is flanked by no less imposing rows of stone seating, though now there are wildflowers growing out of it. Since the war this bastion has served as a grandstand for motor racing events. It's remarkable that it still exists, being an overt demonstration of Nazi expressionism, so it's a wonder the Allies didn't pull it down. Objectively, the main tribune viewed from the rear actually looks like a giant 1930s art deco Roxy cinema.

Along this main straight, the available width of paved asphalt is probably twice as wide as the majority of racetracks. The streets comprising the rest of the circuit are also bounded by three layers of Armco barrier, much of it lined with high mesh fencing to catch wayward debris, or posts offering the possibility of erecting it for race days. From the grid, the circuit disappears clockwise ahead of me down a half-mile straight to the Grundigkhere, one of the circuit's two hairpins, where I end up riding the kerb in the Porsche for my photographer's benefit. I should imagine this has seen

some almighty shunts on the first lap. Then a few hundred yards back the other way towards the tribune, the course jinks sharp right, then sharp left through the Schöller-S, with a long, slightly curving stretch of broad straightaway behind the Steintribüne, easing right before suddenly arcing left into the second hairpin, the Dutzendteichkhere. It's an ad hoc car park during the day, but the scorched tyre marks, red and white kerbing and Armco declare its true purpose. With the lake to the right, the circuit then rushes back into the Zeppelin plaza and onto the start-finish line.

But what about this giant slab of architecture? It's an extraordinary building to find at a racetrack, by any standards; at Dundrod there's the Joey Dunlop grandstand, at Reims there are the 1950s pits and grandstand, and at Solitude the Mercedes race control building. Cerda also has the ancient Targa Florio pits and control tower, all purpose-built for racing. But the nucleus of the Norisring circuit is a structure that in any other context would be magnificent, but now it's both outrageous and intriguing, given the ambitions of the faction who built it. There's no subtlety about it; it's austere, without any exuberant embellishments, just slabs of blockwork.

The main wedge is called the Steintribüne or Zeppelinhaupttribüne, named after the inaugural landing site of the eponymous Count's airship in 1909. From 1933 the National Socialist party used the arena built on the site for their rallies. The tall colonnades that originally flanked it and provided a backdrop to the rows of seating were pulled down in the late 1960s. The Steintribüne was erected between 1935 and 1937, using concrete and brickwork faced with a

The 991 Cabrio stands on the Norisring's main start-finish straight, which runs through the Zeppelin field where the National Socialists staged their military rallies in the 1930s. ANTONY FRASER

cladding of limestone slabs. Architect Albert Speer took his inspiration from the Great Altar in the upper city at Pergamon, which was built about 165 BC. The site was excavated by German archaeologists in the 1870s and reconstructed at the Pergamon Museum in Berlin, so there was clearly an obsession with its place in antiquity.

The Norisring circuit is not that well known outside Germany, though from the late 1960s through the 1980s it hosted major international sports car races and still puts on rounds of the DTM (Deutsche Tourenwagen Meisterschaft), European F3 and German Porsche Carrera Cup. In terms of seniority it's somewhere behind other German circuits founded pre-war – Nürburgring, Avus, Sachsenring and Hockenheim – though older than the Lausitzring and Oscherschleben. As a street circuit its character is more akin to the seaside circuits of Monaco, Porto and Long Beach. The Norisring, however, is on the periphery of a major city, flanked by the Dutzendteich parkland, and the structures that survived bombing in the Second World War provided a readymade setting for a racetrack. Noris is a poetic name for the city, derived from the Latin form, Norimberga. Motorcycle races were held from 1947 and car racing began in 1954. The Norisring was soon one of the top circuits on the German motor sport calendar. During the course of five decades the track layout has changed five times, going from 2km in 1950 to 4km in 1961, including an underpass and flyover, and back to 2km in 1972

The races for sports prototypes and GTs during the 1960s saw plenty of Porsche action, with the likes of Gerhard Mitter, Hans Herrmann, Udo Schutz, Sepp Greger and Heini Walter battling it out in 904s and 356 Carrera-Abarths with Lotus Elans and Elva-BMWs. Later in the decade Jo Siffert,

Cornering hard in the 991 Cabriolet in a bid to emulate the stars of the international racing scene who are still active on the Norisring circuit. ANTONY FRASER

Ben Pon, Vic Elford, Rico Steinemann and Toine Hezemans, piloting 906s, 910s and 908s, fought with Lola T70s, Alfa T33s and GT40s crewed by the likes of Frank Gardner, Brian Muir, Jo Bonnier and Paul Hawkins. In 1968 it was the turn of Brian Redman in a Lola T70 to narrowly win from Elford and Rolf Stommelen in their 3.0-litre 908 Spyders and Richard Attwood in another Lola. As well as Interserie (Can-Am style) races featuring Porsche 917 Spyders, DTM events during the 1970s witnessed battles between 911 RSRs and BMW CSLs. The cast changed subtly, and the 1980 DRM field consisted of Porsche 935s led by John Fitzpatrick and Stommelen against Hans Stuck and Jan Lammers in BMW MIs.

It is time for a lap. I hunker down in the Cabriolet cockpit, and for a few glorious moments I'm Jo Siffert in the Hart-Ski 910, snarling my way in amongst the big banger Lolas, GT40s and P3 Ferraris. I rush down to the far end of the circuit and take a wide line into the Grundig hairpin, which would be quite tight with three or four cars trying to share it, kiss the apex and blast out wide onto the mad rush for the Esses. The nimble Porsche zigzags neatly here, clipping the blue and white rumble strips, but brute power tells on the long run behind the Steintribüne along to the expansive Dutzendteich hairpin, leaning on the tyres and charging out onto the start-finish straight again. That last hairpin was the trickiest bit, according to John Fitzpatrick: 'you approached it at such high speed around a fast corner, and it was easy to miss the braking point.'

Intensity of racing here has been episodic. Through the 1980s there were high-profile DRM (Deutsche RennSport Meisterschaft) and DTM races, and World Cup events staged in 1986 and 1987. A new era for DTM touring cars began in 1990, raising the game in 1995 with the short-lived International Touring Cars Championship (ITCC). More pertinently

Changing down to 2nd in the seven-speed manual gearbox for a hairpin on the Norisring street circuit. ANTONY FRASER

991 GTS (2016–2018)

Layout and chassis
Two-plus-two coupé and cabriolet, unit-construction steel body/chassis

Engine

Type	horizontally opposed, rear-mounted 6-cylinder
Block material	aluminium
Head material	aluminium
Cylinders	flat-six
Cooling	water
Bore and stroke	91 × 76.4mm
Capacity	2981cc
Valves	4 valves per cylinder
Compression ratio	10:1
Fuel system	multi-point injection; twin turbochargers
Max. power (DIN)	450bhp @ 6,500rpm
Max. torque	405lb ft @ 5,000rpm
Fuel capacity	64 litres (14.0 gallons)

Transmission

Gearbox	7-speed, rear-wheel drive manual/7-speed PDK (Doppelkupplung) semi-automatic
Clutch	Hydraulic two plate
Ratios	1st 3.91
	2nd 2.29
	3rd 1.58
	4th 1.18
	5th 0.94
	6th 0.79
	7th 0.62
	Reverse 3.55
	Final drive 3.59

Suspension and steering

Front	steel springs and 20 mm lowering, lightweight MacPherson spring strut suspension, PASM, two manually selectable damping programs with electronically controlled dampers
Rear	lightweight multi-link suspension with wheels independently suspended on five links
Steering	electromechanical rack-and-pinion
Tyres	245/35R × 20ZR front, 305/30ZR × 20ZR rear
Wheels	20in aluminium alloy
Rim width	9in J front, 12in J rear

Brakes

Type	front and rear vented discs with six-piston calipers
Size	350 × 34mm front; 330 × 28mm rear

Dimensions

Track	
Front	1,541mm (60.6in)
Rear	1,544mm (60.7in)
Wheelbase	2,450mm (96.4in)
Overall length	4,528mm (178.2in)
Overall width	1,852mm (72.9in)
Overall height	1,284mm (50.5in)
Unladen weight	1,450kg (3,196lb)

Performance

Top speed	312km/h (194mph)
0–60mph	3.9s

for us, the Norisring also hosts rounds of the Porsche Carrera Cup, where the likes of Sean Edwards and Nick Tandy strutted their stuff. Nuremberg's not so far from Stuttgart, so the Norisring is a natural on the Porsche calendar.

PORSCHE SPARKLES AT SPA

Spa-Francorchamps was once the fastest circuit on the world stage. The lap record for the 14.12km (8.7 miles) road course stands to Henri Pescarolo in a Matra-Simca MS at 3m 13.4s, averaging an incredible 262km/h (162.79mph) in 1973. During Porsche's brief flirtation with Formula 1, Dan Gurney placed 6th and Jo Bonnier 7th in 718s in the

1961 Belgian Grand Prix. Porsche's first major success at Spa was Jo Siffert/Brian Redman's win in the 1969 1,000km (620 miles) in a 908 coupé, followed by the 1970 and 1971 WSC 1,000km victories for Siffert/Redman and Pedro Rodriguez/Jackie Oliver. The endurance event was abandoned in 1975 due to safety considerations, but was revived in 1982 on the modern circuit. Porsche 956s took the 1,000km honours in 1982, 1983 and 1984 with Jacky Ickx, Jochen Mass, Derek Bell and Stefan Bellof at the wheel.

There's no better time to revisit some of these moments than when armed with a 991 Carrera S. After we'd put our press car through its paces on the permanent Spa track, we ventured out to retrace the original circuit on the public roads. With long, sweeping bends like Burnenville and

A trip to Spa-Francorchamps enabled a few laps in a 991 C2S, here flashing up the hill from Eau Rouge to Raidillon. ANTONY FRASER

Holowell, and even longer straights like Masta and La Car-rière, some of them were so empty we even came close to the speeds certain cars would have reached in the circuit's heyday. The points where the old circuit departed and re-entered the modern track are still visible, exiting to the side of Les Combes – where there's a gate across the road – and back in again at Stavelot (though the original Stavelot corner was a couple of miles away near the town of that name). Burnenville is a very long, demanding downhill right-hander. The Masta Straight is 3 miles (4.8km) long, though not entirely straight, and punctuated by the left-right Masta Kink. By comparison the Kemmel Straight is a blink-and-you-miss-it dash. Then and now, Spa-Francorchamps remains an awesome circuit.

I've also sampled it as a punter in a 997 GT3 belonging to trackday specialists RSR. Run by its Dutch founder Ron

991 GT3 (2017–2018)

Layout and chassis

Two-plus-two coupé, lightweight unit-construction steel/aluminium body/chassis

Engine

Type	6-cylinder, horizontally opposed, rear mounted
Block material	aluminium
Head material	aluminium
Cylinders	flat-six
Cooling	water
Bore and stroke	102 × 81.5mm
Capacity	3996cc
Valves	4 valves per cylinder
Compression ratio	13.3:1
Fuel system	multi-point injection, twin turbochargers
Max. power (DIN)	500bhp @ 8,250rpm
Max. torque	339lb ft @ 6,000rpm
Fuel capacity	64 litres (14.0 gallons)

Transmission

Gearbox	rear-wheel drive, 7-speed ZF PDK (Doppelkupplung); 6-speed GT manual
Clutch	Hydraulic multi-plate
Ratios (PDK)	1st 3.75
	2nd 2.38
	3rd 1.72
	4th 1.34
	5th 1.11
	6th 0.96
	7th 0.84
	Reverse 3.42
	Final drive 3.97
Ratios (GT manual)	1st 3.75
	2nd 2.38
	3rd 1.72
	4th 1.34
	5th 1.08
	6th 0.88
	Reverse 3.42
	Final drive 3.76

Suspension and steering

Front	independent by MacPherson struts, aluminium links, longitudinal and transverse links, ball joints, coil springs, gas dampers, anti-roll bar; PASM; 25mm lowering
Rear	independent multi-link by MacPherson struts, aluminium links, lateral and transverse links, ball joints, coil springs, gas dampers, helper springs, anti-roll bar; PASM
Steering	rack-and-pinion
Tyres	245/35R × 20ZR front, 305/30ZR × 20ZR rear
Wheels	20in aluminium alloy
Rim width	9in J front, 12in J rear

Brakes

Type	front and rear vented discs with four-piston calipers
Size	380 × 34mm front; 380 × 30mm rear

Dimensions

Track	
Front	1,551mm (61.06in)
Rear	1,555mm (61.22in)
Wheelbase	2,450mm (96.45in)
Overall length	4,562mm (179.60in)
Overall width	1,852mm (72.91in)
Overall height	1,271mm (50.03in)
Unladen weight	1,430kg (3,152lb)

Performance

Top speed	320km/h (199mph)
0–60mph	3.2s

Visiting Spa-Francorchamps with a 991 Carrera S provided an opportunity to revisit the route of the old 8-mile (12.9km) circuit, as well as the current F1 track. ANTONY FRASER

A few laps of Spa with Ron Simons demonstrated how amazingly capable a modern Porsche 911 is in the hands of an expert. ANTONY FRASER

Simons, the emphasis of RSR's operation shifted from Nürburgring Nordschleife to Spa-Francorchamps in 2016 when The Ring changed ownership, as he explains:

We can only do private instruction on exclusive track days at the Nordschleife and that is simply not enough for the number of customers we have every week. You don't need to look far to see that Spa is the best track in the world, with the best corner in the world. We've created a lot of demand for Spa, and that's why we are the only racing school and driving academy at the circuit.

Ron climbs aboard our 991 Carrera S for a few instructive laps, correcting my imperfect lines, and then helming the car himself. All the time he's commenting as he demonstrates the optimum lines through the turns:

Eau Rouge is the easiest bit, Raidillon is more difficult; get everything right in the compression and it's a big thrill. Pouhon is 500m of sex, the second-best corner in the world, you don't change the steering through the whole turn. Blanchimont – the third best corner in the world, almost flat but not quite ... All three are an easy 120mph on the exit!

We swap seats and trundle slowly up the F1 pit lane, show our 'driver' wristbands to the marshals and accelerate out onto the track below La Source. Here we are approaching Eau Rouge. You have to lift, surely? Well, not necessarily: depends on your entry speed, but I can state that I once took a GT3 RS through there without so much as a jab on the brake. Comparisons come to mind: the Corkscrew at Laguna Seca, Paddock Bend at Brands Hatch, Bergwerk on the Nordschleife. Ron is dismissive: 'whatever people have told you, Eau Rouge is not flat, it is very far from flat and unless you are able to copy your line at least ten times in a row you are not ready for speeding up yet.' The entry to the corner is from the pit wall, veering left. Adhering to Ron's guidance I don't accelerate too soon because there is

With years of circuit driving instruction behind him, Ron Simons is well qualified to advise on my progress over every metre of Spa (and the Nordschleife), commenting all the time on the optimum lines and speeds through the turns. ANTONY FRASER

still a lot of movement in the car; if I accelerate and I don't have any bite on the front, then it gets dangerous. The 991 Carrera S is deceptively quick. Out of Raidillon we're out onto the long straight to the Esses and I concentrate on gaining speed, braking early for the tight right-left followed by a deceptively tight right. Another downward rush before the long, adverse cambered right, no throttle, and another longer run down to Pouhon. Feather the throttle, clip the apex much further round than you'd think, allow the car to drift out, and slightly downhill again to the next right-left. The following sequence seems straightforward: tight right, onto the rumble strips, aim for the blockhouse and veer right, powering hard for Stavelot and the final push for the wrestling match in the wiggle ahead of the pit straight. La Source hairpin is a photographer's favourite because you're almost close enough to touch the cars. I know the optimum line around it by heart and give it my best. Ron calmly says, 'could we be a little further out next time, please?' And the verdict of Ron and RSR?

> *You did really well, but, as I saw a couple of times, don't go into quite a difficult corner like Eau Rouge and be too aggressive on the throttle. It's better to find a slightly higher speed going in and then keep it stable, so what I notice is sometimes you go in maybe a little bit slower than you could, and then you hit the throttle, so you destabilize the car. Next time carry a little bit more speed into it, constant throttle, let the car just find its way through, and as soon as you can you hit the accelerator again.*

Taking a tight line in the 991 C2S around La Source hairpin, before plunging down the hill towards Eau Rouge. ANTONY FRASER

It was also instructive to experience just how amazingly capable a modern Porsche 911 is – and what speeds it can achieve around a racetrack in the hands of a professional. While I'd seen 135mph (217km/h) on Kemmel Straight before braking for Les Combes, Ron was already doing 135mph at the top of Raidillon before hitting the straight. Imagine how exhilarating that made Eau Rouge!

PLAY MISTY FOR ME

The mists of time rolled away as we tackled the legendary Rossfeld hill climb, scene of yet more Porsche successes in its 1960s heyday and, at one time, a significant venue on the international motor sport calendar. The course nestles within a glorious, wild, mountainous setting, the peaks soaring resolutely upward, some sheer, some merely vertiginous. In winter I dare say we'd be deep in snow. This is the land of low-pitch-roofed chalets, their balconies gaily festooned with flowers, external walls muralled with religious iconography and churches with onion-dome steeples.

We've motored down to the German-Austrian border, close to Salzburg, in a 991 Turbo, pausing at Zuffenhausen to check out Gerry Judah's triple 911 sculpture (2015). It's 27m high, featuring three generations of 911 (2.0 swb, 3.2 Carrera and 991) soaring atop a twisted tripod on the Porscheplatz roundabout between the factory and museum. It's all in white, unlike his colourful Goodwood effort of 2013. It's difficult to judge it from the ground, due to the orientation of the cars, but it's doubtless a treat when viewed from the museum's upper levels.

While long stretches of autobahn are under reconstruction, making it a tight squeeze with trucks on the contraflows, there are plentiful sections of derestricted motorway where we can give the Turbo its head. My colleague clocks a majestic 175mph (282km/h), while I manage only a paltry 160mph (257km/h). The Turbo's potential top limit is 318km/h (197mph), so we're not even close, though I can attest to its 0–62mph time, achieved in a blink-and-you-miss-it 3.1s. This is such a competent car that there is little drama, just the sensation of extremely high speed that most of us outside Germany experience only briefly as a plane takes off. Skirting Munich, we find ourselves passing briefly through Austria, south of Salzburg, due to the vagaries of the frontier boundaries. As in Switzerland, a toll is payable for travelling on Austrian autobahns, but our on-board satnav says we'll soon be heading off into the neighbouring mountains, so we desist. We're still on the valley floor when we hit the Alpine resort of Berchtesgaden and plot a course up to Rossfeldstrasse. The road becomes a lane, winding

Rushing up Rossfeld Hillclimb in the 991 Turbo. The impression of high banks on one side and drop-offs through trees on the other is a daunting prospect where barriers are absent. ANTONY FRASER

narrowly upwards, and we emerge beside an incongruously large, modern visitor reception centre serving tourists bent on visiting the Eagle's Nest, an eyrie that served as Adolf Hitler's summer residence. The road system was all pretty new back then, with mountain views to die for on a sunny day, but now the mists are wafting across the steep slopes.

Hill climbs are fascinating events, a cross between a single stage of tarmac rally and a short section of a road circuit such as the Targa Florio or Carrera Panamericana, where the objective is to set the best time by getting to the summit faster than anyone else. Cars are flagged off one at a time and hurtle uphill, snaking through a succession of daunting curves till they pass the chequered flag and time control at the top. Rossfeld-Berchtesgaden is one of the longer ones, at 6km (3.8 miles), rising 505m in altitude from start to the finish at 1,500m above sea level. By comparison, British hill climbs tend to be short and sweet, like Shelsley Walsh, 1,000 yards (914m) long and a 100m ascent. On the other hand Pike's Peak in Colorado is a monster 20km (12.4 miles) long, rising 1,440m (4,700ft) on the way. Rossfeld's heyday was the 1960s, though as we shall see, its origins were in the 1930s, and a clubby revival event is staged annually now. Rossfeld was on the European Hill Climb Championship calendar during the late 1950s and 1960s, along with Mont Ventoux (France), Trento-Bondone (Italy), Ollon-Villars (Switzerland), Gaisberg (Austria) and Freiburg-Schauinsland (Germany), a series contested by top drivers and ambitious manufacturers. We have only got to look at Porsche's works participation with the 910 Bergspyder programme in the late 1960s to see just how seriously they took hill climbing back then, winning the European mountain-climb series twelve times between 1958 and 1969.

In 1927 the notion of a scenic Alpine road known as the Deutsche Alpenstrasse took off, running along the entire mountain range between Lake Constance and the Königssee, ostensibly to promote tourism. Construction of the road began in 1933 at Inzell. The Rossfeld Höhenring-strasse section was planned as a dedicated mountain loop off the eastern end of the Alpine road, winding between the villages of Unterau and Oberau, with superb views of the Obersalzberg mountains along the way. Although construction started in 1938, the last stretch to Hinterbrand wasn't finished until 1955. (The final section to Königssee was never finished, even though that village is but a ten-minute drive along the valley from Berchtesgaden.) In the 1950s the Rossfeldstrasse was classified as a privately owned national road and a toll was introduced to cover building and maintenance costs, rather like accessing the Nürburgring Nordschleife today. The tollbooth also marks the hill climb startline. The whole Rossfeld-Panoramastrasse winds around the moun-

Porsche enjoyed a huge amount of success in the European Hillclimb Championship in the late 1950s and all through the 1960s. Here is Eberhard Mahle in his 166bhp 911 2.0 at Rossfeld in 1966, round 1 of the European Mountain Championship. Mahle finished 3rd overall in the GT Championship, 1st in class up to 2000cc. PORSCHE MUSEUM ARCHIVES

tains for 16km (10 miles), with a maximum gradient of 13 per cent and an elevation of 1,560m (5,100ft) above sea level. It is also Germany's highest permanently accessible road.

The first hill climb events for motorcycles and cars were staged from 1925 to 1928 on the steep, sandy track leading from Berchtesgaden to Obersalzberg. In 1958 the Rossfeldstrasse race became an international venue for touring cars and GTs, sports cars and smaller single-seaters, when it counted towards the European Hill Climb Championship. By this time Porsche had already been contesting hill climb events for a few years. Sepp Greger notched up Porsche's first success at Rossfeld in 1959. Porsche's next victory at Rossfeld came in 1961 from Heini Walter in an RS61. In 1963 the floodgates opened, and Greger took the 1600 class with a 356 Carrera, while Edgar Barth won the 2.0-litre category using a Porsche-powered Elva chassis (like a low-slung Lotus 23). Teammate Herbie Müller drove the regular mountain championship car, a 718/8, while Barth also took the Rossfeld GT class in a 2000 GS Carrera. He went on to win the rest of the 1963 Hill Climb Championship rounds at Trento, Sestrière, Schauinsland and Gaisberg to scoop the title. A charming souvenir of the 1963 event, 'Alpen Bergpreis am Roßfeld 1963 (Bergrennen/Hillclimb)', may be found on YouTube. Rossfeld continued to be a successful venue for Porsche, with Barth the overall victor in 1964 in a 904/8, Gerhard Mitter in 1965 in a 904 and 1966 in a 910 coupé, with Rolf Stommelen victorious in 1967 in a 910 coupé, and Mitter again in 1968 in a 910 Bergspyder.

At 6km (3.8 miles) long, Rossfeld Hillclimb consists of a succession of curves and esses, interspersed with very few straights, perfect territory for the 991 Turbo. ANTONY FRASER

That was the last time Porsche raced at Rossfeld. The mountain-climb events had been a major stepping stone, an arena in which Porsche quickly secured a dominant role, and a proving ground alongside its increasingly concerted assault on the World Sports Car Championship during the mid-to-late 1960s. After the 1969 Le Mans 24-Hours, however, the works team was withdrawn from racing and the competition reins handed to JW Automotive (Gulf) and Porsche Salzburg (Martini).

The 1973 oil crisis brought an end to hill climbs at Rossfeld until Günter and Heidi Hansmann instituted a revival in 1998 in the same spirit as other modern reprises of vintage events. The Rossfeld Historic hill climbs up the Rossfeldstrasse lasted until 2010. Joachim Althammer set up another revival in 2013, identified as the Internationaler Edelweiss Bergpreis Rossfeldrennen, it was grand enough to persuade Porsche, Mercedes-Benz, Audi and BMW to dispatch cars from their respective museum collections, along with 140 other entrants, enabling fans to witness Hans Herrmann driving a 1966 Porsche 2000 GS-GT, Walter Röhrl in his 1987 'Pikes Peak' Audi Sport Quattro E2, Jochen Mass aboard a 1928 Mercedes SSK, and Prince Leopold von Bayern in a 1961 BMW 700 RS. The line-up in 2014 was equally eclectic.

The stage is set, so let's give it a go! The back-end squats and the scarlet 991 Turbo makes an aggressive getaway from the Rossfeld startline. It's 50 short metres into the first left-hand hairpin, adding more rubber to the tyre tracks that already bedeck the asphalt. It sticks like glue, and apexes out onto a quarter-mile straight, snarling through three swift upshifts and back down again through the gearbox as I brake for two more hairpins that rush towards me in quick suc-

cession. It's remorseless and it's also addictive; what goes up must come down, and, having reached the top, I motor back to the start for another crack.

The overriding impression is of high banks on one side of the road and drop-offs through trees on the other. Most of the course is lined with pine forests interspersed with alpine pastures. A final rush through a couple of hairpins takes us past the timekeeper's box, located on a curve right at the summit. There'd be fabulous vistas across the valleys if we weren't up in the clouds – and, by late afternoon, in pouring rain. There's an assembly area below the start, and a collecting layby after the finish line. A paddock just over the summit consists of a hillside web of single-track roads with individual grassy pull-ins where cars are fettled prior to their runs. The Rossfeldstrasse effectively forms a circle, so, unlike most hill climbs where the competing cars have to descend the route they've raced up, in batches after each category has performed, at Rossfeld they can carry on going down the other side of the hill and back to the startline collecting area.

It's very easy to see that, when trying hard, even the slightest distraction would have you off the edge and into the trees. It's pretty fast, well surfaced, and consists of a succession of curves, esses and sharper bends, interspersed with very few straight bits, and a dozen or so challenging hairpins. In a quick car they come up on you very swiftly. Providing my colleague with ample opportunities to snap sharp shots for this feature, I drive around bends that we've earmarked as being somehow special, and that means driving to and fro between safe turnaround points, maybe eight or ten times. There's method in the madness, because it gives me the opportunity to learn some sections of the track quite thoroughly, and as we've driven the whole Rossfeldstrasse in

Tackling the legendary Rossfeld Hillclimb in a 991 Turbo, the author opposite locks around one of the myriad hairpins. ANTONY FRASER

With 560bhp on tap, the 991 Turbo could have proved a handful on Rossfeld's wet tarmac, but its all-wheel-drive system and PSM traction control made progress around the turns exceptionally sure-footed. ANTONY FRASER

both directions several times scouting for locations we've come to know the whole route reasonably well.

I can confirm that this is one heck of a demanding stretch of road, and no wonder they decided to run a competition up it. Our Red Rusher is extraordinarily fast by any standards, and I reflect that, with 560bhp on tap at 6,500rpm, I must be going up the hill at least at a similar pace to a 1960s race car, benefiting from my on-board traction control systems. The turbo cuts in smartly and it's like a rocket blasting off when the car shoots forwards. The slightest throttle pressure has it dropping a couple of gears and the revs soar and off it goes again.

I address the hill climb with a bit more vigour, and I'm surprised to find I've got quite a sweat going on, because it's actually pretty demanding. I surge up to the corners and attack them, finger-tipping the paddles and braking hard

The 991 Turbo sticks like glue, snarling through the curves and hairpins in quick succession. ANTONY FRASER

The 991 C4S Cabrio's ride, handling and stability are of the highest order, with stupendous grip levels on the long, fast curves. ANTONY FRASER

while it drops a couple of gears, and I can turn in with total precision, keeping the throttle on round the apex. I power out again, steaming up the hill to the next hairpin, round that and then hurtle upwards with blasts of power between each curve, left-right, left-right, straight-lining the bends wherever possible to get the optimum line up to the next hairpin. There's an urgency, an incessant, repetitive quality to it.

There must be at least a dozen hairpins on the way up as well as numerous interestingly cambered bends. Some are more open, others tight where the road narrows, with stone walls lining the drop-offs in places, and buttressing the banks in others. Sport mode is irresistible, and there is a real cacophony echoing off the walls. I flash over a couple of bridges too, oblivious to the rushing torrent beneath. There are only a few buildings beside the track, though we break at lunchtime to investigate a couple of café-restaurants overlooking the course.

Halfway up, close to the edge of the track, I pause by a big boulder bearing a workmanlike metal plaque dedicated to Ludovico Scarfiotti, who was killed here on 8 June 1968. It consists of a steering wheel and a painted portrait of the works Ferrari star who'd won Le Mans in 1963 and twice European Hill Climb Champion (1962 and 1965) in a Ferrari Dino. On that fateful day he was handling one of three works 2.0-litre flat-eight 910 Bergspyders. Though the monument is alongside a straight bit, the Porsche actually went off on a nearby right-hander into the trees below. Its luckless driver was thrown out and suffered fatal head injuries. One rumour suggests he was distracted by a spectator, another that the throttle stuck open, and it may be coincidental that he crashed just after his teammate Rolf Stommelen had also gone off lower down the hill, wrecking the car but sustaining only a broken arm. Gerhard Mitter, driving the third works 910 Spyder, posted the fastest time up the hill to win the event and clinch the championship. Motor racing is a tough sport, even something as apparently innocuous as hill climbing: Gerhard Mitter died a year later on the Nordschleife, and Rolf Stommelen succumbed at Riverside in 1983.

The heavens have opened – and up here we couldn't be much closer with our feet still on the ground. We still need a quintessential shot from behind a hairpin parapet with, likely as not, just fresh air behind the photographer and the valley 1,000ft below. We call it a day and ease down the hill, which now resembles a fast-flowing river,

Heading across Germany we try a different route to Calais, hooking off at Karlsruhe for Saarbrücken and then up to Luxembourg. This car just eats up the miles – nothing comes close to it, though we are occasionally overtaken by even more fixated speed junkies. Without exception, they all slow obediently when the 130km/h signs appear. Most

of this is autobahn and, eventually, autoroute, apart from a stretch where they appear to be thinking about dualling it near Kaiserslautern. By Calais our Turbo Rouge has travelled around 2,250km (1,400 miles) on this trip, averaging 28mpg (10.09ltr/100km) in all manner of conditions.

LOVERS' LANE

A hedonistic road trip on Germany's Romantic Road – Der Romantische Strasse – takes the 991 C4S Cabrio driver on a complex itinerary through beautiful scenery, peppered with alluring gastronomic and retail honeypots. The German National Tourist Board has designated a route specifically for the purpose: the seductively named Romantic Road meanders down the spine of southern Germany, 413km (256 miles) from Würzburg to Füssen – give or take deviations and wrong turnings – and it's a really entertaining drive.

But what is a great driving route? Before describing the Romantic Road, let's just analyse the desirable features that any heroic journey needs to offer: it should be more than just an A to B highway; it ought to have designated start and finish points, with alluring hotspots along the way; it should twist and turn and present sufficient changes of geography to entertain the driver, allowing him or her to exploit the prowess of the car and delight the senses.

The Romantic Road ticks all the boxes and the distractions come thick and fast, so it's less of a road trip, more a cultural and culinary outing – and therein lies the romance. You can knock it off in a couple of days, but that would be to miss out on a wealth of architectural, epicurean and bucolic treats. The countryside changes subtly from rolling hills, rivers and pastureland, crossing an arable plateau and concluding in the Alpine lakes and foothills just short of the Austrian border.

Although it's bookmarked by achingly picturesque ancient town centres and villages, in fact the Romantic Road is a relatively recent concoction, with a nod to the old Roman road system – fair enough, because many of the towns are 2,000 years old. It was invented around 1950 by clever marketing people to get Germany's tourist industry up and running after the Second World War, and managed to turn a disparate assortment of B-roads linking a couple of dozen rural settlements into a world attraction. A recent national poll placed 'The Romantic Road' at number 50 in a list of popular Germanic holiday destinations, while several landmark castles, churches and towns along the way came much higher in the standings – including the dramatic fairy-tale Schloss Neuschwanstein, which placed second overall.

But does that make it a great driving route? Absolutely, in

The 991 C4S Cabriolet is docile as a lamb in urban settings, when it emits a deep nasal hum, and powerful as a lion when called upon to tear along the highway.
ANTONY FRASER

so far as there are plenty of sections where you can indulge yourself behind the wheel, from the sinuous blacktop in the northern sections to the alpine hairpins in the south, with the opportunity to max out on the unrestricted autobahn should you fancy a high-revs blast.

Antony Fraser and I have been lent a brand new 991 Carrera 4S Cabriolet by Porsche GB. It is 725km (450 miles) south from the Eurotunnel terminal to Würzburg, the start of the Romantic Road. This is rolling, arable countryside, sleepy villages, big tractors, and tumbledown farmhouses buttressed by log piles for their winter fuel. Our trip coincides with the first summer sun, all the blossoms are out and the woodlands are myriad shades of green. We overnight at Bad Mergentheim on the River Tauber, a mélange of late medieval buildings overshadowed by a castle that belonged to the Grand Masters of the Teutonic Order.

On our way to the first of the major attractions, Rothenburg ob der Tauber, we cross the eponymous river on a B-road curving gently along a valley flanked by hillside vineyards. Almost every forested ridge that can be seen from the road is topped with a pinnacle-turreted castle or an onion-domed church. The prevailing colour of the domestic buildings is yellow, though we've seen mint green, royal blue and a dirty pink; they're mature, half-timbered and fully timber-framed houses, hung with big shield-shaped tiles. We could go faster, but we'd soon be in another village and we'd have missed something on the way. Brown tourist signs identifying the Romantische Strasse stand sentinel at most road junctions, but it is possible to miss them and go the wrong way, especially since many streets and town centres are currently being resurfaced as cobbles give way to slabs. You really need a map of the road unless you are happy just to go from place to place on the back roads. The satnav will pick up the towns, but it is just as likely to overlook the designated route to reach them. Although these B-roads are curvaceous there is nothing particularly demanding or sudden enough to catch out the unwary; in fact most of the curves flow nicely into each other, so it's a relaxing and pleasant cruise.

It's easy to go very quickly in the 395bhp 991, but on these roads we don't do much more than 96km/h (60mph); the Germans stick rigidly to the speed limits, so we tend to be similarly compliant. Mostly it's beautifully smooth asphalt, but surfaces of some of the more rural sections are not that good, particularly where there are no white lines down the middle. In fact these laid-back lanes suit the nature of our transport, and the cabriolet really is a civilized motor. It's a matter of moments to lower or raise the roof – fabric clad magnesium – which can be done even travelling under 30mph by holding the console switch until the electronics have done

Spurning the satnav in favour of an old-fashioned road map, aboard the Eurotunnel Shuttle on the first leg of the journey along Germany's Romantischestrasse in the 991 Carrera C4S Cabriolet. ANTONY FRASER

their thing, unlatched and parked the lid in its compartment between cockpit and engine. Apart from direct access to the elements, another wonderful thing about a cabriolet is that you are aware of all the pungent farmyard smells. Travelling with the roof down and the side windows up, and the wind deflector in position behind us, it's quite cosy, offering fresh air and a breeze without being cold.

This 991 Cabrio is a fabulous all-rounder. It's strong, there's no scuttle shake, and a howling engine note is the only noise at 240km/h (150mph). Several times we hit 273km/h (170mph) on the unrestricted autobahns, where we exploit stupendous grip levels on the long, fast curves, the front and rear of the chassis gently pitching as it follows the surface. Ride, handling and stability are of the highest order. It's docile as a lamb in urban mode when it emits a deep nasal hum, and powerful as a lion when called upon to tear up the highway, the blaring exhaust dropping through its semitone repertoire of engine notes with each gearchange. It's possibly the most competent Porsche I've ever driven, notwithstanding the 'hairdresser' soft top.

After negotiating the diminutive medieval alleyways of Rothenburg, we climb out of the Tauber Valley onto a ridge surrounded by arable countryside with distant hills on the horizon, and head south for Dinkelsbühl, one of the towns, like Rothenburg, Nördlingen and Landsberg an der Lech, whose antiquity is indicated by huge medieval walls enclosing criss-crossing cobbled streets and alleys. After Dinkelsbühl the route follows a three-lane highway clogged with trucks crawling at 60km/h (37mph). That's no fun, so from Nördlingen to Landsberg we leapfrog the major city of Augsburg via the autobahn.

The 991 C4S Cabriolet with a backdrop of Harburg's formidable castle. ANTONY FRASER

Lakes and Alpine scenery mark the southernmost Bavarian end of the Romantische Strasse. Though it's easy to go very quickly in the 395bhp 991, on these roads we don't do more than 96km/h (60mph).

ANTONY FRASER

The silver charger with fairytale Neuschwanstein Castle in the background, just one of the architectural attractions along the Romantic Road. ANTONY FRASER

After Landsberg we are on a three-lane road: for a few kilometres two of them are in our favour for overtaking, and then vice versa. There are plenty of fuel stations along here. The on-board computer says we're averaging 25mpg (11.3ltr/100km), which isn't bad at all considering the different roads we've been travelling on.

Having left Baden-Württemberg, we're now in Bavaria, where every meadow contains a wooden field barn. It's less of a main drag now, more a country lane with meadows on either side, then more wooded hills, a mixture of conifer and deciduous trees. We are now seeing Alpine-style houses with low-pitch roofs and, at last, here come the best driving roads: smooth white top with fast sweeping bends. The Bavarian byways are the most enjoyable on the route, sweeping up and down and curving through the woods.

The next tourist alert is the Wieskirche – the 'Church in the Meadow' – which is an absolute Rococo riot, with every surface florid with paintings and the most elaborate altar, pulpit and organ loft. It's in the middle of nowhere,

Red leather and matching red upholstery make a sumptuous cabin interior for the 991 C4S Cabriolet. ANTONY FRASER

BRENDON HARTLEY INTERVIEW

Le Mans winner Brendon Hartley describes the 991 GT3 as by far the best road car he's ever driven. ANTONY FRASER

A youthful career in single-seaters earned New Zealand driver Brendon Hartley a seat in Porsche's 919 in the FIA World Endurance LMP1-H Championship, taking in the 2014 Le Mans 24-Hours in which he qualified 4th. His experience in Formula Ford, F-Renault (alongside Daniel Ricciardo) and the British and European F3 series led to a season in GP2 with Coloni in 2010, culminating in an F1 seat with Red Bull Racing in 2017.

His taste for long-distance prototype racing began with drives in LMP2 for Oreca-Nissan. After a gritty spell as junior test driver at Red Bull and Toro Rosso, he hooked up with Mercedes in 2012 and still enjoys their retainer, but fortunately this allows him to focus his talents on the Porsche renaissance in LMP1. He outlined his meteoric rise in motor racing during a break in proceedings in Goodwood's Drivers' Club garden in 2017.

JT: You had a spell as an F1 test driver with Mercedes, and you've also driven F1 cars.

BH: The first year I drove Nigel Mansell's Lotus 92 from the early 1980s, and I also drove the current Mercedes F1 car up there, but more showboating than going for a time. I was a reserve driver for Red Bull Racing for two years and I was a test driver for Mercedes for a few years as well. I never did a race, but I did a lot of test laps and a lot of laps on a computer screen.

JT: You kicked off in karts when you were six years old.

BH: Blame a motor sport-mad family. My dad raced all sorts, from Formula Atlantic to speedway, dirt track, Mini Se7ens; he was a real racer, reasonably successful, but racing mad. He builds race engines for a living now, so I followed in his footsteps and I grew up at the racetrack. Even when I was a kid I was trying to learn racing.

JT: Your career from Formula Renault onwards is mostly single-seaters.

BH: I got into single-seaters when I was thirteen. That seems mad, because you're only allowed to start racing at thirteen, and I was very lucky that my brother Ben had developed a car and I hopped straight in and was pretty successful. I had great supporters in New Zealand, and I got picked up by Red Bull and they brought me to Europe, aged sixteen, which was a bit of a fairy tale.

JT: How did that affect your regular education?

BH: It was almost non-existent after that! I had a Red Bull 'young driver' test in 2005 when I was fifteen, and I missed my end of year exams, but I made a decision with my family that I've got the opportunity of a lifetime here, so I took it and moved to Europe at sixteen to start racing. I don't regret it, and obviously I think I made the right decision.

JT: So now your career has moved on into long-distance endurance racing. In 2012 you were in ALMS, and you won at Road America driving the BMW-Riley LMP2.

Brendon Hartley drives the RS Spyder up the Goodwood Hill at the 2015 Festival of Speed.

ANTONY FRASER

BH: Yeah, after Red Bull I bounced back and I found endurance racing in 2012. I did Le Mans for the first time and absolutely loved it. I travelled through the US last year, and I raced in Grand Am as well as test driving F1, and I kept very busy and started enjoying my racing more than ever, and then Porsche noticed it and gave me this opportunity of a lifetime. At the end of 2013 they gave me the test, and here I am.

JT: How different is the Porsche 919 Hybrid to drive from what you've been used to?

BH: Aero-wise it's quite similar to an Audi, which I raced at Le Mans last year, but the 919 is much more complex. It's the most complicated car Porsche has ever built. It's four-wheel drive, and has two recovery systems that generate energy and send it back to the engine, there's an electric motor and gearbox just sitting beside my feet, and it's massively complex how it all works.

JT: Did it take long to get up to speed?

BH: Actually, Porsche have done a really good job to make it feel quite intuitive. I was worried that all this new technology on board was going to detract from the real racing element, but it's nice to find that the skill set that you need to make the car go round the track is the same as a regular car, though obviously you have a few more toys to play with. Most of

it is about changes here and there, filtered down from the engineers who're doing the hard work back in the garage, monitoring everything, and the skills that you need to make the car go quick, brake, accelerator and turning in and feeling what the car is doing through your backside hasn't changed.

JT: What's your personal goal? Where do you see the next step?

BH: Winning Le Mans would be the next step, on a personal level, standing on the podium at Le Mans and hopefully being part of the Porsche family for the rest of my career, and I couldn't be happier where I am.

JT: You've recently driven two of the 919's predecessors, the 1996 GT1 and the 2006 RS Spyder. How do you like those?

BH: They kept reminding me the GT1 is a priceless Le Mans-winning car, but it wasn't possible to be too gentle with it; in a car as good looking and provoking as this, slow and steady is not an option! And I love the RS Spyder; I drove it last year at a Portimao test day, and that's a lovely circuit and the car is unbelievable. I was actually quite surprised at how quick it was, how much downforce it has. It was developed over three or four years, so balance-wise it couldn't be any better. It's actually one of the best cars I've driven in my life, most enjoyable, and it's one of my favourites.

(continued overleaf)

BRENDON HARTLEY INTERVIEW (continued)

JT: Does it feel lighter than the 919?

BH: It is in fact a lighter car, you can feel it. And actually you have a lot more downforce because in that era fuel efficiency wasn't as important as it is at the moment with the current set of rules, where fuel efficiency becomes very important. We are concerned with fuel consumption and harvesting energy, so aero efficiency becomes even more important than total downforce. Obviously, we want to have as much downforce in the car as possible, but as soon as it becomes inefficient it's a problem, so actually in that era there was more downforce in the car, the cars were lighter, but much less efficient.

JT: Does that mean you're not feeling the physical effect of downforce to the same extent?

BH: Oh yeah, we still have a lot of downforce, don't get me wrong. It's just that the ideal way around the lap moves slightly because you have energy requirements to manage. When you put inefficient downforce on the car you're using more fuel in a straight line, which then means you're going to run out of fuel by the end. For a given lap, you have a certain amount of fuel, a certain amount of energy, so it just moves the window a bit where the optimum lap time is downforce versus efficiency. It's just changed the dynamics of how to make the car go quicker.

JT: Are you getting your head around stuff like that as you're going along or is it intuitive?

BH: A lot of that is done off the track. And as to how we manage a good lap time, there are a few little tricks about how we harvest as much energy as we do. But the great thing is that a lot of our energy is harvested on the straight, which would normally be wasted out of the exhaust system, but it is now harvested back to the battery, so that's obviously just by putting your foot down. The rest we generate during braking, which again doesn't affect the driving too much. In actual fact, it's all managed so well that you just wouldn't really be aware of it. You are a little bit aware of the front diff, so as you're turning in there's a slightly different feeling in the front of the car, due to the fact that it is four-wheel drive, but other than that we can drive it as normal. Obviously we have a few little tricks that we can play with

on exit with a four-wheel drive, but generally speaking to get the car around the track it's the same as always.

JT: To what extent does it vary from circuit to circuit?

BH: A little bit, yes, and again, we have certain targets of how much energy we need to recuperate, so that can mean a few little tricks here and there, and again, that's where efficiency comes back into play. If you have a lot of top speeds and a higher minimum speed then you're not going to recuperate as much energy, compared with a slower circuit, so there are a few things you can do just from car set-up. From a driver's point of view actually it doesn't change too much, but the way you set the car up and manage everything is slightly different.

JT: You've raced the 919 Hybrid at Silverstone, Le Mans and Spa, so what comes out as your favourite circuit?

BH: Le Mans! I love Le Mans. Especially if I'm driving through the night, which we don't get to do on any other circuit. There's obviously something very special about racing at Le Mans in a Porsche, and leading Le Mans in a Porsche was a big highlight of my career. I love the topography of Spa, but if you look at Le Mans on a map you don't think much of it, but when you actually drive it, it's so unique. There's no track in the world like it, with such long straight lines, and it's a combination of real race circuit and country road. It's such a unique place with a lot of subtleties, and I love driving there.

JT: You must be stuck for any kind of leisure time.

BH: We get a little bit of spare time, so it's not a normal 9-to-5 job, and we have a lot of testing to do for the next race, so a lot of time goes into training. We'll have prep days in Weissach where they're also developing a simulator program which we'll start working on and then driving laps on the private track. We're very involved in developing next year's car, but at the same time it's not our job to be around every day. It's our job to drive the cars very quickly.

JT: Everybody has a hero, so who would yours be?

BH: I have a lot of respect for a lot of drivers, but obviously there is a New Zealand one who's a bit special, and that is

Brendon Hartley won the Le Mans 24 Hours in the 919 Hybrid in 2017 with Timo Bernhard and Earl Bamber. PORSCHE MUSEUM ARCHIVES

Chris Amon. The only problem is, I wasn't old enough to actually see him race because I was born in 1989, although I do know Chris quite well now. And actually, he is a bit of a hero of mine; he won Le Mans with Bruce McLaren in 1966 (in a 7.0-litre MkII GT40). But New Zealand's got such a rich motor sport history, and we're such a mad motor sport nation. I was just speaking to Howden Ganley earlier. He was the last Kiwi to stand on the Le Mans podium in 1972 (with François Cevert, Matra-Simca MS670) and he tells me I'll be the next! There's actually been a big gap at Le Mans in terms of Kiwis wins, so hopefully I can fly the flag once again.

JT: In 2017 Toyota looked set to bounce back as the favourite for this year's race, taking pole and leading during the opening nine hours, but in the space of three hours on Saturday, all three TS050 hybrids were out of contention, and you went on to take the win.

BH: My heart sank for Toyota during the night when I saw their cars drop out, and I felt quite sad, especially after last year. It's a brutal race. I know how hard everyone at Porsche has worked for this one day, and I know that Toyota will have been working equally as hard. Their fate was brutal, and then seeing our sister car retire from the lead as well. I had mixed emotions when I came by. I saw it was running very slow, and that's when I understood we were fighting for the victory. You can't write these stories; it's Le Mans, it's always unpredictable. Sometimes at the beginning of the race you don't believe it's possible for such a story to exist, but it did. We thought we'd lost our chance for the victory, but this is a moment I'll remember for the rest of my life.

Brendon is a Porsche nut through-and-through now. Having driven a 991 GT3 road car on the Weissach test track, he describes it as 'by far the best road car I've driven.'

Possibly the ultimate 991 model, the GT2 RS Weissach version is 30kg lighter than the Clubsport, with carbon stabilizers and coupling rods on front and rear axles, and titanium roll cage within. AUTHOR

LATEST 991 GT3 R

In May 2018 Porsche announced a new customer 991 GT3 that would be eligible for all GT3 race series worldwide in 2019. Based on the 911 GT3 RS, the lightweight body-skeleton is based on an aluminium-steel composite construction, with roof, front lid and bumper-fairing panel, wheel arches, doors, sill-skirts and tail sections, plus engine lid and interior trim all made of carbon fibre reinforced plastic (CFRP). All windows are made of polycarbonate. Power is supplied by a 4.0-litre flat-six motor developing 550bhp, largely identical to the production engine of the road-legal 911 GT3 RS. Direct fuel-injection operates at pressures of up to 200 bar, allied to variable valve timing adjustments of the intake and exhaust camshafts, with six throttle butterflies.

Transmission is via a Porsche sequential six-speed constant-mesh gearbox with an electronic shift actuator, operated by paddle-shifts mounted on the steering wheel. The electrohydraulically controlled clutch eliminates the need for a clutch pedal, benefiting quick racing starts.

Aerodynamic improvements include air vents in the front wheel arch fairings, designed to increase downforce on the front axle, while the 1,900 × 400mm rear wing provides aerodynamic balance. The tyre circumference at the front axle has grown from 650mm to 680mm, and in consort with new double wishbone suspension, this is said to enhance braking consistency over the duration of a race. The brake system features ABS, with six-piston aluminium monobloc racing brake calipers operating on ventilated and grooved 390mm steel brake discs at the front, with four-piston calipers and 370mm discs at the rear.

During pit stop refuelling the 120-litre FT3 safety fuel cell can now be refilled from the left or right, depending on circuit layout. Doors and side windows can be removed, and the new racing bucket seat offers drivers better protection in the event of an accident. The seats are now bolted in at six points, and in combination with the adjustable pedal box, the driver's centre of gravity is optimized and offers increased safety in an impact, while side impact protection in the driver's door consists of a carbon-Kevlar aluminium matrix with energy-absorbing plastic foam. All controls have been perfectly aligned to suit the needs of the driver and, for the first time, the new GT3 R cockpit provides air-conditioning, ensuring interior cooling during a hot race by means of a direct connection to the seat and driver's helmet. The 991 GT3 R costs €459,000 and is available from December 2018.

For 2019 Porsche offered the 991 GT3 RSR for customer teams to run in GT3 race series worldwide. PORSCHE PHOTO ARCHIVE

though sought out by trippers. Meanwhile the mountains in the background are getting ever steeper as we motor south.

Then we spot it: Schloss Neuschwanstein, jewel of the Romantic Road. King Ludwig II's fantasy Gothic castle is perched on a crag with the jagged Ammer mountains soaring behind it. Built over thirty years from 1869 on the site of previous castles, its theatrical turrets and pinnacles provided the inspiration for Disney's *Sleeping Beauty* and several other movies, including *Chitty Chitty Bang Bang*, in which the magical car is incarcerated in the 'Vulgarian' dungeons beneath the castle. As we draw nearer on a narrow lane another castle emerges from the forest: Hohenschwangau, a more sombre bastion finished in 1837, though magnificent when floodlit. We're at Schwangau, surrounded by four lakes. It is the biggest tourist trap on the whole route, with high-end hotels and restaurants that are way out of our league, pricewise. Nearby Füssen is more down to earth — it's Bavaria's highest town. Close to journey's end, we can now enjoy a bit of R & R – 'Rotwein and Retail'!

The Romantic Road is a real treat: it's one of the more obscure European routes, and because the tourists buzzing the honeypots have travelled by coach rather than car, many of the interconnecting roads are largely traffic free. A great driving road should exhilarate, stimulate and elicit your best efforts behind the wheel. It should cover a distance great enough to allow stopovers to sample nightlife, it needs spectacular landmarks, and a variety of topography to enable you to get the best out of your car's performance. The German Romantic Road offers plenty of opportunities like these for putting your 911 through its paces, though I'd definitely recommend it as a touring holiday where you are not in a rush to get anywhere, and you can afford a week to enjoy the rustic spree through southern Germany. If you're not convinced, think of it this way: for shopaholics there are the retail opportunities in the towns, and for driving enthusiasts there are the winding Bavarian roads. And there's always a Gasthof at day's end.

On the principle of saving the best till last, north to south is the preferred direction of travel because the real driving roads are at the bottom end in the foothills leading into the Austrian Alps. Here's where our 991 really comes alive, fairly whizzing up and down the Alpine passes and lakeside margins. It is a scorcher, delivering faultless turn-in on the hairpins as I floor the throttle at the apex and it eagerly lunges off down the road. I can't resist the sport/loud button, which hardens everything up, including that gorgeous flat-six soundtrack, echoing off the canyon walls. We are in 911 nirvana. This is indeed one heck of a driving route, and the 991 C4S Cabriolet is just the car for it.

The Romantic Road is a collection of curvaceous B-roads with most of the curves flowing nicely into one another, making it a relaxing top-down Cabriolet cruise. ANTONY FRASER

GENERATION GAME

Nothing stands still for long in the world of Porsche: scarcely a day goes by without my email inbox receiving some missive to do with its racing activities and corporate affairs. The latest stop-press item concerns the next generation of 911, designated the 992 Carrera, and due for launch in 2019.

The 992 Carrera is the eighth-generation 911. In terms of its appearance, wheel arch extensions imply a wider track, endowing the upcoming model with increased high-speed stability and more space for rear-seat passengers, though its overall length remains unchanged. There's also more of a hunched back aspect to the rear quarters. The new monocoque's skeleton employs more high-strength steel sections and aluminium than previously in order to lower its weight, while a full-width retractable rear wing enhances aerodynamic stability and downforce.

Ahead of the launch, project director August Achleitner declared that 'the 992 Carrera is more advanced than the 991 Carrera, and it's one of the last cars to drive autonomously (as opposed to taking care of the driver's role), though the driver is able to switch off the assistance systems too.' It isn't a totally electric model, though a fully-EV Porsche 911 is growing ever closer. The new model's back-end features revised light clusters, a raised engine lid and vertical vents. The entire 992 range, including the GT3, will employ turbocharged 6-cylinder engines, marking the end of naturally aspirated units, though the Gen 2 991 line-up had almost reached that point. The 992 GT3 will deliver more than 500bhp, while the standard models offer an extra 10–15bhp over the 991 Carrera and Carrera S, rated at 364bhp and 414bhp, respectively. Like its predecessors, the 992 will also be produced in Targa form, although that too will be a couple of years down the line.

The range-topping 992 Turbo S borrows engine hardware from the 991 GT2 RS, so its output rises by 50bhp to 630bhp, edging it to within 30bhp of the rival Ferrari 488 GTB, while the regular Turbo deploys 592bhp, which is 61bhp more than the 991 version, lifting top speeds in all cases to more than 200mph (322km/h). The current 991 Turbo S's astonishing 0–62mph time of 2.9s will be eclipsed, while the upcoming 992 Turbo will duck beneath the 3.0s mark for the first time. Of the Porsche cars in production after the 992's launch, only the electric Mission E will be quicker off the line, though that won't be released until 2020.

The hybrid 992 model will be introduced in 2020. It will use the turbocharged flat-six, allied to an electric motor, providing limited all-electric and performance-boosting functions, which could produce in excess of 700bhp and feature an electric boost button. Upcoming CO_2 regulations for 2020 spurred on the hybrid model's development under director Erhard Mössle.

The 992 Carrera is the next generation of 911, due for launch in 2019. PORSCHE MUSEUM ARCHIVES

CHAPTER SIX

SPECIAL VERSIONS OF THE 996, 997 AND 991

COASTAL COMMAND

If you take the ultimate road-going examples of the 996 and 997 and let them loose on North Norfolk's rolling coast roads, which one wins the jackpot at day's end?

Faced with a dilemma calculated to confound anyone with a Porsche addiction, how do you choose between a 996 GT3 RS in white, with brilliant blue graphics, and a 997 GT3 RS in classic Viper Green with black detailing? No question, the earlier model has the purer shape, compared with the

later one's cut-and-thrust extremities. But, of course, it's not that straightforward. You'd probably want the subtle refinements and superior performance of the later car, but, as we'll find out, the older car has enough tricks up its sleeve to readily stand its ground.

We're on the enchanting strip of Norfolk coast between Hunstanton and Sheringham in the east. Our subject Porsches have been provided by Martin Pearse of MCP Motorsport, who knows all the back lanes that we can drive them on to best effect.

To bring us up to speed on spec, the 381bhp, 3.6-litre 996 GT3 RS was in production from 2003 to 2005, with a miserly 682 cars built. A no-frills, go-for-it track weapon, it was the basis for the Carrera Cup cars of that era. The RS has a slightly different engine spec to the 'ordinary' GT3, with reshaped inlet and exhaust ports for race homologation, though officially there was no increase in power. The RS suspension features progressive rather than linear springs, while its dampers are uprated from between 10 to 15 per cent stiffer than the GT3's, while the top mounts can be

Back lane boogie: a pair of GT3 RSs swing through the trees. AMY SHORE

Gulf-Porsche 991 GT3 RSR rides the kerbs at the Ford Chicane at Le Mans 2016. SIMON MAURICE

Esplanade promenade: the 997 GT3 RS and the 996 GT3 RS beside the beach. AMY SHORE

rotated 120 degrees to achieve a Cup Car compatible position. Front and rear control arms are adjustable, and the RS ride height is 3mm (0.1in) lower than the standard GT3, itself a low-slung 30mm lower than the 996 C2. The RS can accelerate from 0–60mph in 4.3s, with a top speed of 306km/h (190mph).

Martin tells me that a previous owner had some trouble at the Nürburgring. Manthey, which is based nearby, fixed the bodywork and installed the K410 conversion, costing about €8,000, at the same time. Two owners later and it's still done a meagre 29,000 miles. Martin is currently looking for £130,000, though he may hang on to it as he likes it so much. What gives it the edge over its RS siblings is its Manthey tuning kit, consisting of manifolds, ECU remap and exhaust, yielding 410bhp on Manthey's rolling road at the Nürburgring, hence the kit being identified as the K410.

Inside the 996 cockpit there's a suede wheel-rim, Alcantara headlining and similarly upholstered handbrake and gear lever gaiters; the sculpted Recaro bucket seats are straddled by blue Schroth five-point harnesses and matching blue regular belts, plus a half roll cage in the rear portion. Otherwise there's not much to choose between the two GT3 cabins. Both have fire extinguishers in their passenger footwells. There's an RS logo on the gear knob, the handbrake lever and the rev counter, validating the exalted spec. In a car like this, the driving position is critical. I find the Recaro seat has me sitting slightly higher than in my own 996 and that's something that might need addressing, even though in practice it doesn't diminish the RS experience.

The more numerous 997 GT3 RS came out in 2006, with 1,909 3.6-litre Gen 1 cars made, providing a homologation model for a number of racing series, with a 444bhp 3.8-litre Gen 2 version available in 2010 (another 1,600 units built).

**Dark Alcantara dominates the 996
GT3 RS cockpit.** AMY SHORE

**Cross-braced scaffolding forms the roll cage
in the 997 GT3 RS cabin.** AMY SHORE

The RS is 20kg (44lb) lighter than the 'ordinary' 997 GT3, tipping the scales at a relatively modest 1,375kg (3,031lb), thanks to its adjustable carbon fibre rear wing, polyester engine lid and perspex rear window. The RS's rear bodywork is 44mm (1.7in) wider than its GT3 counterpart because of the Carrera 4 shell that clads it and enables a wider track for enhanced cornering potential. This is at the expense of straightline speed due to increased drag, not that you'd know it in normal motoring. While the 996 GT3 RS is confined to white bodywork with either red or blue graphics and detailing, the 997 GT3 RS panels and paint scheme are specifically designed for this competition-oriented model, with a small range of bright hues available, such as Viper Green.

The 997 version has much more developed aerodynamics than the earlier model: it's got a bigger front splitter, with channelled scoops that direct cooling air to the brakes, plus larger air intakes. Overall the ducting and contours of the front panel are less intricate than the older 996 model, plus its sidelights and indicators are in housings separate from the headlights. They both have Kevlar rear wings – aerofoils, even – and the 996's front lid is also Kevlar-reinforced fibreglass. The 996 also has an aftermarket under-bonnet 'external' ignition ring-pull off switch by the washer fluid reservoir, which surprisingly the 997 doesn't have.

The 997 RS cockpit feels more claustrophobic than a normal 997, partly because it's dominated by a range of competition-focused equipment including the bright red Schroth five-point harnesses and the complex scaffolding of the half cage in the rear compartment, while the chairs too are predominantly black, apart from the matching Viper Green centre tunnel, Alcantara armrests and headlining. The factory steering wheel, in gunmetal grey with Alcantara suede rim and yellow band around the top to centre it, is a classy feature. Viper Green was one of the least popular colours when the model was launched: there were more takers for the conservative hues. Martin is confident, however, that the rarer paint job will ultimately make it a more desirable commodity.

The thorough once-over the car was given after it was imported certainly seems to have paid off in the ride and handling behaviour, which is just sublime. It's had a new starter motor fitted and a Sharkwerks bypass exhaust, made by Alex Ross in California. Martin thinks the Sharkwerks bypass kit seems to make it a little bit quicker and certainly the noise is better, 'emitting a boom like an aircraft breaking the sound barrier that comes on song at 4,000rpm!'

Drive away. A 997 GT3 RS in Viper Green and a 996 GT3 RS in white with blue graphics: which would you choose? AMY SHORE

We ease the precious pair out of Sheringham and through rolling countryside, wriggling through a succession of dreamy villages. The coast road opens out into a swirling sinuous blacktop artery and we blast west to Langham airfield, where we're allowed to run the cars on what's left of the Second World War Lancaster bomber station. At one time it would have been on a par with similar airstrips like Snetterton and Silverstone. That's far from the case today, but it does mean we are unconstrained by other traffic. I'm surprised to find the 996 can stay with the 997 in the higher reaches, though it's not as zesty on take-off as the 997, less inclined to want to come out and play immediately, though that's a relative observation. This is pretty exhilarating stuff, two RSs on roads that we both know well enough to know where we can go fast.

Tyres are a critical matter in our drive. The 996 GT3 RS's ten-spoke RS wheels are shod with Michelin Pilot Sport Cups, 295/30 ZR18 on the back and 235/40 ZR18 on the front, while the 997 GT3 RS is running on 235/35 ZR19 Continental ContiSport Contacts up front and 305/30 ZR19s at the rear. Both cars have drilled and vented ceramic discs. As Martin says, 'the ContiSports are really nice, grippy in the wet and in the dry; the only snag is that Porsche won't issue a warranty with them on because they are not N-rated.'

On the other hand, the 996 proves quite twitchy, and everything happens very rapidly on these back roads. It turns in sharply, but it is bobbing about a bit. It has a bit more of a weaving tendency, which could be down to the tyres; they feel as if they're really gripped to the asphalt and reluctant to change direction, making each high-speed turn a tad snappy. This may not be a bad thing on the expanses of a race circuit, but it's a trifle unnerving on a bendy back road. All is forgiven because I reckon I can hold the 997 on these winding warrens. And I love the view out of the windscreen where you've got the white tops of the front wings on either side, while the haunches

A rural ride in north Norfolk aboard a 997 GT3 RS and a 996 GT3 RS. AMY SHORE

viewed in the side mirrors are neat, though less muscular than the 997's C4-sourced arches. As I follow the white 996 RS with its blue decals I admire the way that the blue line comes around the rear flanks and fades towards the number plate, and it's nice on corners to see the blue wheels – arguably the best colour combination – offset by the yellow plate and the red rear lights.

I love the firm, thoroughly planted ride of this 996 RS and the fact that you feel every little undulation of the road surface. This is a harder ride than the 997, which may be due to the 997's recent comprehensive makeover. The 997 has quite a sharp clutch, and the gear linkage is delicately notchy. Acceleration is astonishingly vivid: off it goes with the slightest accelerator pedal pressure. The ride is agreeably firm,

Beautifully colour-coded ten-spoke alloy wheel on the 996 GT3. Elegant nosecone disguises aero splitter beneath. AMY SHORE

Black detailing and graphics on the 997 GT3 RS includes matching ten-spoke alloy wheels. Rear wing is cantilevered on engine lid spoiler. AMY SHORE

A balmy day in rustic north Norfolk with the 997 GT3 RS and 996 GT3 RS. AMY SHORE

A fruity couple: the 996 GT3 RS and the 997 GT3 RS take a comfort stop. AMY SHORE

and I'm feeling all the different nuances of the road surface. It's also good being in a left-hand-drive GT3. The green car is wonderfully manoeuvrable and everything feels right about the driving position, the comfort of the seats, the way your body is hugged. I think this could be my ultimate 911 because it's so user-friendly and less complicated than a 991 GT3. Travelling at low speeds through the Norfolk coastal villages, the sound of the Sharkwerks exhaust booming off the flint walls is not quite spine-tingling, but it's certainly announcing its presence. On the open road there's that delirious sonic boom at 4,000rpm in 4th, which is where it really takes off.

We roll the cars down onto the promenade at Sheringham. I'm surprised that the white car attracts more attention from holidaymakers than the green one; perhaps the later model's more extreme aero mods make it less comprehensible to the untutored viewer. If I had to choose one it would be the 997, in spite of its in-your-face ducts and

spoilers. Viper Green is vibrant, redolent of the 911's halcyon days, and it's just so well sorted. It is always possible, however, that the purity of the older model's lines would swing the balance when the white car has new tyres and its suspension has been sorted out.

THE SPECIALS

Car manufacturers commemorate the most significant anniversaries with limited editions. There's an element of self-indulgence here, because these two special edition coupés happen to be among my favourite 911s. They're slightly quirky, somewhat idiosyncratic, and make an appropriate comparison for a back-to-back feature: the 997 Sport Classic, which has inspired much heart searching as to what to do with my own 996, and the 991 50th Anniversary model, celebrating a half-century of the 911.

For a closer appraisal, I'm visiting the JFD collection at Kontich, Antwerp, where they currently reside under the patronage of Johan Dirickx. These two cars may seem a strange choice given his appetite for classic 911 RSs, but before discovering why they appeal to him, let's first pin down the specs. The slightly older 997 Sport Classic deliberately set out to evoke, if not recreate, the company's illustrious history, rather like the 991R. Johan's is one of just 250 cars built, introduced at Frankfurt in 2009, on sale from January 2010 and priced at £140,000. The most obvious references to an era not so far ago are the ducktail engine-lid spoiler, the pair of retro racing stripes over the roof and front lid, and the Zagato-style double-bubble roof. The front panel is bereft of a splitter, but retains minimal lower air scoops sculpted from the valence, plus black grilles.

Parting shot: the 996 GT3 RS and 997 GT3 RS head for the horizon. AMY SHORE

Special editions rarely get any better: the 997 Sport Classic and 991 50th Anniversary models. ANTONY FRASER

Is it Two-Tone? It's certainly one of The Specials as far as limited editions go. The aerodynamic profile of the sills is different from standard, and there are vents behind the rear wheel arches to disburse hot air from the brakes. Lights are subtly different front and rear, while the stone guards on the leading edges of the rear wheel arches are in matching grey. The fuel cap purports to be classic alloy, and the doors are also in aluminium. The Sport Classic runs on 19in factory-made Fuchs alloys, shod with Pirelli P-Zeroes, 235/35 ZR19 on the front and 305/30 ZR19 on the back, and the offset of the front rims manages not to look too shallow. The Carrera S 3.8-litre flat-six develops 23bhp more than standard, giving 403bhp, achieved via mods to the intake manifold, airflow and special exhaust system with split twin tailpipes. It's coupled to a short-shift six-speed manual gearbox rather than an overly modern PDK gearbox, enabling a top speed of 301km/h (187mph), while 0–62mph takes 4.6s.

The 997 Sport Classic runs 19in black-centred Fuchs-style wheels, and its pert ducktail spoiler and blunt front help present a compact profile. ANTONY FRASER

The 997 Sport Classic's 3.8-litre flat-six develops 403bhp, thanks to modifications to the intake manifold, airflow and special exhaust system. ANTONY FRASER

Under the ducktail lives a carbon air-intake box that's described as a Porsche Exclusive Power Kit, and it's refreshing to see something a bit different inside a modern Porsche engine bay. Anachronisms are all very well, but not at the expense of safety and efficiency, so the 997 Sport Classic is fitted with decidedly non-classic ceramic composite brakes. It's also equipped with a limited-slip differential, and the suspension consists of PASM with 20mm lower ride-height and wider rear track. The body is 44mm broader-beamed, and finished in Sport Classic Grey with pale grey stripes that deliberately underplay the racing allusion; they are so pale in certain lights that you can only just make them out. It may be wilfully retro, but it's certainly nothing like as ostentatious as the early 1970s RSs it aims to celebrate.

Cabin interior of the 997 Sport Classic, upholstered in Espresso brown and Houndstooth woven leather and tweed, while the basket weave is echoed in the door panels. ANTONY FRASER

The Espresso Brown and Houndstooth woven leather and tweed cabin is also agreeably different to standard fare, and the Recaro seats are comfortable and supportive, while the basket weave upholstery is echoed in the door panels, so the impression is of a largely brown interior. It's also got a proper handbrake lever. The paired grey racing stripes are echoed on the gear lever knob and the rev counter too. Surprisingly, the dinky rear seats are present as well, and the 911 Sport Classic legend is embossed in the headrests, scripted in chrome on the door sills, while on the glovebox it reveals that this car is number 069 of the 250-off limited edition run.

Barely perceptible, the Sport Classic graphics include a pair of darker grey stripes, visible on the underside of the ducktail spoiler. ANTONY FRASER

Johan's fancy was captivated by this entire package when he saw it at a contrived Porsche publicity shoot that put the Sport Classic together with a 1973 2.7RS. He thought it was a fabulous looking car, one of the Exclusive Department's first experiments to make a short run series, but he was deterred by the price of more than €200,000, roughly €60,000 or €70,000 more than a normal Carrera 2. In time, however, he heard about a Sport Classic for sale. Despite having just 15,000km, which made it usable on the road, its value had dropped to its lowest level, well below the original price. Having bought the car, Johan had the factory's Exclusive Department buff out a couple of flaws in the paintwork to get it back to pristine condition, and reproduce a 'Genesis' book about the car that the original owner had ordered but which had become separated from the car. This factory visit proved even more fruitful when an artwork of the car emerged that had been done when the first owner bought the car.

The 50th Anniversary 991 is based on the broader Carrera 4S body with wider track and consequent suspension changes, including reprogrammed PASM. Styling tweaks include Sport Design mirrors and 20in Fuchs wheels. ANTONY FRASER

Johan now owns both examples of the 997 that he aspired to: the Sport Classic and the 4.0 RS:

In my opinion, the 4.0 RS and the Sport Classic are the two 997s you want to have, and I'll keep both because they are beautiful and distinctive. The Sport Classic is the touring car, the car to go to the South of France in, whereas the 4.0-litre RS is the track car, the one you're going to take to Francorchamps to enjoy yourself and drive back on the road. That's the way I look at the Sport Classic, it's more the bour-geois car compared to the racing bias of the 4.0 RS.

The 991 50th Anniversary is another story. It's preceded in the pantheon of 911 birthday honours cars by the 25th

Cabin interior of the 50th Anniversary 991 has an austere quality redolent of the era it celebrates, featuring Houndstooth check, plus '50' logo on headrests and dashboard. ANTONY FRASER

Anniversary 3.2 Carrera of 1989, the 964 wide-body 30th Anniversary from 1993, and the turbo-fronted 40-Years 996 Celebration of 2003. It's also a little bit outside the normal realm of what Johan would go for, not having the RS suffix that embodies the majority of cars in the JFD Collection. The 394bhp 3.8-litre flat-six is carried over unchanged from the Carrera 2, augmented by an optional power kit. It's based on the broader Carrera 4S body with wider track and consequent suspension changes, including reprogrammed PASM, styling tweaks include Sport Design mirrors and 20in Fuchs-inspired wheels, which are the brashest aspect of an otherwise understated party girl. The external birthday gift trappings are the darkened headlight bezels and chrome highlights across the engine cover. Whereas the Sport Clas-sic retains the 997's more rotund front wing contours, those of the 991 Anniversary are suppressed, and that tends to support the Sport Classic's retro aspiration.

A limited-edition plaque confirms it is number 1,678 out of 1,963 units built. ANTONY FRASER

The 911 50th Anniversary cabin features special stitching and Houndstooth check, with the '50' logo on the headrests and dashboard, and a limited edition plaque confirming it is number 1,678.

Dials are black with green numbers, and I note it's done just 5,536km. It was registered to Johan on 19 May 2014, with a scant 8km on the odometer. He was originally consid-ering buying just one special edition 991 for the JFD Collec-tion, and the 911 50th Anniversary seemed like a sound idea, fitted with the power kit, seven-speed manual gearbox and ceramic brakes. Johan also ordered the 'Genesis' book so the car would be complete. A total of 1,963 examples were built, representing the first year of 911 production. That was quite a big number compared with the 250 Sport Classics;

the 996 Celebration model offered in 2003 was also limited to 1,963 cars, in the same way that the 986 Boxster S 550 Spyder 50th Anniversary model from 2003 spawned 1,953 examples.

Johan believes Anniversary 911s are becoming quite sought after:

> I think all the cars found customers, and now people are starting to search for them, especially when they have a power kit and a manual gearbox. At the time when I was going to buy one, everybody said, 'you need a PDK', but I didn't want a PDK, and that's why I ordered the manual gearbox, and there are very few cars built with that combination of manual gearbox and power kit, especially in Europe. In the US every car had a power kit, but then again, they almost all had a PDK too, but European buyers at least had the option.

Johan has since also bought a 991R. It says much for Porsche marketing acumen that a classic RS connoisseur, who brooks no nonsense in matters 911, can be tempted by modern special editions. Does he feel the same degree of attachment to the 991 Anniversary car as he does the 997 Sport Classic? 'The thing is, as I bought it new I have a kind of commitment not to sell it, but actually, if somebody came by and wanted to buy it, I would sell it. Now I have the R, I don't actually need another special edition 991.' Johan believes that too many special editions devalue the concept of what they are meant to be celebrating, and make them seem trite.

The one-off 1,000,000th 911 is this green machine, a 991 Carrera, parked on the concourse of the Porsche Museum in 2017. AUTHOR

On a recent visit to the Porsche Museum I encountered the ultimate special edition, the Millionth 911, in Irish Green. Johan is sceptical about its status, even though it is badged as the 1,000,000th 911:

> We will never know whether that was the millionth or the millionth-and-one car. I'm sure they have four or five cars like that lined up, just in case they smack one up. It will be in the region of the millionth 911, that's for sure, but I'm not convinced that it is exactly the millionth car off the production line. But I like that colour combo and interior with the wood veneer and houndstooth seats. It's a good PR stunt, and I wouldn't be surprised if they made a small series of Millionth cars – about twenty of them, like they did a green one with a ducktail for the presidents of the Porsche clubs.

Porsche is very creative with special editions, but he thinks the moment will come when people have had enough of them.

> You remember the Le Mans 991, a red, white and black car with the red stripe in the Le Mans livery of the 919? You might as well buy yourself a white car and put on the decals yourself and get the wheels painted black. But with the Sport Classic you have something a bit special: at least you have new pieces of bodywork like ducktail and double-bubble roof, and that makes it different, but I don't see the point of having a Le Mans edition, unless you are totally obsessed with Le Mans or you have a taste for Martini! We've come a long way since the Martini striped 924 of the 1970s, and I think that Porsche should make a little bit more effort than just putting some decals on a car and saying it's a limited edition. It's too easy.

That may be so, but they have been diligent when it comes to creating standout models. Apart from strands of engine capacity, body types, trim levels and technical specifications, they have gone for the bullseye when making special versions of the 911 – the RSs, the Jubilee cars, the GT2 and GT3 – and it's feasible that without these tantalizing short runs and the publicity they generated Porsche might not yet have reached a million 911s. As Johan says, 'you do need those limited series, be it for racing or to sell, to make people feel they want to have something special, and all those things put together are very seductive.' And the upgrades that create special editions do provide targets for one's own personal modifications.

We cruise out into the arable countryside south of Ant-werp. The Sport Classic has now logged 32,000km. How does Johan rate its handling?

I never actually put this one on a track, so I never drove it sideways, but it's a good street suspension set-up. I don't think it's a great track suspension because it will be way too soft. I see this car a little bit like the evening opera tour: you go to the opera and have something to eat and drive back home. A car for special occasions, and it's very well suited for that; it's got the beautiful, almost bespoke, interior that's only made for one series.

It's a superb driving position, arms bent and close to the wheel, a taut ride, though not bouncing overly on the bumps, and secure handling. From the outset it's beautifully respon-sive on the throttle, accelerating without drama but still going hard, and there's a different exhaust note as I ease through the gears. Johan believes the exhaust note changes over time: 'after 10,000km some things in the exhaust start to burn in, then you have a different sound to what it started off as. I'm almost sure that you would not get away with the sound restrictions that you have now when the exhaust is open.'

Time to try the 991/911 Anniversary. At idle, the sound-track is soporific. Does it stand comparison with the GT3? 'The GT3 is much peakier, though this has a much more usable power band, whereas the GT3 you have to really go into the higher revs. So, it's like a touring car.' Some touring car, though it does have decent air-con. At 3,500rpm the power kicks in, bringing with it a different exhaust note, and it emits a lovely popping on the over-run in Sport Plus. The chassis is a bit stiffer and the throttle response is a bit faster. Dropping down to a lower gear it blips the rpm, faking a heel-and-toe double declutch. The 991 is smoother, and you sense the evolution logic of the 911 better in the 991 model than you do in the 997, which is closer to the 996 than it is to the 991. The Sport Classic is more challenging because it's livelier than the Anniversary. The 991 suspension mani-fests itself at different levels depending on the road surface, and is very efficient. There's not a lot to choose between the two cars' engines. It's more to do with the feel of the brakes and the chassis, and it's clear that the Sport Classic is the sportier model – still more Grand Touring than track car, though.

We chase up and down the country lane for the camera-man's benefit, and I conclude that the Sport Classic, with its wilder exterior, is the one with the sexier personality. The driving experience, however, suggests that the 991 Anni-versary is a bit more efficient, more planted. The 991 has more brake horsepower – it's 430bhp and the Sport Classic is 403bhp – while the Sport Classic is slightly higher-geared than the 991. The car that evokes the classic 911 is the more raucous party animal than the one that's actually celebrat-ing its anniversary. For me, lost as I am in the imagery of RS ducktails and Zagato double-bubble roofs, the choice is clear: I'd have the Sport Classic. But maybe in the real-life drivability stakes, the 991 has the more valid claim to celebrate the 911's birthday. Still, any excuse for a party: so, many happy returns to the specials.

BACK IN THE FAST LANE

What does 1,000 horsepower feel like under your right foot? Some time ago I reached for the horizon in a couple of 9ff's finest. Where would we be without unrestricted auto-bahns? It's a rhetorical question, because, frankly, with my concentration buried in the controls of 9ff's white charger – the so-called GTurbo 1000 – I couldn't care less. It's one of those 'wouldn't be anywhere else' moments, the 1,000bhp rush matched by my 1,000-yard stare as I focus on the van-ishing point, eyes focused as far down the autobahn as I can see as the sparse traffic and scenery rushes up to meet me in a barely comprehended blur. This is the life!

Housed in a spacious workshop on the outskirts of Dort-mund, 9ff was set up by Jan Fatthauer in 2001. Today he runs the business with his wife Frauke (that's where the 'ff' in the name comes from, looking conveniently similar to '911') and a staff of fourteen focused firmly on producing high-performance Porsches. There are at least fifteen cars in the throes of tune-up and restoration. Legacies of the supercar

The 50th Anniversary 991 is powered by the 394bhp 3.8-litre flat-six, augmented by X51 power kit. ANTONY FRASER

era are a couple of low-slung, mid-engined, wild GT9s being prepped for customers. I notice a spaceframe chassis under wraps, potentially the makings of another of these signature supercars. Output of all 9ff models totals an impressive 200 cars a year.

Jan has provided a couple of examples from his current line-up for us to try: the black and gold F97 GTronic 750 and the white GTurbo 1000. They are almost from opposite ends of the 9ff spectrum, broadly akin to the difference between a 911 Turbo and a GT2: one's a benign experience whereas the other is, potentially, a rowdy one. Of the GTronic 750, he says:

> some details are very special, and it will be a show car first and then sold to a customer. It's twin turbo without any visible intercooler, because we put in a water intercooler so you don't need any kind of wing or special hose; we take out the air conditioner and use the place for the intercooler. It has a six-speed Tiptronic gearbox and it's four-wheel drive. It's got the flared fenders (wings) with the distinctive 9ff front panel and splitter, the rear wing and rear apron and side skirts, so this is actually a conversion that we sell quite a lot of, but which is not that well known worldwide. Most people think we do only 1,000bhp cars, but this is a bolt-on 750bhp kit.

As well as discrete front splitter, broad air intakes and sill skirts, the GTronic has a rear diffuser with twin exhausts, two grilles either side of the rear valance and two in the back of the rear arches, and a huge air intake on the front of them. Both cars sport vast rear wings.

The spec of the GTurbo 1000 is based on a GT3 with twin turbos, so it's 1,000bhp. The conversion is also bolt-on, so it looks nearly stock, but it has bigger modifications that mean it's more of a technically modified car with rear-wheel drive only, no traction control and no PSM. Mechanical enhancements start with the brakes, as you need to have the means to haul that much power back to reality when the 130km/h signs come up.

> We upgrade the brakes and the suspension relative to the different weight set-up. The gearbox has new ratios and stronger internal parts, and we use the GT3 race engine because it's the old Mezger engine. It's very similar to the 997 Turbo engine, but we have to modify many parts like pistons with lower compression ratio and camshafts with different timing, more for turbo and not so much for high-revving naturally aspirated work. Then we have to install the complete turbo system, which means headers, turbochargers, intercoolers with other special intakes and the complete new exhaust system. We use the driveshafts from the 997 Turbo, which are really strong: we use them in all our cars, even the 1,400bhp cars, without any problems. We have a better clutch too. Last step is always the most difficult to adapt, and that's the electronics.

The sequential linkage, manufactured by the Czech company SQS, works very well. It's an external attachment, so there's no gearbox intervention, and it converts the standard H-pattern to a sequential shifting mechanism. It's simplicity itself to operate: six clicks back towards me, and one

White tornado: the 9ff GTurbo 1000 is based on a GT3 with twin turbos, with 1,000bhp, rear-wheel drive only and no PSM traction control. PETER MEISSNER

Incredible as it may seem, 9ff's GTronic 1000 serves up literally 1,000bhp from its twin-turbo GT3-based engine, as well as being rear-wheel drive with no traction control, nor PSM. ANTONY FRASER

push forward to engage reverse, and there's a handy digital indicator telling me which slot I'm in. However, I do have to operate the clutch and accelerator conventionally with each shift, and it does call for a strong clutch foot. Jan says the shifter has a reputation for long reliability, whereas a fully sequential gearbox needs rebuilding after fifty hours. There's no PSM (Porsche Stability Management) on the GTurbo 1000, 'for the simple reason that the factory traction control is made to cope with 450bhp and not 1,000bhp, so it wouldn't really work'.

But why not start with a 997 Turbo in the first place? Simply because in this case the donor car is a GT3 provided by the customer:

> and it's more economical to modify the GT3 engine than to exchange it for a Turbo engine. The characteristics of the GT3 engine are more suitable for this kind of car. It's more GT3-like because it's higher revving, and it can do 8,000rpm with the turbo engine. We like to do this conversion in a GT3 because in my opinion the GT3 is the nicest driving car in the whole 911 range. It feels light, it feels very direct and sporty, it's comfortable enough but it's not too much comfort. I don't like these limousine style 911s like the Turbo.

Jan favours two brands of tyre to cope with the huge amounts of power on tap. The Michelin Pilot Sport 2 is recommended for sporty drivers as it offers a good compromise of grip in hot, cold and wet conditions, and it can also be used on the track without losing out too much in comparison with the Cup tyres. Drivers who use their cars just on roads

9ff founder Jan Fatthauer explains that his particular fondness for the water-cooled 996 Turbos is because they were new in 2001, the year he started the company. ANTONY FRASER

and autobahns are advised to fit Continental ContiSports: although they don't provide so much grip, they are the best for all-round use and give a comfortable ride with low noise levels:

> When you're generating that much power, the tyre is more significant, and that presents another problem, which is that your top speed also goes up, and so we need homologation from the tyre company to allow us to reach these high speeds. This really is a serious issue for us, and only Michelin and Continental give us homologation for 360km/h. All the others, like Bridgestone, stop at 300 or 320km/h and that is not enough. If they can allow us to do 350km/h and more they did a good job developing their tyres.

The most extreme conversion carried out by 9ff is the GTronic 1400, based on the 997 Turbo Tiptronic from 2007 to 2009. 'The Tiptronic gearbox made by Mercedes-Benz is extremely tough. The manual gearbox would struggle to cope with this kind of power, so we have to have Tiptronic.' The complete body conversion comes with bumpers, sideskirts, engine lid and wing, some interior parts, front and rear suspension, Supercup brakes, 20in O.Z. Superleggera wheels, and – here comes the clincher – a 4.2-litre twin-turbo flat-six, endowed with special crankshaft and bigger pistons and cylinders, developing 1,400bhp. Although the GTurbo 1000 is a manual, Jan is a fan of Tiptronic:

> The Tiptronic is perfect because it is very comfortable to drive. If you have 1500Nm of torque, with a manual gearbox you need an extreme four-disc clutch to handle such a big amount of torque and that would make daily use a little bit tiresome. No normal organic clutch can handle this kind of power. It's quicker with a manual, sure, and for speed trial events a manual is better and quicker, but for ordinary drivers I prefer to offer Tiptronic.

Jan selects wheels for his cars according to price, weight and aesthetics, depending on which model they're fitted to. He finds that many customers prefer the O.Z. wheels: 19in is a stock size, but the tyres also work well with the 20in wheels amd there is hardly any difference in comfort and ride.

9ff cars all feature distinctive aerodynamics, the result of careful honing in the Audi wind tunnel in Neckarsulm. It can test up to 300km/h, whereas most others can only go up to 200 or 250km/h. It also has a proper rolling road underneath the car and so the wheels can turn. Since a lot of turbulence is caused by the wheels rotating and by the road surface under the car, the Audi tunnel gives the most realistic results. A trip to the wind tunnel is an expensive proposition, however, and three or four cars that are in the build stage may be tested during each time slot to assess the best combination of aero parts:

> *You cannot modify the cars in the tunnel; you only can change panels over, trying out different combinations and configurations till you get the best measurements. We don't do it that often, and a good test driver who has a good sense of feel for the car can measure a lot on the street with very elementary electronic tags in the car. You have adjustment for the ride height, and it's measuring the actual height of the car front and rear. We have a special electronic sensor that we can monitor on our laptop telling us the amount of lift and downforce at 200 and 300km/h, and then we see if we can get more downforce, so it's very easy to test on the street.*

A low drag coefficient is really important on a high-velocity Porsche.

As the supply of donor Mezger engines has dwindled, 9ff has been using the modern 9A1 engine from the 991:

> *The Mezger engine was one of the best engines ever, but now we have a solution with the new one. And the Mark 2 twin-turbo DFI engine with PDK is very smooth and elastic. It's a good engine, maybe not as strong as the old Mezger engine, but for sure it's not worse. The Mezger engine is the legend that it is because of its strength, you couldn't kill it. All the engines we have over there waiting to go in the cars outside, they're all Mezger engines. We also did some 4.4-litres but they're always called a 4.0-litre S. We can get nearly 600bhp from a naturally aspirated engine at 9,000rpm, in a car weighing only a little over 1,000kg, and there's an immediate response. We always use double ring pistons like the best racing engines because then engines can have 50 or 60 hours' lifetime; my philosophy is always to have reliable engines and I also prefer simple solutions.*

The GTurbo 1000 uses a Garrett GT1000R turbo, Pankl forged aluminium pistons, steel liners and titanium con rods with special 9ff cams, while the GTronic 750 is equipped with a KKK K24 turbocharger and free-flow intercoolers. Jan elected to use these particular turbos after trying several different permutations by trial and error. He claims to have built about 500 engines in the previous fifteen years and each one is slightly different, as there's always something that can be optimized. A K24-750, for example, is easy to install because it doesn't need water lines: all the oil lines and oil reservoirs can be taken from the stock engine, making it good for small conversions.

Jan has a fondness for the water-cooled 996 Turbos because they were new in 2001, the year he founded 9ff. An occasion that helped to establish his reputation was the annual top speed shoot-out held by *Auto Motor und Sport* magazine at Nardò, near Naples, in 2004, setting his first world record in the V-400 (marketed as the 840bhp 911-based GT9) and lapping Nardò at 387.9km/h (241mph).

9ff's GTronic 750 has masses of power available, above and beyond the expectation of a normal turbocharged 911. PETER MEISSNER

The 9ff GTronic 750 and GTurbo 1000 all set for some full-on lappery at the F&T LaSiSe motor industry test track near Dortmund. AUTHOR

I'm not sure if I would drive this car now! It was very dangerous; it was bumpy and we drove without any spoiler or any rear wing because of the drag coefficient, so although it had good aerodynamics the car was constantly drifting on the steering, with a minimum 5-degrees angle at 388km/h! Since that time our philosophy has always been to break any kind of world record to give us a good marketing platform, and I would say it really works. So, it's not only for my pleasure that I have a car which can do over 400km/h; if you ask my wife or my two boys, they will say, 'we want to go to Bremen, but let mum drive because then we will be quicker!'

All of 9ff's mechanical and assembly operations, as well as bodywork creation, take place on site. 'We have a small bodyshop in the back where we fabricate all the glassfibre and carbon-fibre. Our welding area consists of two rooms, where we make all the headers, exhaust systems, roll cages, tube frames for the GT9 chassis: we do everything in-house.' Jan thinks that supercars like the GT9 have had their day and there's more of a market for cars like the GTronic 750. The GTurbo 1000 is sold as a complete package to a single specification, whereas the GTronic 750 can be specified to order with as few or as many modifications as you fancy or can afford. You could, for example, opt for just the bolt-on engine conversion without internal modifications, or a different transmission, upgraded brakes, bigger wheels and uprated suspension. It is the same with the bodykit, although specifying just a front splitter would not make it a GTronic.

In order to put the cars to the test we have come to the F&T LaSiSe test track at Selm, north of Dortmund. In the normal course of things, you're more likely to be sharing

track space here with trucks and tractors as that stands for Forschungs & Technologiezentrum LadungsSicherung Selm GmbH (Research & Technology Centre for Cargo Securing Selm), which specializes in lorry logistics and agricultural vehicle research. I slide into the black-and-gold F97 GTronic 750. A button on the door console makes the exhaust note louder or quieter, and just driving it away from the factory it's booming like a bittern, so I press the quiet button to make it less obtrusive.

It's a firm ride, though agreeable in a business-like fashion. There's masses of power on tap, above and beyond the normal expectation of a turbo 911. The boom comes when I back off when it's on over-run, so when I floor it the boom is replaced by a snarling roar, and then I back off and the boom comes back. So, it's a rev thing, below 2,500rpm. But a quick jab of the right foot on the accelerator sends the revs soaring round to 5,500rpm and the car jumps out of its skin. The further I go the more attuned to the car I become, and the blissful power and mellifluous gear changes are very seductive. It corners beautifully flat and is absolutely controllable.

Not only are we able to sample super-swift on the autobahn, we can really lean on the suspension on the uninterrupted test track, which has a wonderfully smooth tarmac surface to play on. Soon I am blatting around the infield loops with 9ff's chief mechanic and skimming between the lorry cobbles on the rustic back road. It's a car journalist's heaven. Here I can lean on the GTronic far more than I could on the open road, and it's beautifully taut, yet supple, as I glide through the turns.

The white car is quite a different kettle of fish, fundamentally because it is rear-wheel drive and manual transmission,

Trying out 9ff's black and gold F97 GTronic 750 on the motor industry F&T LaSiSe test track at Selm, near Dortmund. PETER MEISSNER

aside from possessing 250bhp more. Its hard-edged character is immediately evident as I hoist myself into the cockpit over the door bar constituent of the roll cage scaffolding. The whole sensation is of a firmer, more acute suspension in a more sports-oriented attitude rather than a dedicated highway approach. The comprehensive roll cage is not so intrusive but I am aware it's there, defining the pugilistic potential. I'm a lot more attentive about the controls than I would be in the black car; the whole driving experience is more of an operation. The controls are all at odds with one another: I need a strong left foot because it's a stiff clutch, whereas the brake pedal doesn't need too much effort to slow it, but I need a delicate right foot because the power spins up immediately. On the other hand I need a firm hand on the shifter: each shift is accompanied by the characteristic exhalation of the wastegate blow-off valve, and there's incessant popping and rumbling on the over-run. There aren't quite enough gears to be able to play a tune, but it manages half an octave. The boost button is just ahead of the gearshift and I've got sport mode and boost control for the journey back to the garage. The boost gauge is located atop the dash where the Sport Chrono clock used to be. The 1,000bhp monster has way more attitude, defined by greater power, louder noise and a more track-focused turn-in and handling, which is manifest as I swing it around the same course as its well-mannered sibling. If it's extrovert full-on performance you seek, look no further!

We leave the test track and hit the autobahn for the blast back to base. It's here that I taste the incredible power of 1,000bhp. It's like a rampant stallion kicking its legs in the air and taking off at a flat-out gallop, the closest I'll get to emulating the rearing horse on the Porsche coat of arms. In

an instant I am surging down the straightaway like a guided missile, working the shifter swiftly through the gearbox into 6th. I search for terms of reference. Ruf's CTR-3 might be a more civilized proposition, though I saw 200mph in one at Bruntingthorpe. A JZM-tuned 997 GT3 with similar SQS shifter that I handled at Silverstone is getting there. The F1 Prost-Peugeot AP03 3.0-litre V10 with similar output that I drove at Circuit du Var truly was a wild animal in comparison with the GTurbo 1000. Here you immediately appreciate the power on tap, but it's harnessed, controllable, nailed down, which is not the case at all in a twenty-year-old F1 car. No, the GTurbo is a fabulous piece of kit, a devastating performer at every level. Its serene sister is the antidote, the warm-down, though no less rewarding in its own right. I really am back in the fast lane.

DOUBLE DUTCH

911Rs are rare, so two together is a
special moment. ANTONY FRASER

Beautifully taut, yet supple, gliding through the turns, the GTronic 750 is equipped with a KKK K24 turbocharger and free-flow intercoolers. PETER MEISSNER

The 997 Sport Classic cuts a period dash in the atrium of Porsche Center Gelderland, home to a private classic car collection as well as Official Porsche Center, restoration facility and Porsche Classic dealership. ANTONY FRASER

In just ten years Porsche Classic Center Gelderland, owned by Mark Wegh, has become one of the largest specialist dealerships in the world, selling an amazing twenty cars a week – classic and modern. Mark has just asked if I would like to drive a brand-new 911R, the sportiest road-focused (as opposed to track-biased) incarnation of the 991. And there was also a chance to get behind the wheel of the iconic 997 Sport Classic.

Mark is proud of his rapid success, starting from scratch in 2006. Clients come from all over the world to a state-of-the-art showroom that's full of the current product line-up, mainly in black and dark grey. Another showroom contains upwards of thirty classic Porsches, ranging from a 356 Carrera Spyder to 964 Carrera Cup NGT, all of which are for sale. I don't see a single one with a windscreen sticker price of less than €200,000, even the unrestored and deeply distressed 901 Maine barn-find, and especially not the pretty Gulf Blue 2.7 RS or the 356 Carrera Speedster.

Mark Wegh, proprietor of Porsche Center Gelderland, boasts a 100-strong private collection including this 356 Speedster. ANTONY FRASER

To the rear is a vast workshop with ten lifts bearing cars undergoing service or restoration. I contemplate a soft-window Targa hull installed on a jig, which looks like the kind of basket-case that would have been written off not so long ago, but the sums paid for air-cooled Porsches mean it will eventually run again. Mark's not fazed by the difficulties of sourcing increasingly rare parts:

Everything is out there to be found, though when you need it tomorrow then you have a problem. So when you're starting on a restoration like this you must already be searching for the parts you'll need. That's the mistake a lot of people make. They go looking for the parts only when they need them, and then it takes longer and it's more expensive.

I gaze in wonder at the space and cleanliness, but the real surprise is above on the first floor, where Mark houses his 100-strong collection of vehicles. They're not all Porsches (probably half are VWs), but without exception they are special and ultra-low mileage. There are plenty of high-end Porsche 911s, RSs, GT2s and GT3s, two 918 Spyders, plus rarities like a 901 masquerading as a wide-body SS, a Jäger-meister-Kremer RSR that came 9th at Le Mans in 1975, a 356 that's done the Mille Miglia – cars to die for. There are some touching counterpoints in the collection too: 'A few years ago, you could get front-engined Porsches virtually for free, and this 924 Turbo with only 30,000km cost €2,500.' Alongside it is the 928 CS given to Hans Stuck by the factory in recognition of his 1986 and 1987 Le Mans wins.

Cars are in Mark's DNA and he has been collecting them for more than twenty-five years. His favourite is a 356 Speedster, '41,000 miles, never repainted, only a new roof, the rest is completely original'.

I'm not going for the value of the car; the history and purpose of the car is my thing. I know a lot about the cars, and I like what I have. I have cars that are worth from €3,000 up to €300,000, but it's the story behind the car that's important, as well as low mileage. I like limited editions, or the first or the last in the line. I prefer to give more money for an untouched, un-restored car than a cheap car with a high mileage and then have to restore the car.

Unsurprisingly Mark also collects Porsche paraphernalia and scale-model 356s.

The car I'll be driving out of Mark's collection is a 997 Sport Classic, one of just 250 cars built, fitted with the six-speed manual transmission rather than an anachronistic

Triumphal trio: the 997 Sport Classic, 911R and 991 Carrera S outside Porsche Center Gelderland. ANTONY FRASER

PDK gearbox. Born in the heady days of Porsche's classic revival, when 911s of all ages were being furiously backdated, the 997 Sport Classic was introduced at Frankfurt in 2009 and went on sale from January 2010 priced at £140,000 in the UK. This car was first registered on 12 April 2012 and it's done 16,585km. Its stand-out features include a pert ducktail engine-lid spoiler, a pair of retro racing stripes over the roof and front lid, aluminium doors, Carrera GT Zaga-to-style double-bubble roof, a front panel bereft of splitter but retaining minimal lower air scoops sculpted below the valence, plus black grilles. The aerodynamic cut to the sills differs from the standard, and there are vents behind the rear wheel arches to dissipate the hot air from the brakes. The lights front and rear are subtly different, while the stone guards on the leading edges of the rear wheel arches are also in matching grey. The fuel cap purports to be classic alloy too. It runs on 19in factory-made Fuchs alloys, shod with Pirelli P-Zeroes, 235/35 ZR19 on the front and 305/30 ZR19 on the back, and the offset on the front rims manages to look right and not too shallow.

The Carrera S 3.8-litre flat-six develops 23bhp more than standard, giving 403bhp, achieved via modifications to the intake manifold, airflow and special exhaust system with split twin tailpipes. It's coupled to a short-shift six-speed manual gearbox, enabling a top speed of 187mph (300km/h); 0–62mph takes 4.6s. Under the ducktail there is a carbon air-intake box that describes itself as a Porsche Exclusive Power Kit. It's interesting to see something a little out of the ordinary inside a modern Porsche engine bay.

The 997 Sport Classic is fitted with decidedly non-classic ceramic composite brakes, a limited-slip differential and PASM sports suspension with 20mm lower ride-height and

The roadside scenery flashes by in a blur as the 997 Sport Classic whizzes through the country lanes of the central Netherlands. ANTONY FRASER

The Sport Classic gives a very taut ride, plus dazzling performance and secure handling around the bends. ANTONY FRASER

wider rear track clad in 44mm broader-beamed bodywork. Known as Sport Classic Grey, of course, the body colour – and the stripes for that matter – is a matter of taste; pale grey is a deliberate understatement, and the stripes are so pale you can only just make them out in certain lights. It is certainly different, and nothing like the ostentatious hues of the early 1970s RSs that the Sport Classic seeks to celebrate. I drop into the Espresso Brown woven leather and tweed cabin, instantly comfortable in the retro yet supportive Recaro seat. It's the work of moments to shuffle into the optimum driving position. I feel so at home here. First thing I notice is that there is a proper handbrake.

The racing stripes are echoed on the gear knob and the rev counter, too.

The basket weave seat upholstery is echoed in the door panels, so it's a largely brown interior. The rear seats are present as well, and the 911 Sport Classic legend is embossed in the headrests, scripted in chrome on the door sills, while on the glovebox it reveals that this car is number 106 out of a 250 Limited Edition run. From the outset, it's beautifully responsive on the throttle, and there's a different exhaust note as I ease through the gears.

For the most part we're on country lanes, but occasionally we hit a stretch of A-road – dualled, even – where I can

Cabin of the 911R, with Houndstooth-upholstered bucket seats, white stitching, carbon fibre strip across the dashboard, and plaque on glovebox lid.
ANTONY FRASER

open up the Sport Classic. It's a very taut ride, firm but not bonking over bumps. This is a fabulous car; it has the looks, the ergonomics and controls, plus dazzling performance and secure handling that enable me to say that, at last, I've discovered my ideal 911 … for now, anyway. It feels like my favourite armchair and it's powerful, handles superbly, and I might even see if I can replicate it in some way.

Back at the Classic Center, I'm handed the keys of Mark's own 911R, number 718. With a warning not to put too many kilometres on it, we ease out once again into the Gelderland countryside. As much as I'm smitten by the Sport Classic's trip down memory lane, at least in its cabin architecture, the R takes the nostalgia spree a stage further, offering substantially more purposeful competition-style seats upholstered in houndstooth tweed, but lacking electrical adjustment, and a harder-edged seating position and performance to boot. A carbon fibre strip across the dashboard provides a nod to modernity, while RS-style pull handles on the door take you back in time, with '911R' embossed in the headrests. There are no rear seats or half-cage, and I'm also sitting lower and closer to the steering wheel, more of an attack-the-Nordschleife posture.

The R has a similar double-bubble Carrera GT style roof to that of the Sport Classic, but the ducting goes the other way in the rear valance, and it's got reflectors and the different shaped 991 styling, plus the carbon detail on the door mirrors. The ten-spoke wheels carry Michelin Sport Pilot

Cups, 245/35 ZR 20s on the front and 305/30 ZR 20s on the back, with enormous RS discs and calipers visible behind the 20in wheels. This is a 991 GT3 RS in an older wolf's garb that somehow contrives to look modern, and of course it delivers scintillating performance, acceleration and the tautest ride and handling you could wish for in an on-road context. We take a loop around the intersecting polder back roads; for that reason, this isn't a full-on blast, but I am so glad to have driven it.

Is it a benchmark 911? It's what you'd expect, a hard-edged, up-to-the-minute GT3 RS, with retrospective looks to match. I don't have to travel far to appreciate the enormous volume of noise that fills the cabin as I power up the 4.0-litre 500bhp Mezger engine, snarling along the dykes and notching just the middle ratios of the six-speed gate. It's endowed with four-wheel steering geometry, so swings easily in and out of turns. It's alive from the start, and it's much more of a raw beast than the Sport Classic. On the other hand, having driven three of the original 911Rs from 1967 and 1968, I can discern no similarity whatsoever, apart from a certain raucous rawness. With those cars, R might just as well stand for 'Raw', not 'RennSport' or 'Race'. The new 991R dabbles in the nostalgia fountain, rather than fully immersing you. Who cares, this is what the state-of-the-art 911 has become, but for all that I don't quite like it as much as the quirkier 997 Sport Classic. That's the real deal, and possibly my favourite car in the whole book.

Roadside attraction: the 911 R is a hard-edged, up-to-the-minute version of an RS, with retrospective looks to match. AUTHOR

CHAPTER SEVEN

MOTORING WITH THE 997 AND 991

COUNT OF MONTE CRYSTALS

I've covered the Monte Carlo Rallye Historique eight times since 2008, following the action in my own Porsches and reporting on it for several Porsche magazines. Like the perennial rally crews, I'm drawn back every January, even though it'll probably mean standing out in the elements, ankle deep in snow in some godforsaken wilderness, culminating in that slithering haul round innumerable icy hairpins up to Col de Turini. It's just so fascinating, especially when there are always that many Porsches to follow. Variously, I've gone in my own 964 and Boxster, plus press Cayenne Turbo, and in 2010 I travelled with Antony Fraser aboard a 997 C4 Targa, enjoying a journey through wintertime in northern Europe and a blast of sunshine in Monaco at rally's end. Here's how it panned out.

A dearth of snow on most stages meant most of that year's competitors finished the event unscathed, though there was still unmelted ice and snow up in the Ardèche. It was another good year for Porsches, with fifty-six entered, mainly 911s and a sprinkling of 912 and 914/6s out of a total entry of 341 classic cars. To put that into historical perspective, works or works-supported Porsche participation brought wins in 1968 for Vic Elford and in 1969 and 1970 for Björn Waldegård, with Jean-Pierre Nicolas victorious in 1978 in a Carrera 3.0 prepared by the legendary Alméras Frères of Montpellier. It's hardcore,

Deep in the snowy Ardèche hill country, the 997 C4S Targa on a transit section between the Burzet stage and the Saint Agrève service halt. ANTONY FRASER

no doubt about it, and competitors who tackle the Monte Carlo Rallye Historique are brave souls. They're frequently travelling at speed on single-track roads over uncertain surfaces, against the clock, going at least a day or two with no sleep, and always battling the elements. Oh, and not forgetting the mechanical vagaries and esoteric handling of 40-year-old classics. Many of the more than 300 entrants return year after year because they're addicted to this heady formula, though in the teeth of a blizzard at midnight, the word 'masochists' springs to mind.

Four decades on from their 1969 and 1970 Porsche victories, Björn Waldegård and Lars Helmér topped the listings, posted in separate 911s by the cars' Stockholm-based owner Mauritz Lange. He'd recruited another Swedish veteran, Hans Sylvan, to co-drive Waldegård, while he himself took Helmér as navigator. This just had to be recorded for posterity, so we followed the event from start to finish in the 997 C4 Targa, kindly lent to us by Porsche GB.

With start points designated at Glasgow, Oslo, Copenhagen, Barcelona, Turin, Bad Homburg and Reims, we tagged along at Reims, pausing to snap our Ginger Targa beside the semi-restored Grand Prix pits complex. It may be a cliché,

but it's too good to miss; the ghosts of drivers and mechanics are undoubtedly abroad, and in traffic-free moments it's easy to conjure up the halcyon days of the 1950s. The competitors then wended their way to Monte Carlo before an about turn north to Valence on the River Rhône for a day's stages in the remote forested gorges of the Ardèche mountains. We made straight for Valence.

There was more snow in northern France than we'd left behind in southern England, but there were no dramas for our sure-footed 997 C4 Targa, and it gave us a decent five-and-a-half hour run to get the feel of the 997. The on-board economy meter showed a creditable 28.5mpg, cruising between 70 and 90mph (113–145km/h); we hadn't gone over 100mph in deference to traffic police. We tried it on the back roads with the Porsche Stability Management switched off just for the fun of it, but the 997 has so much traction that even in the snow it isn't really necessary: the mark of a good chassis is how much control it provides without the electronics switched on. It's supple, yet broad shouldered like an all-in wrestler. Even though I'm a lifelong adherent of the manual box, the PDK auto transmission is uncannily intuitive, spot on in exactly the right gear at the right time

The 911 Ts of Bjorn Waldegård/Hans Sylvan and Mauritz Lange/Lars Helmer pull out of a layby near Sisteron after a routine service on a transit section of the Monte Carlo Rallye Historique. ANTONY FRASER

in any situation, power on or off. It's also operable via finger and thumb shifts when needs must on the steering wheel, selecting manual mode by flicking the lever left. Not having to have clutch control on steep hills has its advantages as well: you put it in D, press your foot down and off you go without the jerkiness that you sometimes get with clutches. How to have a good time in the snow? Manual mode, 2nd gear with traction control off; there's enough power to break traction without having to go very fast. Plus, we've got winter tyres: everyone should keep a set somewhere in the garage, mounted on a spare set of wheels.

In the 1970s studded tyres were highly controversial. Several different types were in use – spikes, chisels and studs – with differing quantities embedded in tyres according to weather conditions. While the AC de Monaco sanctioned them, local councils through which the rally would be passing objected on the grounds that 300 rally cars on studs would tear up their tarmac. So, pre-Monte, chaos reigned while teams juggled service arrangements and numbers of tyres required from suppliers and the organizers dithered, finally allowing that studs would be legal when the reluctant council capitulated, just a fortnight before the start. In 2011 the Norwegian 911SC crew Tore Berntsen and Lasse Hansen drove from Copenhagen on studs and elected to keep them on throughout the rally, as Lasse explained:

> there's so much better traction with studded tyres, even though they wear down quickly on bare tarmac. A fresh set gives you so much more grip on icy sections. On the other hand, another red SC [Aril Amundsen and Anstein Hagen] came down with us from Copenhagen with no studded tyres at all, and they really regretted that as they were having a very difficult time.

Where snow is guaranteed, winter tyres matter, and in Germany they're a legal requirement: your insurance is invalid in the event of an altercation without them. They're also essential when covering the Monte Carlo Rally. My 964 was shod with Nokian Hakkapelittas and my 986 Boxster S runs on Vredestein Snowtracs, though as things turned out in 2010, we encountered very little snowy action.

The day we'd saved by not belting down to Monaco was spent on a reconnaissance of the Ardèche stages, getting back into Valence for a rendezvous with the Swedish teams and the first of two hilarious evenings at the Bistrot-des-Clercs in the medieval heart of the city.

The array of classic cars in the expansive Champ de Mars next morning ranged from Alpine-Renault A110s and A310s, homespun Renault-Gordini R8 and Simca 1100, BMW 2002,

Winter wonderland: with all-wheel drive and winter tyres, the 997 C4S Targa is much at home in the snowy Vercors mountains. ANTONY FRASER

Opel Kadett and Mercedes-Benz tin-tops, to more focused Fiat 124 Spider and Lancia Fulvias, easy-riding Citroëns Light 15, SM and DS, plus a smattering of small-engined exotica like Autobianchi, Steyr-Puch, NSU, Ami 6 and a DKW that leaned precariously through the turns. The retinue was led away by Marc Duez in a big red Healey, with Bruno Saby an early starter in his perversely matt-black Alpine A110, and former GP star Eric Comas not far behind in another French blue one. Numbered 5 and 6, the Swedes' 911s were also in the vanguard, so once they were away we headed for the vast limestone escarpment to catch them on a stage.

You can't watch every stage if you hope to see one or two specific cars, because you'll miss them on the next one, plus we hoped to see the maintenance crew in action at a service

The 997 C4S Targa on the transit section between Burzet stage and Saint Agrève service halt during the 2010 Monte Carlo Rallye Historique. ANTONY FRASER

halt. We made our way up to St Cheylard and over to an access road we'd earmarked leading to the second regularity stage, Burzet, and settled in at a wiggly section of country lane where there was a foot or so of snow, with mostly clear tarmac but ice and slush on bends untouched by the sun. There was time to take stock. The backdrop of forested gorges and triangular peaks contrasted with dazzling white meadows populated by a few horses and cattle. The 997's temperature gauge revealed it was −6°C and I was grateful for thermals and parka.

Soon the course cars raced by, clearing the way for the competitors. Rasping race engines droned in the distance, growing closer with each gearchange. Even after the first stage they'd got out of sequence: first up came a Simca 1100 wearing number 7, then a Mustang hove into view. The Duez Healey had been an early leader but fell back with mechanical problems, and then the Swedish 911s appeared, the orange car leading the red one by several minutes. Such are the rigours of regularities that most cars bimbled past at jaunting pace. When we met the retinue after Burzet we were caught up by the very cars we'd just seen go by on the stage: the snarling orange 911 blasted past, followed by an R5 and an Alpine A110. Cars slithered this way and that, and some, spotting our lenses, stepped out the back end, just for us. They were going like hell and it was all we could do to stick with them through the serpentine B-roads winding up to Saint Agrève. We were living the dream!

Even major work has to be done at impromptu road-side halts because the paddocks are parc fermé – at Valence that's the expansive Champ de Mars formal public gardens and at Monaco it's the harbour front that serves as the F1 pits and garages at Grand Prix time. Out in the boondocks,

Motoring along the Route Napoleon beside the River Var, the 997 C4S Targa is a sublime grand touring car. ANTONY FRASER

The Monte Carlo Rallye Historique follows in the tyre tracks of the big-time FIA rally, and many of the villages still have the banners promoting the event still in place, as at Saint Agrève in the Ardèche. ANTONY FRASER

like at Saint Agrève, snow-filled lay-bys, village squares or fuel station forecourts are taken over, setting up as much as an hour before their charges come hurtling through. The little marketplace at Saint Agrève was packed with crews and admin cars, so many teams elected to do running repairs out in the country, ad hoc, on the way to the next stage at St Bonnet-le-Froid.

A couple of stages had been cancelled in the Alpes Maritimes coming up from Monaco, snow restricting visibility to a few feet, but not this one. Luckily this looping stage didn't present too much trouble. As the tortuous route wound its way south-east for the Lamastre to Abloussière stage the snow petered out except in the wooded bits where icy hazards lurked. These rustic roads incorporated every possible camber change, pothole and deformity, occasionally through farmyards and most of the time with a sheer drop to one side or the other. Gaps between cars ranged from thirty seconds to a couple of minutes, with a few overtakes witnessed. Then it was back to Valence for a return match with the Swedes.

Peter Bergqvist was organizing the servicing schedule and showed us where, two hours down the route, we could rendezvous to watch the action. Playing safe we were up at 5.00am to catch their start from the Champ de Mars. Leaving them to their own devices, the two service vans, followed by our 997, rushed south-east through Crest, Die and Digne-les-Bains, pulling into a snow-lined lay-by at dawn near Sisteron to await their charges. Two mechanics to a car, they were refuelled, oiled, screens cleaned, systems checked, limbs stretched, and powered away for the day's second – and last stage – at Villars-sur-Var before the run down to Èze.

Everyone should drive this bit: it's without doubt the most stunning scenery on the Route Napoleon. Perpendicular crags and pinnacles form gateways to the gorge of the River Var. Overhanging cliffs have been undercut to accommodate the road, lofty bridges taking it from one flank to another, swathed in netting like a collage of giant hammocks to halt rock falls. Huge pendant icicles decorate tunnel roofs and clad sheltered cliffs like frozen waterfalls. It presents the ultimate sports car challenge, following the route Napoleon took across the Alpes Maritimes, from Cannes to Grenoble,

after he escaped from Elba in March 1815. The network of roads he used, covering 350km in seven days, became known collectively in 1932 as the Route Napoleon and they offer some of the finest driving in Europe.

It's no coincidence that the Monte Carlo Rally uses stretches of it between stages, though we're doing it the opposite way to the Imperial march, heading south-east from Valence to where the Route hooks up into the Alps proper at Digne-les-Bains. We parked some 50 or 60ft above the River Var to snap the rally cars belting through a tunnel. The 997 made short, thrilling work of one last hairpin climb before the descent to the Autoroute at Nice and the duck-down to Èze time control.

At the Èze check-in area, dazed by the warm Mediterranean sunshine, there was time to take stock of our vehicle. Its paddle shifters are stationary on the column (as opposed to buttons, which turn with the wheel) and these are more practical in the heat of the moment; PDK is also idiot-proof as it will revert to auto if you forget where you are with the paddle switches. In manual mode it lapped up most of the hairpins in 2nd, though 1st was sometimes useful on the tightest and blindest. Being four-wheel drive you can't use the swing-out tail as a means of getting round the corner as there's just too much grip, unless there's snow on the ground. The winter tyres are progressive too, complement-

Paused beside the Route Napoleon, the 997 C4S Targa takes a break while Fraser snaps the rally cars in transit – in this case the 911 that placed 2nd. AUTHOR

ing the chassis in their communicativeness. Steering is light, though lacking in feeling compared to an old 911. Turn-in is spot on and you can get on the throttle early and streak out the other side of the bend. Brakes are fantastic and the ride is equally refined, soaking up the backstage potholes with no trouble. It's so competent that you can afford to stretch its legs and see just how fast it might be, especially where the roads are a bit more open.

Spurning the harbourside parc fermé and the one-by-one starting ramp, we hurled the 997 up the endless hairpins to the Cols de Madonie, Braus and Turini to catch the spectacular night stages. The longest was 60km, and with very little snow or ice on the roads it was strictly regularity. As much as it's an arduous rally stage, Turini is also a social gathering. The Monte's like that: anything can happen. Soon a klaxon sounds, and we don't have long to wait before the cars come through, exhausts crackling in the crisp night air, batteries of spotlights piercing the darkness, matched by a haphazard fusillade of camera flashes. How come the drivers

aren't blinded by this, and how come we're not run down? Freezing snow-melt causes black ice and it's even tricky to walk, which makes the competitors' rapid pace even more awesome. A 924 Turbo spins, though the 911s scuttle past with varying degrees of drama.

It's hypnotic, but also cold, so after an hour we pull the plug and head downhill in the 997 during a break in the running to claim a different vantage point. Now there came a succession of cars we'd not seen before – Volvo 122 and 144, Stratos, 924, Giulietta, VW notchback, Matra Djet, Saab 99 and Sonnet, and a two-stroke 96 that backfired eerily through the forest. God, it was cold. But worth it. By 1.00am the stragglers had petered out, so we made the hour's run back to Monaco where latecomers were still making their way to parc fermé.

A sunny stroll mid-morning between the assembled ranks of classics revealed mercifully few casualties, unlike 2009, when black ice on Turini caught out most, and even Vic Elford's 911 succumbed. Björn Waldegård was less than

Sunset over Monte Carlo: the 997 C4S Targa heads up the mountains towards La Bollène-Vésubie and Col de Turini. ANTONY FRASER

The 997 C4S Targa makes the obligatory pit stop on Reims' restored Grand Prix circuit start-finish straight. ANTONY FRASER

enamoured of the timing situation. Though navigator Sylvan struggled occasionally with their new on-board clocks and trip-meters, they felt too much pressure from the official timekeepers who hurried them on, anxious to stick to schedules. There were no time cards to stamp like the 'olden days' and no means of matching their own calculations against those of the organizers. Times change. In 2018 I followed Jürgen Barth and Roland Kussmaul in their 924 Carrera GTS. Like the majority of crews, they relied on the latest Blunik device, which tells them exactly how fast they need to be going on a stage, and even the lines through the corners for best effect. It's a compact system for maintaining segment and connection section times accurately, specifically in regularity rallies. It embodies a clock, chronometer, speedometer, odometer, speed table, calculator and calibrator in a single device. It enables the navigator to view total and partial distance, average and instantaneous speed, time and distance remaining to finish the sector, with a constant display of the sensor readings. Significantly, it displays the regularity maintenance numerically, so that, if it shows a negative number, the driver needs to accelerate. Conversely, if it's a positive number then he must brake. If it shows 00 he's going perfectly. It allows the crew to schedule regularity segments, with or without changes of average, connection sections, and memorizes different calibrations.

Classic Porsches make great historic rally cars, though regularities are a different discipline entirely from the halcyon days that Elford and Larrousse emulated a decade ago on the Monte retrospective, casually racking up the penalties without a care. Late morning next day, bleary-eyed competitors begin to drift into parc fermé to check out the results, declared official at midday. Waldegård and Sylvan were surprised to be down at 29th overall. Mauritz Lange

and Lars Helmér were 219th, legacy of a detached gear lever that meant doing a whole stage in 2nd gear. Instead of copying the 911 victories of 1968 through 1970, the regularity spoils were carried off this particular year by an innocuous (and frequent victor) Opel Kadett GTE. A 911 did finish 2nd, however: the 1965 2.0 car of Mario Sala and Maurizio Torlasco. In fact, to make it to the finish is an achievement in itself, so we headed for a celebratory tipple at the Tip Top. Thus mollified, we climbed into our Targa and headed for home.

CANAL DREAMS: 997 TURBO CABRIOLET

Blasted by blizzards, we barge into Scotland with a 997 Turbo Cabriolet by way of the Cumbrian and Northumbrian fells and the Cheviot Hills. Not surprisingly, we get what we deserve: a dump of snow and an abundance of ungritted roads – the perfect formula for another memorable road trip. At least the canopy is weather-tight.

Starting and finishing at Porsche GB's Reading HQ, the drive is intended to take in two civil engineering icons: the Falkirk Wheel, located midway between Edinburgh and Glasgow, and the restored Anderton Boat Lift, near Northwich in Cheshire. Both edifices hoist pleasure boats up and down the height of a five-storey block, from one waterway to another, and I am curious to see what these colossuses are like in the metal.

Launched in November 2009, the seventh-generation 911 Turbo delivers 500bhp from its new 3.8-litre, direct-injection, twin-turbo flat-six, up almost 25bhp on its predecessor. While coupés can be ordered with PDK transmission, our Cabriolet comes with six-speed manual, which means no paddle shifts or 'SportPlus Launch Control' – and it's all the better for that, bearing in mind that the pure 911 experience is supposed to be about feel and character. On the whole, it's a neat, articulate shift, especially through the higher gears, but I never quite master a baulky third-to-second downchange, or the throttle-versus-clutch balance when pulling away in first, ending up with too much of both. This clutch is quick to bite, so there's a tendency to overcompensate on the throttle. The other minor frustration is the reluctance of the driver's seat memory to retain its settings; whenever it's unoccupied, it reverts to the default cramped position. Top speed is a claimed 194mph (312km/h), with 0–60mph accomplished in a lag-free 3.7s. The dashboard digital readout says it's returning 24mpg at legal road speeds, though more enthusiastic driving drops this to 20mpg.

The Turbo is a broad-shouldered bruiser, and the soft-top 997 is not as pretty as a Boxster, but it's still an exquisite

Twilight of the Gods: taking the turns in the Meteor Grey 997 Turbo Cabriolet as dusk falls. With heater at full blast the cabin is still warm enough to have the top down. ANTONY FRASER

sports car with stonking performance, the sense of exhilaration amplified by the unfettered blue-sky view, with no hint of wind buffeting or scuttle shake to mar the experience. Its Meteor Grey finish has unremitting grey upholstery. The overall impression is muted and the cockpit cries out for a touch of loud leather to echo its sheer pulling power, though the fabric roof with smaller rear windows makes the cabin more cosseting than the coupé. Where we're going, the Porsche's ground-gripping arsenal of four-wheel drive, trac-

tion control, Active Suspension Management and Porsche Torque Vectoring, which caps understeer by moderating the inner rear-wheel brake in cornering, inspires confidence, and I need every weapon I've got to keep us stuck to the road.

A 5.00am start means we're in Cumbria by breakfast. Sleet turns to snow as we blow through northern England, sweeping horizontally towards us like a hail of bullets. Taking a deep breath, we forsake the A1 for the gorgeous A696 and A68 routes that wind up through the Cheviots to Jedburgh. Roadside pines pale under their icing-sugar dusting, and the 997's grey camouflage disappears into the heavy-laden sky. The two-way roads are slushy from a recent salting, although the central strip over the white line is still powdery enough to deter overtaking, while the multiplicity of speed cameras encountered once into Scotland forbids it altogether. Fortunately there are still plenty of twists and turns to revel in the Turbo's indefatigable thirst for freedom, its flawless handling, solid ride and, when summoned, that violent power delivery. The Turbo's sound effects department has an entertaining addition to the flat-six repertoire. The whistle generated on a trailing throttle is reminiscent of wind shrilling round a pylon, a beguiling noise that I provoke as often as possible.

Just over the Scottish border at Carter Bar, a truck in the ditch alongside a straight section provides pause for thought. We fill up in Jedburgh, pass through Lauderdale and head on towards the Lammermuir and Moorfoot Hills, south of Edinburgh. The grim country is home to sheep, deer and a few stationary grouse. It's clear enough to see the whit-

Backdrop for the 997 Turbo Cabriolet, the spectacular Falkirk Wheel hoists barges and river craft, rotating to a height of 75ft (23m), from the Forth and Clyde Canal to the Union Canal. ANTONY FRASER

ened slopes, but hilltops are shrouded in cloud. After the Edinburgh ring-road, we take the faster M9 to the exit for Falkirk, where the Porsche's satnav guides us to the Wheel.

It's vast, an ingenious engineering sculpture whose 75ft (23m) high stainless-steel rotor hovers above the canal basin, giant talons clawing the air as its caissons rotate from one watery level to another like a giant food blender in slow motion. At the upper level, the aqueduct channel is supported on a series of five hoops to create an illusory tunnel, which rises off piers that gain height as they march down the hillside. Conventionally, the job would be done by a flight of locks, but the Falkirk Wheel performs the lift in one semicircular motion. It's open to waterway traffic every day except Christmas Day and, right on cue, a couple of boats perform the elliptical orbit as we clean the car. And then another blizzard promptly dumps on us. Nevertheless, the Porsche gets admiring glances from Wheel visitors who

want to know if it's a Carrera. We put them right with a guide round the engine lid's Turbo badge and distinguishing air scoops in the rear wings. As dusk falls the Wheel is transformed by coloured lenses changing every half-minute: blue morphing to yellow, green to magenta, reflecting carnival-style in the water.

Nocturnal snaps taken, we retrace our snow-laden tracks and the Turbo's headlights pierce the gloaming, reflecting off the predominantly white Borders landscape. Above 15mph (20km/h) the 997's front corner spotlights come on, revealing the kerbs and verges just a little bit better. Thanks to more thorough gritting, our pace improves at Coldstream and we push on to our Geordie home-from-home.

More snow's fallen, so it's an early start for the 200-mile (320km) journey to Cheshire. The scheme is to traverse the country from north-east to south-west via Hexham, Alston and Penrith. That way, we'll really get to grips with the wind

Light show: Falkirk Wheel illuminations spotlight the cockpit of the 997 Turbo Cabriolet, showing supportive seats, manual shift, satnav and sculpted steering wheel arms. ANTONY FRASER

Motoring through Gilderdale Forest near Alston, Cumbria, in the 997 Turbo Cabriolet; its all-wheel drive enabled safe progress on the county lanes. ANTONY FRASER

and weather. We cross Hadrian's Wall to pick up the trans-moorland A686 at Haydon Bridge, and instantly it's a grit-free zone. The higher we climb, the deeper it gets, yet the Porsche plugs gamely on. Firs droop with snow and the dry-stone walls criss-crossing the moors exaggerate the whiteness. All our Porsche traction control systems are working feverishly, the secret on-board army apportioning a bit of drive here, a little rallentando there. I stab the brake to feel for grip, in case we're actually riding on sheet ice beneath the snow. Not yet, apparently. To try and gauge the limits still further, a burst of power has the back-end twitching, though it's eminently controllable. Next step, press the Sport button, just for the hell of it, but that's not such a great idea, after all. By the time we're up on the tops around Whitfield Moor, I'm fairly confident we'll get through.

The sun's out, so we're living the rag-roof dream, top down, coats on and heater belting out max therms. The 997 Cabriolet's one-switch system for retracting the soft top is entertainingly efficient: dip your left wrist, finger the switch up and the mechanism springs into action. First the windows drop, and immediately the hood unclips itself from the windscreen header-rail, eases backwards overhead like a concertina, to be swallowed neatly in the gaping maw that's opened in the rear scuttle. The door windows do a double shuffle and emerge in the up position. To re-erect it, simply press the switch down for the duration of the action – a repeat performance in reverse. It won't operate above 30mph (48km/h), but on a snowbound fell road in a sudden blizzard that counts as excess speed, in any case. You can't do a road trip in a drop-top and not do the deed. But up on the Northumbrian moors?

Closer to Alston the gritters have been out. After Hartside Top there are serious corners to contend with. The flu-

Slide rules: an opportunity for a wheelie in the 997 Turbo during a pit stop at Hartside Top Café on the A686, the highest café in England at 1,904ft (580m) above sea level, on the return run from the Falkirk Wheel. ANTONY FRASER

ency of the Turbo's four-wheel-drive chassis and the adhesion of its 235/35 and 305/30 × 19in low-profile Michelins through the tight corners enables mind-bogglingly rapid progress between Alston and Penrith. It goes precisely where I point it, and any over-anticipation of apex or radius is instantly correctable. Instant gobbets of power have us hurtling breathless towards the next corner – proving again and again that this is a first-class sports car working out on one of the country's top driving roads. If there is a downside, it's the cacophony of road noise emanating from the broad tyres, loud enough to smother the mellifluous flat-six burble except when on full throttle. The tyre din varies in volume according to smoothness of surface, and their squat profiles make for a choppy ride on a rough road.

Down at Hexham, we eschew the motorway and take the A6 for Shap. The snow has yet to arrive here, so progress is swift as we shadow the M6 on a thrilling blast along sweeping curves up and over the northern Lakeland hills and down to Kendal, before joining the M6 motorway at Carnforth.

Anderton is not far from Northwich. With a little help from TomTom, the on-board satnav brings us straight to the water's edge. Like the skeleton of a cathedral nave made out of cylindrical metal poles, the recently renovated boat lift is another monumental engineering feat, dating from 1875. The stewards kindly let us bring the Turbo close to the giant trusses for a photo op, just as a pair of narrowboats glide into the lower caisson, ready for their 50ft (15m) aerial journey.

It's a slower ascent compared with the modern motion we witnessed at Falkirk, but canal dreams are best leisurely paced. Fast is for fools on these waterways. Reopened in March 2002 after a six-year, £7 million renovation programme, the 150-year-old Anderton Lift raises and lowers vessels 50ft between the lower-level River Weaver and the higher Trent and Mersey Canal. The principle is the same as for using a lock: an ascending boat slides into the original 252-tonne caisson tank and, as one water-filled trough elevates, so the other descends. It would need a flight of at least five normal locks to achieve the same elevation with economical use of water. The first Anderton lift was constructed in 1875 to serve local salt mining and, later, chemical industry freighters. It consisted of the bare bones of the present structure, but employed a hydraulic ram to elevate and lower the pair of caissons containing the barges, coasters and narrowboats. The problem was that the river water was saline and corrosive, so in 1908 an upper deck was erected carrying the cogs and pulley wheels driven by electric motors suspended over the sides of the frame on new buttressing stanchions. The structure fell into disuse in 1981, but then the restored lift reverted to the hydraulic principle, making the top-deck apparatus redundant.

Ancient and modern: the 2009 997 Turbo beside Cheshire's 19th-century Anderton Boat Lift. ANTONY FRASER

With the Christmas exodus in prospect, there's a new urgency about our southbound progress. When you really want to go for it, the car is of a similar mind. The new Turbo has proved itself entertaining and hugely capable on as wide a range of roads and traffic conditions as you could wish for. But is it a vastly better performer than its predecessor? For now, the elements decree that has to be taken on trust, though given the fun we've had, I can't think of any other car I'd rather have driven northwards, westwards and back again, with the lid off, anyway.

A BIT OF R&R

The original 911R is a potent legacy to live up to: fifty years on I tracked the RennSport recipe at Abbeville Circuit, courtesy of Johan Dirickx, who loves nothing better than to drive his Porsches in the manner for which they were designed. His favourite venue for this activity is Abbeville circuit in northern France, and I have been invited to join him

there to sample the 911R, along with its latest stablemate, a recently acquired 991R, sibling of the one I drove at OPC Gelderland (*see* Chapter 6).

Back in 1967 Porsche's race director Ferdinand Piech delivered his opening salvo on the 911's inexorable pathway to on-track invincibility in the shape of the 911R. There are no two ways about it: the R is a spartan competition car and one of the rarest of 911 derivatives, with just twenty cars bearing the RennSport R chassis number. The specification included the 210bhp 901/22 engine (similar to the 901/20 Carrera Six), which meant it was technically a prototype and thus eligible only for the GTP class on the international stage. At the time it was categorized by the FIA as a Group 4 car, requiring a maximum of fifty units built in twelve consecutive months, compared with a minimum of 500 units built in a year for the 911S in Group 3 race trim. The factory race department retained six of the twenty 911Rs, and the remaining fourteen units were sold to privateers.

Johan's 911R is one of the six factory cars, commissioned in June 1967, chassis 11899002 R, and completed on 6

Two generations of 911R: the 991 acknowledges a debt to its 1967 ancestor, the pared-to-the-bone racer. ANTONY FRASER

November 1967. It debuted in Vic Elford's hands the following month at a Hockenheim press day, and was retained by the factory as a test and race car until invoiced on 29 September 1969 to Dr Mario Daolio, a motor racing fan practising in Asmara, Eritrea, then under Ethiopian rule. As far as Johan knows, his 911R was campaigned only once, in the XII Circuito di Taulud road race at Massaua, Eritrea, driven by Nino Ronzoni (Eritrean champion from 1951 to 1956). Johan bought it in 2010 for the JFD Collection and a complete engine rebuild was implemented at 911Motorsport, Antwerp.

Back in the day, the 911R's power output was quoted at 210bhp. In a very light, narrow bodyshell, tipping the scales at less than 900kg, that is a potent mix that took radical surgery and wilfully minimalist construction to achieve. Every panel except the basic shell was replaced with fibreglass items. Bumpers, valances, front and rear lids, doors and front wings are all in resin, while the door window frames are aluminium, the panes glued in with silicone, and the engine lid hung with the simplest of hinges. There are no door liners, no roof lining and leather thongs hold up the windows. Distinctive louvred air vents in the plastic rear three-quarter windows each have a little drip tray to catch rain ingress. There's no radio or glove compartment, no cigarette lighter, minimal carpeting over the side sills, and the simplest of rollover hoops, braced from the rear seat mounts. Sidelights are sim-

ple aftermarket items, and indicators are sourced from the contemporary NSU 1000 TT. What appeals as an intriguing concoction today was simply a pared-to-the-bone racer in 1967. I mention this because it's the spec that Porsche paid homage to when it introduced the limited edition 911R in 2017. Fifty years on, unsurprisingly the Rs are as different as chalk and cheese.

Clearly Johan is a huge fan of the 911R, and placed an order when he heard that a retrospective GT3-type model boasting a manual gearbox was on the stocks at Zuffenhausen. Soon enough he learned it would be the limited edition 991R, commemorating the fiftieth birthday of the 911R. Out of the production run of 991 cars, Johan was keen that the chassis number of his new 991R would match his 911R, which meant it would have to be 002 991, but Porsche explained that number 2 was reserved for the CEO, so instead Johan decided to go for 603 because his first RS was 1603. Then came the delicate matter of matching the hue of the 911R. There are many shades of white on the Porsche palette, and in consort with Andreas Preuninger he settled on a light ivory with matching mirrors, and a racier red for the stripes than worn by other 991Rs. There's a reference to the old car's chassis number in the new one's door sills, too, so that, as he explains, 'Basically, they are a pair now, we cannot separate them; they are like twins, with 50 years' difference.'

On the track these Rs are from opposite ends of the vehicular spectrum. Let's take the 911R. After ten minutes' frenetic lappery Johan's got it well warmed up, and I can head out on track too, where it's a joy to handle such a properly sorted car. Vivid acceleration accompanied by that aggressive snarl, rising to fever pitch as the revs soar to 7,000rpm in each gear. The handling's equally sharp and turn-in taut as I balance it through the bends, perfectly weighted steering making it a joy to swing from corner to corner. It's pretty stiff, though inevitably there's an element of period 1960s roll. But what a beautiful 911 this is, so responsive and so chuckable, and all the while I'm treated to that manic roar of the on-the-cam 2.0-litre flat-six. It's agile, precise, and there's loads of grip, with plenty of feedback. As I brake the car pivots itself on the front end, the back-end sticks, thanks to its Dunlop Green Spot tyres, which match the R's short chassis geometry, and round it goes. No doubt this tight circuit suits its abilities very nicely.

The 991R is a different matter altogether. It dabbles in nostalgia rather than imparting the full immersion provided by its senior sibling. Take the cabin, which is dominated by houndstooth-upholstered competition-style seats that lack electrical adjustment. A carbon fibre strip across the dashboard provides a nod to modernity, while RS-style pull-handles on the door-cards take you back in time, and the '911R' embossed in the headrests remind you of what you're sitting in. There are no rear seats and no half-cage. It has to be viewed not as a trackable GT3-style car but as a consummate old-school grand tourer. It's a wonderful seating position, and the houndstooth seats are firm and supportive, gripping me at the midriff. I'm relatively close to the wheel, and the relationship of feet-to-pedals and to steering wheel and shift-lever feels spot on. The tops of the front wings provide a tantalizing frame viewed through the sides of the windscreen. A badge identifies this car as a tribute to 11899002R, Johan's other R, and as number 603 out of 991. The ten-spoke wheels carry Michelin Sport Pilot Cups, 245/35 ZR 20s on the front and 305/30 ZR 20s on the back, with enormous RS discs and calipers visible behind the 20in wheels.

Even with my lid on it takes less than half a lap to appreciate the enormous cacophony that fills the cabin, road car or not, as I stoke up the 4.0-litre 500bhp Mezger engine, snarling around the twists and turns using just the 2nd and 3rd ratios of the six-speed gate. It's alive from the start, and its four-wheel steering geometry ensures it swings easily in and out of the corners. It's a supremely responsive car, but with the best will in the world you could never describe it as raw, in the same way that the original R wears its heart on its sleeve. In fact, having driven four of the

Little and large: 50 years separate the two incarnations of the 911R. In terms of driving experience there is no comparison: one is a totally raw race car, the other refined and sophisticated. ANTONY FRASER

Complexity versus simplicity: the broad-beamed tail end of the 991-based 911R harbours aerodynamic aids, while the 1967 911R offers lightweight fibreglass panels perspex windows and minimal aftermarket sidelights. ANTONY FRASER

Taking a turn at the wheel of the 911R at Abbeville Circuit in northern France. The relationship of feet-to-pedals and between steering wheel and shift lever feels spot on. ANTONY FRASER

original twenty 911Rs in recent years, I can discern no similarity whatsoever with their modern namesake. If you need proof, check out the 991R's cup holders. But who cares: this is what the state-of-the-art 911 has become – a special edition GT3 with the manual shift that the model was denied until very recently.

Does the 991R live up to the legend, or is it just a cash-in special? Obviously it has almost nothing in common with the 911R, physically or conceptually. How could it, when everything, from automotive technology to safety legislation, construction methodology and racing regulations, not

to mention marketing objectives, has moved on so far? Five decades is a long time, so it's small wonder that the 991R is a descendant of the original R in badge only. Nevertheless, it's a very fine car in every respect.

KIWI CAPERS

This could be the ultimate road trip: a whistle-stop 1,700km (1,060-mile) tour of New Zealand's beautiful South Island. Highway heaven, indeed. It's January, and New Zealand's summertime climate is balmy, traffic is light, even though it's peak holiday season, flora and fauna are amazing, nothing bites or stings, and the only snaking is the sublime hill roads. And to top it all, I've been let loose in a 997 C4S. Porsche paradise!

My son Alfie was living in Nelson at the top of the South Island and demanding a visit, so this was combined with an offer from Brent Jones, who had just finished making a replica of the 911 RSR R7 that finished 4th at Le Mans in 1973, to lend us his 997 for a week's sightseeing around South Island's beauty spots.

As well as an itinerary, Brent's briefing includes instructions on how to operate the radar detecting devices installed in the 997, something of a necessity for inveterate speeders on account of the national limit of 100km/h (62mph) – and the New Zealand cops don't mess about. Thus primed, we set off from Christchurch on the main A1 east coast highway, which is mostly two-lane north-to-south with passing lanes, flanked by a single-track railway line and the Pacific beaches about 5km (3 miles) over to the right. Traffic is relatively heavy, much of it going our way because the road further north is still out of use following the November 2016 earthquake at Kaikoura.

We turn off left at Waipara and head for the Lewis Pass on State Highway 7. I'm glad of the radar detector, because the cops are vigilant and several times the apparatus alerts us of surveillance. Not that we're going particularly fast, it's more to do with habitual wariness. It bleeps, I slow to well below the speed limit and around

A road trip around New Zealand's spectacular South Island in a 997 C4S was one of the best ever, here parked up by Lake Wanaka. AUTHOR

An example of New Zealand's charming timber-framed buildings, the Historic Empire Hotel at Ross, a tempting overnighter for the 997 C4S. LAURA DRYSDALE

the corner there's the Holden patrol car. We're on sweeping driving roads through the valley so we press on to the spa resort of Hanmer Springs.

We hit the road early. The route heads on up to Maruia Falls, meandering beside the river and interspersed with a few hairpins approaching the summit of Lewis Pass. There's a real feeling of passing into a different weather system crossing from east to west, and suddenly we're in the clouds, driving through a forest of black beech.

Large yellow advisory speed signs preface many corners, and a bend involving the slightest difficulty will have a sign with a recommended velocity for you to negotiate it at, ranging from an 85km/h sweeper to a 15km/h hairpin. Like all New Zealand road signs, they've been in kilometres since the country went decimal in 1967 – so we're in a right-hand-drive 997 with a speedo in km/h. As for these suggested speeds, it's possible to better them by some way in a four-wheel-drive 911. I might drop it into 5th for a '65km/h' bend and hoof it round at 85km/h, just for the hell of it, but in any case the C4S chassis takes everything in its stride.

Down from the higher slopes the climate changes and we're seeing enormous ferns again. We've got the road pretty much to ourselves as it's winding through the forest, mostly beech, birch and fir. Now and again, beside the river we see abandoned coal mining settlements. At Reefton there's a living facsimile of a miners' encampment, where they're trying to promote a town that was on its knees after mining, of both coal and gold, finished in 1951.

It's 415km (258 miles) from Christchurch to Nelson on

this particular route. The Buller Gorge heads north via Murchison on the 69 and then the 6 to Nelson, where there's a plethora of amazing plants and birds, including the sonorous Bellbirds. A mellow breeze counters the glorious summer heat. Further up the coast on the 60 we crash at a cosy backpackers' at Collingwood on Golden Bay – glorious beaches, tidelines higgledy-piggledy with washed up driftwood.

As we approach Westport on the Tasman Sea coast, the vegetation becomes lusher with masses of tree ferns. A limestone escarpment beside the Buller River features huge cliffs and overhangs to our left and there are single-file cuttings to negotiate. The road twists and turns endlessly along the craggy coastline with glimpses of black sand to our right, the cliffs all covered in bush.

We climb the lighthouse at Cape Foulwind and a little further on we pause among the tourists to view the amazing Punakaiki Pancake Rocks, incredible layered limestone formations jutting out into the sea where they've been sliced and undercut over millions of years. You would not want to get caught in the tidal surges, currents and blowholes here. The main road's pretty straight now down to Greymouth, an aptly named port serving a mining community where the Grey River flows into the Tasman Sea. We're billeted in the bush in an Airbnb caravan: it's snug, but gusting winds and the rain pelting on the tin roof make it impossible to hear the telly! So much for the privations of camping.

Next day it's brightened up, the sky's blue and the road has flattened out, with a bank of exotic trees on one side and sea on the other. Broad rivers are in full spate, churning milky-water channels and grey pebble eyots, mostly spanned by single-track bridges, sometimes shared with the railway

Filling stations are not numerous down the west coast of the South Island, so brimming the tank when half full was a precautionary measure, carried out here at Whataroa. LAURA DRYSDALE

line. A short distance south is the artisan town of Hokitika, where jade jewellery, hand-blown glass and greenstone are crafted into shapes that apparently all mean something in Maori folklore.

At modest main road speeds the 997 is proving economical but, mindful of a potential absence of filling stations the further south we go, we refuel at Ross. It becomes hillier and the road winds through densely packed forest. We're in a designated ecological area, getting into the Southern Alps, the backbone of South Island, and the tall trees are covered in parasitic plants, from mosses to lichens to yuccas.

We ascend a serpentine road up Mount Hercules: mostly 4th gear, a bit of 3rd, 80km/h, just the kind of road this car is made for. Route 6 must be one of the world's great driving roads: it's 417km (259 miles) from Westport to Haast, where it tracks inland towards Wanaka. Our next geophysical phenomenon is the Franz Joseph Glacier. Tinged pale blue, it's a wall of ice, a mile or so from the viewing embankment, filling an entire 12km (7.5 mile) valley and 300m deep. We learn that it's receded that mile in the last 100 years, due to 'global warming', leaving behind a sprawling, icy river.

The 20km (12 miles) between the Franz Josef Glacier and the Fox Glacier is unadulterated ecstasy, a succession of hairpins going up one side of the mountain and down the other, traversed as quickly as possible at 3,000 or 4,000rpm, 3rd gear, 4th gear, sheer dynamic bliss as the C4 kisses the apexes and hugs the white lines out. There are far fewer tourist traps at Fox Glacier and, despite the short distance between them, the foliage is very different with taller trees, all covered in the most incredible mosses and ferns, though the bush is less dense.

Motoring south on the coast road again, there's a succession of broad river valleys with fast flowing currents crossed by single-track bridges. We're heading into sub-tropical forest again. The plant life is effusive, lustrous and shiny, with so many different textures of leaves and fronds, encompassing every shade of green. Despite minimal traffic there are occasional road-kills – possums mostly, and a few pheasant-sized wekas.

Just short of Bruce Bay we turn onto an unmade road. Our Airbnb accommodation is a cabin set just behind the beach levee in a wooded water meadow. As far as you can see around the bay, the beach is strewn with huge pieces of driftwood, whole trees and root systems that have been washed down the rivers and out to sea, and then flung back again. This coastal strip has a backdrop looking east at Mt Cook (3,724m) and Mt Tasman, New Zealand's two highest mountains, which may be glimpsed whenever the cloud and the mist clears, revealing a little snow right on the tops, with the ridges enfolding and superimposed on each other into

the distance. There's a whole weather system evolving just in this one bay, where it's raining at the cape to the south, yet brilliant sunshine where we're standing, while the air is full of spray from the crashing waves.

Although I've been told there are more Porsches per head of population in New Zealand than anywhere else worldwide, the number we actually spot on the road is not large: maybe a dozen Cayennes, half-a-dozen Boxsters and a 996 GT3. After breakfast we hit the road again. Approaching Haast, we turn inland on the 6, where there's an extremely long single-file bridge over the Haast River. We press on along the river valley, where the tarmac steams as the sun dries it. According to our road map, the mountains on either side are all personified: the Snob, the Joker, the Pivot, the Deuce, and so on. They are very steep and forested all the way up to the limit of the tree line, above which lies tundra

Crossing a wooden bridge with the 997 C4S beside the coast at Bruce Bay. LAURA DRYSDALE

Sleek and purposeful: the rear three-quarters of the 997 C4S, unencumbered at rest by retractable spoiler. Most bends are signed with recommended maximum velocities, as here, approaching Lake Wanaka. AUTHOR

Much of the time the magnificent scenery negates against fast motoring, though occasional straights such as this one flanking Lake Hawea on the way to Wanaka and Queenstown provide an excuse to open up the 997 C4S. LAURA DRYSDALE

and then the snow. Some of the tops are hidden in cloud. At Makarora we're suddenly in a broad valley with serrated pinnacles ahead, heralding the vast, turquoise waters of Lake Wanaka lying in their midst. The winding lakeside road switches from one bank to another at 'The Neck' to run alongside another inland sea, Lake Hawea. There are glorious vistas in every direction.

Our target is Queenstown. There's a broad plain between khaki hills, and I suppose winter snow suppresses plant growth up there, but now there's a vivid profusion of wild lupins. We're entering another pass into the Crown Range between Wanaka and Queenstown, a winter sports road with successive signs indicating places where you should fit your snow chains. Heading down from the pass towards Queenstown the landscape is a lot mellower with mown meadows and sheep grazing. Queenstown has a vibrant harbour on Lake Wakatipu that draws milling crowds to its open-air gigs with buskers, fire-eaters and jugglers.

It's 265km (165 miles) on the SH6 and SH85 from Queenstown across the Otago plains to Palmerston on the Pacific seaboard. We make for Cromwell, passing Highlands Motorsport Park and numerous vineyards. After Dunstan Lake and its big dam there's more terracing around Clyde, with apple and cherry orchards. At Alexandra we abandon the 6 in favour of the 8 and the 85 towards Ranfurly, as there's even less traffic going this way. It's fast, two-lane blacktop with some nice cambered curves in an undulating landscape, and the tourist hot spots are now far behind us. Agriculture lies at the heart of the rolling Otago region. with livestock on rough pasture cladding a strange moorland moonscape, corrugated hillsides with jagged peaks beyond.

It's another two or three hours still to Palmerston and the Pacific, 100km (62 miles) of blissfully deserted roads. Palmerston's Victorian church spire and a beacon on top of a conical hill greet us. We've crossed from coast to coast and arrived at Shag Point, and then it's north on State Highway 1, which goes from Dunedin in the south all the way to Picton and the Wellington ferry, 700km (435 miles) to the north. Or it will, once the road's repaired at Kaikoura.

Downtown Oamaru is a big surprise with its immense, neoclassical limestone buildings, civic and commercial, a legacy of Victorian aspiration when they envisaged a major port matching San Francisco. Many of these are now given over to indoor markets and art galleries, like the SteamPunk Museum and Classic Car collection.

It's 250km (155 miles) from Oamaru to Christchurch on the A1, heading north towards Timaru. At Geraldine, however, we veer left off the main drag onto the 72, the signposted 'scenic route' to Christchurch via Mount Hutt, with long, long straights traversing the flat coastal plain. It's warm and sunny and, unusually, the 997's sunroof is open. The rushing wind noise from the open top obscures the Beltronics' warning bleeps, and inevitably I get nicked for speeding. The fine for doing 129km/h on an arrow-straight road is 230 New Zealand dollars. I count myself lucky: 140km/h is a ban.

The 997 C4S on the jetty at Moeraki. LAURA DRYSDALE

Back in Christchurch I take the 997 around Hagley Park to a carwash before returning it to Brent. It's an awkward denouement: when I try to move off from the carwash, it won't budge. I phone Brent. The assumption is that the clutch has gone, and he's philosophical: 'I've done a few trackdays with it, and it's ten years old, just one of those things. Lucky it's happened here and not in the middle of nowhere.' Trailered ignominiously away, it's discovered that the dual-mass flywheel has split in two. It appears that the rivets that hold it together had all sheared off.

The last few days of our trip are spent at Brent's holiday home at Akaroa on the spectacular Banks Peninsula. There's also an opportunity to have a go in his newly built 911 RSR replica on Ruapuna circuit. It's a faithful copy of the Martini RSR with the 'Mary Stuart collar' rear spoiler that came 4th at Le Mans in 1973, and was built in Christchurch by Jason Burke at Burke's Metalworks, and was assembled and fettled by Wayne Graves of Autothority, using NOS parts sourced from TwinSpark Racing in the Netherlands. It's a real pleasure to drive on the track, and Brent has since raced it successfully in NZ historics.

Our 997 road trip has covered 1,757km (1,091 miles) on the most fabulous roads and through the most gorgeous scenery. It's been a total pleasure and I can't wait to go back, especially if a 997 is involved.

The 997 C4S pauses amidst the majestic 19th-century architecture that defines Oamaru on South Island's east coast. AUTHOR

CHAPTER EIGHT

THE SPECIALIST TUNERS

CALLING THE TUNE

For almost as long as Porsche has been in business, specialist tuners have sought to improve upon the standard product, some more successfully than others. They have had varying degrees of expertise and levels of enhancement, ranging from straightforward body kits to complete reconstructions, incorporating integral roll cages, reupholstered cabins and substantially increased performance levels. I visit several of them regularly to discover what tweaks they have up their sleeves. There is a perfectly valid argument that insists that you can't improve on the standard car, such is the level of commitment Porsche puts into design, development and race-bred technology for its products. There is a great deal of truth in that, but many enthusiasts, including myself, cannot resist going an extra mile and tuning up the basic models. What follows is a collection of impressions having driven a number of such commercial offerings.

VANISHING POINT

A silver arrow with a vengeance, the FVD 996 GT2 is a 730bhp monster, propelling us towards the horizon faster than a howitzer shell. The landscape flashes by, the autobahn's edges a grey-green blur. Bridges zoom into view and zap overhead as we whizz past. I look as far into the distance as possible, gauging gaps between vehicles to see who's likely to pull into the overtaking lane

The author drives FVD Brombacher's latest 991 Carrera GTS show car at the summit of Freiburg-Schauinsland hillclimb in September 2018. With revised sills and modified aero, new exhaust and remapped software, it produces 580bhp. ANTONY FRASER

Despite its race-slanted nomenclature, the 996 GT2 was built as a road car, while its GT3 sibling served on the circuits. This one has received FVD's workover, including bigger bores, taking it up to 4.1 litres. ANTONY FRASER

on this unrestricted section of blacktop. Fortunately they check their mirrors in Germany. A glimpse at the speedo says 300km/h as we streak from one *kreuz* intersection to another. That's 186mph. All too soon it's over, but it's a taster of just how mental this GT2 can be when 730bhp is unleashed. For now, just relax.

We have come to Freiburg in the picturesque Black Forest region of south-west Germany to pay our annual visit to Willy Brombacher of the components, tuning and restoration specialists FVD. He always has a project car for us to try out. This time it's a customer's 996 GT2, with which FVD's techies and backroom electronics wizards have been tinkering for the last twelve months. Always questing for the ultimate in performance gains, or some other esoteric goal, Willy is more than happy to tweak any top-line Porsche that's to hand as FVD's test bed.

The turbocharged 2WD 996 GT2 was announced in 1999, primarily as a road car, unlike the competition-focused 993 GT2; the 996 GT3 would do duty in the racing department. Just 1,300 GT2 996s were built during a five-year production run before the unveiling of the 997 GT2. As befits its flagship power status, the GT2 has the widest version of

the 996 bodyshell with modified nose and fixed rear wing, plus those giveaway NACA ducts in the leading edge of the rear wheel arches serving the intercoolers. The suspension is set up with a ride height 10mm lower than the four-wheel drive 996 Turbo. Developing 462bhp (later 483bhp) from its 3.6-litre flat-six, the normal 996 GT2 derives its speed from two KKK turbochargers. It's rear-drive only, with six-speed manual gearbox. So much for the standard car. After its technical makeover, the FVD GT2 tops even the 997 GT2 RS's 610bhp by more than 100bhp.

The compact FVD workshop is a hive of activity. They have a 997 being fitted with Ohlins shock absorbers, the subject of FVD's latest venture in the damper department. There's a Volkswagen camper still here that was being restored on our last visit, and half a dozen engines and gearboxes in various states of disassembly. Our GT2 test car has been at FVD longer than expected because the owner had a slight accident bringing it over, which required a new front end, though the technical aspect then took priority, beefing up engine and brakes. Evidently it had previously received mechanical work in its home country that needed rectification, as Willy explains: 'I tried my hardest to convince him that it will have enough power with normal sport cams and not race cams, but he wouldn't listen … noise doesn't mean it's powerful, but if I was his age maybe I would do the same.'

I'd been expecting something a little more ostentatious, but then this is a customer car. Apart from the FVD graphics that identify the car for our shoot, there are no modifications to the regular bodywork, nor the wild striping that bedecks other FVD specials. Anyway, silver is still understated cool. Compared with some GT2 rear wing excesses, this one is not excessive. There are four exhaust pipes, paired in different diameters. 'The sports exhaust system is a little bit noisy,' Willy acknowledges, 'but he demanded that. Maybe in Malaysia there's no law against it like there is in Germany.' Willy explains the methodology of extracting 730bhp from the GT2's Mezger motor. First they fit bigger bores, taking it up to 4.1 litres. That in itself has become an area of FVD expertise. Then it's down to more subtle adjustments:

We control it by adjusting the turbo boost and the timing, and it is easy to do that now with electronics, but actually it's most fun when it's 650bhp max, then the handling is nice, you still have control over the car not the car over you. It's actually sport mode, what you'd normally use in a race car, so that's fundamentally the secret, but we were able to program it so it's working perfectly at 2,000rpm, even though it's a turbo, so you don't need to change gear because it's very torquey — 980Nm at 4,500rpm.

Willy Brombacher of FVD is more than happy to tweak any top-line Porsche. ANTONY FRASER

There's nothing novel in the transmission department: the gear ratios are standard GT2. Willy calls it 'a race car for the street', noting that it will actually do 343km/h (213mph) at 7,300rpm.

That's all well and good, but you need something special for the brakes: six-piston Brembo calipers on 380mm ventilated discs. Willy describes these as the best combination for street use:

> Eight-piston calipers are OK for racetracks, but six pistons are fine for the street. That's the system we've been selling for almost ten years without any changes, for all cars, and it works really well. That's the system we get from Brembo. It's black and grey so there is not much to do. It's that easy to install when you change the original brake discs during routine maintenance.

The split-rim BBS wheels are shod with Michelin Sport Pilot Cup tyres, which work well when they're on a dry track but are less grippy on a wet road. On the backs they are 325/30 ZR19s and on the front they are 255/55 ZR19s. 'When it's dry on a warm road it's like a go-kart, but you need to be very respectful with the tyres when there are wet spots because it's a little bit nervous, but you get used to it.' Chance would be a fine thing – getting used to 700bhp on a damp road on trackday tyres.

The cabin is seductively purposeful. Strangely, it's a right-hand drive that belongs to a customer from Malaysia and it's bound for Singapore, where they still drive on the left as a legacy of Empire. Though there are decent roads in the south of Malaysia there are no derestricted sections, so the power-hungry owner will be hard-pressed to perform a legal max-out. Guarding against a worst-case scenario, FVD installed a Porsche original equipment Eisenmann roll cage. 'If you have a car like this I always highly recommend fitting a roll-over cage, because it's better you have it as a safety feature than not.' There's also an FVD-supplied Momo steering wheel, specially tailored in Alcantara and exquisite to the touch.

I nestle into the all-embracing Recaro seat and embrace the controls. When I fire up the 996 GT2 flat-six it plunges into a colossal booming cacophony. The noise of the lightweight flywheel, in concert with the gearbox, is also quite noticeable. There's a slight tremolo to the throttle at low revs because of the special cams, hinting at the tremendous power available when it comes on song. To begin with the roads are damp after a shower, and Willy urges caution on account of the Sport Cup tyres, imperious on a warm dry track but like slicks in the wet: 'It goes absolutely crazy when

FVD installed an Eisenmann roll cage and Momo steering wheel in this right-hand-drive 996 GT2, bound for Singapore. ANTONY FRASER

you have damp roads, and if you accelerate at all hard you would just lose it.' No problem, it's perfectly happy to burble along at a low-velocity 1,500rpm, a docile kitten easing through Freiburg on our way up through the forest to the Schauinsland hill climb photoshoot.

New Bilstein PSS10 coil-over dampers are fitted, and the handling is peerless, irrespective of Willy's new enthusiasm for Ohlins shocks and Eibach springs. 'The customer demands Bilsteins, so that's what we've fitted, because he wants to have it a little bit stiffer, and you can actually feel that on the road.' Turn-in is very sharp and assured on the incessant twists and turns and 2nd gear hairpins of the Schauinsland hill climb, and in a lot of corners I'm giving the wheel a little bit of an old-school jink to assist the grip. We pause at the halfway house restaurant and wooden timing booth before motoring over the top and westward towards

Turn-in is sharp and assured on the incessant twists and turns and 2nd gear hairpins of the Schauinsland hill climb. ANTONY FRASER

the vineyard terraces. Circulating repeatedly round our loop through the back road vines for the benefit of the camera, I sense the wonderfully compliant chassis, the vast grip in the turns and the bottomless resource of power. An awesome machine.

When we hit the unrestricted autobahn I floor the throttle to see what happens. It's like being in a catapult, firing you forward relentlessly in every gear, no matter how tight the belts; your body's restrained but your head nods helplessly. It feels like being on a plane taking off without leaving the ground. Splendid backfiring on the over-run, popping and banging like a good 'un. We've been in 5th gear all the time on the autobahn: 'Normally you wouldn't need to do that because the engine is so elastic, so even in 6th gear you know you have power to accelerate. That's how torquey it is.' Happily, it stops pretty thoroughly as well. It's just that you can be maxed out on an unrestricted section and all of a sudden there's a 130km/h sign, likely as not followed by a 120km/h, and without exception everyone reacts dramatically and falls into line, even in the overtaking lane. That's what governs maximum speed in Germany: rigid adherence to the limits. As Willy declares, 'Now you understand why we need the big brakes'.

Although Willy is proud of this GT2 masterpiece, he would run a 996 Turbo Cabriolet for his own enjoyment:

> I love the cabriolets now, because it's an ideal driver's car. If you want to enjoy the car and the scenery as well as be street-wise, then you would definitely take a cabriolet. If you go for sport and you go to race tracks, then of course you'd go with a coupé, but right now to have fun, a cabriolet 996 Turbo Cabriolet or even a 997 Turbo Cabriolet is the way to go. Nobody can do anything on the 991 really, tuning-wise, as there is still a big issue with program control units.

We know FVD's extensive online parts and components business, but we're less familiar with the specialized tuning and bodywork restoration side, so Willy takes us on a guided tour. There are pure gems in the lockups, including a 964 Turbo 2, a 964 RS and 2.7 RS, all newly restored by an ex-Zuffenhausen painter. A very special project is under construction in the bodyshop. 'We also do normal maintenance stuff, small things like suspension and brake system changing, the regular tuning, and that is not a big deal, but when it comes to restoration, that means building a complete car and that takes a lot more time.' FVD has two cars involved in the Supercup series through FVD Switzerland and won the Belgian GP support race at Spa for the first time. The company is also involved in GT Masters.

The FVD-tuned 996 GT2 is an awesome machine, providing a bottomless resource of power and a wonderfully compliant chassis. ANTONY FRASER

In terms of FVD's core components business, Willy has recently noticed that more people are queuing up to buy parts for air-cooled cars, especially for 964s and 993s. This is because many owners used to have their cars transformed or facelifted with fancy body kits, or updated to 964s and 993s, but now collectors want to restore them to their original condition. That means original fenders, front bumpers and everything else to give the car back its original look. It's no surprise that FVD is catering for the spirit of the time: 'And then the cars get driven, so they need maintenance, and you need the parts to repair them because they drive them more. There has really been an increase in the demand for spares for air-cooled cars. but then we always did specialize in them a little bit more than water-cooled.'

Willy also has an eye on the future of the 996 GT2: 'I told him we need to get this car in nice shape because in ten years it will be worth a lot of money, collectable, definitely, because they didn't make that many 996 GT2s.'

This car has widened the goalposts in a typically extravagant, yet determinedly logical, FVD manner. It's no different externally to a factory GT2, yet it operates in an even more hard-core fashion. There can be few cars capable of delivering so dominant a performance and transporting you across continents in such a robust way. Put into perspective, the vanishing point may be an unobtainable goal, but FVD's 4.1-litre GT2 will have a darned good stab at getting you there.

RUF SCR 4.2 RtR AND 'THE ULTIMATE'

No external Porsche specialist is as prolific or innovative as Ruf Automobile of Pfaffenhausen, Bavaria. In 2017 the firm, a registered manufacturer in its own right as well as an Official

In 2017 Alois Ruf introduced two neoclassic masterpieces, the SCR 4.2 and the 'Ultimate', both very special in their own separate ways. ANTONY FRASER

Porsche Centre, created two neoclassic masterpieces – the 'SCR 4.2' and 'the Ultimate', each radical in its own, inimitable and innovative Ruf way. Alois Ruf introduced this pair at the Geneva Salon earlier in the year, and it took six months' fine-tuning to hone them to perfection.

It's been clear that Alois Ruf has espoused the 'period look' over recent years. The 'Hippie 917' graphics on the CTR-3, the 4-cylinder 911-based engine powering his 356 and the 911 Carrera RSR replica are three standout examples, and now the pair we have at our disposal present themselves overtly as 964-generation cars. The ratio of new-to-old Rufs is manifest in a tour of the main workshop, which reveals six 'classic' 911s and just three modern creations, mostly in service or under construction for customers. But Alois does not do things by halves, and the spec of the SCR and the Ultimate are jaw-dropping.

The SCR 4.2 is finished in burnt orange, and it's a very special package because, although it resembles a 964, it's actually based on a 993, featuring the multi-link rear axle and suspension. 'We wanted the most modern rear axle found on an air-cooled 911,' says Alois's son Marcel. It's not that they then clad the 993 shell in un-guttered 964 panelling – all classic Ruf bodies are smoothed off like that – it's that the

total wheelbase is increased by 7cm (2cm on the front axle and 5cm on the back). But the total length of the car stays the same, so it's the wheel arches that have shifted in the bodyshell by that much in each direction, forward and backwards, and that of course means the distance from bumper to wheel arch is less. The internal cabin dimensions don't change – the extra wheelbase doesn't gain any more room

The SCR 4.2 is based on a 993, featuring multi-link rear axle and suspension, but with overall wheelbase lengthened by 7cm. ANTONY FRASER

Engine bay of the Ruf SCR 4.2 housing the liquid-cooled, normally aspirated 4.2-litre, 525bhp 997 Mezger engine, driving through a six-speed manual gearbox. ANTONY FRASER

in the footwells. Those sumptuous bulging wheel arches are hand-beaten and hand-welded, and are rather broader than those on the Ultimate, due to a slightly wider track. They house five-spoke 19in Ruf alloys, wearing Michelin Pilot Cup 2 tyres, 285/30 back and 245/35 front. The SCR's extended wheelbase is only discernible when the two cars (or a standard 964) are standing next to each other. Ruf believes that the extended wheelbase brings better stability for high-speed driving: 'the main reason we did this was to have the same wheelbase as a 996 or 997, to give more stability at high speed than the 964 or 993, which can seem a little choppy.' There's a perfectly good reason for that because of what they've done with the SCR's powertrain.

They have installed a liquid-cooled, normally aspirated 4.2-litre, 525bhp 997 Mezger engine, driving through a six-speed manual transmission. Or more simply, they've turned an air-cooled 993 into a 997 GT3 kettle, and presented it as a 964. The fundamental reason they didn't add turbos is simply down to space for the radiators – there just isn't room for intercoolers (though you can bet they'll eventually find a way, just like they did with accommodating batteries in the electric Greenster). The radiators are behind the 964-style front panel and the central air inlet. In fact the entire water cooling system passes through the whole car, because there was no other possibility than to use the front panel for the radiators; all the cables and coolant tubes pass through the car, while the central section of the front bumper is an air intake as well as the two ducts to supply cooling air. The slats in the rear valances of both cars dissipate the hot air. It's all very impressive.

The SCR's doors, front wings and front lid are in carbon fibre and the rest of the bodyshell is steel. While the imme-

diate impression is that of a 964-derived car, in the cabin the dash and gauges are the only broad references to that model. Marcel describes the specification:

> For the SCR 4.2 we made everything as modern as possible. So for the rear axle we took the 993 multi-link, and in the front we retained the regular MacPherson wishbones as fitted on the 964 or 993, incorporating the package that we've developed with Bilstein, with our own springs and shock absorbers that have been spec'd for this car. The six-speed manual gearbox and rear-wheel drive incorporates a very strong differential so the traction goes the right way. The rest of the car is classic Ruf, with the integrated mirrors, rain gutters deleted, and the integrated roll cage within the cabin, though for most of the interior we have been very restrictive: the cars have no door pockets, just carbon fibre plates; there's no radio, though we do have air-con, which is a minimum feature that everybody wants today.

The SCR dash sports typical Ruf instruments, black background with green dials, and the distinctive Ruf steering wheel, aluminium pedals, lightweight carbon door panels with RS-style door pulls, and still offers electric windows and mirrors. Closing the doors on both cars, they feel infinitely light. The carbon applications are carried through on the dashboard, the handbrake and shift lever. The back seats are absent because the rigid bucket seats deny access to the rear cabin, where a removable cross bar creates additional torsional rigidity. The carpeting is Ruf-monogrammed, as are the kick-plates on the door openings. The bucket seats are carbon fibre for minimum weight, but very well padded and upholstered in an Op-Art black-and-white chequerboard pattern. 'You can choose to spec the interior as you wish;

The RtR is the latest incarnation of a model Ruf first produced in 2001, though it's a formula that dates back to the first Ruf product, the Turbo Coupé of 1977. ANTONY FRASER

you can have more luxury, but these two cars are now absolutely down to the minimum to reduce the weight.'

While the SCR 4.2 and Ultimate project the prevailing obsession with the classic 911 image, the RtR that Ruf launched in 2016 reflects the modern water-cooled look, albeit in highly modified format. The RtR is four-wheel drive, based on the 991 Turbo, paradoxically with a manual gearbox - though you can have a PDK double clutch gearbox if preferred, and that's something that Ruf has always offered: you can have any drivetrain configuration you like, and you can choose whatever propulsion you want. The RtR is the latest incarnation of a model Ruf first produced in 2001, though it's a formula that dates back to the first Ruf product, the Turbo Coupé of 1977. The blue RtR body of the current car was created by inserting additional material in the wings (fenders in US parlance), incorporating carbon-fibre in the front arches and steel in the rear. Marcel talks us through the spec:

> The RtR uses the same powertrain as the CTR-3 (Ruf's mid-engined supercar) and the RT-12R, and that's the old, tried-and-tested Mezger engine. We can tweak 800bhp out of that without compromising any safety and security reserves on the car; that's the reason why we use this well-established engine. We can also offer a six-speed manual gearbox for the RtR, which is an exclusive feature because normally you would only be able to have the PDK transmission in the Turbo today.

The front lid is carbon-fibre, and the cabin is another Ruf *piece de resistance*. It has the same colour co-ordinated blue steering wheel boss, extended as highlights around the dash panel, the centre console surround, door panels, and the rear of the seats - with blue stitching in the leather as well. It's a marvellous environment for an uplifting driving experience. Ruf looks after the details too: stashed in the luggage compartment of the RtR is a plastic Ruf-logo'd case containing a continental travel kit.

'We created a new Ruf modular wheel,' Marcel tells us, 'working together with OZ, and both front and rear are running very wide tyres, and on the front we have 255s and 325s on the rear, so you can really see how much wider the track becomes by the offset of the wheel rims.' The brake discs are carbon-ceramic items, at 410mm the biggest possible diameter on the front, allied to six-piston callipers, with 390mm discs and four-piston callipers on the back. Short of a racing car, I've never seen such big brakes on a road car.

The inspiration for the wide-body look came in the first instance from Estonia – the glamorous Mrs Ruf – who had

The RtR uses the same tried-and-tested Mezger powertrain as the Ruf CTR-3 and the RT-12R, generating an awesome 800bhp. ANTONY FRASER

some renderings drawn up a couple of years ago to illustrate her vision. She explains, 'I talked with a customer who was interested in a more aggressive look, and I called the design "Turbulence," which is a play on words!' As she acknowledges, 'it's kind of ironic that our reputation stems from the amazing speed achieved by the narrow-body YellowBird back in the late '80s, and here we are, doing a wide-body car that contradicts our original values.' Nevertheless, they do cater to a particular market segment that prefers extreme aesthetics, and we all have our particular foibles.

And now for the chance to drive the RtR on the long, looping Swabian backroads, arcing up and down between pasture and arable, forests and tiny villages with onion-spire churches and 100ft Maypoles, fabulous for evaluating the chassis in the bends and undulating cambers. I'm driving the blue RtR first, and I'm struck by the opulent cabin with its wonderful driving position in the Ruf lollipop seats, and as it's a manual left-hooker I familiarise myself with the six-speed gate. Foot on brake, twist the key and it bursts sharply into life. The guttural soundtrack says it means business. The clutch is extremely sharp and it takes a couple of goes to get if off the line, though all is resolved once out on the open road. A delicate throttle and strong clutch foot is all that's needed. However, this is a much more nervous animal than I was expecting, as I apply the slightest throttle pressure and it surges forward. The feedback from steering and chassis is acute too, as it's feeling every nuance of the road surface. I'm hearing a whistle from the wastegate as the turbo boost cuts off between gear changes. The brakes are equally as sharp – what else was I expecting from those dinner plates? – and the slightest pressure has it jerking, so I need to be extremely smooth on the pedal. There's also an amazing roar between 5,000- and 6,000rpm as the turbo kicks in and we rush away. This could be addictive. The way the RtR accelerates in 3rd and 4th, right round to 6,000 and 7,000rpm is just staggering. When is it going to tail off, I wonder, but it doesn't stop – it just keeps on accelerating. But even when I floor the throttle the power delivery is very smooth; there's no particular kick in the back, it's just a smooth onslaught of muscle. It's also fun to play a tune with the engine note going through the gearbox. I press the Sport exhaust button so its strident bark is sounding twice as loud, totally awesome, and my hosts use the moment to record a video of the sequence of gear shifts as I move up and down the 'box while travelling through the landscape. Handling is slick through the esses, with the pegged-down assurance of the four-wheel drive chassis. The other side of the coin is that I can also cruise along in 6th gear in a very relaxed way. That's the sign of a classy grand touring car: to provide the excitement in the corners and go touring like a lounge lizard. Having a manual box with a turbo engine is especially unusual, and it's a joy to drive a manual car with so much power on tap in each gear. The whole thing is extraordinarily smooth and sophisticated. Alois Ruf sums up:

The RtR cabin has colour-coordinated blue steering wheel boss, with blue highlights around the dash panel, centre console surround, door panels, and seatbacks, with blue stitching in the leather. ANTONY FRASER

The blue RtR is an extreme car; it takes you to the maximum. It's for people who like the wide body look, with big wheelarches and huge tyres that puts the full race car image on the road, and therefore we had to stay with the good old Mezger engine which we have given our 802bhp package, and that cannot be combined with the double clutch (PDK) gearbox, so we had to go manual, and there are still plenty of people around who miss the stick shift, although the double clutch gearbox is perfection today. The engineers have worked miracles to make all of that happen, but there are people who've lived all their life with a clutch and stick shift, so it's for those individuals, a custom-tailored car. It's just about the widest bodied car that's practical on the road, and that's about the maximum rear-engined turbo power you can go to as well.

It's easy to imagine Alois, Marcel and their designer and engineers sitting around a table bouncing ideas off one another, but the bottom line is that much of the product is customer driven. Marcel explains that their client base wants carbon fibre, as it saves weight and it's up-to-date technology: 'We brought those messages together and made a new package to satisfy all those demands.' Although the Ultimate takes it to the stars with its unprecedented body-chassis, it is driven by a typical Ruf air-cooled turbo powertrain, whereas the SCR is more fundamentally innovative in offering a modern driveline and running gear in a traditional bodyshell.

That was the next step, to see how we could bring together the higher performance and, let's say, more convenient water-cooled technology, because air-cooled cars always have their downsides, so that's the reason why we wanted to stay with the reliable 993 chassis but combine it with the last evolution of the normally aspirated water-cooled Mezger flat-six engine.

The Ultimate has its own VIN number and is probably the harbinger of more similar models. Type approval regulations govern what manufacturers can produce and sell, and Ruf is a manufacturer in its own right. Since obtaining type approval generally means water-cooled engines, that is the way forward, in whatever guise.

These two are our demonstration cars, and they represent the fruits of all the knowledge that we've gained over the years, decades, and that's also what makes us unique. We are still experimenting with

the SCR, because we are still improving and integrating the two electronic worlds: the water-cooled 997 electronics and the 993's twenty-year-old electronics. It works fine, because we have our own computer in between that's translating the signals back and forth, but we still have to refine some settings to really bring it to everyday usability. It's a big piece of development, because when you stretch a wheelbase then you really get into the real bare metal of the car. The Ultimate will probably be for sale next year, but we had to build it with the carbon fibre skin so we knew how to do it, see how to mount the carbon fibre to the roll cage with glue and rivets, and this is the first car with that technology. Then we needed to do the testing, to put kilometres on the car. The orders are there, so we'll build the first cars this coming winter.

As for price, the Ultimate costs €480,000 and the SCR 4.2 €430,000.

When you talk about spending between €400,000 and €500,000 on a car, you have to look at what's comparable, and then the exclusivity, and what is the real unique package, and then you can see that we're no more expensive than other brands in our segment. We're talking about ten cars a year for one model, and we really do have the customer base that is craving cars like these.

When Ruf unveiled the cars at Geneva it was the ardent cognoscenti who visited the stand to discuss them. 'No one really knew what they were as they look like a twenty-year old car, though the connoisseurs were intrigued, because at Geneva we couldn't say too much.'

The **SCR 4.2** controls feature typical **Ruf** instruments, **Ruf** steering wheel, aluminium pedals and **RS**-style door pulls, while the bucket seats are upholstered in an **Op-Art** black-and-white chequerboard pattern. ANTONY FRASER

There's always a feel-good factor about visiting Ruf, where we're warmly welcomed by all the staff and family. The icing on the cake, though, is driving the cars, and that time has arrived.

I'm at the wheel of the SCR 4.2. Fabulous seating position, and I'm fairly close to the wheel – the chequer pattern is reflected in the shiny carbon door panel. It's a booming exhaust note, and the car feels light and eager on take-off. Initially it does feel like the 993 donor – albeit an RS version – and its longer wheelbase is not detectable in a straight line. It's a fairly stiff clutch, and I feel I'm reaching top gear in the six-speed gearbox thanks to the instant power delivery and lightness. I wind it round to 4,500rpm and it really does start to go. Changing gear, the revs drop imperceptibly between each shift. It's a linear power delivery, a vast surge of pace and speed that's difficult to comprehend when all my senses are focused on the road ahead and how the car is gobbling up the tarmac as the horizon rushes up to meet me and the scenery hurtles by on either side in a blur. It'll go all the way to 322km/h (200mph), given an unrestricted autobahn. Meanwhile I'm enjoying its very fine handling, and I'm sensing the longer wheelbase in cornering. It may not be as intuitive as a 964, but it is totally sure-footed. Small wonder, given the enormity of the tyre package, evoking an RS-like image that strikes me as I glance in the mirror at the other car following behind.

The SCR is extremely powerful and I am inclined to liken it to a 997 GT3 in that respect. Does it feel like a 964? Not surprisingly there's an ambiguity about the controls – the dash, gauges and seating posture tell me that's what I'm driving, while what I'm feeling are the sensations of controlling and riding in a modern, high-revving 997.

The wheelbase of the **Ruf SCR 4.2** is the same as a **996 and 997, providing better stability at high speed, and is barely discernible, even in profile.** ANTONY FRASER

The Ruf Ultimate offers a more track-focused driving position, and the semi-competition clutch pedal travels a long way before it bites. ANTONY FRASER

As the automotive world increasingly espouses electric cars, it would be remiss not to mention the Ruf Greenster, based on the 997 Targa chassis and running gear, and powered by a pair of Siemens electric motors, operated via a single forward and reverse gear lever. ANTONY FRASER

I switch to the more track-focused bucket seat of the Ultimate and something as subtle as the seat height immediately tells me this is the more aggressive of the two. The hardest thing to get used to is the clutch pedal. My foot comes back quite a way before it bites, and I learn later that it's a semi-competition clutch, fitted because so much torque (720Nm) passes through the rear-drive transmission. Originally they also tried a single mass flywheel, but it was abandoned in favour of the dual mass flywheel. I also feel the subtle difference between the gearshift of the two cars: the Ultimate's is a mechanical rod linkage, whereas the SCR's is a cable linkage. The noise it emits at low revs reminds me of a didgeridoo, but above 4,000rpm it is positively roaring.

The acceleration from the Ultimate's twin-turbo air-cooled flat-six is dynamic, and the way it takes off and the power comes in is quite amazing. It's as if the whole car envelops me and catapults me forward; I become part of the whole package. It's capable of 339km/h (210mph) and I don't doubt it would do that on an autobahn. Steering-wise, it feels more familiar in a 964 or 993 context than the long-wheelbase SCR, though that in itself makes the SCR more intriguing. There's a real surge of power that's overwhelming when my senses try to tell me I'm in a 964 — apart from the air-con, which on the hottest day of the year is working absolutely fine (as it probably wouldn't in a regular 964). Is Ultimate too much of an overstatement? At this point in time, no. It certainly is radical, but you just know that, even now, Ruf is aiming to set the bar higher in the Ultimate challenge.

One or the other? The main character-defining difference between the two cars is the powertrain — air versus water

— as well as structural and dynamical differences. The blue car is the ultimate hooligan and yet the driver is part of that wild package, while the orange car provides the more civilized experience of the two. Both exude quite different personalities, but there's no mistaking their purpose: they are out-and-out sports cars, grand touring with very much a sporting edge, so that they are like over-excited 964s. The Ultimate is the full-on kiddie, but the SCR 4.2 is the more comfortable laid-back incarnation of the two. And that's precisely what Ruf was aiming to achieve.

TECHART 991 GTSTREET R

The TechArt GTstreet R is an explosion of art and attitude, based on a 2017-model year 991 Turbo S. ANTONY FRASER

WHEN THE GOING GETS RUF

It doesn't come much tougher than a trackday at Hockenheim, at least as far as high-speed cornering's concerned. That series of sweepers into the start-finish zone is awesome.

At least once a year the Ruf family clubs together for a rally in a blissful scenic location, which often incorporates a trackday session on a race circuit. Ruf owners at this year's gathering number a dozen cars, plus a few regular Porsches of the GT3 persuasion, as well as our road-trip 718 Cayman.

A presentation and dinner at the Hockenheim-Ring hotel has been arranged for the Ruf-owning (and aspirant owner) attendees, although Alois and Estonia are late, having had a slight altercation with a Golf en route from Pfaffenhausen in their SCR 4.2.

Next day the Ruf and Porsche cars form up in the pit-lane in gorgeous sunshine, divided into three groups according to competence. First up, we are shown onto an expansive skidpan within the paddock where a pair of instructors demand we emulate their GT3-style antics on the coned route around the tarmac. Some drivers perform better than others, even in my 'experienced' group. Two hoses are gushing, so as I'm circulating the car is getting a drenching. 'More aggressive application of throttle and brake,' my instructor yells at me through the window, 'and use just 1st gear,' so I jab the pedals accordingly, relying on tyres and the Ruf's poise while twirling the wheel to avoid rotating the car.

Next I have the thrill of driving the SCR 4.2 really hard on the wide expanses of the actual circuit – an awe-inspiring experience in itself – and it's great once more to be in the car I drove at Pfaffenhausen a year earlier. Judging braking distances around Hockenheim is key, because I'm travelling extremely fast, using all the revs and diving into the turns, aiming at marker points on apexes, riding the kerbs a little bit and powering out onto the straights. It is a thoroughly riveting exercise, and I am very warm indeed. The instructor in his 996 GT3 dictates the pace, followed as closely as possible by a retinue of Rufs and a handful of modern 911s. Each one takes it in turn to follow him, so after completing a lap when you've been right behind him you peel off and the next guy follows on behind the instructor. Is he being kind to me? I have the SCR pretty well up behind him, and on the longer straights, of course, I have no trouble holding onto him. I fancy I can brake later into the turns but he is swifter out of them. Anyway, it's academic as it's so much fun, lapping a circuit with such a poignant depth of history as Hockenheim has, in among the Ruf fraternity. The German Grand Prix will be staged here in July 2018, and it's amusing to reflect that I've driven the Sachs-Kurve flat, in an SCR, ahead of the stars.

Driving the Ruf SCR 4.2 at Hockenheim in 2017. It resembles a 964, but the wheelbase and engine correspond with those of a water-cooled 997 GT3. ANTONY FRASER

Lapping Hockenheim in the Ruf SCR 4.2, diving into the turns, aiming at apexes, riding the kerbs, and powering onto the straights, a riveting experience. ANTONY FRASER

Among the coterie of specialist tuners and tweakers orbiting the Stuttgart galaxy, TechArt are probably the most prolific purveyors of Porsche bling. It's all tastefully done, provided you like your Porsche given the carbon fibre workover along with its performance hike. Current TechArt masterpieces are the 718 Boxster S and 991 Carrera 2, and they have just been joined by the GTstreet R, as wild an incarnation of the 911 bloodline as you could wish for.

TechArt creations are all about standing out from the crowd, and nothing has more cred than the new 991 Turbo-based GTstreet R. It's Daphne Green, a trifle effete for such a dynamic bruiser, but you can't argue that it's not eye-catching: especially given the striping that's both subtle and not so subtle, and detailing that's sometimes intricate and sometimes plain shouty. While factory-issue 997 Sport Classics and 991 Rs are relatively restrained, the GTstreet R is an explosion of art and attitude. It's based on a 2017-model year 991 Turbo S, and in this guise, it's a 720bhp 3.8-litre twin turbo, four-wheel-drive rocketship. To give an idea of the sort of performance upgrade their Techtronic power kit enables, recent runs at the Ehra Lessien test track produced 0–100km/h (62mph) in 2.7s; 0–200km/h (124mph) in 8.5s; and 0–300km/h (186.5mph) in 23.3s. That's not hanging about. 'That's great for us,' says PR Tobias Sokoll, 'because it's faster than a McLaren.' Faster than everything, pretty much.

Once my eyeballs have become accustomed to Daphne and her vivid graphics, I focus on the detailing – what TechArt describes as its 'genetics'. The TechArt badge is resplendent on the front lid, and the model is identified on the doors and the engine cover. On the underside of the front lid is

TechArt's 991gt is based on a C2S, finished in Air Force Blue, fitted with the firm's Aerokit front spoiler and splitter, side skirts, rear diffuser, roof spoiler and rear wing, all in carbon fibre. ANTONY FRASER

the embossed TechArt logo in big letters, and on the floor mat inside the front boot is the lovely yellow stitching with the GTstreet R legend sewn into it. The green pin-striping that continues from the roof and down the back window relies cleverly on the darkness of the glass to perpetuate the colour scheme. It sports a sort of biplane rear wing incorporating ducktail and spoiler, whose cantilevered top deck is so high that I could be flying a Sopwith Camel – though it has to be said, in somewhat greater luxury. It's said to apply 321kg of downforce at 186mph (300km/h) – on the autobahn rather than the street, naturally.

TechArt's split-level premises is fronted by a rotunda showroom displaying four vehicles: two Macan Magnums, which seem to be their current staple, and a 991 and 997 Cabriolet, all featuring the TechArt twists. Not only does it have a busy workshop with four hoists, TechArt also has the advantage of having a dedicated in-house upholstery shop, affectionately known as 'the Saddlery', where all the trim is fabricated from a riot of dyed hides and miscellaneous templates festooning a wall, while steering wheels are intricately hand-crafted from scratch.

Tobias describes the thinking behind the GTstreet R:

> The main idea is to have the sort of look and down-force and on-track feeling like you have in the GT3 RS, but with the benefit of turbo thrust, great handling and the practicality of everyday use. It drives like a turbo with more boost and more downforce, but you don't have the hard ride and steering of a GT3 RS, which in any case you probably wouldn't want to drive every day. The car we've got here is the Clubsport version, so you've got the roll cage, and in the back seat we provide a helmet and a bag to store it in. You can order that with the car.

The cage is made specially for TechArt and is lacquered to suit the Daphne Green finish, while the black dots you see are the screws holding the tubes together. The price in this configuration, including the special colour and the generous interior, is about €390,000 for the complete car. 'The transformation to the GTstreet R starts with the aero kit, mounting, lacquering, then the wheel set and the exhaust, the interior kit and the 640bhp power kit, so you're up at nearly €400,000 inclusive of German tax, and all mounted on the 991 Turbo donor car.' Tobias explains that the market is split between buyers for whom money is no object and who will order a brand-new car, and those running a 2015 model and like the idea of upgrading it. 'It's also possible to build the GTstreet R on the previous model, so that's quite interesting for guys who have had their car for two years now and want to buy something new but don't know what, so they can now have this one for 400 grand.' The transformation could be accomplished in six to eight weeks. A client proffering a 2015 car could get the new three-dimensional rear lights fitted, plus the fog lights that also came in with the facelift. That way it would look identical to the Gen 2 car, apart from lacking the mode switch on the steering wheel.

There's a lot going on with these bodywork extensions: the workshop starts by removing everything surplus to requirements from the car. All the new GTstreet R body parts are carbon fibre, including the lacquered ones. For instance, the bumper panel is all carbon, the front lip and splitter is new and projects forward automatically – the same mechanism as the turbos – and it can be overridden. The rear wing extends vertically by 5cm, and it also angles up to 15 degrees. 'If you don't push the button or change the mode it's speed-driven, and when you go in Sport Plus or use the button for the spoilers you can operate it by yourself,' explains Tobias. They've angled the oil-cooler differently too, so that cooling air passes over it and exits via the extractor slots in the front panel. The front lid is carbon fibre, as are the side skirts and bargeboard flaps surrounding the front corners of the car. There are nine louvres in the front wing (fender) tops, in matt-lacquered carbon fibre, like the wheel arch extensions, though it can also be ordered with all-gloss body colour. The prominent intakes ahead of the rear wheel arches are calculated to enable the engine to develop more power by allowing greater air ingress to the intercoolers, in consort with the air intake on the top of the engine lid. The vents behind the rear wheels duct the hot air behind the car. The GTstreet R runs on 20in forged TechArt 'Formula IV' Race centre-lock wheels, shod with the more road-friendly option of Michelin Pilot Sport Cup 2, with 265/35 ZR 20s front and 325/30 ZR 20 on the rear. The 21in option wheels wear Continental ContiSports, with whom TechArt have a tyre contract. In this case, the 20in wheels are finished in black, enlivened by a tidy Daphne-coloured rim bead.

The mechanism of the spoiler's supports has been upgraded, and it all looks very formidable. There are two grilles below the engine lid: one is open and one is decorative, echoing the shape of the three-dimensional rear by transferring across the whole back of the car. At the bottom is the rear diffuser with defined spaces for the twin paired titanium tailpipes. The two central ones are darker than the outer ones as they operate at more pedestrian speeds; the blue-grey outers come into play during fast motoring. 'The colours also change depending on what you do with the car,' says Tobias. 'When you pull hard on the autobahn they take on a different colour compared with driving through the city.'

The Clubsport version is mostly upholstered in Alcantara, which is wonderfully tactile. The standard interior is removed, and TechArt's saddlery snippers make up the trim panels. According to Tobias, 'Our designer used special stitching that matches the exterior colour, so all packages feature this cheeky street art stitching on the seats, on the door panels and in the roof, so the continuity is even there when the sunshine roof is open.' The yellow stitching theme is carried through the beautifully made TechArt steering wheel, fashioned in-house in the saddlery. It is not quite circular (it's flat across the bottom for better thigh clearance), but it carries the shift paddles and the regular audio controls, and there's a big boss in the centre with the TechArt shield and half-moon symbol, and the Sport control button at lower right. The coloured sewing also extends into the detailing on the back of the paddles, the steering wheel and the gearshift gaiter. The customer can choose whatever colours he wants. I notice a discrete plaque stating that this is 001, the very first GTstreet R. I take a peek in the glove compartment and there's a hand-made GTstreet wallet containing the vehicle documents, which is another nice touch.

Everything is negotiable, so if the customer wants a different power kit on it, there are several different opportunities with regard to performance. You've always got the basic Turbo and Turbo S, and our Techtronic power kit puts out 620bhp when fitted on the pre-facelift Turbo S, and 640bhp on the facelift Turbo S, and then the really big power kit like this car has delivers 720bhp. So, you've got five different power kits depending on what model you have, and whether you want the big one or if 620bhp is enough. It's down to what the customer wants to do with his car and what he is dreaming of.

The aerodynamic modifications are evolved in a wind tunnel.

We put the car in a wind tunnel to optimize the aero, and also to be sure it's safe when you drive at 340km/h: you want to know it's not going to misbehave. We now know that, when you are on stage three of the active aerodynamics with every spoiler extended, you've got 321kg of downforce at 300km/h, so you really feel when driving the car that it is firmly pressed onto the street.

When honing a car such as this it's helpful to have a stretch of the local autobahn handy. The GTstreet R is TüV approved: 'We don't crash the complete car, but we always have to do the test for pedestrians, and we have to drive into the

TechArt's GTstreetR's body kit is entirely made of carbon fibre, with aerodynamics honed in the wind tunnel. ANTONY FRASER

dummies to see how it reacts when the head lands on the bonnet and when somebody's leg is hit.'

TechArt has upgraded the suspension with shorter springs, and the wheel rim offset broadens the track. 'It has the options that Turbo S normally has, like air suspension, and it works quite well. And if the customer wants to have the car more tracky, for example, there's also a coil-over set-up that we can fit. We can apply virtually anything from our full range, depending on what the base car happens to be.' Like the 991 Carrera S that I sampled earlier (see Chapter 5), I'm grateful for the nose-lift kit on our photoshoot, which raises the front of the car so the spoiler clears any ruts or rocks as I perform endless turnarounds in forest tracks and lay-bys to provide my colleague with panning and cornering shots as he stands mired in the middle of a field. The nose-lift facility is activated by a button on the centre console, and it happens very quickly, which of course is a good thing, with the front happy to levitate and descend when the car's travelling at under 15km/h. The suspension retains the PASM and PDCC (Porsche Dynamic Chassis Control), and it's been slightly upgraded with beefier springs that TechArt has developed especially for the car, and it sits 30mm lower than its progenitor. The brakes are the same carbon ceramic items as on the Turbo S. As Tobias says, 'There are things that work well that you shouldn't change.'

All the modifications on TechArt cars are driven by a technical and aesthetic impulse, contemplated, assessed and agreed by a panel of employees, from marketing to technical and styling, with the last word from CEO Thomas Behringer, as Tobias explains.

Our in-house designer Thorsten Stroda draws the whole thing, not only the external modifications and

the sticker kit, but he also designs the interior too. The technical guy also has to approve what's proposed, and then the designer builds his ideas around that, and then they're discussed again and again until a final format is agreed.

Not only does TechArt have its own trim shop, its carbon fibre facility will shortly relocate to a new building under construction.

It's a growing business. There are currently four guys working in carbon-fibre, and they have so much to do, fabricating everything from Magnum to GT parts, so right now they are also looking to recruit another person. Normally they do all the interior parts, the mirrors and things like that, but the GTstreet R is the only body kit that's completely in carbon fibre. We've also integrated the active aerodynamics that we tested in the wind tunnel.

The GTstreet R was a year-and-a-half from design inception to production, which is pretty good going, suggesting that it was an ongoing progress that didn't get bogged down. There was a great deal of careful thought and evaluation during the application of the detailing process. The result is undoubtedly one of the more spectacular transformations of a standard Porsche. They've very much gone their own way, and it's a very neat creation.

As well as in-house development engineer and test driver Moritz Renner, who's occupied the role for ten years, TechArt also engages the services of 1992 Porsche Carrera Cup champion Uwe Alzen to hone the cars' performance. Alzen's career also includes scoring 2nd place at Le Mans

The GTstreetR sticks like glue through the bends, and neither lifts nor bottoms out in the dips and troughs. ANTONY FRASER

in 1998 in the works GT1, and along with his brother Jürgen he's an expert in the VLN race series and Nürburgring 24-Hours in their privately prepped GT2. 'Uwe established our record on the Nordschleife with the pre-facelift Turbo S,' Tobias tells me. 'It was also clocked at 3.4s to 100km/h (62.1mph), maxing out at 345km/h (214.37mph).' For the record, that's 0.1s quicker than a 3.8-litre 991 GT3.

My first impression when sitting in the car is how womb-like it feels; I'm cosily enveloped in the Alcantara of the seats. In fact there's Alcantara everywhere: door liners, A-posts, the roof lining, and it's also in the boot. However opulent the donor car's cabin interior may be, it is completely removed and switched for TechArt's swisher in-house Alcantara cladding. The control button on the steering wheel is zeroed at 0, with 'S' for Sport and 'SP' for Sport Plus, and there's also 'I' for 'Individual', so you can program your personal setting too. The exhaust is connected to Sport and Sport Plus, and if this was Spinal Tap we'd be up at Eleven in SP volume. If you have it on 'Individual' you can just have the exhaust open, without engaging the performance changes that are made to the engine that apply in Sport and Sport Plus modes.

I'm being fairly circumspect on a wet road to start with, bearing in mind that we're on Michelin Pilot Cup Sport 2s — and, as Moritz Renner says, 'this car needs race tyres to suit its character, so we have no choice, we need the Pilot Sport Cup 2s, everything else would be illogical. But, if you've got a long run to do, ContiSports are also a very good tyre.' Indeed. But this really is a very exciting car in normal mode, let alone going into Sport and Sport Plus. Applying Sport Mode produces an instant leap into a different auditorium, while things get sharpened up in the handling and acceleration departments. This car is extremely competent and so efficient. It can do everything at slow pace, as dictated by traffic, and if then given minimal pressure on the accelerator pedal it responds instantly with storming accelerative motion. The steering is beautifully weighted and I can feel the car around the corners on this lovely curving Black Forest road.

If Sport is a sonorous delight, instantly firming the ride and sharpening the responses and sustaining the revs for a tad longer, Sport Plus is positively explosive, and you feel the repeated backfiring on the overrun through the seat. You'd have to be really committed to exploit it to the full. As it is, it's possible to deploy the GTstreet R's vast power resources on some of the local back roads — one outing I do with test driver Moritz takes us onto the most amazing switchback blacktop where they regularly take the cars for suspension development and compression test analysis. Here my life flashes before me as we hurtle downhill toward the forest at breakneck ski-jump speed, the driver matching

Hurtling into the forest: the TechArt GTstreetR has upgraded suspension with shorter springs, 30mm lower, and the wheel rim offset broadens the track, plus 991 Turbo S air suspension. ANTONY FRASER

the car twitch for twitch with a hint of opposite lock on the damp roads. As he says, 'today it's very slippery and there are some corners with wild cambers and blind summits a bit like the Nordschleife, so it is a little bit tricky. But,' he says reassuringly, 'I have driven this car about 8,000km during testing, so I've got a good understanding of its performance and I know what it can and can't do. It's very easy to handle, so you can make really spectacular moves without being a professional race driver.' It's a lesson, though, and I now know that I can confidently make overtaking decisions with this car that I wouldn't contemplate in my 996. It gives plenty of feedback, so it's inspiring, knowing that I won't be running into trouble. The roads have dried out later on and traction is not an issue. It sticks like glue through the bends, and in the dips and troughs it neither lifts nor bottoms out. This is a staggeringly efficient, potent machine. It's beautifully built, looks fantastic, with staggering acceleration, planted handling, solid as a rock, and one of the most joyous rides I've experienced since … I was last at Pfaffenhausen.

CARGRAPHIC 991 CARRERA TURBO CABRIOLET

Sooner or later you'll need to replace your exhaust system, or you'll be seduced by the notion of upgrading for the sake of performance increase, or merely making more noise. Chances are, your research will bring you to Cargraphic, which is based in Landau, in the heart of the south-west German region of Pfalz. The firm has been marketing Porsche exhausts for more than twenty years, since Thomas Schnarr went into partnership with Simon Young, who manufactures Cargraphic's own manifolds, catalytic converters, silencers (with or without integrated flaps) and Active Sound exhausts for diesel engines at his Cullompton factory in Devon. Cargraphic's aftermarket Porsche accessories catalogue also features performance components such as its own three-piece wheels and AirLift kit, a front-axle lift system for cars with lowered suspension and limited ground clearance.

Thomas Schnarr is constantly upbeat about his products:

All our silencers are assembled in the same way, wrapping two or three layers of stainless steel wire-wool around the baffle, plus a layer of needle mat (glass-fibre blanket) around the inside of the insulator case, and then we fill the void with glass robing, which is like fibreglass in a continuous filament so it doesn't break down. This is then pushed into the silencer under pressure. These machines squash the case to the right shape for the baffle so the internals retain the shape.

The exhaust side of the business represents around three-quarters of the firm's turnover. More recently the new Active Sound System has become Cargraphic's second most popular product line. This is followed by the company's own series of road wheels, available in six different styles, including Motorsport split-rims, and then various performance upgrade components, such as throttle bodies, intake plenums and lightweight flywheels.

All parts are test-fitted, dyno-tested and TüV approved in Germany.

We have a prototype system or a component part made in England, then we get type approval; we receive an order and the finished article is produced and despatched. Our business is divided 80 per cent through dealers and 20 per cent private orders. We are constantly expanding, and we have a lot of growth potential in new markets like South America, South Africa and India, and we're doing a lot in Australia and New Zealand now. China has declined a little bit, but India and Malaysia are doing very well. India is a very big growth market, because they have loads of Cayennes and SUVs, if not sports cars.

Cargraphic has a register of agents worldwide, including Parr Motorsport in the UK, and runs the mail-order operation from its Landau premises. The way dealers order items and components has altered radically:

Motoring top-down in the Cargraphic 991 Carrera C4S Cabriolet, it is easy to be seduced by the notion of upgrading the exhaust system for the sake of a performance increase, or merely making more noise. ANTONY FRASER

Whereas before we had dealers in America who bought containers full of stuff and kept a stock of it, this is no longer the case; they buy items as and when they need them, and that's because distribution systems like UPS and Fedex mean we have competitive freight rates, so we can send, for instance, a 997 Turbo system today to the East Coast of the USA overnight for about €150. Because everything goes via Memphis, it takes another day to reach the West Coast, but it would be there within two days for €175. Then the dealers despatch to the customers.

Cargraphic has a spotless workshop with three hoists and state-of-the-art equipment to carry out virtually any task on your Porsche. To demonstrate the Cargraphic range, Thomas has three cars for us to try, each featuring very different Cargraphic apparatus. First up is a Macan V6 diesel; it may not be especially dear to Porsche aficionados, but nevertheless it is an extremely capable vehicle. When fired up it sounds less like a diesel than a big-block American V8 petrol guzzler. The question is, not so much 'why,' as 'how?' Up on the hoist Thomas points out a pair of bulbous speakers mounted just before the tail pipes, which are programmed to emit a petrol V8 rumble, which you can modulate to high- or low-pitch V8 via a smartphone app. But Thomas says that's the exception:

We try to make our systems fit with OE parts, whereas other makes won't do, and in some cases you can't just replace the tail pipes or rear box because their systems won't match with the existing parts. Design-

wise, with the Cargraphic products, we always try to maximize flow, maximize power but still keeping it within a respectable – and legal – sound level. Because of the constraints with TüV in Germany, we can't have a system that's absolutely unfettered, so there has to be a compromise between the level of sound and the performance that can be gained, but our systems do tend to be more driveable and more user friendly as a result. You don't have that horrible droning in the back of your head over long distances.

How they gauge whether a particular configuration of silencer and header and tailpipes, plus catalytic converter and heat exchangers is going to enhance the car's performance is, according to Thomas, 'very much an experience-based thing. We have a decibel meter and we measure the car as standard and then we can do our own work and then measure the car.' That's done static and drive-by, rather than rolling road. Increasing bhp is also down to past experience:

It's what we've learned over the years. We can work out primary diameters, primary lengths and cats we know always give an improvement with the modern 200-cell, tri-coated T38 platinum, rhodium, palladium Cargraphic exclusive cats. There's an immediate gain to be had in fitting those when the factory parts are usually 600-cell, so immediately you've increased the flow by three times. If you're going for maximum power you should consider those, as a lot of the factory headers are particularly restrictive. And there are good gains to be made in replacing the stock headers with our free-flowing headers.

Sampling Cargraphic's 991 Gen 2 Carrera C4S Cabriolet in the picturesque Pfalz vineyard countryside, featuring a state-of-the-art Cargraphic exhaust system. ANTONY FRASER

Another car to benefit in this way is the 991 Gen 2 Carrera C4S Cabriolet, which I sample out in the picturesque Pfalz vineyard countryside, featuring state-of-the-art Cargraphic exhaust and cat sections – a wonderful car on a sunny afternoon.

Cargraphic's *pièce de résistance* is a 1987 3.2 Carrera, finished in Blood Orange and backdated accurately, aesthetically at least, to a 2.7RS lookalike, complete with Carrera graphics on the lower flanks. The orange 3.2 backdate reflects where Thomas sees the trend going in 911 ownership:

I see the direction as classic, especially as new cars become more and more tightly regulated. So I want to have a baseline for the next twenty years. With our facility and our knowledge and what we can produce, I see the direction heading towards classic cars, because the next generation of regulations will make it very difficult for us, especially in this range. There will always be people who want to upgrade their performance or maybe want a performance exhaust sound from their 996s or 997s or 991s, but for classic Porsches the possibilities are limitless. We have so many classic parts in store, and this is in addition to our range of exhausts and tuning equipment.

My own 996 is equipped with Cargraphic silencers, and sounds – and goes – all the better for it (see Chapter 10).

KREMER '997' K3

Fans of the legendary Kremer Racing Team can emulate their heroes in a genuine slant-nose K3 road car, a copy of the firm's current VLN-championship slant-nose racer, built in-house as a 997 Turbo-based road-going supercar.

The name Kremer Racing probably conjures up slant-nose 935-style Porsche racers, with absurdly drooped snoots and the widest rear haunches possible, perhaps focusing on the team's amazing Le Mans win in 1979, when the 935 was in its heyday. Certainly, one of Porsche's most favoured customer teams, Kremer ruled the GT class for much of the 1970s and early 1980s with its extraordinary 935-based racing cars, evolving from the K1 in 1976, the K2 in 1977 and the K3 in 1978. The last of these turned out to be the most successful 935 variant, due to its air-to-air intercooler instead of the air-to-water units used by the Porsche factory. After that, the even more radical K4 of 1980 featured a space-frame chassis (like the factory's 935 Moby Dick). Following a change of race regulations, the CK5 of 1983 was a custom-

built Group C prototype based on a 936, while the 962 CK6 was a take on the factory 962, followed by the CK7 Spyder, an open-cockpit prototype using 962 mechanicals. Finally there came the K8 Spyder, which was an improved version of the K7 for the International Sports Racing Series and Le Mans 24-Hours. Kremer even built a 917 for the 1981 Le Mans 24-Hours using leftover parts. Although the racing ground to a temporary halt in 2001, there's a consistent back catalogue of results, with the 935/K3 era probably the standout years.

Kremer's principal Eberhard Baunach explains the motivation for launching the K3 as a road car:

Parked outside the admin building and workshop, the Jägermeister 935 Kremer K3, raced in 1981 by Axel Plankenhorn and John Fitzpatrick, stands alongside the latest 997 Carrera Cup-based K3. ANTONY FRASER

I took on the business in 2010. I used to come to Kremer as a customer with my air-cooled 911 and saw so much passion for Porsche and historic race cars. I thought it should be more celebrated and it would be good to have a renaissance because it's such an iconic race team. The idea of doing a Kremer edition for the road was a straightforward means of endorsing the team's fifty-year racing heritage – as well as having some business success. The K3 was the most successful car from the house of Kremer, so we took that bodyshell and adapted it onto the 997. We started the project in October 2014, so it's taken two years. It's quite a big job for a small but dedicated company, and to mount a K3 silhouette on a 997 was really an adventure. It has TüV approval, and now we are nearly ready to productionize it. We have had enquiries and expressions of interest from Germany, Japan and the States.

Re-launching the K3 was not on the original agenda, though, as the original idea had been to rebuild the spaceframe K4 as a recreation of a historic race car, but there were no blueprints or construction drawings, only a K4 chassis that could be copied. Instead it was decided to go with the K3, which uses the 930 chassis as its underpinnings.

When Eberhard took over, Kremer were handling only historic and air-cooled cars. He realized the company had to move into water-cooled Porsches by doing it in the way

Eberhard Baunach took over as proprietor of Kremer Racing in 2006. ANTONY FRASER

that had made Kremer successful: racing Porsches in long-distance endurance events, at an international level.

The Nürburgring is close by, so let's start there with the VLN. The plan was to push the racing for five years and then hope that a big sponsor would take over. We have just finished the sixth year and there is no big sponsor yet, so it looks as if we'll have to reduce racing next season, although if someone comes along and says, 'OK, I've got €1.3, €1.5 million for you', we are totally in the game. But as you know, the race business is making fire with hay: very bright and shining but nothing left after it's burned up. After two years you have an old race car, so to be on the top level with a potential overall winner you have to have a new car every third year. We started with a 997 Carrera Cup car, and we did a good job even though it wasn't an overall winner. So I decided we would sell driver seats, but when you consider nearly 200 cars

are starting every race weekend, with three drivers per car, there's a lot of competition for us and the fees we can ask are not great. So, we have a couple of in-house drivers and a pay driver and that works quite well.

Nevertheless, it's a hard-nosed business, and even worse if the pay driver crashes their car.

For example, an overall winning car – a 991 R – is about €450,000, and then you need another €100,000 for spare parts and it hasn't even raced yet. Insurance is so expensive that you can even afford to absorb two crashes before insurance cover is worth having. Anyhow, that's the racing game, and it is unstable, so we have the workshop and the garage as a stable base for the company, and the other business idea is to do a Kremer special edition, hence the K3. We want to push the name, to say, 'we are back', with the same things that Kremer was successful with in the past. If you are able to prepare a car for the 24-Hours of the Nürburgring it demonstrates that you mean business. And now we are on the edge where we have to change our business focus, so maybe we will race less and push more on the K3 development, and we are very close to the goal with that.

Let's see how it's getting on, then. Among the assorted Porsches is a Jägermeister-liveried 1980 K3 that was raced in 1981 by Axel Plankenhorn and John Fitzpatrick. There's also a spaceframe 1981 K4 chassis, a maze of triangulated scaffold tubes, awaiting restoration. Eberhard expands:

Kremer Racing boss Eberhard Baunach explains that the team's programme in the VLN race series was obliged to embrace water-cooled 911s. ANTONY FRASER

The K4 panels clad the spaceframe, whereas when you strip the KI, 2 and 3, you still have the basic Porsche 930 bodyshell. The KI is single turbo, and then in 1977 the K2 became flat-nosed 935 style, 2857cc single turbo, followed in 1978 by the K3 flat-nose, with twin-turbos and upside-down gearbox to get a little lower ground clearance. They had a locked differential so the wheels always turned at the same speed, too.

Kremer's main workshop is replete with a broad cross-section of Porsches, including a 356 being stripped out for restoration, a narrow body S, a 964 and 993 for service, and an SC/RS being converted back from race to road. At the rear of the workshop are five different engines on stands in various stages of rebuild: air- and water-cooled, 4- and 6-cylinder units. Several shelves and cabinets display massive trophies that the team has garnered during its racing career. There are five hoists – a couple occupied by cars in service – and there's a separate engine shop occupied by the Kremer team's 997 GT3 R that saw action in the N-24 earlier that year. A set of dedicated Fuchs wheels shod with ContiSports awaits the road car – huge rim offsets and black centres. Kremer are Fuchs agents, and a set for a 996 would cost €700 a wheel. The overall impression here is neatness and efficiency.

My eye is drawn to the white K3 race car that Kremer has had accepted for the German VLN series. It's this car that's provided much of the inspiration and know-how to produce the K3 that we're reviewing here. The road car is currently up on its own built-in air-jacks, one of which is under the front axle and one either side in the rear footwells. Beneath

The latest Kremer K3 race car, based on a 997 Carrera Cup car with bodywork by Zimspeed, is scheduled to appear in the German VLN race series. AUTHOR

The engine bay of the Kremer K3 houses a normally aspirated 997 Carrera Cup engine with carbon air filter housings. ANTONY FRASER

the skin it's a 997 Carrera Cup car, and the conversion begins with the removal of much of the 997 exterior panelling. The K3 bodywork is produced by Zimspeed, run by Holger Zimmermann, son of the proprietor of DP Motorsport, which provided Kremer Racing with 935 panels forty years ago. 'It's a neat relationship,' says race mechanic Liam Fraussen, 'Kremer Racing used to get 935 bodywork from DP Motorsport and now we are getting it from Zimspeed.' Zimspeed evolved the modern version of the slant-nose bodywork in a wind tunnel. The whole car is 60cm longer overall than the 996 Carrera Cup car. The shell is 2m wide, which is the limit permitted by VLN regulations, but the sloping nose differs from the original K3. In effect, they are copying not so much the original Vaillant or Jägermeister 935-based cars so much as the latest racer, the white K3, and road-going regulations and TüV approval means complying with headlight regulations – hence the main- and dip-beam Hella lenses in the leading slopes of the front wings. Fans were ecstatic when they first saw how the race car reverted to the Group 5 retro look.

Specifically, the two circular mesh grilles either side of the front oil cooler grille feed fresh air to the water radiators mounted ahead of the front wheels. The two horizontal banana-shaped slats are for cooling the brakes, and the eight louvres on top of the front wings allow the hot air to escape, which is also the function of the open ends at the rear of the wings, rushing the expelled air along the sides of the car. Among the K3's neatest design cues are the finned top edges of the front wings. In the leading edges of the rear arches there are blanked off openings that will supply cooling air to the 997's turbos, as that is the K3 road car's designated power plant; meanwhile it's a normally aspirated 997 Cup Car engine.

The slats in the rear three-quarter windows are taped over to prevent rain ingress, though the finished production car will be appropriately civilized. The rear wings (fenders) are attached to the inner shell by Dzus fasteners, seven each side, along with three tucked-away Allen screws. The rear wings/fenders are also open ended to allow hot air to escape, along with seven cooling slats. The original 997 rear wheel arches are cut back by about 75m (3in). The rear spoiler consists of a ducktail surmounted by an adjustable wing, with a small Gurney flap to trim the aero. The whole spoiler and engine lid ensemble is made of substantial fibreglass, though perfectly installable by one person; the two arrowheads fit into housings in the car's rear shell either side of the rear window, and the ensemble is secured with four more Dzus fasteners.

It's been an on-going learning curve, creating and fine-tuning the road car, with subtly different permutations evolved during the VLN race series on the K3 race car by Kremer's lead driver Wolfgang Kaufmann, who evaluates sizes and settings during testing. 'You can see that everything comes straight from the race track,' Liam says:

> not just from the tunnel, and Kremer fans love that. We have spent a year evolving the race K3 aerodynamics, so pressure is good front and back – we don't have such a big spoiler on the back so we are allowed the enormous diffuser at the rear for racing, but we can't have that on the road car. We don't need it on the road anyway.

The Hella rear lights must be visible from 1m back from the car. A hallmark of the original K3 was the huge single headlamps mounted just above ground level either side of the front valence. In the modern car we find Hella LED driving lights in a similar location, though slightly further back in the wings, which Liam says may be mounted so they swivel with the steering. The rearview mirrors are Carrera Cup items and seem perfectly adequate on the road.

The front lid is clipped shut, with the central Cup filler nozzle prominent. The bars from the roll cage feed into the engine bay at the top of the shock turrets, with triangulated tubes leading diagonally back into the cockpit. There's no need for a strut-brace, though when they employ a 997 Turbo

as donor car they won't have the Cup cage and will doubtless fit a strut brace. As well as the tank, there are reservoirs for brake cylinders, ABS, power steering and air jacks.

The doors are fibreglass, in this case 997 Carrera Cup items – in fact the doors and the roof are the only visible body parts from the donor car. There are normal handles for opening the doors, and the in-car camera that records racing incidents is still present. The roll cage is also state-of-the-art GT3 Carrera Cup, massively braced and reinforced in the triangulations, most noticeably in the door openings. It's unlikely that a customer for the K3 road car would want to go to such lengths, but such a construction is entirely possible if required. There's a fully automatic fire extinguisher system with spray points all around the cabin, which is fitted with Recaro race seats, six-point Schroth harnesses, OMP steering wheel with paddle shifters and buttons for headlight flasher (red), pitlane speed limiter (green) and car-to-pits communication. The lower buttons don't function in the car's road-going role. There's a fly-off handbrake and the clutch pedal is necessary to get it going, though during my run out in the car I am grateful for its presence while making shifts on a damp, leaf-strewn road surface. The wheels are composed of 18in BBS split-rim centres with rim offsets stepping out another inch to create a 19in diameter wheel. Tyres are Michelin Pilot Sport Cup 2s, regarded as the best compromise for road and trackday use, with 325/30 × 19 on the rear, and fronts at 254/35 × 19. Peering into the engine

Homage to the legendary 935 K3 race car. Kremer Racing offers this 997 Carrera Cup-based road car so fans can emulate the team's Le Mans win of 1979. ANTONY FRASER

bay the most obvious ancillary is the Kremer-branded twin-inlet pipe with a pair of air filters at either end.

Driving the K3 on the road is an intriguing prospect. It is still, as far as the controls are concerned, a 997 Carrera Cup car, and the productionized 997 Turbo will be as civilized as you'd care to specify it. I clamber over the cross-braced scaffolding of the roll cage and settle into the supportive racing seat. Liam buckles me up in the six-point harness. The OMP wheel has a beautiful feel to it, and the carbon fibre paddles are easy to use, right-hand paddle for up and left-hand for down. My seating position is close up to the wheel. Eberhard hovers like an anxious parent.

We are on a little-used back road a few kilometres from the workshop, dodging showers so the road is damp and strewn with sodden leaves. It's a tad daunting, but opportunities to drive a proper Kremer racing car don't come along that often. There's no gear lever, just the paddles, but that's not an issue. I also have the clutch to facilitate the gearchanges. However, the clutch is of the on-off variety; it's not muscle building, but it is a matter of accurately synchronizing the engine revs with the clutch take-up. I let the pedal come up till I feel it bite, and then ease on the gas – and it's very difficult to get it right at first. There's very little in the way of a turning circle too, but soon enough I'm rolling. Every gearshift is quite violent – it's bang, bang, bang with each one as the car shudders momentarily. Mostly I don't get out of 3rd, especially in the woods, though on the open straight I have time to find 4th and 5th. One time going into 4th there's a twitch from the back-end on account of the damp road. Woah! On the road every gear is a sort of compromise, and it's difficult in traffic to find exactly the right gear to be going

On the back roads the Kremer K3 is out of its element, and it's rare to get out of 3rd gear; every gearshift is violent, making the car shudder momentarily. ANTONY FRASER

along in, whereas on a track you'd be slotting ratios to fit every corner. Nevertheless, when unfettered the grin factor sure is a big one. As for the noise, it's pure Nordschleife! At turnarounds, I'm noting the engine temperature on the Motech speedometer and it's consistently reading 8.5°C.

All the controls are race oriented at the moment, and maybe this is what you'd want with your Kremer street car, but you could always stick with the standard 997 Turbo apparatus when you place your order. As Eberhard says:

> when we're making the proper road-going 997 based K3, it will have the interior of the normal 997 Turbo road car. We have two directions: one is to build on a 997 Cup base like this, so the interior will be like this, or you get a 997 Turbo or GT2, whatever you want, and we make the K3 on that. The flat-nose is good for racing because the engine and gearbox are at the back, so you have more pressure on the back wheels, plus the flat nose is not only good looking, it has aerodynamic advantages too.

All of which filters down to the price, which is roughly €100,000 on top of the donor 997, including work carried out at Kremer's Köln workshop. Eberhard has the last word:

> No bodykits; we do the work in house so it's done right; that way it's a proper Kremer conversion too, with the kudos that brings. It's the right time for the K3 too. Porsche recently brought out the 997 Sport Classic, pale grey with a little ducktail, and it was immediately sold out, so this retro look is working.

Based on a 997 Carrera Cup car, the Kremer K3 cabin spec includes a comprehensive safety cage, an OMP wheel with carbon fibre paddles, race seats and six-point harnesses. ANTONY FRASER

The K3 may reprise the halcyon race car, but it looks awesomely modern too.

ON THE RACETRACK

With its sixteenth overall Le Mans victory under its belt, from 1999 Porsche turned its attention to the development and deployment of near-standard racing versions of the 911, thus returning to its motor sport roots. Instead of sending a works team to the tracks, the company supported customer squads by providing works drivers and expertise gleaned from five decades at Le Mans. In 1999 the 911 GT3 R made its grid debut. Powered by the 415bhp water-cooled 3.6-litre flat-six engine, Manthey Racing's Grand Touring entry outpaced the entire competition, even the larger GT class entries and several prototypes. Uwe Alzen, Patrick Huisman and Luca Riccitelli secured a clear LM GT class win ahead of another GT3 R fielded by the American Champion Team with factory support. What followed is reminiscent of Porsche's legendary beginnings at Le Mans: Porsche customers lifted six more consecutive class victories up to 2005.

In 2000 three American teams and three French teams, plus a squad each from Germany, Switzerland, Belgium, Australia, Japan and Spain, all fielded 911 GT3 Rs at Le Mans. Best-placed was Japan's Taisan team, although success didn't come without some jitters. On the Thursday Hideo Fukuyama seriously damaged his Porsche in the course of doing a double somersault, and his mechanics worked a 40-hour shift to rebuild the 911 in time for the race. It was a major success for Porsche, as the 911 GT3

Drama of a nocturnal pit-stop during the VLN Nürburgring 24-Hours' enduro. AUTHOR

Rs took the first seven places in the GT3 class. For 2001 Porsche Motorsport rolled out a successor endowed with further developments, majoring on improved aerodynamics. The 911 GT3 RS took up where the R left off, and once again, the first seven places in the LM GT category were taken by Porsche customer teams, with Seikel Motorsport highest placed and coming 6th overall.

The following year the US Racers Group team were blessed with works support in the shape of factory drivers Lucas Luhr and Timo Bernhard. Ranged against them was the 911 GT3 RS fielded by Manfred Freisinger's team, starring works drivers Joerg Bergmeister, Romain Dumas and Sascha Maassen, who eventually crossed the finish line only a single minute behind the US Porsche. Another North American crew took the victory in 2003. This time it was the turn of Alex Job Racing, who joined forces for the Le Mans event with Petersen Motorsports. The two squads normally competed against each other in the ALMS (American Le Mans Series), but their cooperation paid off, despite poor weather conditions affecting the race. Of the eight 435bhp GT3 RSs to start, seven went the distance, though only three of these seven managed to complete the whole 24-Hours.

Its 3.6-litre engine now delivering 445bhp, the 911 GT3 bore the traditional RSR designation. Suspension and aerodynamics had undergone further upgrades accordingly, and for the first time a sequential transmission was fitted. Thus equipped, the joint US White Lightning/Peterson Motorsports team lifted the Le Mans trophy in 2004, and the following year it was Alex Job's turn once more. The seventh consecutive class win for a racing Porsche based on the 911 GT3 was also the eleventh win in a row for a 911. Then in 2006, in what looked like yet another sure-fire victory for the 911 GT3 RSR, just before the finish the leading Seikel Motorsport team's RSR gearbox gave trouble, relegating them to 2nd place.

Next time around, in 2007, Porsche teams locked out the entire GT podium, with the French IMSA Performance Matmut squad scooping the 24-Hour honours, as well as winning the inaugural environmental Michelin Green-X Challenge, establishing that the GT3 RSR was the most efficient car in respect of fuel consumption and average speed. This used to be called the Index of Thermal Efficiency (an assessment based on speed, weight and fuel consumption). In fact, Porsche won this particular accolade every year until 2011.

A four-minute lap time was generally seen as the holy grail or, in other words, the benchmark barrier to break for the GT2 class in which the 911 GT3 RSR was competing. In 2008 American works driver Patrick Long turned in a qualifying lap in the GT3 RSR of 3m 58.152s. During the race, however, the two fastest Porsches were running

one-two when they managed to collide. Porsche was also represented by customer teams in the prototype class, and the RS Spyder was the marque's first sports prototype to contest Le Mans since the 911 GT1 98 clinched overall victory in 1998. Prepared in accordance with the regulations for Le Mans Prototypes 2, the RS Spyder was not built as a contender for outright honours, rather a likely candidate for victory in the small prototype class. The aerodynamic open-top racer, which was powered by a 3.4-litre V8 producing 476bhp, was required under the race regulations to have a starting weight of 825kg, so Weissach technicians had to add ballast. Even so, the Dutch Van Merksteijn Motorsport RS Spyder won the P2 class by seven laps ahead of the similar car of Danish Team Essex.

For 2009 the engine capacity of the 911 GT3 RSR grew to 4.0 litres, but air intake restrictors limited the output to around 331kW (450bhp). The rivalry between factory pilots Joerg Bergmeister and Marc Lieb made waves as they jousted for highest grid position in the GT2 class, and Bergmeister was a scant three-hundredths of a second faster. It didn't go too well in the race, as Lieb's Felbermayr-Proton 911 GT3 RSR was sidelined with a defect in the fuel system, while Bergmeister had to park the Flying Lizard Motorsports GT3 RSR after a collision with a rival. In 2P, the Essex team's RS Spyder bettered last year's 2nd place with the class win.

For 2010 the GT3 RSR was fitted with its most powerful engine yet, developing 455bhp from its 3996cc flat-six, also running wider front tyres and revised aerodynamics: with this Felbermayr-Proton won its class as well as the Green-X Challenge. A year later, in 2011, works driver Marc Lieb took fastest race lap in the Felbermayr-Proton car, though unprecedented tyre wear caused the Felbermayr, Matmut and Flying Lizard cars to drop back to 4th, 5th and 6th, respectively. The following year was the end of the story for the 911 GT3 at Le Mans, though IMSA Performance Matmut scored 2nd in the GTE AM class using the previous year's RSR.

In 2013 the factory team returned to Le Mans after a fourteen-year interval. Team Manthey fielded a pair of brand-new 911 RSRs against strong opposition in the GT category. The RSR is based on the seventh generation of 911, designated the 991. While the well-proven 4.0-litre engine still delivered 460bhp, many innovations were concealed beneath its partly carbon fibre body, including the new lightweight racing gearbox. The front axle comprised a wishbone layout instead of MacPherson struts, and the wheelbase was expanded by 10cm. It was a double victory for Porsche, with success in the GTE PRO class for Manthey's Leib/Lietz/Dumas. In the GTE AM amateur class, the previous year's Matmut GT3 RSR took the win for Vernay/Narac/Bourret, recording the marque's 101st and 102nd class victories.

One of the work's 919 Hybrids in the pits garage at Le Mans ahead of the 2016 24-Hours race. This is the Timo Bernhard/Brendon Hartley/Mark Webber car, with Webber in discussions with technicians. AUTHOR

The new set of rules that applied for the World Endurance Championship (WEC) for 2014 were clearly focused on efficiency and required the use of the latest hybrid technology. The aim of the new rules for the upcoming season was to significantly reduce fuel consumption and the new Porsche LMP1 therefore needed to deliver optimum efficiency as well as maximum performance. The best placed 919 2.0 turbo V4 Hybrid came 11th, driven by Lieb/Dumas/Jani, with the highest placed RSR in 17th. It was a different story in 2015, with factory 919 Hybrids coming 1st and 2nd, a lap apart, for Earl Bamber/Nick Tandy/Nico Hulkenberg and Timo Bernhard/Brendon Hartley/Mark Webber. More relevant to our story is that the top LM GTE RSR came 22nd overall and 2nd in class, driven by Patrick Dempsey/Patrick Long/Marco Seefried.

Outright victory in 2016 went to Lieb/Dumas/Jani in their works 919 Hybrid, a lucky win by any standards as the leading Toyota retired on the last lap, while the Gulf GTE AM RSR of Mike Wainwright/Adam Carroll/Ben Barker came 33rd overall and 6th in class. What's evident is that there's been a level of consistency in podium results in the GT class commensurate with Porsche's achievements in what now seem like the halcyon days of the 1970s, though somewhat overshadowed in recent years by the amazing success of the 919 Hybrid in LMP1: three wins on the trot can't be overstated.

The 991 RSR of Frédéric Makowiecki and Richard Lietz ran in the Pro class of the 2018 World Endurance Championship series. PORSCHE MUSEUM ARCHIVES

Running in the GT-Le Mans category in the WEC, the two factory 991 RSRs of Laurens Vanthoor/Gianmaria Bruni/Earl Bamber and Nick Tandy/Fred Makowiecki/Patrick Pilet placed 12th and 10th respectively in the 2018 Mobil 1 Sebring 12-Hours. PORSCHE MUSEUM ARCHIVES

The Manthey-prepared factory 991 GT3 RSR of Henzler/Makowiecki/Pilet finished 41st overall, and 10th in the GTE Am class at Le Mans in 2016. AUTHOR

Lap one of a round of the US Carrera Cup series at Lime Rock circuit, Connecticut, 2014. AUTHOR

THE CARRERA CUP AND SUPERCUP

Deserving of a book in its own right, the Porsche Carrera Cup and its close relative, the Porsche Supercup, started in 1986 as the 944 Turbo Cup series. The forerunner of the multi-national Carrera Cup and Supercup series, the 944-based one-model series was Porsche's calculated contribution to recreational motor sport, implying that anyone could have a crack at it, given the wherewithal, of course. In the inaugural seven-race series, hobby drivers went head to head with professionals in virtually bog-standard 944 Turbos, the forty contestants sharing a DM45,000 purse at each race. The higher you finished, the more you earned. Initially the curtain-raiser for the ADAC Supercup Group C races, the Turbo Cup blossomed into the 964-based Carrera Cup in 1990, for which Weissach built fifty cars, and by 1993 the Supercup was tagged onto F1's coat-tails. After the air-cooled 993 Cup Cars became obsolete it was the turn of the 996 GT3 to fulfil that role. It has had a hugely successful racing career in the one-make national and regional Porsche Carrera Cup and GT3 Cup Challenge series, as well as the international Porsche Supercup races supporting the FIA F1 World Championship. It has won many championships and gruelling endurance races, including the GT class of the

ALMS (American Le Mans Series) seven times, placed 1st overall in the Daytona 24-Hours, and 1st overall at the N-24 Nürburgring 24-Hours six times.

Its successor, predictably, was the 997 Carrera Cup race car, based on the GT3 RS. Its spec included a 44mm (1.7 in) wider body, 15mm (0.59in) lower front splitter, 1.7m (67in) rear wing from an ex-GT3 Cup S race car, LED tail lights,

The Racer's Racer: Super Mario in the driving seat of a 997 GT3. He was fond of saying, 'If everything seems under control, you're just not going fast enough!' ANTONY FRASER

Mario Andretti raced a 996 GT3 Cup in the Supercup round supporting the 2000 US Grand Prix at Indianapolis. PORSCHE MUSEUM ARCHIVES

The transmission includes a paddle-shift, race-bred, pneumatically activated six-speed developed specifically for the track. It uses lightweight materials in its construction, plus stripped-out cabin, complete with a full roll cage, racing seat and all the safety gear required for competition, weighing in at 1,175kg.

Porsche celebrated its third consecutive victory at Le Mans in 2017 with the 919 Hybrid, calling time on the WEC (for how long, one wonders) and moving into single-seater Formula E for 2018, increasing its GT programme with the 911 RSR and 911 GT3 R. Time will tell if trends are electric, though it does smack of jumping on a bandwagon. Alongside this apparent aberration, however, two GT3 Cup Trophies, ten GT3 Cup Challenges and eight Porsche Carrera Cups operate worldwide, culminating with the internationally contested Porsche Mobil 1 Supercup, which tours selected rounds of the F1 championship. The Porsche one-make Cup series, which includes the Porsche Carrera Cup GB, is one of the most successful international racing programmes and provides a realistic stepping stone to becoming a potential Porsche factory driver.

Entering its sixteenth year in 2018, Porsche Carrera Cup GB is a principal fixture on the British motor racing calendar. A key element is that grids of more than twenty identical cars put drivers' skills in the spotlight, inevitably producing close racing, backed up with top-class facilities for teams and drivers. Run by Porsche Cars Great Britain (PCGB), it has raised interest in Porsche motor sport in the UK and provides a pathway for young drivers to climb the racing ladder through the Carrera Cups and Porsche Mobil 1 Supercup, up to World Championship GT racing. Two drivers who have recently raced their way to the top of this pyramid are Nick

racing exhaust system with fully controlled catalytic converter and Porsche Ceramic Composite Brakes. It had 9.5J × 18 front alloy wheels with 24/64-18 Michelin racing tyres and 12J × 18 alloy rear wheels with 27/68-18 racing tyres. There were additional Unibal joints on the track control arms, front and rear sword-shaped anti-roll bars with seven position settings each, a additional vent in the upper part of the front lid, and steering wheel-mounted Info Display with six switches.

Porsche next introduced the 991 GT3 Cup for the 2013 Porsche Supercup season, based on the 991 GT3. Like the 991 GT3 road car, its improvements over the 997 model included revised aerodynamics, an improved roll cage, new wheels and a revised chassis. The direct-injection 3.8-litre flat-six produces 338kW at 8,500rpm and drives the rear wheels through a mechanical limited slip differential.

The 919 Hybrid of Hartley/Bernhard/Bamber won the 2017 Le Mans 24-Hours, taking the lead two hours from the finish. PORSCHE MUSEUM ARCHIVES

The Porsche Supercup invariably provides close racing and plenty of thrills and spills. Here at Mexico City, Dennis Olson leads Dan Cammish and Josh Webster in their 991 GT3 R Cup cars. PORSCHE MUSEUM ARCHIVES

PETER DUMBRECK INTERVIEW

**Peter Dumbreck is the lead driver in the
Falken Team's 991 GT3 R.** AUTHOR

Peter Dumbreck is the lynchpin of the Falken Tyres racing team, bringing their Porsche 997 GT3 R to the podium at the Nürburgring 24-Hours in 2015. If you'd flipped a Le Mans car into the woods at 190mph (305km/h) and walked away, you'd probably be content to rest on your laurels. Not Peter Dumbreck: the resolute Scotsman carried on racing in the DTM and the WEC, driving for Mercedes-Benz, Spyker, Aston Martin and Opel, with a best result of 3rd at Le Mans in 2013. In 2005 Peter guested in a 997 GT3 at the Silverstone round of the Porsche Supercup, followed up by four seasons driving a Lexus in Super GT, and two seasons for Nissan in GT1. In 2018 he signed for his twelfth season with Falken Tyres, specializing in the German VLN series and the Nürburgring 24-Hours. He scored 3rd place on the N-24 podium in 2015, which is where we chatted in the Falken hospitality suite.

JT: You had a hugely successful career in single seaters, notably Formula Vauxhall-Lotus and F3. Why did you move into the WEC?

PD: Sure, everyone on the singe-seater ladder wants to get into Formula 1, but I had an offer from Mercedes-Benz to drive at Le Mans in 1999, and I was also doing Formula Nippon in Japan. There comes a point in everyone's career where you have to make a pragmatic move, and I could have carried on in Formula Nippon with no contract, but the offer of a works drive in the WEC and DTM from Mercedes was too good to pass up. Other drivers like Paul Di Resta have made it back into F1 from there, but you have to win the DTM championship and I came 2nd.

JT: Do you ever think of the somersaulting CLR incident?

PD: Not really; it seems like a world away now. Mine was the third flip – Mark (Webber) had already gone over twice, but mine was the one that made them pull the plug on the race and their whole programme in ALMS as well. It was in the back of my mind that it could happen, that it could flip, and as soon as it started to happen I knew what was going on, but I didn't have that 'life flashing before my eyes' moment. I thought, well, Mark's survived so there's no reason I shouldn't. I tend to fight it to the end, holding onto the wheel and take the force of the impact with my body. I didn't black out, but I was very conscious of the G-forces, and you just think, 'I'm having an accident here', and I just braced myself and tried to make it as easy for myself as I could.

JT: You spend most of your time racing in VLN these days. What's the Ring like for a racing driver?

PD: Here, I'm always pushing the car to the limit, and the undulations in the track are constant, plus the fact that you leave the ground with all four wheels off, three or four times in a lap, and then there's the slamming down, not just the kind that you get as you come off one camber onto the other: there's a big hit, and then you bounce out of that camber and go the other way. The N-24 is one of the hardest races in motor sport, in the world, even, and this track is brutal on the car and the driver. It's the focus of my year, the N-24, and Falken's too. It's also one of the few events where

Highly sophisticated and complex environment of the Falken 991 GT3 R cockpit features an electronic circuit map on the steering wheel boss. AUTHOR

you have top pro-drivers paid by the manufacturers, plus gentleman drivers out to enjoy themselves, and guys who aren't so wealthy but just love their racing. And we have to pass around thirty cars per lap, which isn't always easy when you're coming up behind an inexperienced amateur driver, because you don't know where they're going.

JT: Effectively the N-24 is run on two different (though interconnected) circuits: the sanitized F1 track with its vast gravel run-off areas, and the Nordschleife, where there's a sliver of grass but the barrier is mostly right up against the track. Do you think racing here is still relevant?

PD: Yes, maybe more so. We all know how dangerous the place is, and you're punished if you make a mistake, but it has a unique appeal for 700 drivers and 300,000 spectators.

We like the challenge of it because it's forcing us to explore the limits. There are lots of elevation changes and it's very bumpy. Actually, it's like one very long street circuit, and that's why the manufacturers love honing their products here too. When you're on the Formula 1 circuit you know you've got two-and-a-half-miles where there's much more room to manoeuvre with plenty of run-off, though you can never relax. Our tyres are designed for the Nordschleife; they don't work quite so well on the track surface of the Grand Prix circuit, but from a driving point of view we're still pushing hard on the Grand Prix circuit, just with more room.

JT: Your car is a 997, built on a 2014 chassis, running an ECU that dates back to 2010, so does that explain why your qualifying time isn't as fast as the opposition?

PD: Pretty much, yes. For the past two years Porsche have concentrated on the 919 Le Mans car, and for homologation reasons we haven't been able to update the ECU to help us match the Audis and BMWs technically, though Porsche have helped with the on-board speed limiter. We shall have another car next year; either a new 991 GT3 R or a Falken RSR from the States.

JT: How do you practice for the VLN?

PD: We spend a lot of time trying different tyre compounds, and in fact this is one of the few series where there's a tyre war going on. Michelin are our biggest rivals, and that's our benchmark, but basically you can run whatever you want.

JT: How long are your stints behind the wheel?

PD: Normally as long as a tank of fuel lasts, nine laps, but no longer than three hours each. It might vary if we have to pit for tyres if it comes on to rain, and then we'd maybe double stint.

JT: What's your personal race strategy?

PD: I treat each stint as its own race, because the thought of still running this time tomorrow scares me. So I try and do the best job I can in my stint, hand the car over in as good a condition as I can. We have a couple of containers in the Falken paddock enclave where we can get a physio massage, take a shower, eat something, and have a power nap. By then I'll know roughly what time I'm getting back in the car for my second race stint.

(continued overleaf)

PETER DUMBRECK INTERVIEW (*continued*)

Atmospheric twilight shot of Brunnchen on the Nordschleife during the 24-Hours. AUTHOR

JT: How do you pace yourself? Do you take maybe half a lap to dial yourself in, or are you on it straightaway?

PD: If you're on brand new tyres, just out of the heaters, you'll let them bed in first, but by the time you arrive at the Nordschleife they'll be ready to go hard. And you might take half a lap of the Nordschleife to get really acclimatized.

JT: Do you have a personal 'red mist' control?

PD: Yes, I'm often talking to myself! Say someone's really wound me up, I'm saying 'Calm down, calm down!', and likewise if I start drifting off, I'm going, 'Focus, focus! Keep your head here.' Because at any time something could happen, and dealing with it has to be a reflex action.

JT: Do you have a preference for driving during the day or the night?

PD: Dusk and dawn are the two nicest periods and, for sure, you're going to drive at least once during the night, but the best times to drive are just as it's getting dark or just as it's getting light, because you can adjust so you keep your speed. And that's how I tend to look at 24-hour races.

JT: What were the major dramas during this year's race?

PD: We were careful with the tyres, and when it started to rain in the night I pitted for intermediates and took it easy till it eased off and a dry line emerged. Then I came in for slicks and double stinted for another six laps. It was during that time that a lot of crashes were happening, people got caught out on slicks; the Haribo Merc, the Frikadelli Porsche (Sabine Schmitz's rival GT3R) went out at that point. The guys with the Bentley were really ragging it, and Steven (Kane) overdid it, slammed on the brakes and I went into the back of him, luckily no damage to the radiator. There was a bit of needle as Wolf (Henzler) had hit him earlier!

JT: It's such a long race that you must come across the same cars again and again, so you get to know which ones will be cooperative and which ones to watch out for.

PD: Yes, every three or four laps, in fact, so you might pass them three times in one stint. Some guys stick out and you know to be wary; others you know they're a good crew and they'll know where you are and when to pull over. Occasionally there'll be one car where none of its drivers are paying much attention because they're just trying to keep on the track, and they're the challenge.

JT: How was it in the speed-restricted sections?

PD: Yes, this is all in the aftermath of the accident (involving the death of a spectator in 2016) in the first VLN round. The drivers have had to go back to school to learn the new rules, which meant seven hours in the classroom, familiarization bus rides around the circuit and a driving assessment with an instructor over eight laps, but the marshals don't seem to have learned the same lessons. There was a lack of consistency about the marshalling, so that if you arrived somewhere and a yellow flag was being waved, and at the

Wolf Henzler won the 2004 Porsche Supercup series in a 996 GT3-R, the 2008 American Le Mans Series with a 997 GT3 RSR, and the GT2 Class at Le Mans in 2010 in a GT3 RSR. He also helms the Falken 997 GT3 Cup in Grand Am, ALMS and the VLN series, as well as Manthey and KCMG operations in the WEC, including the Le Mans 24-Hours. AUTHOR

next one there was a single yellow board, then you'd wonder, should that be two yellow boards, which means a Code-60. But then at the next post there could be two yellow boards, and a green flag after that, releasing you from the Code-60, after which the quick cars are doing 200km/h, only to come upon another two yellow boards, with a couple of slower cars doing 60km/h. Nowhere to go except on the grass. Very dramatic! But we don't need that: there should be some consistency and some warning you're about to enter a Code-60 zone.

JT: What about the on-board speed limiter?

PD: When we did the last VLN race we had to adjust the speed manually, which meant you were continually looking from the road to your speedo and trying to drive a race, and that meant you weren't paying enough attention to the

road. Now, with the limiter you just hit the button and it holds the car at the right speed. We all understand why the speed limits have been brought in but personally I think that makes it potentially more dangerous because you're not focusing on your driving. You're focusing on your speed and the other cars that you might normally go by easily, but now, in the restricted zones, you can't go by because they can do 200km/h as well. I hope they find another solution so we can run free again.

JT: How does the limiter work?

PD: It's gear-related; in first gear we do 60km/h, in fourth gear we do 200km/h, and in 5th and 6th gear if you press the button you do 250km/h. Ironically, I can go through Flugplatz flat in 4th now, and I've never been able to do that before. Because it's on the limiter and it goes ba-ba-ba-ba-ba at 200km/h, and once you're through the section you go up a gear and that lets the limiter know to switch off – like cruise control – and you can go up to 250km/h. And thankfully none of us got caught speeding during the race – you only get two warnings.

Indeed, Peter and his three co-drivers (Wolf Henzler, Martin Ragginger and Alexandre Imperatori) stayed focused, and in spite of a couple of altercations – one with a Bentley that misjudged its braking point, hence the application of reams of gaffer tape – they brought the Falken Tyres' Porsche 997 GT3 R home in a well-deserved 3rd place. They'd actually led the race at midnight, as the top three cars – Audi R8 and BMW Z4 – swapped places as one or the other pitted for tyres and fuel.

Despite the Porsche's vast rear wing and the downforce it exerts, there are several places on the Nordschleife where cars become airborne, such as the Flugplatz where the Falken 997 GT3-R takes off in the 2014 N-24. ANTONY FRASER

Tandy and Earl Bamber. From his first appearance in Porsche Carrera Cup Asia in 2013, Bamber quickly progressed to the Porsche Mobil 1 Supercup in 2014 as a Porsche Junior and signed as a Porsche works driver for 2015. That year he joined fellow Carrera Cup and Supercup graduate Nick Tandy and F1 driver Nico Hulkenberg to take the first of the 919 Hybrid's three wins in the Le Mans 24-Hours. Bamber was again part of the winning team in 2017.

Nick Tandy, the first British driver to win Le Mans in a Porsche since Allan McNish in 1998, made his debut at the Porsche Carrera Cup GB in 2008. After winning the Porsche Carrera Cup Deutschland in 2011 and the prestigious Porsche Cup in 2012 as the best private Porsche driver worldwide in a 911, he became a works driver and progressed through the Porsche racing series. His impressive achievements earned him a seat in the third entry for the Le Mans 24-Hours in 2015, where he went on to win the toughest car race in the world. Nick claims that the Carrera Cup taught him to become a winner and ultimately a champion driver. 'When you compete against so many top-line drivers in identical cars, it forces all of you to raise your game, otherwise you don't win! So many world-class drivers have developed that skill racing in the Carrera Cup.' Indeed, many drivers seeking careers as professional sports and GT racers have used the Carrera Cup as a launch pad.

Former Porsche Carrera Cup GB champions Richard Westbrook, Michael Meadows and Damien Faulkner have built careers as professional racers, and 2012 Carrera Cup GB runner-up Ben Barker raced a Porsche 991 GT3 RSR in the 24-Hours of Le Mans in 2016 and 2017. An unprecedented number of Porsche Carrera Cup GB drivers participated in the 2017 Porsche Mobil 1 Supercup, including Josh Webster (2016 Porsche GB Junior champion), Dan Cammish, Tom Sharp, Paul Rees, Ryan Cullan, Sean Hudspeth and Mark Radcliffe. The new 911 GT3 Cup is to be imtroduced in 2018, plus changes to the race format and points structure: 'The new car is faster, more durable, more efficient, and even safer than the previous model. It is quite simply a pre-bred race car and a precision instrument for the race track – the next step in our vision to creating the perfect race car.' With more than 3,500 units sold, the 911 GT3 Cup is already the most numerous sports racing car among motor sports teams and drivers. The improved 911 GT3 Cup design includes new front and rear aprons, four-point LED headlights and tail lights with contemporary aero. Other design improvements include the new front and rear aprons, which optimize the air flow, and FIA rain lights have been integrated for the first time. Safety has also been dramatically improved by an enlarged roof hatch providing easier access to the cockpit of the aluminium and steel hybrid

One of the stars of the **US IMSA GT3 Challenge, Christina Nielsen drives Wright Motorsports' GT3 R, partnered by Patrick Long.** AUTHOR

bodyshell. Developed from scratch, the new 4.0-litre flat-six engine delivers 485bhp at 7,500rpm, and 480Nm torque at 6,500rpm. Transmission is via a racing clutch and a Porsche six-speed sequential dog-type gearbox, making it the fastest one-make race car in the UK.

LONG DAY'S JOURNEY INTO NIGHT

Pounding the Nordschleife big dipper for 24 hours really is the greatest test of man and machine. I've covered it several years running, and in 2016 I followed Falken Tyres' 991 GT3-R's steady rise up the running order, and greeted the dawn with the crazies in the forest.

It's a seductive recipe. Take 180 assorted cars – models you might conceivably expect to see on the road – turn them into racing cars, and let them loose for a day and a night on the most amazing racetrack in the world. That's the Nürburgring 24-Hours, run on a combination of the Nordschleife and F1 circuit that totals 25km per lap. The N-24 is one of the best events on the motor sport calendar because of the wildness of the terrain, the rollercoaster topography, read-

The Falken 997 GT3-R on the Karussell at Nürburgring Nordschleife during the 24-Hour race in 2014.
ANTONY FRASER

ily identifiable 'road cars' – and the fact that they are driven pretty much flat-out for a whole day and night. Each of the car's four drivers treats every nine-lap stint as a sprint, and if the car holds together and stays out of serious trouble, it stands a good chance of a decent finish.

It's the forty-seventh running of the event, which, since the demise of world championship events on the Nord-schleife, has become the most important meeting on the fabled circuit's calendar. The N-24 is a standalone race, sharing rules and regs with the ten-round VLN Lang-streckenmeisterschaft Nürburgring (VLN Endurance Racing Championship Nürburgring). It's important enough to

The Falken 991 GT3 R leaving the pits during the 2016 N-24. Crewed by Peter Dumbreck, Wolf Henzler, Martin Ragginger and Alexandre Imperatori, the car went on to finish 9th overall. AUTHOR

attract manufacturer support for the teams and a significant number of professional racing drivers. The entry list kicks off with an eye-watering mix of supercars, ranging from Audi R8 LMS, Mercedes-Benz SLS AMG GT3, Aston Martin Vantage GT3, Porsche 911 GT3 RSR, Bentley Continental GT3 and BMW Z4 GT3, to Chrysler Viper, Nissan GT-R GT3, Lexus ISF CCS-R, and two-off Ferrari-based SCG. The sponsors' artistic palette has really gone to town, especially on some BMWs. Of the 700 or so drivers present, top-line aces include Augusto Farfus, Tom Coronel, Wolf Henzler, Peter Dumbreck, Rob Huff, Sabine Schmitz, Patrick Huisman, Claudia Hürtgen, Bernd Schneider, Uwe Alzen, Frank Stippler, Pedro Lamy and Richard Westbrook. Most of them are N-24 regulars.

Cars are parcelled into three 'grids' according to specification and qualification times, and released from 4.00pm Saturday afternoon at 3-minute intervals by successive rolling starts. The lower echelons consist of Audi TTs, Porsche Caymans, BMW M-coupés and 325s, and finally, a host of Golfs, Clios, Leons, Astras and Corollas. They'll represent the greatest challenge for quick pro-drivers who know the circuit's twists and turns intimately: dealing with inexperienced amateurs in the third wave's hatchbacks, who are focused on negotiating the corners and fighting each other, but not looking in their mirrors. So there's a great deal of second-guessing. There are thirty-six 911s, ranging from out-and-out 991 and 997 GT3 R to GT3 RSR, Cup and GT America, along with six Caymans, S and R. Top independent Porsche teams like Manthey (essentially the factory squad by another name), Kremer, Black Falcon, Frikadelli and Falken

Grid girl glamour at the N-24: unlike other echelons of the sport, the Nürburgring 24-Hours still retains some traditions. AUTHOR

TV star Sabine Schmitz is a regular competitor in the Nürburgring 24-Hours in her Frikadelli Racing 991 GT3-R. AUTHOR

Tyres have cars running, and I'm following the fortunes of the Falken outfit to see if they can top the 3rd place that they achieved last year now they have a new 991 GT3 R. Regular drivers Peter Dumbreck, Wolf Henzler, Martin Ragginger and Alexandre Imperatori have represented Falken's driving force for several years now, so if anyone can pull it off, they can.

At 2.00pm the cars are wheeled out onto the grid. With half an hour to go the drivers show up for a photocall, by which time the start-finish straight is rammed with milling fans, grid girls and pit crews. There's a hands-off attitude to crowd control at this event and the fans are well behaved. Though they stray into the pitlane during the race, they're moved back with velvet gloves. A small posse comprised of Falken PR people and a few fellow journos make our way out to the Nordschleife to catch the thundering pack on the first lap. At 4.00pm they burst into sight, led by the long-

nosed Merc SLSs, mid-engined Audi R8s, BMW Z4GT3s, Aston Vantages, a Bentley, Nissan GT-R and Lexus ISF. Somewhere in the midst of the cacophonous horde is the mint-and-blue Falken GT3. Between gaggles of cars we stroll further. The leading batch roars by again, a little more spread out. Within a couple of laps, they're lapping the backmarkers. Then, twenty minutes gone, we see red flags. The race has been stopped, and we peer into a marshal's tent to see their monitor. There's been an almighty hailstorm on the far side of the circuit and eleven cars have gone off one after another, blocking the track. The recovery vehicles begin to trundle by. The hailstorm reaches us, frozen stones the size of marbles. A restart is scheduled for 6.30pm, so when it's dry again we walk back to the pits complex.

I fill in time chatting with drivers. Erstwhile Top Gear presenter Sabine Schmitz started racing Porsches in 2005. 'We built our own team, my boyfriend and me,' she says; 'Frikadelli means meatballs, so we are the meatball racing team; my boyfriend is a German sausage king!' Has she seen conditions like this very often? 'Yes, plenty of times, sure. I got stuck in the snow one race.' And the new car?

We've had it since December, and we did the Daytona 24-hour race with it, and three long distance races so far. It's slower than the old car, and we can't develop it because of the handicaps; we have to add on weight and the air restrictor is very small, so we don't have a chance against the others. Mercedes, BMW, Audi, they play with us at the moment, so we're here because our fans were so upset when we said we don't want to start, so we said, 'OK, we go'. On the Nordschleife the big Mercedes are so strong. We got a blue light so that helps get people out of the way. Yeah, the conditions are really awful, but we like awful weather because we're used to it and we are not afraid of the rain. And I think we need a lot of rain tyres. I ordered some very hard tyres because sometimes you have half and half, and you're never sure so if it will rain or if it rains heavy, and it could be dry here and wet over there, it can change three or four times a lap.

Even so, it must go without saying that the Nürburgring is your favourite circuit? She grins: 'Everything else in the world is boring!'

This year Peter Dumbreck is philosophical about his chances on his fourteenth N-24. The length of the circuit and Nürburgring's fickle climate meant they didn't get their quick qualifying laps in when it was dry. Although they were potentially one of the quickest cars in the lead bunch, their qualification time was outside the top thirty, so they didn't get the hallowed blue light to display in their 991 GT3 windscreen to denote a fast car coming up to overtake a slower one:

We didn't get a lap in that was good enough. Theoretically we had a fast-enough car, but we had traffic and rain, and we're still learning with the car. We started 21st last year so we're another eleven places back from there, but anything is possible. I'm not sure we ultimately have the dry pace; in qualifying

Night-time pit stop for Sabine Schmitz's Frikadelli Porsche 991 GT3-R, 2016. AUTHOR

yesterday the Mercs were doing an 8m 15s lap. We can't do that, but in the wet we have a more realistic chance. We'll all be pushing like crazy so you've got to be lucky and survive the race. The usual story, just get the car through until first light and see where you are and act accordingly.

This wasn't the first race they'd done with it. In VLN rounds earlier in the year there were issues with the power steering, which went down four laps from the end, and in the second race they finished 10th but, as Peter admits:

Everyone's here now, so the competition is that much stiffer. Last year we went into the race saying, 'If we get a top five we'll be happy', but this year the target is going to be top ten. We've all done this enough times to know that if we can stay out of trouble and keep the car on the track and just pump in a decent lap time then we will come up the order. There's something like thirty-six GT-E cars on the grid that are the same speed and have four fast drivers, and we don't know what they've got left in the bank. We're running pretty much maximum, so there's guys sand-bagging maybe.

It's an uphill struggle in more ways than one.

The rule makers can decide in between qualifying and the start of the race whether to add a bit more weight or smaller restrictor to the front-running cars because they think they're too quick. So no one really wants to show too much. But when you see an 8m 14s in mixed conditions with a double yellow flag, I think they've shown everything. Even if we had an absolutely clear track with the best conditions possible we couldn't do that time, not yet anyway. The old car [997 GT3-R] was different because we were allowed to run a lot more power and have a lot more straight-line speed. This [991 GT3-R] is a much better car, but we've got smaller restrictors so we're not as quick out of the corners and we're not as quick in a straight line, so the goalposts have moved. The car feels really hooked up in the corners, but we just don't leave the corners as quick as the other cars because we're not able to put the power down. We're not allowed to use the power that's available, which is disappointing because we've got a better engine as well. So, if we were allowed to run open, for sure we would be on it. But that's modern GT3 racing, they are just trying to level off, otherwise one manufacturer would *develop their car so much that the end result is the car would end up costing a million rather than half a million, and that's why they brought the restrictors in so that they control it all and there's no benefit in spending all this money.*

All the new Porsches have the same problem:

We're a bit off the pace of the Manthey cars as well, but then they're not at the front either. Their highest one is 12th and the other one crashed in qualifying and the Frikadelli car is mid-pack, maybe 20th, so none of the Porsches are excelling like last year. You almost start the cycle again with a new car and gradually build up, and even tyre development goes back to square one. We had it all sorted with the old car, but this car develops a lot more grip, traction, and the tyres we had on the other car aren't strong enough for it, so we've had to develop stronger tyres for this car and, fingers crossed, we can do full stints with the tyres. In the beginning it was questionable because we were getting issues with the tyres, just as the other Porsches were with their Michelin tyres. In fact all the Porsches were having problems about going the full stint distance on one set of tyres, so that's something we've had to work on because safety is paramount. It's no good for the driver or for the result to get seven or eight laps into a stint and the tyre blows and you're somewhere out on the back of the circuit. So, knock on wood, we have a fighting chance with the tyres now, so we've got to work on performance.

The restart is delayed until 7.00pm, even though it's still raining. I stroll down to the first Esses complex on the F1 circuit to await the maelstrom. Cars that have been stuck out on the circuit are re-fettled in the pits and drive by for a warm up. The crowds in the stands cheer like mad. When somebody has to come in and have some work done and rushes back out they all cheer again. The first two passes are behind the pace car as they assess the conditions, and finally they're away again. Being Porsche fans to the core, we're apt to deride rival makes, but those big Mercs, Audis, BMWs and Astons look and sound absolutely awesome. Porsche GT3-Rs are the most numerous marque/model in the first starting group, and this bunch is followed a few minutes later by Group 2, comprised of 997 GT3 Cups, Cayman Ss, Audi TTs, BMW M3s, Vantage V8s and hot Astras. Another gap, and along come Group 3, the hot-hatch Clios, Siroccos, Civics and Minis. And, quaintly, a 1970s Opel Manta, a per-

One of the most distinctive corners on the Nürburgring Nordschleife, the banked Karussell demands a specific technique to negotiate it. As cars circulate there's an additional soundtrack of tortured fibreglass splitters grazing the concrete. AUTHOR

ennial entry, which does not disgrace itself, even though it looks like it's absconded from the historic race. All told, 185 cars are out there, and in a matter of three laps the fastest Group 1 GT3s are in among the tin-tops. There is never a dull moment.

The top snappers' vantage point is the outside of the Karussell. The tarmac lane peters out and we're on forest roads. Soon enough we're stomping through the undergrowth and up to the Armco surrounding the most famous hairpin of any racetrack. Cars rush up the approach and are pitched into the banked concrete loop, hanging a front wheel as they do so. The drone of the engines is intercut by the scraping of Kevlar fins and airdams, the air heady with the stench of Castrol R and burned plastic, mixed with the wafts of barbecues from across the track. Welsh track marshals are on duty and there's a Union Jack enclave inside the apex. This is undoubtedly the place to see the cars at their wildest, cocking wheels as they drop into the banking, suspension compressed by G-forces as they hurl around the 180-degree turn, then another wheel wags as they're shot out at the other end, climbing again on the way to Höhe Acht. Cars being lapped or ones with damaged bodywork stay out of the banking and circulate on the tarmac apron. Peter Dumbreck describes the methodology here:

In the Karussell it's boom, boom, boom, all the way through it and you're driving as hard as you can, but you can't just stick the throttle down flat as it would under-steer out and hit the wall. But because it's banked you drop the car down and it sticks, and then you load it up and get back on the throttle and gradually drive it through the corner.

It just looks awesome.

We trundle round to Brünnchen where the track is almost completely graffitied by the fans, who are magnetized to the fence. Diverse factions colonize particular areas on an annual basis, staking their claim with asphalt scrawls. The volume of the babbling German PA commentator mostly drowns out the music, but the solstice reverie is clearly brewing.

Cars hurtle through from Wippermann, and we ease along to Pflanzgarten to see the cars in flight, one of several places around the Nordschleife where cars get airborne for a split second. Cars plummet downhill and, just before slowing slightly and turning right into Schwalbenschwanz, they get all four wheels off the deck.

Hardly a metre of the Nordschleife lacks the attention of the graffiti artists; here the Falken 997 GT3-R pounds the Schwalbenschwanz in 2014. AUTHOR

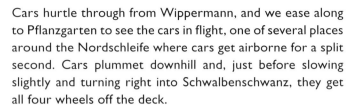

The Falken 991 GT3 R leans into the Karussell during the 2016 Nürburgring N-24, eventually placing 9th overall. ANTONY FRASER

A routine midnight pit-stop and driver change for the Falken squad's 997 GT3-R. AUTHOR

The topography is so varied that each bend and every dip provides a different aspect and backdrop to see the racing. What's most impressive is the velocity of the big R8s, SLSs, GT3 Rs and Z4s, the indomitable noise, the speed differential between them and the hot-hatches – most of whom stay well out of trouble – and the decibel factor, possibly won by the Lexus, which sounds amazing. After a while we can recognize each distinctive multi-cylinder engine note as they pelt through the 'green hell'. Most of the faster cars including the Porsches deploy flashing lights as they come up to lap slower cars. During the night, the Falken boys move resolutely up the running order. 'It's smooth on the Grand Prix circuit,' says Peter, 'so you push slightly more there because it's wider and you've got a margin for error and you can make up a bit of time here. If you've got a gaggle of cars in front, you want to try and get through them all while you're on the Grand Prix circuit.' The Falken wet tyres seem to be more effective than rivals' too.

We head back to the pits to see the driver changes, well-rehearsed operations accompanied by wheel swaps, screen cleaning and refuelling, which takes the longest. A siren blasts, cars rush in, waved into their designated garage by a

Spectating at the N-24 is a hardcore experience: fans have camped for a week ahead of the event, built themselves stands and shelters, and during the night braziers burn, thunderflashes explode, beatboxes boom, and the racing is incidental to the prevailing hedonism. AUTHOR

lollipop mechanic, on-board air jacks elevate them, and the job's done by two mechanics per wheel and two to refuel, while drivers help one another out and in, belting up in the process. Unless there's some bodywork to gaffer tape, the car is stationary for less than three minutes.

Hundreds of thousands of spectators line the circuit, mainly clustered in designated areas. Out in the country they've packed the woodland dells and trackside margins for a week with all manner of imaginative camping facilities, a mix of tents, tepees, caravans, trucks and multi-tiered scaffold platforms, hugger-mugger in the woods as well as right up against the paths alongside the circuit wire. The weirdness in the woods at night is a heady blend of *Apocalypse Now*, *Mad Max*, Burning Man and Glastonbury, a smoky welter of campfires, braziers, fireworks, thunderflashes, strobes, a magical mystery tour set to the pounding backbeat of disco, techno, alco, whizzo, and all the while the race cars hammer by. Out here the race is kind of incidental, but mesmerizing nonetheless as the cars snarl past.

Night moves, and nocturnal shots are called for, so we head out to the loony bin on the outside of Brünnchen, where the atmosphere among the favelas of tent city is heady with Ramstein heavy metal vying with dub-reggae, drum 'n' bass and techno providing a driving counterpoint to the incessant snarling race engines and generators.

A haze of smoke from campfires, barbecues, hot dog stalls and fireworks drifts this way and that, strobes, torches and bonfires illuminating the arena as race car headlights glide serenely past, defining the curves of the track, fading into tail lights and brake lights. The smells too, not only Castrol R, but cooking aromas and hot engines, a heady mix indeed. Someone offers us a beer: it would be rude not to. As for the drivers, Peter Drumbeck says that the fans' nocturnal craziness doesn't faze them:

> You think, 'is that fog, or is it smoke, is that a barbecue? I smell sausage so that's a barbecue.' Then you come through the other side of it and it's clear again. Or I see a green light, and I think, 'why have I got a green light?' but it's actually a fan's decoration for his house in the forest!

We head back to the GP circuit to catch the vibe and the finish in the Falken pit garage. At 4.00pm the chequered flag is waved and that's it. The mechanics, techies and fitters are tired but elated, and with good reason: the mint-and-blue-hued GT3-R has been in the mid-teens most of the day, going up to 9th an hour-and-a-half before the finish. A top-ten finish was what Wolf Henzler said would be good enough, and it is the highest placed Porsche. All told, it's

The combined lap distance of the Nürburgring F1 circuit and Nordschleife is 25km (15.5 miles), and in 2014 the top two cars completed 159 laps, or 4,035km, in 24 hours. AUTHOR

been a relatively trouble-free race for the Falken crew. The other Falken drivers are equally upbeat, exchanging hugs and handshakes with all around them, as Wolf enthuses: 'The car worked perfectly, it was great teamwork. A bit of black tape is nothing in a 24-hour race like this.' But actually, the result goes down to the wire: one of the black Haribo Mercs has led for a third of the entire race distance, shadowed part of the time by a white Merc (the AMG-Team's Black Falcon car driven by Schneider/Engel/Christodoulou/Metzger) that never quite gets the traffic in its favour to grab the lead. But on the penultimate lap the lead Merc is obliged to pit for a splash and dash, allowing the white Merc to close right up. As the two cars pitch into the Esses at the end of the pit straight, the white car delivers a slight nudge on the black one, punting it wide, and the white car is off into the distance into an unassailable lead. After 3,400.65km, just 5.697 seconds separates the first two cars, the closest margin in the event's history. Afterwards there is fury in the Haribo garage: the team manager holds his head in his hands and two of the drivers can't bring themselves to climb the podium. That's racing, say the stewards.

GULF STATE

The halcyon days of Porsches resplendent in Gulf colours were in the early 1970s, but the iconic livery is still racing on a Porsche 991 RSR GTE. I followed the team's fortunes in the European Le Mans Series (ELMS) at Le Mans in 2015.

A familiar colour scheme barrels into sight, weaving through the Ford chicane and onto the pit straight. It's the iconic pale blue-and-orange livery, but it's not cladding a 908

or 917 – the shape's too modern. Yes, it's a 991 RSR GTE, the Gulf Racing Team's ELMS contender. I've come to Le Mans ahead of the 24-Hour race, and while the works 919s wow the crowds, I've discovered this intriguing car that harks back to an earlier era.

Owned and run by Mike Wainwright and Roald Goethe, Gulf Racing is based at Milton Keynes alongside the Gulf Aston Martin squad with its four DB9 Vantages. The Porsche team was set up in 2012 to contest the five-round ELMS challenge. Mike Wainwright, Adam Carroll and Phil Keen did well to win the LM GTE Class of the first round of 2015 at Silverstone on 11 April, finishing half a lap ahead of the 2nd placed car. Starting from P5, Keen worked his way up the order to claim the lead after forty minutes, and the team kept the car ahead until the chequered flag came out four hours later. ELMS championship dates are well spread out. After Imola in May, which didn't go so well for the Gulf squad, the series shifted to the Red Bull Ring in Austria in July, Paul Ricard in France in September, concluding at Estoril on the Portuguese coast in October.

On the basis of their success – they're lying 2nd in the title race after Imola – they'd been invited to the preliminary Le Mans test, though being a leading contender in ELMS didn't guarantee them a run at La Sarthe, such is the complex nature of the championships. As we chat in the Gulf hospitality enclave in the paddock behind the vast Le Mans pits enclave, Mike Wainwright explains how it works:

> If you're in the WEC [World Endurance Championship] you have a guaranteed place at Le Mans. Then for all the other entries, it's a question of where you finished in certain championships last year; in the European Le Mans series, if you finished 1st and 2nd, you get an entry in the 24-Hours. Between all the different classes and the different manufacturers, that takes up 90 per cent of the entries, and the rest is by invitation. Our invitation was to the reserve list, and normally by this time we would be on the grid.

They're second reserve for the moment, but it turns out that, due to the high volume of Asian entries this year, they don't make the cut. For now, it's back to concentrating on ELMS.

Mike's been racing since 2010, debuting at the Dubai 24-Hours. He started off with a Lamborghini Gallardo, followed by an Aston Martin Vantage GT2, and then set up the team in 2012 running McLaren MP4-12C GT3s in the European-based Blancpain Endurance Series. In 2014 he switched allegiance to Porsche with a borrowed 997, acquiring the team's current 991 RSR GTE in July in order to do the last two ELMS races of the season. While circuits such

Gulf Racing Team's 991 GT3 RSR, a contender in the European Le Mans Series, cruises the Le Mans pit lane ahead of the 24-Hours, 2015. AUTHOR

as Spa and the Nürburgring have exalted status they're not on the ELMS calendar: elusive as it is, Le Mans has the aura, as Mike explains:

> At this level of GT racing people look to the 24-hour races. From that perspective, Le Mans is special. It's a big circuit, it has all the manufacturers, it has all the different classes of car and it has this palpable atmosphere, which you really do feel when you turn up. There's a sense of anticipation here that's quite unique. As a driver it's very special because you have the combination of the race circuit and the road sections, and some unique, very fast corners – the Porsche Curves, Indianapolis, Arnage – all these places are really quite special.

The Gulf livery was acquired in a quite pragmatic way.

> We went to Gulf and said, 'we want to race under your banner'. Roald owns the ROFGO collection of Gulf racing cars and we asked if we could race in the Gulf livery, and through that we built the relationship. They can access the car collection, and we can drive under their livery, and it works very nicely: we get the benefit of Gulf's iconic colours, and from an international corporate perspective, they get the recognition in return, because the car and the colours are always out there. It's one of the best-looking cars on the grid, irrespective of whether it's a Porsche or not, because it's so eye catching.
>
> The core of the team is based at the workshop in Milton Keynes where the car's prepared before and after every race.

> They look after the car there, they do all the prep, and all the transportation comes from there. We do testing in March and the beginning of April and then I don't do that much because that's the balance between a full-time job, family and racing, so a lot of my testing actually happens in the car at race meetings.

That includes Le Mans, where the tricky bits for him are through the back part of the circuit, from Mulsanne corner all the way round to the Ford Chicane.

> The high-speed sections and through the Porsche Curves is where I lose time, which is normal because of the technicality of it, where I'm less on the edge than the pro drivers. It's about being safe, being consistent, and for us as AM (amateur category) drivers the more time you have in the car, the more comfortable you get with it and the easier it gets. It's constant blue flags because of the LMP1s, which are far quicker, even the LMP2s, because there are so many long straights, and they are naturally quicker than us, so the traffic is fairly constant, but the marshalling system is good. It's nice to look forward the whole time but you tend to be looking in your mirrors an awful lot.

From my vantage points above the pit lane and down at the Ford Chicane, the Gulf Porsche looks every bit the part of the works Manthey cars as it hurtles by. Porsche probably made fifteen examples of the 991 GT3 R, of which seven are customer cars, and the rest are factory team cars – running under the Manthey banner. 'The 997 GT3 R was on its limits as an old car,' reflects Mike:

> and it was at the end of its racing life, which is why the 991 RSR GTE is at least 2s per lap quicker. That's largely down to telemetry and technology, and of course the engine's a bit better, and there's been a big step forward on the aerodynamics of the car. It's got a smoother front and much better aero. The revised front end and the new rear wing provide a better balance, which gives greater stability in fast corners. They've advanced on pure performance, which is engine and turbo, but the big advance is now in the aerodynamics of the cars.

The RSR GTE's centre of gravity is also significantly lower than that of its predecessor, thanks to extensive use of carbon fibre, from which the front and rear mudguards, front

Artwork of this Gulf-liveried 997 Turbo tuned to 650bhp by 9ff was painted specially for the book by French watercolourist Laurence B. Henry. LAURENCE B. HENRY

The Gulf crew formulates its pit-stop strategy for the 991 GT3 RSR ahead of the 2016 Le Mans 24-Hours. AUTHOR

and rear lids, doors, underbody, wheel arches, rear wing, dashboard and centre console are all made. Similarly, all the windows are made of especially thin polycarbonate, plus the lightweight lithium-ion battery also contributes to weight reduction. That's the broadest comparison between a 991 GT3R and a 991 RSR GTE.

To refine the definition of GT3 and GTE, according to the Porsche Motor Sport press office, these two GT categories are as fast as each other, but accomplish their performance in quite different ways. A GTE car's spec is developed within a defined set of regulations, while a GT3 sports a bigger wing on a chassis with wider bodywork. That makes the GT3 relatively cheaper because it doesn't require as much development time and money to build and develop the car. For example, the 991 GT3 R costs €304,500, whereas the 991 RSR GTE costs €498,000. 'The RSR GTE is much more of a proper sports-racing car,' Mike tells us:

> because the balance between the road-going car to the outright sports-racing car has gone more that way, so they're all designed off the basic road car, but GT3s only go so far, so there's more of a road-going car in a GT3 than there is on a GTE car. As far as the rules are concerned, the GTE specifications are much stricter than GT3: GT3 has much bigger aero, and out of the box tends to be quicker than the GTE cars, and the GTE cars are quite restricted in that respect: comparing the aerodynamics of a GT3 to a GTE, the GT3 has a bigger spoiler, bigger splitter and should therefore be faster, but where the RSR GTE benefits is a better engine and better build.

And while the car is running, live on-board telemetry transmits more than 200 different measurements straight to the team's pit wall stand via an antenna on the car's roof, which keeps the engineers in the pits garage up to date with all rel-

Driver's complex workstation in the cockpit of the Gulf-Porsche 991 GT3 RSR, shared in 2015 by Mike Wainwright, Adam Carroll and Phil Keen. AUTHOR

evant vehicle data. The car's new FT3 safety fuel tank, with its lower centre of gravity, also makes it easier to refuel under race conditions: all weekend we see refuelling and tyre-changing rehearsals taking place up and down the pit lane.

There are six 991 RSRs in the Le Mans pits garages today, including the Gulf Porsche entry, which is a single car operation, unlike the early 1970s when the work's backed Gulf-JW Automotive squad normally ran three, sometimes four cars. Back at the Milton Keynes workshop there are four full-time mechanics, one full-time engineer, the team manager Matt Beers and the secretary, while at a race meeting there'll be at least ten people working on the car, including the mechanics, the tyre guys and the race engineers. Roald Goethe, who was injured in the 2015 race when his Aston crashed, divides his time between the Gulf Aston Martin camp and the works Aston team. Mike is dedicated to the Porsche effort. There are two sub-categories in GT: AM and PRO, within which there are three different levels of driver ability: Pro, Silver and Amateur.

The pro here is Adam Carroll, the silver-rated up-and-coming pro is Phil Keen, and Mike Wainwright is the amateur. As a pro, Adam has a top-line record: in 2005 he was test driver for BAR-Honda, was A1GP champion in 2008 and 2009, with stints in IndyCar, F-Renault, Auto GP and McLaren in the Blancpain pro category. As Mike explains:

The trick from a competitive perspective is have a good 'Am' driver and then the best from the silver and gold category. You are only allowed one from each category in the Pro-Am class. I've been racing with Adam for the last year and a half, and as he's a pro, so he looks for work, and if you get the desired team bonding effect, pros tend to stay with a team for quite a while. Someone like Phil, or any silver-rated driver, is more transient because a good silver becomes a gold, and then he has to go somewhere else because you can't have him in the car anymore, unless he takes the place of your previous professional driver. I'm the slower driver so they minimize my time in the car. There's a minimum I have to do in the race from a time perspective, and in ELMS the Pro driver has a maximum he's allowed to do. At Le Mans there's no maximum for the Pro, though he's not allowed to do more than four stints in a row. Obviously, the car's at its most competitive when your best driver's in the car.

Ironically, even though it's a European-based championship, the ELMS does not visit Spa-Francorchamps, which is, however, on the WEC programme. The only double header is at Silverstone, which runs separate WEC and ELMS races on the Saturday and Sunday. Mike raced in ALMS in the States in 2011, but personal commitments prohibit the dedicated week necessary to commit to a race there. Of the tracks on the European series, he cites Imola as one of his favourites.

The Gulf 991 RSR GTE riding the kerbs at the Ford Chicane during the 2016 Le Mans 24-Hours.
SIMON MAURICE

We had a good result at Silverstone. It was our first victory as a team, so it's nice in that sense, but from a driveability perspective I find Silverstone quite tough, because it's quite technical with fast parts and very complex curved sections. People say Imola is quite technical, but I think it suits the Porsche more than Silverstone, but they're proper circuits, rather than small Mickey Mouse circuits where you can't even stretch the legs of the car properly.

As far as rivals in GT are concerned, the Ferrari 458s and Corvettes always tend to be quick, and as Mike says, 'this year we're competing against four good Ferrari teams and one of the Corvettes, but we are competitive, and though we didn't have such a good result in the last race – through bad luck more than anything – if we have a chance, we do well. The target is to get a guaranteed place for the race at Le Mans next year.' On Sunday's test day Adam Carroll demonstrated what the 991 RSR GTE could really do, and with a clear lap he posted a 4:01.208 lap time, ending the day third fastest in the GTE Am class. Gulf team manager Matt Beers told me, 'We've had a great test day. The car was quick, the setup was good, but for now it looks like we will just have to remain focused on winning the ELMS so we can avoid this situation next year.'

In 2016 Gulf Racing GB stepped up from ELMS to WEC, with Keen replaced by Ben Barker. The season started badly with a crash at Silverstone, but fifth in class in their first Le Mans, and a strong finish to the end of the season showed that they had the potential to emulate the feats of their blue-and-orange predecessors of almost fifty years ago.

GULF STREAM

The Gulf Racing saga goes way back to the 1930s, but the current sequence of the name's history started in 1966 when Grady Davis, vice-president of Gulf Oil, bought himself a Ford GT40 and teamed up with John Wyer, team manager of JW Automotive. The following nine years witnessed one of the most successful commercial partnerships in racing history. The team's Ford GT40s, Mirages, Porsche 908s and 917s notched up three World Championships – plus three outright victories at Le Mans – and were associated with some of the world's greatest drivers. Superstars of their day, Pedro Rodriguez and Jo Siffert set new records everywhere they raced the Gulf Porsche 908s and 917s, and their exploits at Brands Hatch, Le Mans, Spa-Francorchamps, the Nürburgring, Targa Florio and Daytona are legendary. The Steve McQueen movie *Le Mans* endowed the Gulf Porsche 917 with iconic status, while Gulf won the 24-Hours again in 1975, returning to Le Mans with Derek Bell in 1994 with the 6th-placed Kremer Porsche K8. In 1995 Gulf partnered Ray Bellm in the Gulf McLaren F1 GTR, winning the BPR Global Endurance Series in 1996 and the GT Class at Le Mans in 1997. In 2001 Gulf sponsored Stefan Johansson's winning Audi R8 in the European Le Mans Series, and since 2011 Mike Wainwright and Roald Goethe have run the Gulf AMR and Gulf Porsche squads in WEC and ELMS.

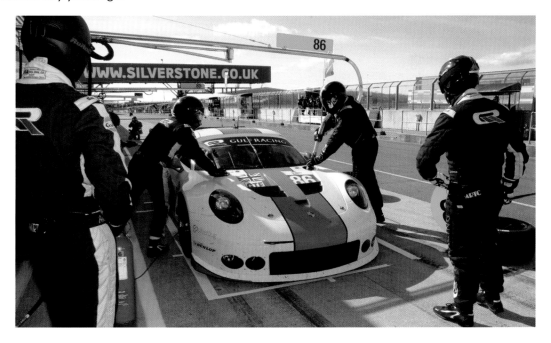

Driven by Mike Wainwright, Adam Carroll and Phil Keen, the Gulf 911 RSR GTE won its class at the 2015 Silverstone round of the ELMS races. SIMON MAURICE

CHAPTER TEN

BUYING, MAINTAINING AND MODIFYING

It's possible to do just about anything you want to a mainstream 996. The newer the model – 997 or 991 – the less the need, or perhaps the inclination to tamper. But why bother? A standard 996 is plenty quick enough and supremely nimble to start with, and if you want one that's both significantly quicker and more agile still, then you probably ought simply to buy a GT3. It might even work out cheaper in the long run.

But it doesn't have to be a performance upgrade; if you're content with the performance and handling, you may want to update the appearance to that of a later model, or customize it so it stands out from the rest at a club meet. Probably the most obvious upgrade for the earliest 3.4-litre 996s with their fried egg headlights is to fit a set of clear indicator lenses. This makes a big difference to their appearance, and is easy enough to do, but the parts will cost you probably £1,200. They could make the car more attractive to a potential buyer when the time comes, but are unlikely to add anything to its value. As time passes, the 3.4-litre cars have acquired a charm of their own, and no one seriously cares about the eccentric shapes of 996 headlights any more.

Wheels and tyres can make a big difference to the look of a car, though not always for the better. Choose your style and size carefully, or you could easily compromise both the aesthetics and the ride. Fitting shorter, stiffer springs and dampers will give you something of the GT3 feel at a fraction of the cost. Again, though, be wary of going too low and too stiff, as I'll explain later on. As for the brakes, fit harder pads, perhaps, together with braided flexible hoses, track-specification brake fluid and maybe some additional ducting for cooling air, but it's more important to ensure the discs are smooth on both faces.

Power upgrades start logically enough with an ECU re-chip, and a performance air-filter and exhaust system, which can certainly make the car sound better, even if it won't necessarily go substantially better. And since there's no sub-stitute for cubic inches, a straightforward engine change is probably the most cost-effective route. Porsche upgraded the M96 engine from 3.4 to 3.6 litres, and with a re-chip boosted the latter as high as 345bhp in the special edition 40th Anniversary model. Autofarm can potentially offer as much as 4.0 litres from its Silsleeve units, as evidenced by Josh Sadler's own 996.

How much to spend depends on your budget, naturally, and what model and extras are on the wish list. Starting with a 996, by perusing the online sales sites, looking at what's in the bargain basement is not such a grim prospect as it used to be. It'll be a 3.4-litre car, Tiptronic, four-wheel drive C4, Cabriolet body, and probably in Arctic Silver, and weirdly hued upholstery: Wimbledon green, anybody? A smidgeon under £10,000 in UK money. High miles? Not necessarily, though 70,000 is probably the lowest I've seen. But do we care, provided the service record's reasonably up to date? Some say that the higher the mileage the more likely it is that issues like the IMS bearing will have been dealt with long ago, and anyway the 3.4 has two rows of bearings in its IMS race and is therefore stronger than the Gen 2 996's 3.6 motor. That's the downside of an old 996 that's fallen off the desirability radar. But actually, there are enough opportunities out there that have been cared for. Now, can you live with a Cabriolet? The 996 Cab hardtop is a rather bulbous affair, but in a convertible context the 996 Cab's lines are pretty sleek, and there's nothing wrong with a zany interior – my Boxster's is flesh-tone pink, after all. And what about Tiptronic? You see where I'm going with this? The full hairdresser: a 996 C4 Tiptronic Cabriolet! If you allow a ceiling of £10,000, it might just get you into 911 territory, albeit at the cheap end. You might point out that, not so very long ago, a 3.4 could be languishing at a couple of thousand less than that, but you had better not take too long over this as 996 values have turned a corner, and they'll carry on going up as more people aspire to Porsche ownership at what we'll call the affordable side of air-cooled prices.

A test drive ahead of a purchase is an essential facet of the buying procedure, whether in this instance, a 991 Gen 1 C2, 997 C4S, or 996 Turbo, all available for similar money. ANTONY FRASER

Buying from a reputable specialist is key to Porsche acquisition and ongoing ownership support: Ash Soan takes delivery of his 997 C4 at Williams-Crawford. AUTHOR

Between £15,000 and £20,000 buys a perfectly decent 996, and like everything, the higher you go, the better the spec and more recent the model. Above £25,000, you'll get a later car with more options, and you'll also be into the realm of the Carrera 4S, moving into 997 territory. As for Cabriolets, for some reason they've become less desirable than coupé equivalents, so, in general, expect to pay around £3,000 less than for the equivalent coupé, but make sure that it comes with the high-quality hardtop with which it would have been sold when new. By the same token, a Targa is generally worth about £1,000 less than a comparable coupé. It seems that earlier Carrera 4s are less desirable than the equivalent Carrera 2, despite the fact that you get more kit for your money. Probably the most valuable thing about the earlier C4 is that it has PSM, which the Carrera 2 didn't get as an option until a bit later. Manual transmission or Tiptronic? Most buyers want a manual shift. Colour makes a difference to desirability, though. Brighter hues, Red, Yellow, Grey, anything that stands out from the Arctic and Polar Silvers that used to be flavour of the moment. Cabin upholstery too, with the Terracotta and Savannah beige lightening things up over a sea of black. Satnav is the most desirable optional extra, though to be fair, an updated TomTom or the Google Maps on your iPhone will provide you with way more up-to-date information than the on-board satnav. The DVD-based PCM2 system that came out in 2003 is better still. In all cases make sure you get at least a reasonably up-to-date set of discs: they're not cheap. Parking sensors are well worth having, too. Last, but by no means least, always go for a car with a good service history.

'PIG ENERGY'

Here's how I bought a kettle. Seeking a blank canvas for my project car, in the wake of my late lamented 964 ('The Peppermint Pig'), I selected a 996 C2 Gen 2 3.6. Its name? Check the number plate – P16 NRJ, or, if you will, 'Pig Energy'. Bob Dylan fans cried 'Judas!' when he spurned acoustic in favour of an amped-up Fender. The same happened to me, though I've yet to receive the mandatory thirty pieces of silver – just one rather large silver nugget. Why a 996, though? When you've lived with 911s for almost two decades you miss the cabin architecture, no matter how captivating the sights and sounds of the great outdoors that you enjoy with a Boxster. There's a simple logic to a 996 though, and that's the money. 'They've gone north', said a friend on Facebook. And indeed, they have. In the short time I'd been looking for one, prices had not only hardened, they had actually risen for certain versions like the C4S and 40th Anniversary models, and you can forget about GT3s and Turbos. I could see that clean, high-spec 996 C2s were also on the rise, and certainly not hanging around very long. I missed at least a couple of good ones by havering about the price.

There was another agenda too. Perhaps one way forward would be to acquire a spent 996, a 3.4 Gen 1 basket case with knackered engine, and gradually fix it up, colour-wrap it, fit a GT3 bodykit maybe, and just see where we got to with it. Appraising one or two cars of this disposition was disheartening, both visually and in the driving experience. I resolved to set my sights higher, but the quest wasn't quite so simple.

Ironically, my regular dealers were fresh out of affordable 996s during my hunt. There were some tasty GT3s and Turbos about, but beyond my fiscal reach. I avidly scoured the online channels and the classifieds, but to no avail. Factor in manual transmission and coupé body and the opportunities are halved. Not averse to left-hand drive, I perused the northern European websites too.

Eventually the search boiled down to a Speed Yellow C4S – with no engine – at dedicated Porsche breakers Van Zweeden at Middelburg in the Netherlands, a potential venture supported by Paul Stephens and Autofarm, who offered a rebuilt 3.6 engine to put in it; or, closer to home, one of two silver C2 coupés gracing the showroom at Porscheshop, Halesowen. A commission in Belgium enabled Antony Fraser and I to visit Van Zweeden en route, our Cayenne Turbo hooked up to a trailer just in case. On the face of it, this project could have been a cheap C4S. It was right-hand drive too, not that I minded about that one way or the other. But there were just too many unknowns for someone with limited means: most of the documents had been destroyed, for example, allegedly in a marital split, and there was no rational reason why a British car should find itself in the Netherlands without an engine. Cosmetically it wasn't perfect and I decided it was a great project for a specialist with reserves. With a tinge of regret, we drove away.

When I enquired about his 996s, Ian Heward at Porscheshop immediately offered to equip the lower mileage of the two with one of his carbon fibre Y-pipe induction kits, installed with a pair of K&N cone filters at either end. He'd get the ECU remapped too. In addition, it already had a short-shift gear-lever, Alcantara headlining, Dansk exhaust and GT3-style sills. The other 996 was resplendent with Gen 2 GT3-style bodywork add-ons, always a come-on, though at this stage in the proceedings I preferred not to make any ambiguous claims about the specifi-

cation of my next car. We can work up to that, but for now the less adorned car would be the way forward. Plus, it had clocked less than 46,000 miles. As I searched in vain for a car in a 'loud' colour, the notion of the blank canvas of this silver machine took precedence.

If a standard 996 is a good bet – a sound investment, even – why compromise that by fiddling about with it? Of the twenty-five or so cars I've owned, the ones that stand out most are the ones I've tweaked, tuned or pimped in some way. Apart from the 'Peppermint Pig', recently departed these shores (endowed with fresh 911Motorsport engine, Bilstein and Eibach suspension and Specialist Components' 964 induction kit), the car that endures in the memory better than most is my 1969 Alfa Romeo 1300 TI sedan, which, during the mid-1980s, rose in capacity via successive engine transplants to 2.0 litres with LSD and lowered suspension. I'm an incorrigible tarter-upper, and no doubt it won't end there.

I sorted the finance while Porscheshop fitted their induction kit and got it MoT'd. I travelled up to Halesowen, frankly with no great expectations, and in the Porscheshop garage I clapped eyes on my new car for the first time. It was a revelation. It turned out to be special order metallic Arctic Silver (92U), a lighter silver than I'd expected, and absolutely pristine, inside and out – so good I could hardly believe it. First registered in 2001, it was originally sold by OPC Glasgow, and the documentation revealed it'd had three previous owners. For the last few years it'd been serviced at Autofarm and I asked for their opinion, pre-purchase, without

The Gen 2 996 C2's 3.6-litre flat-six had an ECU tweak and was fitted with a EuroCupGT Y-pipe and twin air filters, supplied by Porscheshop. AUTHOR

The Gen 2 996 C2 'Pig Energy' quayside at the Hook of Holland, wearing five-spoke Carrera wheels shod with Vredestein winter tyres. ANTONY FRASER

to like? As for the Pig Energy number plate, that's a bonus, as the car declares its own moniker. As one wag commented, 'does that mean it runs on methane?' If only, though the on-board computer suggested it was doing 28mpg (10.09ltr/100km) of five-star on the 185-mile (297km) run from Birmingham. And that turns out to be about par for the course, comparing realistically with the lighter 986 Boxster's broadly 32mpg (8.83km/100ltr) average.

LOW LIFE

There's nothing wrong with the 996's standard suspension; positively a magic carpet ride compared with its predecessor. But I decided mine needed lowering, if only on aesthetic grounds. Cue a set of shorter H&R springs. Brands Hatch: so much to answer for. Blame it on childhood visits to watch tin-top tyros and halcyon heroes battling it out on the twists and turns of the Kentish black-top, sparks showering from ground effect-induced bottoming-out suspension as they swept around Paddock or Clearways. From

prejudice – 'good car', they said – and that was the clincher, because there's no better recommendation than that.

What's next? Porscheshop stock a vast range of goodies for the whole line-up, especially 986, 987, 996 and 997, from powertrain to suspension, aftermarket wheels, lights, cabin and external panelling. There's a raft of accessories and enhancements that will gradually find their way onto the car. Meanwhile, as Ian Heward says, 'the Y-pipe and a re-map are the best first mods everyone does when they buy a 996 Carrera, and after that it's the exhaust and an 82mm throttle and plenum. But get used to the re-map first!' And he was right.

As I drove the car home from Halesowen I grew to like it more and more. The controls are pretty much identical to the 986 Boxster I'd become accustomed to, though the seats aren't quite as figure hugging. It drives perfectly: there's no veering to one side, its handling is taut, no play in the controls, everything nice and tight. Changing gears means being firm and positive with the short-shift lever. I reckoned it'd been standing for a while, as about the time I reached Newmarket it suddenly seemed to wake up. Great acceleration, deep exhaust note, pin-sharp turn-in, sublime ride. What's not

Comparison of original equipment spring and H&R spring, a set of which lowered the ride height of the 996 C2 by 30mm to provide more focused handling and turn-in, if a harsher ride. AUTHOR

1340cc Ford Anglia to 964 Peppermint Pig, with at least five Alfas and a Beemer along the way, pretty much every car I've owned has been slammed. Well, apart from one or two Citroëns with hydropneumatic suspension that, at rest, sat on the ground in any case. So why change the habit of a lifetime?

Pig Energy 996 was always going to be a project car, no matter how wonderful the basic unadulterated car. The magazines are full of adverts from the springs and dampers specialists, and selecting the new kit for the 996 could have been like closing my eyes and sticking a pin in a page. But I'd had H&R springs before on the Peppermint Pig, and so I asked their advice about what would work on the 996 C2. As with Pep Pig, I visualized a fresh coil-over system, but I'd not reckoned with the overarching on-board presence of PSM. I got a full and frank lecture from their press officer Yvonne Menzebach, the gist of which ran like this:

We don't do electronic shocks at H&R, so there is no possibility to connect the PASM wires to our shocks to retain the adjustment. So, we recommend you just fit our lowering springs, which will drop the ride height by 33mm, and fit our thicker anti-roll bars. To mount our monotube coil-over kit to a PASM car, which is possible, you would have to do the following: remove the PASM shocks, reprogram the Porsche ECU to 'non PASM car', isolate the PASM wiring and fasten the wires safely in the car so they don't get damaged or interfere with any other suspension parts; rasp off the protrusion from the washer for the front – or use a new OE washer with a round

bore. After this you can fit our coil-overs. But there are other issues to address. As soon as you take the PASM shocks off a car with a Sport Chrono Package Turbo, the overboost will run to an error that is not easy to correct and the overboost may not work anymore at all.

There could be warranty issues too. Porsche is very severe when it comes to their warranty, so when using an aftermarket suspension where you're not only changing the mechanical stuff but also the electronics, they can easily limit their warranty. To cut a long story short, the main problem is the wiring, which cannot be connected to most aftermarket shocks, plus the reprograming of the ECU to 'non PASM car'. None of which applied to me because I was not about to ditch the 996's PSM, but nevertheless it's a cautionary tale for anyone who might be contemplating doing so. I duly ordered H&R's lowering springs and roll-bar kit, and a couple of days later two large boxes arrived from Trockenbrück, north Germany. I booked 'Pig Energy' into STR in Norwich, and mechanic Chris Lewis took charge.

With the car on the ramp and wheels off, Chris undid all four corners, He removed the spring assembly from each corner, dismantled it, put the new replacement spring in, and then built them back up again. The springs were quite a straightforward job to do really. The worst bit was accessing the rear mounts because there's a bit of trim behind the seats that has to come out to gain access to the rear mounts. In a Porsche 964 the access is in the engine bay, but here it's inside the cabin.

Hertfordshire-based specialists RPM Technik produce a range of modified Carreras under their CSR Programme, employing aftermarket suspension, modified bodywork and re-engineered mechanical componentry to create bespoke versions of 996s and 997s, emulating the exclusive 997 Sport Classic. This is Phil Churchill's 997 CSR Retro, shot in 2018. On the road, the CSR is similar in character to a 997 GT3 Touring. ANTONY FRASER

In the 996 Chris removed the carpet behind the seats, but it went back in easily enough, so that was not a problem. The H&R springs were a perfect fit: the old springs looked like the original standard Porsche ones, so, at 45,000 miles they'd probably never been touched.

Both front and rear anti-roll bars have drop links that mount them to the suspension, so Chris first had to take those apart:

> You've got to undo them anyway, then the rear anti-roll bar is then literally held on with four bolts, so you just unbolt that and then bolt the new one on. It's quite simple, whereas the front one needs the bit of cross bracing for the chassis support and the front suspension brackets to come down, and then you have to wriggle the old anti-roll bar out, and do the same to get the new one in place. It's not a difficult job, it's just a bit more fiddly than undoing four bolts.

The new anti-roll bars were supplied with new bushes, and again everything fitted perfectly. The front anti-roll bar is in a fixed position but the rear anti-roll bar is adjustable, so you can adjust the roll stiffness as required. There are three settings, of which medium is the best option for regular road use: 'When you've got three positions to choose from you might as well start on the medium, and then if it is too stiff you can go soft, and if it is not hard enough you can go harder.'

Having reassembled the corners, Chris applied STR's four-wheel alignment apparatus and realigned the camber and toe-in, so all four wheels point in the right direction.

Front corner of the 996 C2, showing H&R lowering spring, MacPherson strut, tidy disc and brake caliper. AUTHOR

The front wheels just needed a very slight tweak to get right, but the back wheels were quite a long way out. After he took it out for a road test. Chris said, 'It's definitely a firmer ride, not uncomfortably firm, because it doesn't crash and bang over pot holes and bumps and in fact it seems quite composed.'

One of the most taxing journeys I've done since having it lowered, deliberately avoiding all motorways, took me over the Pennines via Macclesfield and Matlock and the heinously restricted Cat-and-Fiddle pass, where the 996's handling was subjected to the most strenuous of test sessions. It's all good news. The shorter H&R springs have quite radically altered the character of the car, so it now behaves like I want it to, which is to say, akin to the old 964, in that it's much more firmly planted. It feels much more dynamic, and instead of its previously serene gliding characteristics, its latent animalistic spirit is released. I can feel all the nuances of the road surface intimately through the steering wheel and through my backside, and that's partly what keen driving is about. On a long stretch of motorway and the rustic rides of north Norfolk it now lacks the luxury magic carpet ride, but then that was what I was trying to divest myself of. I'm back in touch with the tarmac in a positive way, and I can proceed through a series of bends more quickly and with more confidence and precision, because I know where the car is going to go. It's telling me, 'I'm going to tuck in here, duck out there.' Up at the ton on a fast bend, it's as if it's on rails – it just doesn't waver, I just steer it round and it's uncannily sharp compared to how mellow it was; it hugs the ground like a truffle hound. But the main thing is, it's achieved the stance that I wanted, and it's brought the car to life in both its handling and its aesthetics. It's come alive and it's even better than the Pep Pig – way faster too.

Among the mechanical and cosmetic projects, maintenance issues included routine servicing such as attending to the brakes. Not that the braking potential was particularly compromised, but I was conscious of a scratching sound that's normally associated with a stone getting lodged between caliper and disc. Sure enough, there was scoring – but the inside faces of the two front discs were also badly corroded, and the only remedy was a fresh pair of discs. I ordered a pair from Porscheshop, packaged as a EuroCupGT kit with a two-year guarantee, for £164.99 delivered. German discs and Pagid pads. By one of those weird coincidences, the anti-roll bar drop-link bushes on the front right corner had suddenly started rattling loudly on the bumps, so I got a set of those at the same time, costing £45 a pair. I checked the car into STR in Norwich, and the bill for fitting was £130, give or take, and braking is now spot on.

The Gen 2 996 C2 had its engine lid and integral electric spoiler replaced with a notionally lighter swan-neck double-decker rear wing from a Gen 1 996 GT3. AUTHOR

ON A WING AND A PRAYER

Keen to complete the transformation from standard 996 to something more akin to my penchant for 911 competition cars, I had it fitted with a 'swan-neck' Gen 1 GT3 rear wing. Going for a wing, indeed any wing, wasn't a clear-cut choice. For starters, the simple rounded contours of the 996's unadorned rear quarters are perfectly pleasant, aesthetically, until the electric spoiler deploys at 75mph (120km/h). But there needed to be a match with the newly fitted Carrera Cup style front panel, so it then became a question of what style and profile of rear-end aerodynamic extension would look best, given that I wasn't bent on imitating any hot 911 in particular.

The wider I cast the net, the greater seemed the potential cost, which restricted the final option to a certain extent. Having endowed the 964 Peppermint Pig with a ducktail, there seemed to be no good reason not to steer my 996 Pig Energy down that route too, especially when we find the doyen of fast 911s, Alois Ruf, fitting ducktails on his supercars and being perfectly content with the downforce created. Like all Ruf-made kit, however, his ducktail would have been expensive. I examined the carbon fibre ducktail made by RPM Technik, a lovely piece of kit, but again more than I could stump up for; ditto Getty Design in the USA. Both Porscheshop and Design 911 offered some attractive GT3 Gen 2-style rear wings that would have been contemporary with the age of the car.

But I can now reveal that I have long held a sneaking admiration for the gorgeous compound curves of the swan-neck

wing that adorns the Gen 1 GT3 and what's more, despite its complexity, the fibreglass version is slightly cheaper than a ducktail. My mind was made up. Ian Heward at Porscheshop dispatched a swan-neck wing complete with 996 C2 engine-lid to Wayne Parker at Norfolk Premier Coachworks.

Now the serious business kicked in. The wing had been slightly damaged in transit, so that needed fixing, but all the surfaces bore ripples that required smoothing. First of all, though, Wayne needed to see how well the new engine lid fitted the 996's engine bay aperture. Off came the old lid, complete with its retractable wing, and with hinges and catch swapped over, the new lid with its integral wing took its place. Where the panel gaps were uneven, Wayne and his boys modified the new lid accordingly. It was then refitted and checked for alignment, removed and fine-tuned, and put back on once more. Once they were happy that it was completely flush, off it came again and the laborious task of fettling, filling, sanding and honing the wing and its swan-neck supports was carried out on the workbench and trestles.

A primer guide coat was then sprayed on before block sanding. This highlighted any remaining imperfections in the primer and any such blemishes were attended to. After sanding, the wing and attendant lid were cleaned up with degreaser and the complete assembly primed with a fine surface coat of Arctic Silver. Luckily Wayne had enough paint left over from when they painted and fitted the front panel. When it had been prepped and block sanded, the wing and engine-lid were ready for the topcoat, with a final blow-down and a thorough degrease. The assembly was mounted on a panel stand in the paint booth, wiped down, and the first Arctic Silver topcoat was applied. Two more applications of basecoat were sprayed on, followed by a fourth and final drop-coat to even out the metallic content. Then came a fifteen-minute flash-off in the oven, after which the painter applied the first clear-coat, followed by a last full wet-coat to finish off with. After flash-off, the wing-and-lid unit was baked in the oven for forty minutes at 65°C. The painter let it cool down, then flatted out any tiny imperfections in the clear-coat with 1500-grade wet-and-dry paper. It was then polished back until all scratches were eliminated. The final act was to adhere the black-painted 'gurney strip' on the lower wing section. It looked the complete business.

As with the front panel, the engine lid also contains two air intakes. While Wayne was able to clad the ones in the front panel with the mesh supplied, the rear lid's apertures proved inaccessible from underneath: there are still two cavities that need closing off with appropriate mesh panels to keep the autumn leaves out. That said, the wing looks absolutely awesome and suits the car down to the ground. Well, that's its function after all, to provide downforce, which it did admirably at high speeds, for example on an outing to Abbeville circuit in northern France. I revelled in nocturnal outings where the central rear brake light illuminated the wing too. One small side issue: the car still thought it should be launching and retracting its electric rear wing, issuing a red warning light when no wing issued forth, so it had to be dissuaded from doing this by blanking off the contacts.

DUCK OR GROUSE

In the never-ending quest to individualize my long-suffering 996, in time I could no longer resist a ducktail spoiler, going right to the top and getting one first-hand from Alois Ruf. You either like it or you don't, but I think it looks fantastic, completely transforming the character of the car.

On my last visit to Pfaffenhausen to review the fabulous new SCR 4.2 and the all-carbon Ruf Ultimate (see Chapter 8), Alois offered a 996 ducktail of the kind fitted to his own GT3-based RGT model between 2000 and 2005. Let's not forget that the very latest Ruf Turbo Florio Targa also features a ducktail (without an extending wing), so there can't be much wrong with the concept. 'We can fit it here for you when you next visit, or you can take it with you, have it fitted and bring the car back and we will put our badge on it,' he laughed. One ducktail doesn't turn a car into a Ruf, but it was a warm-hearted gesture and so I brought it home.

The new spoiler was painted and 996 'Pig Energy' was booked into STR in Norwich. The swan-neck engine lid was unbolted and removed, the catches and hinges were swapped over, and then the Ruf ducktail was carefully aligned and fitted. The central brake light under the rear window is

Fitting the ducktail spoiler engine lid at STR, provided for the author's 996 C2 by Alois Ruf. AUTHOR

The pert ducktail rear spoiler gives the 996 C2 a hint of a classic RS look, though to be fair, at 20 years old, the 996 is now almost a classic in its own right. AUTHOR

now blanked off with a filler section that Ruf supplied, and the new more prominent brake light in the centre of the spoiler lip is wired up instead.

I have to say I'm thrilled with the car's appearance: it's pert, it's neat, and it's wrought a complete transformation when viewed from anywhere apart from full frontal (because you can't see the rear end from there). It's tidied up the rear-end no end, now that it's lost the complex, if elegantly contorted, swan-neck wing. It's an amiable look, far less aggressive, some would say less pretentious, than the GT3 swan-neck, and I now realize it is the look I've been striving to achieve, basking like so many of us in an idealized past.

But what would be the effect on the car's aerodynamics or handling? I wondered whether there'd be any noticeable difference in downforce, so I turned the wick up around some well-known swift curves. It seemed a trifle livelier than with the swan-neck wing, possibly, but around the wiggly lanes heading up to the Cromer Ridge it positively came alive – not unlike the ducking and diving of dear old Pep Pig in spirit. It's not just the appearance of the car that's fundamentally altered but the handling too. I had to ask whether I was fooling myself, but on the way back I had a similar experience; seemingly quicker turn-in, delightfully fresh attitude, and more poise around the curves. How could this be, just by switching to an old-fashioned ducktail? Is there an element of Alois Ruf's tuning magic working away behind me? That would be nice, of course, but realistically I can only assume that removing quite a hefty piece of kit – albeit fibreglass, like the Ruf item – from the back end of the car and replacing it with something that must be less than half the weight has had a profound effect on the overall mass, allowing the chassis to access depths of ability previously untapped.

SHOP TILL YOU DROP

Porscheshop in Halesowen, near Birmingham, is one of the foremost purveyors of OEM service items and branded aftermarket componentry for the marque. Porscheshop sponsored my 914 on La Carrera Panamericana in 2011, and I bought 'Pig Energy' from them in 2013. Ian Heward, who raced a 911 2.2E as a student, turned a hobby into a business in 1992, maintaining his own car and helping fellow Porsche competitors run their cars. Its current premises covers 12,000 square feet (1,115sq m). The firm has always been mail-order focused:

> We started off with the older cars, racing the 924s and 944s and the early air-cooled 911s, and as the used parts dried up we supported the racing with new parts, like brake discs, pads, service kits, clutches and that sort of thing. In those days Porsche was only making four or five models, so you only really had the air-cooled 911s, 924s, 944s and the 928, so it was quite concentrated though fairly basic kit.

Porscheshop gradually expanded into more exotic niche market equipment, like the replacement Turbo nose they fitted on my 996 (see Chapter 3).

> The performance and tuning market really grew out of the motor sport, because you were always allowed to fit the next model's spoiler or the next model's bumpers or aero kit of whatever its generation was, so the 944s would get a facelift to 944S2 and the 911s would get a Carrera facelift, and things like that. So, there was always an element of that which grew out of motor sport.

The introduction of the water-cooled models in 1997 opened fresh possibilities:

> As the modern cars came along, that brought in a whole new generation of owner-enthusiasts, along with a whole new range of cars and parts with interchangeability, because of course the Boxster shares a lot of the 996 generation of 911 parts. All the bumpers are interchangeable, the headlights, the bonnets, the rear spoilers, wheels, brakes, it's almost like a Meccano or Lego situation, and owners and enthusiasts picked up on that. They realized that you can ape a GT3 with a basic 996, by swapping its suspension and aero and things like that. The whole thing's definitely customer driven.

The expansion of online sales has greatly reduced the staff required to run the company. Porscheshop used to provide technical customer support as well, but now most people needing technical information about their vehicle, its fitments and applications do their own research online. Some customers, however, still choose to call in person, not just to have their car serviced, but to get a sense of what's new and see the products at first hand.

Ian perceived a surge of demand for upgrading parts and equipment from about 1998:

> Without a doubt, the car parts business grew four-fold effectively overnight. Pre-1998 it was predominantly owner-enthusiasts: you owned one Porsche and it was a prestigious race-bred sports car, even though it was quite yuppiefied at times. Once they were widely available from 1998, the demand for more modern water-cooled parts quadrupled because they were more affordable and interchangeability made it more cost-effective for Porsche to make a lot more cars using the same parts. It didn't devalue a Porsche in terms of its prestige, but it broadened the market and enabled four times as many people to own a Porsche as could do a decade previously.

Though 1998 seems to have been the key year, it wasn't an overnight phenomenon.

> It crept up on us, and it probably took another three to four years before we saw real growth, so it wasn't until the early 2000s before those cars came into our domain en masse, post manufacturer's warranty. The growth was steady from about 2001 onwards because of course it's exponential as those early water-cooled cars are handed on to a second or third owner and the original are buying new again.

The Porscheshop Gen 2 996 GT3 on the Hill at the Goodwood Festival of Speed. AUTHOR

Ian reckons the real expansion started around the launch of the 997 in 2005.

The 997 reverted to a more traditional looking 911 and those cars really took off, because people with older air-cooled 911s decided they'd have a modern Porsche with traditional looks, and things suddenly leaped a generation, and that expanded the market again. All the way through the Noughties this demand for tuning and styling parts continued to be an exciting and affordable part of Porsche ownership.

Nowadays, Ian perceives three different generations of Porsche owner. Owners in their mid-twenties to late thirties will most likely own one modern Porsche, of between five and fifteen years old. Those in their early to mid-forties will probably own a modern Porsche as a daily driver, but they will quite often also also own a classic Porsche, such as a 944. They'll do all their performance tuning, styling and servicing on the modern car and use that every day, and the classic car they'll use at weekends or for special occasions, like shows and trackdays. They probably weren't old enough to drive when those cars were new, but they are buying into fond memories of what their heroes drove in the 1980s. That has brought about a rebirth in the classic parts and servicing kit for cars being restored back to standard. These are all OEM quality replacement parts, apart from modifications such as a K&N filter or a Momo steering wheel, or similar upgrade.

The third generation of Porsche customers is aged from 50 to 70-plus. They remember the cars in the 1960s, 1970s and 1980s, and probably have a newish Porsche of some

Porscheshop regularly supply a wide range of kits and parts to enable routine maintenance on water-cooled 911s. AUTHOR

denomination, but they also have a fairly valuable and well-maintained classic from that era. They are investing in higher-end products for those cars, quality OEM suspension, brakes and so on. Ian sees this as:

a direct split of vehicles, pre- and post-1998, and three different generations of passionate owners. We've been through all those phases ourselves, and we continue to be part of that generational enthusiast movement, relating to the owners and enthusiasts and being part of the Porsche culture. Most of our customers that enjoy Porsche ownership get bitten by the bug like we did. It's infectious. You love your Porsche and you never want to sell it, or if you do, you buy another one. The car ticks certain boxes from your memories and aspirations, and every single owner will invest as much time and money as they can afford into their car, because that's the nature and the passion for the brand, without a doubt.

Now that classic Porsche values have risen to such an extent that they have become either unaffordable or impractical as everyday transport, I wonder how this has affected the components market.

Prices of air-cooled 911s have gone through the roof. Over the last ten years we've seen a growth in the sale of restoration and maintenance parts, so that where it was probably 25 per cent of what we supplied, more recently it's become 50/50 with the modern cars. As the classic 911 models have increased in value, people have moved onto something else that's more affordable, like a 924S or a 924 Turbo, or a 944 Turbo, a 968 perhaps. They've restored the old 911 and sold it on and looked for something else as a new challenge. So now we see it's 50 per cent maintenance, parts and performance tuning on the new water-cooled cars, and 50 per cent in parts, maintenance on the older cars. There isn't a stigma between the water-cooled and the air-cooled cars anymore: they're all part of that perfect Porsche brand.

Ian is finding that he's needing to remanufacture certain parts.

Porsche have been discontinuing parts for the older cars due to a lack of volume, and some of the front-engined water-cooled cars are lagging behind. A lot of the products that we developed in the 1990s, like our fuel-line kits, suspension bracketry, body mould-

ing kits, different products that we developed over the years, died off a little bit when the cars became unfashionable over a ten-year period, say from 2002 to 2012, when there was a lot of enthusiasm for the air-cooled 911s and the 996s. There were too many Porsches around for people to really care about the older ones. So we stopped producing a lot of those items that were popular in the 1990s. Over the last four or five years the demand has come back, and we've put those items back into production; we've even had to ask people to come out of retirement to re-engineer and machine parts for us, because the demand is back again.

Another new front adorns the 996 C2 'Pig Energy', this time from a 996 Turbo, supplied by Porscheshop complete with GT2 upper vent. AUTHOR

Porscheshop's 997 GT3 R engine out for a rebuild. AUTHOR

Indeed they are: I've had two sections of bodykit from Porscheshop, the 996 GT3 swan-neck rear spoiler and more recently a 996 Turbo front, prepped and fitted by Porscheshop in a bid to finally end the incessant kerbing and graunching over traffic calming humps and speed bumps. Ian was generous enough to incise it with an extra GT2-style inlet at the upper face of the nosecone. The general opinion is that the whole balance and presentation of the aesthetics are much better than previously with the Carrera Cup style front, coupled with the ducktail rear spoiler.

Porscheshop has been running a 997 GT3 RS race car for a few seasons.

> We race because it strengthens our brand, and we test and develop products through motor sport. We use it as a form of R&D, so we're sure that the product works. Things like performance brakes, suspension components, we use them on our own vehicles, and if we sell it, it works. Third-party branded products have to have our seal of approval, too. And then there's the EuroCupGT range, a lot of which is designed, tested and made in-house.

They restore racing and road cars, but avoid ground-up and concours rebuilds because that's more specialized: 'We'll do road-going restorations, whether it's air-cooled engine rebuilds, and we'll also do bodywork and interior restoration work, again mainly to keep vehicles on the road or bring back to a nice road-going standard.' There's the thing: Porscheshop specializes in cars that actually get used, which is what should be happening to them.

THE ART OF NOISE

Noise sells cars, that is, if you subscribe to the notion that a vehicle's exhaust note is a powerful draw when it comes to coveting that car. My 996 received a pair of Cargraphic silencers, and the resulting soundtrack was achingly, lustfully strident. Bent tubes and baffled boxes: who knew the subtleties and complexities inherent in an exhaust system, plus the variations in volume and sound quality available to the roar connoisseur.

After having its IMS bearing sorted, as well as a lengthy list of renewables fitted and fettled, it wasn't long before I detected the exhaust was blowing, growing louder with a gradual basso profundo crescendo. It was discovered that the left-hand concertina section of the silencer pipe was ripped by corrosion. Instead of having a new section welded in, I decided to go for a fresh pair of Cargraphic silencers (see Chapter 8), and 996 'Pig Energy' was taken to the Cullompton factory run by Simon and Jon Young.

Simon gives me a tour of their three main workshops. As well as the individual fabrication booths, there's a machine shop, pipe-bending machine, the polishing room, an area where brackets are made, and the chamber where silencers are assembled. Here there's a guillotine and a machine tool that seam-welds cases. We walk past racks of pattern systems for all manner of Porsches, beside which technicians in curtained-off booths labour on work benches fashioning convoluted pipework, stainless-steel cylinders and panels, with flickering welding torches accompanied by the brouhaha of angle grinders, polishers and pipe benders.

The 996's Cargraphic silencers are fabricated in pairs at the Cullompton foundry. AUTHOR

The 'horrible droning in the back of your head' that Thomas Schnarr described to me in Landau is what I've been hearing with my 996 pipe blowing over the last few weeks. How they gauge whether a particular configuration of silencer and header and tailpipes, plus catalytic converter and heat exchangers, is going to enhance the car's performance is very much down to experience. Cargraphic's best-selling item is probably the Cayman GT4 manifolds, available in both cat and non-cat versions, and they can't make them quickly enough, which begs the question why the factory don't fit something similar: 'They are starting to produce their own sports equipment but the key is that they need to produce an exhaust system that is legal in all countries and, given the worst-case scenario, probably California where they have to comply with all regulations, where we are probably side-stepping some regulations.' All parts are test-fitted, dyno-tested and TüV approved in Germany once developed. In practice, Cargraphic receives an order in Landau, the parts are made in Devon then shipped back to Landau, and dispatched from there to the customer anywhere in the world. The time scale for manufacturing a complete exhaust system is difficult to quantify because everything is produced to order in small batches. It probably takes about a week to produce a working set and a pattern set:

The process is to jig the original parts and then to build our part in that jig, so our part will then fit with an OE rear silencer, but if we were producing manifolds, cat sections, centre section, rear boxes and tail pipes, that could be three- to four-week's work, particularly if we're building it on the car. By the time we've built our patterns and then jigged our patterns and then produced one out of the jigs to make sure it fits the car, that could be as much as a month's work. It may need refining, but hopefully it's perfect first time.

That sounds almost like the creation of a prototype system, and at very least they're refining the OE equipment. I ask Simon which he regards as the most impressive exhaust system that he produces: 'Probably our 911 flat-six system for the earlier cars, the 3.2 Carrera maybe, and I also like our 996 GT3 race system, or our 991 Turbo system that features on the Cargraphic video with flames coming out of the tail pipes.' It's a real eye-opener to see just how many different facets there are to creating an exhaust system; we tend to take it for granted, but the complexities that go into its creation are amazing.

Cargraphic exhausts are fabricated from 304 stainless-steel, which is an austenite or gamma-iron, so it's non-magnetic. Cheaper grades of stainless-steel like 409, which is a steel with a high chromium content and not much nickel, are magnetic and will rust over a period of time. According to Simon, the cheaper grades will probably last ten years. Most stainless manufacturers offer a lifetime guarantee to the original purchaser, but the likelihood that somebody keeps their car more than ten years is not that great, If the car's just for high days and holidays, however, it will last as long as 304.

The steel arrives on a palette in $2 \times 1m$ flat sheets, and the tube comes in 6.1m lengths in a range of diameters in $\frac{1}{8}$in increments. The raw material is cut, rolled, bent and polished to produce a finished exhaust system.

We machine all our sensors, flanges, olives and system parts, using the manual lathe where we can modify the flanges. There's a milling machine where we can do things like boring at an angle or counter boring, or machining grooves. Our bending machine can bend anything from 35mm ($1\frac{3}{8}$in), right the way up to 76mm (3in). It's got all these flexible knuckles that sit inside the pipe while the pipe is being bent. It's attached to a hydraulic ram, and after the bend is finished the ram will draw back and iron out any wrinkles or any imperfections in the bend, so we end up with as near to the full diameter of the tube as possible while it's being bent.

Some parts for flanges and brackets are bought in, again in 304, but basically everything is made in-house.

Sparks fly as the 996 silencers are created in the welding shop at Cargraphic's Cullompton factory.
AUTHOR

We have developed several different systems on a dummy 993 engine. It's a matter of taking off the relevant parts that put it back to this 3.2 state. The manifolds were 964 manifolds we'd already produced, so we've got that as a starting point. From there we then hook up a rear silencer onto our engine and then basically plumb in between. It would be nearly impossible to do that on a bench; you either need a car, an engine or an original part to copy. For example, when an order comes in for a set of 964 manifolds, the technician refers to the pattern section. All the bending and cutting information is saved on spreadsheets, so we'll print out the spreadsheet for three sets of 964s. The material is cut and then bent. At that stage the particular job would go to one of the final assembly welders, who get the jig and the pattern, and trim and self-assemble all the pipes, because it's not possible to bend all the pipes in one piece. The welders would then trim all those pipes, tack them together in the jig, group them altogether as they go to the polishing shop, and then the pipes come back into the jigs to be finally assembled and welded. That's the tip of the iceberg really.

Air-cooled versus water-cooled?

The water-cooled systems tend to be simpler, purely because they're more conventional, whereas the air-cooled car with rear engine and lack of space seems to set up a lot more vibration within the system. I'm not sure what the reasons are for that, but it's

Attaching the new Cargraphic silencers to the 996 exhaust system at the company's Devon workshop. AUTHOR

another factor that we have to always be aware of when doing air-cooled parts, for fear of them failing and fracturing. As far as quantities are concerned, it's very difficult to put a number on how many systems we make in a given period because the systems are so different.

I had very little idea that the internals of a silencer were so complex, nor indeed that aural volumes are deliberately altered according to the amount of material contained within the silencer box.

As for my 996 silencers, that's one of the more impressive stages of the process. Everything – the baffles, the cases, the lot – is produced in-house. The baffles start off as a perforated blank plate that's sculpted to form the centrepiece of the silencer box. It's then wrapped in steel wool, placed inside the silencer chamber, which is wadded with fibreglass string, pumped in by a modified airgun system. A similar process is used for all silencers, including the classic flat-six's banana. Variations on the theme include the vacuum flap silencer, which enables the driver to modulate the volume of sound the car is making at the press of a switch. 'When the vacuum flap is open the gases can go straight to the tail pipe, and when the vacuum flaps are closed the gases are forced down the spur pipe into the long run on the silencer. They then go into the centre return and drop back in onto the tail pipe outlet.'

I also notice that some systems employ spring attachments where there's a risk of fracture. The springs allow the system to expand and vibrate, giving 'the system a tremendous amount of flexibility and the ability to expand when it gets very hot without the risk of fracture. They're important on our race and trackday systems.'

There are three different grades of internals for a wheel-arch silencer such as the 996's.

Three different variations of sound, effectively, so you have what would be considered an OE sound, which we call an ET, and then our TüV box, which is a little louder than standard and called an ETR. The export version is an ETS. Each one of them has slightly different box internals, one is a little bit more powerful than the others, and obviously they are packed differently as well. From the outside you couldn't tell which is which without looking at the type plate. There's a type plate on each silencer with the part number on, so for your car it would be Car P96ET and then a TüV number, and then the TüV box would be Car P96ETR, and the last one would be Car P96ETS, which would have no TüV number.'

The 996 C2 receives a new pair of Cargraphic silencers, made and fitted at the company's Cullompton foundry. AUTHOR

While the shiny new 996 Cargraphic silencers are being installed I examine the abandoned old ones. Clearly the concertina-join sections were the Achilles heel, and in fact belonged on a Tiptronic rather than a manual car. It is suggested that the previous owner may have bought them on eBay: apparently the flexies absorb some vibrations and frequencies that are produced by the Tiptronic, but aren't found in manual gearbox cars. A single silencer is quite heavy, so a second person is needed to hold it in place while the catalytic converter and tailpipes are slotted on and it is then bolted up onto the mounting bracket to the side of the engine, which is very awkward to access. 'Pig Energy' is lowered on the ramp and the engine is fired up. An appreciable growl rises to a vociferous snarl at 3,000rpm. On the way home 'Pig Energy' gives voice with a harsher, bellowing rasp than at any time in the past: this is a new vocabulary. Power delivery is smoother, swifter too. It's an amazing transformation as I bask, boy-racer style, in the welter of sound that reverberates off walls, barriers and bridges.

ACROSS THE BOARD

Predictably, if the earliest 996s are £10,000 and upwards, and high-quality 997s linger between £20,000 to £30,000, there's another significant plateau at the £50,000 mark. I recently gathered a trio of 911s together to highlight the

On the premise that you have £50,000 to spend on a Porsche 911, options might include a Gen I 991 C2, a Gen 2 997 C4S, or a 996 Turbo, all available at roughly the same money. ANTONY FRASER

points on the price graph where certain 996 and 997 models intersect with the 991, as the older cars grew more valuable while the newer one depreciated. As it turns out, if that sum is within your means, you're spoiled for choice.

Armed with a budget of £50,000, there are several interesting ways of spending it. Steering clear of the rarefied air-cooled coterie, let's assume you're after a modern 911 that you can use on a daily basis. We've reached a milestone where the cheapest 991s have eased back from their 2012 £72,000 showroom price to the £50,000 mark, and that is a significant yardstick. There are plenty to choose from, as I found at Ashgood Cars, located close to Heathrow Airport, who had half-a-dozen 991s in stock, all within a whisker of that £50,000 purse.

If you prefer to venture into the realms of something a shade older and more exotic, but are not necessarily stirred by the 991, you might think about a 997, which is just as well made and, some say, retains more of the delicacy of feel and fluidity that's become veiled in the 991. If so, how about the 997 C4S, which represents the top of the conventional 997 range without getting involved with the more exotic GT3 and Turbo. Our third contender in this notional £50,000 affair is the 996 Turbo, such as the example here lent by Paragon Porsche. At this budget – and the word 'budget' seems somehow incongruous, given that for many of us £50,000 represents a veritable treasure chest – you could also take an even more sporting route and drive away in a Gen 1 996 GT3.

Three modern Porsches, then, each presenting a different personality and slightly different hue. The 991 is Agate, the 997 is Meteor and the 996 is Seal, making this a Grade A grey day. It's interesting to contemplate their dimensions, which vary less than might be supposed: the 991 contrives to look the bigger car, the 997 C4S is in fact marginally larger, while the 996 Turbo is fractionally shorter and lower, though a tad wider than the 991. This particular 991 C2S was first registered in March 2012 and had done 57,000 miles, with full OPC service history. The 997 C4S is scarcely two years older, registered in December 2010, since when it's clocked 52,000 miles with full main dealer history. Both these cars have seven-speed PDK transmission. The 996 Turbo is a 2004 car equipped with Tiptronic transmission, having done 56,500 miles with full service history.

I'm at Longcross Studios, the former MoD Chobham test track, where the previously luxuriant arboreal surroundings and tortuous trialling routes are being steadily eroded by the sprawling film sets being constructed for epics such as *War Horse* and *Doctor Strange*. Lynden Bairstow, Ashgood's sales exec, has some interesting comments about the differences between the cars:

The 991 is a completely new chassis, yet they've kept the bodyshell much the same size as the 997. The C4 version of the 991 is slightly bigger, but all cars tend to do that with successive generations – even though parking spaces aren't getting any bigger. It's quite interesting to see that these examples of the three different generations are all about the same price – £50,000 – but I think there's still a bit in it as the 991 is still depreciating, whereas the 997 is pretty firm now, and in fact some of them are going up, especially the more sought-after versions like the C4S. The purist will tend to want the normally aspirated non-turbo because of the engine noise, though the new ones are maybe appealing to the next generation.

I think the 997 has more of a sports car feel to it, whereas the 991 is more of an executive car, and that applies to Porsche in general, including the 911s and the Boxster and Cayman. They've gone from being very well-built German sports cars to very quick executive cars. You've still got that Germanic feel about them because it's very well manufactured. But you jump in that 997 and instantly you feel you're in a sports car, whereas if you jumped in the 991 and you didn't have any badges to refer to and someone said you're sat in a Mercedes or an Audi, you'd believe them. It's like a two-seater Panamera. They are very exclusive, very classy, bespoke almost, but not the sports car you expect to jump into in the same way that you would with the 997. But, at the same time, they have to keep up with the technology curve, and legislation too, which is why they went turbo.

The aesthetics of the 996? One man's sculpture is another man's fridge. That business of the fried egg headlight that everybody derided for so long has faded into history, and that very much went with the times. But it's still a Marmite thing in the Porsche community: people either love the 996 or they don't. In any case, I prefer the more upright lenses of the 997.

To refresh our memories on the design origins for a moment, the 996 was styled in the early 1990s by Pinky Lai under the auspices of Harm Lagaaij, the 997 in 1998 by Grant Larson, and the 991 in 2008 by Michael Maurer. The progression is clear. Our three contenders are sufficiently different stylistically that preference and desirability boils down to the specification and driving experience; it's not a question of aesthetics, because they haven't necessarily improved the look of the 911 with the 991. 'It's very subjective,' says Lynden. 'Regarding the proportions of the cars, if you were to look down on the 991 from above – the drone's-eye view – it looks a lot squarer, whereas the 997 is quite long and thin, while the 991's haunches look quite stocky on the road.' The 991's roof line is flatter, but the rear end gets ever higher, and the differences in the tail treatment are marked as well, par-

ticularly the rear light clusters; the 996 and 997 are similar, while the 991 rear lights have gone LED. The way the tails fall away is also different, and the 997 is the most sloping of the three, even allowing for the 996 Turbo's spoiler being erect. But what makes the 996 Turbo look its age, in this company, is those smaller wheels; if you put it on 19in diameter rims or the 20in of the 991 it would bring it closer in poise and stance to its younger siblings.

Lynden recounts the tale of a customer who had bought a four-year old 991 from an OPC, and after six weeks he traded it in at Ashgood for a ten-year-old 997 C4S.

When we got it, it still had over two-and-a-half year's warranty on it; we had a 997 C4S in stock that had done only 12,000 miles, and he part exchanged his 991 against it. Obviously, we gave him money on top

Interesting juxtaposition of three generations of water-cooled 911 tails: the 996 Turbo (closest to the camera), the 997 C4S and the 991, displaying similar contours yet arched subtly differently. ANTONY FRASER

of it, but he was over the moon. It wasn't that he was dissatisfied with the 991, just that he loved the colour of the 997: it was a unique spec with a cream exterior, a brown roof, with mustard interior. He just had to have this colour combination, but even so, that's still quite a radical move to go back in time just to get the colour combo that suits you.

Like, a mint green 964 for instance? And there it is, I couldn't avoid mentioning a classic.

If the 991 is on a downward trajectory on the depreciation scale, can we assume the opposite is true of the 997 C4S and 996 Turbo? We can safely say that values have stabilized, certainly hardened, a trend that's also seen the previous 996 base models start to climb out of the bargain basement. I've collected the 996 Turbo from Paragon Porsche at Mayfield. Sales manager Jamie Tyler provides a considered view about the ballpark £50,000 market, 'Yes, now you can get a 991 for that, although the mid-£50s is more likely, but you'd find a high mileage one on the £50,000 mark.' As the prices are hardening for the earlier 997 and 996 models and the 991 is still in depreciation mode, they are meeting one another on the sales graph. Does a customer think, I was after a 997, but now I can actually get a 991?

The market for 991s is very good, and they look exceptionally good value for money now for a relatively new-looking model, and we do get a lot of demand for them. The people that will buy a 991 are those who will probably use it on a daily basis, while the 996 Turbo is going to be used more on high days and holidays and as a weekend fun car, as well as being a bit more of a long-term investment. The last of the naturally aspirated 6-cylinder 911s are going to be good news in the future, now that everything is turbocharged.

Rear tracking shot of the 991 at the Chobham proving ground, highlighting the svelte rounded contours of the car's hindquarters. ANTONY FRASER

The base model 991 was £71,449 at launch in 2012, so the drop of around £20,000 in five years is hardly staggering. 'We've only been selling 991s over the last couple of years,' says Jamie. 'The first ones we were selling were higher spec cars in the £70s and £80s, and now as they come down into the £50s that seems to be where the market is levelling off for an early one. The Carrera S is mid £50s to early £60s, and then 4Ss would be mid- to late £60s upwards.' That's how it looks in Paragon's showroom, but shop around and there are cars on offer privately for less. It's swings and roundabouts, though, as Paragon has an inestimable reputation for supplying quality cars.

What's Jamie's take on the 997 market?

The 997 market is brilliant, especially for early ones. Not so long ago a very good example of a 2005 Carrera S would have been mid-£20s, now they're late £20s. Generation 2 cars are very good news:

they're holding their value still in the £40s, some into the early £50s, especially the rarer versions, and it's £70 upwards now for a GTS, so they're doing well. We can't buy enough of the ten- to twelve-year-old ones now.'

To be in that sort of price league with a 996, does it have to be a GT3 or a Turbo?

Yes, although standard 996 models are all creeping up as well. The post-2002 Gen 2 facelifted versions that we were selling for late teens a year ago are now early to mid-£20s for good examples. The market for those is creeping up as well. The whole thing about the fried egg headlights is disappearing, and now everyone thinks 996s are cool again: they're good cars.

Aside from these 911s, what else would your £50,000 buy?

Predictably, the 991 C2 felt the most modern of the trio, though not necessarily having the most appealing spec. ANTONY FRASER

You're looking at newer 718 Caymans and Boxsters, or very high spec 981s, possibly a Cayman R. For the same sort of money you can get a 987 Spyder, and we could have snuck in a high-miles Gen 1 GT3, though generally they're a little bit higher: we've recently sold a Gen 2 at £72,000 on 47,000 miles with carbon brakes, and another at £65,000. Normally you wouldn't want to let a GT3 go for anything less than £65,000, and upwards of £70–80,000 if it was a nice one.

It's time to make use of the delirious fact that we are on an unfettered test track, armed with a trio of 911s capable of speeds well in excess of 180mph (290km/h). Not that we're permitted to approach these velocities, but we can pretty much please ourselves in the certain knowledge that there won't be anything coming towards us. First up, the hard-edged 991 C2, with its seductive red leather cabin interior. Its bark complements its bite; it is lean, mean, and its steering is way more acute in feel than the four-wheel-drive Turbo and 997 C4S – a tad skittish on the damp surface, though. Notwithstanding, it inspires confidence and I clip those apexes with unerring accuracy and ride the 90-degree banking like a Daytona ace. Chobham's Snake is a decent substitute for the Nordschleife and Millbrook, dispensing a delicious mix of sweeping cambered curves and unnerving rollercoaster dips and troughs, through which the 996 Turbo is a kid gloves affair, the C4S a safe pair of hands, but the 991 is a tiger in attack mode.

The 997 C4S has the best manners and is the best-balanced chassis of the three, and its front axle feels more attached to the road than the 991's. It presents as the most docile too. Does that mean mundane? Perhaps it also says it's the one that would work best as an everyday car. Well, not necessarily. I've driven the 996 Turbo perfectly placidly from east Kent to west Surrey and there's nothing to suggest it's a tearaway tornado. I'm immediately transported into a somnolent disposition thanks to the relaxed driving position, augmented by the Tiptronic shift. There's a firm feel to the suspension, and its four-wheel drive is perhaps less obvious than the 997 C4S's, and that's partly because of its slightly smaller diameter (18in) wheel-and-tyre combination.

On the Chobham straightaway it's the 996 Turbo that provides the most vivid acceleration of the three. Yet for all its turbocharged prowess, it feels unnecessarily dramatic. But it does have the advantage over the C4S of having the unburstable Mezger engine. Even with a steady throttle application, at moderate speeds the Tiptronic is shifting from gear to gear of its own accord, and on a gradient it's making those judgements on my behalf. Then there's the Jekyll-and-Hyde scenario, where I apply the throttle and it's away like a dose of salts, with brilliant traction on the twisty sections. The 420bhp Turbo has that enormous reservoir of power available, so in any real-time situation, whether overtaking or just getting away from a busy road junction, I am some distance up the road in short order. Of the three automatic shifts on offer, the 996's Tiptronic is the easiest to negotiate and manipulate. There's not much in it, compared

Beautifully proportioned rear three-quarters of the wide-bodied 997 C4S cornering on the unfettered rural roads at Chobham proving ground. ANTONY FRASER

ABOVE: **The 996 Turbo's all-wheel drive and stunning power delivery make it a very attractive proposition in the £50,000 shoot-out.** ANTONY FRASER

Taking a tight line on The Snake at Chobham's Longcross test track in the Gen 1 991 C2. ANTONY FRASER

Plush red cabin upholstery in the 991 Gen 1 C2 is a positive sales attraction. ANTONY FRASER

with the 997 and 991's PDK shift controls, but the 996's are the most basic controls of the three, especially compared with the 991's plethora of switchgear, which undoubtedly satisfies the demands of modern driving conditions. The 997 C4S occupies the middle ground and is the trusty trooper, whereas the 996 Turbo is super-dart fast, but it's also fairly basic, predating LED lights and the stop-start function. I've driven the 996 Turbo further than any of them on this particular gig, and become quite attached to it.

What these three cars amply demonstrate is the evolution of the modern 911. They're all potentially everyday cars.

I've surprised myself, however, to find that the one I want to take home from our day at Chobham is the 991. It is the one that's still depreciating, but it provides the most modern driving experience (as you'd expect), both to sit in and to look at. It's a very together car, and I just adore the red upholstery. So, here's the thing: automotive market analysts predict that the 991 values could continue to fall to perhaps £30,000 by 2020. Shrewdly, you might perhaps want to hang on for a while before taking the plunge. But take the plunge you should; you'll have so much fun.

Artwork by Sonja Verducci of Porsche and BMW rivals plunging into the Nürburgring banked Karussell bend. SONJA VERDUCCI

INDEX